Organ - Preludes

An Index to Compositions on Hymn Tunes,
Chorales, Plainsong Melodies,
Gregorian Tunes and Carols

Volume II — Tune Name Index

by

Jean Slater Edson

The Scarecrow Press, Inc.

Metuchen, N.J.   1970

Table of Contents

A Child Is Born (Pennsylvania
Dutch)

> Johnson, A. H.
> Variant:
> Ein Kind gebor'n

A Child Is Born in Bethlehem
  See: Ein Kind geboren (14th
  Century)

A Child This Day Is Born
  See: Sandys (English)

A la venue de Noël (French)

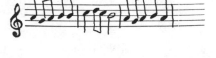

> Balbastre, C. (2)
> Daquin, L. C.
> Variant:
> Noël - Carol of the Birds

> Bitgood, R.

A Little Child on the Earth
  (Flemish)

> Hokanson, M.
> Variant:
> Er is een Kindeke geboren
> op aard

> Mudde, W.

A Little Child There Is Y-Born
  See: Vom Himmel kam der
  Engel Schaar (Susanni)

A Minuit (Noël)

> Bingham, S.
> Faulkes, W.

A Solis Ortus Cardine (Plainsong
   Mode 3)
   See: Christum, wir sollen
   loben schon

A tro, det er aa legge
   See: Ach, bleib mit deiner

A vous je viens m'offrir (French   Tune not found
   Noël)

       Alain, A.

Aa, du som kjenner all (Kocher)

               Z 854

       Karlsen, R.
   Variant:
   Nicht eine Welt, die

Aa, fikk jeg kun vaere den
   (R. Karlsen)

       Karlsen, R.

Aa, fikk jeg kun vaere den
   minste kvist (Lindhjem)

       Nielsen, L.

Aa, Gud, mitt hjaerta stundar
   (Koch)

       Nielsen, L.

Aa, Herre, lat meg heilt
   See: Psalm 105

Aa, hjertens ve
   See: O Traurigkeit

Aa, kom dog, hver som
   (Lindeman)

       Nielsen, L.

Aa liva, det er aa elska
   (Steenberg)

       Nielsen, L.
       Sandvold, A.

Aa salige stund uten like
    (Steenberg)

    Karlsen, R.

Aa var eg meir deg (Orheim)

    Gangfloet, S.
    Nielsen, L.

Aanden opgav enkesoennen (Schop)

                Z 4895

    Thuner, O. E.
    Videroe, F.
    Wuertz, J.

Aardsche machten
    See: Psalm 29 (Dutch)

Abbey (Scotch)

    Rimmer, F.

Abend wird es wieder (Rinck)
    See: Fager kveldsol smiler

Abends (Oakeley)

    Haase, K.
    Means, C.
    Oldroyd, G.
    Peeters, F.

Abermals ein Jahr
    See: Freu dich sehr

Aberystwyth (Parry)

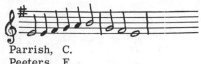

    Barnes, F. M.
    Cassler, G. W.   Parrish, C.
    Goode, J. C.   Peeters, F.
    Groves, R.   Penick, R. C.
    Huston, J.   Stewart, C. H.
    Johns, D.   Vaughan-Williams, R.
    Ley, H. G.   Whitney, M. C.
    Near, G.   Willan, H.
    Noble, T. T.   Young, G.

Abridge (Smith)

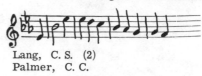

   Adams, T.
   Coleman, R. H. P. (2)   Lang, C. S. (2)
   Garlick, G. T.   Palmer, C. C.
   Gray, A.

Accourez pastoureaux (French   Tune not found
   Noël)

   Busser, H.

Ach bleib bei uns (Calvisius)

   Anonymous
   Asma, F.   Hering, J. C.
   Bach, J. S.   Kaeppel, G. C. A.
   Baldamus, F.   Karg-Elert, S.
   Barlow, W.   *Meibohm, D. (3)
   Beck, A.   Mueller-Zuerich, P.
   Couper, A. B.   Reuter, F. (2)
   DeLamarter, E.   Wettstein, H.
   Dupré, M. J. J.   Wickenhausser, R.
   Haase, K.   Zipp, F.

   Variants:
   Uns ist ein Kindlein
   Wo willst du hin

Ach bleib bei uns
   See: Breslau

Ach bleib bei uns (Klug)
   See: Erhalt uns, Herr

Ach bleib mit deiner Gnade
   (Vulpius)
                    Z 132

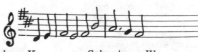

Abel, O.	Kuehn, K.	Schuetze, W.
Boehner, J. L.	Kuntze, C.	Taylor, C. T.
Brieger, O.	Leupold, A. W.	Tuerke, O.
Brosig, M.	Merikanto, O.	Wedemann, W. (2)
Cassler, G. W.	Merkel, G.	Werner, F.
Doles, J. F.	Micheelsen, H. F.	Zierau, F.
Fischer, M. G.	Oechsler, E.	
Fluegel, G.	Papperitz, B. R.	
Gradehand, F.	Peeters, F.	
Guentersberg, H. C. C.	Piutti, K. (2)	
Hasse, K.	Rebling, G.	
Heinrich, J. G.	Reger, M.	
Karg-Elert, S. (2)	Rippen, P.	
Karow, K.	Rudnick, W. (2)	
Koeckert, C.	Schaab, R. (2)	

Variants:
A tro, det er aa legge
Ach blijf met Uw genade

Nieland, H.

Beim letzten Abendmahle

Ahrens, J.   Stehle, J. G. E.
Doebler, K.   Walther, J. G. (3)
Pachelbel, J. (2)

Christus, der ist mein Leben

Bach, A. W.   Markull, F. W. (2)
Baldamus, F.   Marpurg, F. W. (3)
Barner, A.   Mendelssohn, A.
Beck, A.   Merkel, G.
Bender, J.   Metzler, F.
Boehner, J. L.   Micheelsen, H. F.
Bornefeld, H.   Michel, J.
Claussnitzer, P. (3)   Muehling, H. J. (2)
David, J. N. (2)   Mueller, S. (2)
Ehinger, H. R.   Nagel, W.
Enckhausen, H. F.   Oley, J. C.
Fiebig, K.   Pachelbel, J. (4)
Fischer, M. G. (3)   Palme, R. (4)
Fluegel, G. (2)   Papperitz, B. R.
Forchhammer, T. (2)   Peeters, F.
Friedrich, H.   Pepping, E.
Grosse-Weischede, A.   Pisk, P. A.
Gulbins, M. (3)   Piutti, K.
Haase, K.   Raasted, N. O.
Haase, R. (2)   Reda, S.
Hamburger, P.   Reger, M. (2)
Hark, F.   Reuter, F. (2)
Heinrich, J. C. (2)   Rinck, J. C. H. (5)
Herrmann, W.   Roth, F.
Hoernig, O.   Rudnick, W. (2)
Hoyer, K.   Rumpf, W. (2)
Huth, A.   Sachs, J. G.
Karg-Elert, S.   Schaab, R.
Karow, K.   Schaeffer, A.
Kickstat, P.   Schneidt, S.
Kittel, J. C.   Schilllng, A.
Klotz, H.   Schrenk, J.
Koeckert, C.   Schuetze, W.
Kranz, A.   Schwencke, J. F. (2)
Krause, P. (2)   Seitz, J. A.
Kunze, K.   Stiller, K.
Lorenz, C. A.   Stolze, H. W.
Lubrich, F. , Jr.   Strebel, A.
Manz, P.   Streicher, J. A. (2)

Ach bleib mit deiner Gnade (Vulpius) (cont.)

  Christus, der ist mein Leben (cont.)

    Thomas, G. A.   Wolff, C. M.
    Tuerke, O.   Wolfrum, K. (3)
    Vierling, J. G.   Zehrfeld, O.
    Volckmar, R. W.   Ziehr, E.
    Walther, J. G. (5)   Zierau, F.
    Wedemann, W.   Zipp, F.
    Wettstein, H. (4)

  Med straalekrans om tinde
    (Vulpius)

    Frellsen, E.   Karlsen, R.

  Min doed er mig

    Andersen, E.   Nielsen, O. S.
    Godske-Nielsen, H. (3)   Raasted, N. O. (3)
    Hamburger, P.   Rosenkilde-Larsen, E.
    Jeppesen, K.   Vaerge, A.
    Nielsen, J. M.   Woeldike, M. A.

  O Gud, det aer min glaedje

  Song 8 (Dutch)

    Stulp, G.   Wilgenburg, D. van

  Song 162 (Dutch)

    Wilgenburg, D. van

  Song 214 (Dutch)

    Westering, P. C. Van   Wilgenburg, D. van

  Uns ist ein Kindlein

  Willkommen, Held im Streite
    (Vulpius)

    Brosig, M.   Herrmann, K. H.
    Hasse, K.   Trenkner, W.

Ach, bleib mit mir

    Dienel, O.   Tune not found

Ach blijf met Uw genade
  See: Ach, bleib mit deiner Gnade

Ach, erkennet, liebste Seelen
  (Freylinghausen)
  See: O Durchbrecher (Halle)

Ach Gott, die armen Kinder dein
  See: Aus tiefer Not (Strassburg)

Ach Gott, erhoer mein Seufzen
  (Erfurt)

Z 1831

    Krebs, J. L. (4)   Volckmar, T.
    Rinck, J. C. H.   Walther, J. G. (2)
    Vierling, J. G.

Ach Gott, tu dich erbarmen
  (Calvisius)

Z 7228c

    Walther, J. G. (2)

Ach Gott und Herr (Schein)

Z 2050

Bach, J. C.	Kauffmann, G. F.	Schaab, R.
Bach, J. S. (3)	Kempff, W.	Schneider, J. G.
Baldamus, F.	Kickstat, P.	Schueler, H.
Beck, A.	Klaus, V.	Schurig, V.
Braehmig, B.	Koerner, G. W.	Sittard, A.
Brieger, O.	Krause, P.	Streicher, J. A.
Buxtehude, D.	Lorenz, J. F. (3)	Sumsion, C. C.
Claussnitzer, P. (2)	Markworth, H. J.	Trautner, F. W.
Dupré, M. J. J.	Marpurg, F. W.	Vierling, J. G. (3)
Enckhausen, H. F.	Meibohm, D. (4)	Walther, J. G. (5)
Eyken, J. A. Van	Merk, G.	Weber, H.
Fischer, M. G. (2)	Merkel, G.	Wedemann, W.
Franke, F. W.	Metzger, H. A.	Wettstein, H.
Graedener, H. T. O.	Muehling, A.	Wickenhausser, R.
Grote, H.	Palme, R.	Wolff, C. M.
Haase, K.	Pisk, P. A.	Wolfrum, K. (4)
Herzog, J. G.	Piutti, K.	
Hesse, A. F.	Reichardt, A.	
Hessenberg, K.	Reinhardt, A.	
Hiltscher, W.	Richter, E. F.	
Hoyer, K.	Riedel, H.	
Johnson, D. N.	Rinck, J. C. H. (5)	
Kaeppel, G. C. A.	Roeder, E. O.	
Kammeier, H.	Rudnick, W.	
Karg-Elert, S.	Rumpf, W.	

Ach Gott und Herr (Schein) (cont.)

Variants:
Jour de Seigneur

    Hess, C. L.

Zeuch uns nach dir

    Spiering, G.

Ach Gott und Herr II
    See: Fuenf Bruennlein sind

Ach Gott, verlass mich nicht
(Darmstadt)
    See: Was frag ich nach der
Welt

Ach Gott, verlass mich nicht
    See: O Gott, du frommer Gott
(Hannover)

Ach Gott vom Himmel, sieh
    darein (Erfurt)
              Z 4431

Anonymous (2)	*Merk, G. (2)
Bach, J. C.	Metzger, H. A.
Bach, J. S.	Micheelsen, H. F.
*Baldamus, F.	Mozart, W. A.
*Borg, O.	*Mueller-Zuerich, P.
*Claussnitzer, P. (2)	Nicolai, J. G.
David, J. N. (2)	*Oley, J. C.
Enckhausen, H. F.	Pachelbel, J. (4)
* Fluegel, G.	Penick, R. C.
Geist, P.	Piutti, K. (2)
Haase, H. H.	Raphael, G.
Haase, K.	Reda, S. (3)
Hanff, J. N.	Reinbrecht, A.
*Herzogenberg, H. von	Rinck, J. C. H. (3)
Hoyer, K.	Scheidt, S.
Isenberg, K.	Speth, J.
Kaeppel, G. C. A. (2)	Stephan, J.
Kaminski, H.	Sweelinck, J. P.
Kauffmann, G. F.	Telemann, G. P. (2)
Kickstat, P.	Trautner, F. W.
*Kittel, J. C.	*Trier, J.
Krebs, J. L. (2)	Vierling, J. G. (2)
Kuehn, K.	Walcha, H.
Lorenz, J. F.	Walther, J. G.
*Meibohm, D. (4)	Wickenhausser, R.
	Zachau, F. W. (3)

Variants:
Ak, Gud, fra Himlen se herned

Jensen, S.   Thuner, O. E.
Nielsen, T. H.   Videroe, F.
Noergaard, P.

O Gott im Himmel, sieh darein

Philipp, F.

Ach Gott vom Himmel, sieh
darein (Walther)
See also: Psalm 23
                Z 4432

Ach Gott vom Himmelreiche
(Praetorius)
                Z 5368

Barlow, W.   Haase, K.   Peeters, F.
Grote, H.   Meibohn, D. (2)   Piutti, K.

Ach Gott, wie manches Herzeleid
(Psalmodia Nova)
See: Breslau

Ach Herr, mich armen Suender
See: Herzlich tut mich verlangen

Ach, Herre Gott, mich treibt
die Not
See: Ich dank dir schon durch
deinen Sohn (Praetorius)

Ach Jesu, dessen Treue
See: O Gott, du frommer Gott
(Hannover)

Ach, Jesu mein

Hofmeier, A.

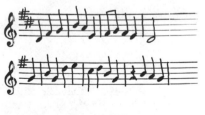

Ach Jesu, meiner Seelenfreude
(Witt)
                Z 3010
Sittard, A. (2)

Ach Jesu, meiner Seelenfreude
(Heinlein)
                Z 8399
*Piutti, K.

Ach, lieben Christen, seid
  getrost
  See: Wo Gott der Herr nicht
  bei uns haelt (Klug)

Ach lieber, Herre Jesu Christ
  See: O Jesulein suess

Ach lieber, Herre Jesu Christ
  See: Breslau

Ach, Liebster, zeuch mich von
  der Erde

    Gulbins, M. (2)

Ach mein Herr Jesu, dein Nahesein (Gregor)
  (built from Nun bitten wir)
                    Z 2029d
      *Claussnitzer, P.

Ach mein Herr Jesu, dein Nahesein (Knoedel)
  (See also: Herr Jesu Christ
  meins Lebens Licht-Nuernburg)
                    Z 2033

    Franke, F. W.   *Piutti, K.
    Hoyer, K.   *Streicher, J. A.
    Kickstat, P.   Weber, H.
    Magnus, E.   Wettstein, H.

Ach mein herzliebes Jesulein
  See: Vom Himmel hoch

Ach mein Jesu, welch Verderben
  (Bremen)
                    Z 3751
      Toepfer, J. G.

Ach, sagt mir nichts
  See: O dass ich Tausend
  (Koenig)

Ach schoenster Jesu, mein Verlangen
  See: Erquicke mich, du Heil
  der Suender (Kittel)

Ach, sieh ihn dulden (Knecht)
                    Z 3078

    Barner, A.   Rumpf, W.

Ach, wann werd' ich dahin
  kommen (Witt)
                          Z 1294
    Stolze, H. W.

Zopff, H.

Ach, was bin ich, mein Erretter
  (Geneva)
                          Z 3542

    Franke, F. W.   Kuehmstedt, F.
    Hoyer, K.   Pfaff, H.
    Kickstat, P.

Variant:
Hueter, wird die Nacht

    Fromm, H.

Ach, was ist doch unser Leben
  See: Aus der Tiefe, rufe ich
  (Herbst)

Ach, was soll ich, Suender,
  machen (Altdorf)
                          Z 3573b

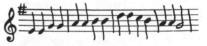

    Albrechtsberger, J. G.   Loewe, J. K. G.
    Bach, J. S.   Luetzel, J. H.
    Baldamus, F.   Markworth, H. J.
    Beck, A.   Marpurg, F. W.
    Brieger, O.   Meibohm, D. (3)
    Claussnitzer, P. (2)   Merkel, G.
    Doles, J. F.   Oley, J. C. (2)
    Drischner, M. (2)   Pachelbel, J. (2)
    Droebs, J. A.   Piutti, K. (2)
    Fink, C.   Rinck, J. C. H. (3)
    Fluegel, G. (3)   Rudnick, W.
    Franke, F. W.   Schmidt, F.
    Grote, H.   Schneider, J. G. (2)
    Gulbins, M. (2)   Schrenk, J.
    Haase, K.   Schuetze, W.
    Hoyer, K.   Seiffert, U.
    Huth, A.   Toepfer, J. G.
    Kaeppel, G. C. A.   Tuerke, O.
    Kickstat, P.   Vierling, J. G.
    Krause, P.   Wagner, F.
    Kuehn, K.   Walther, J. G.
    Kuntze, C.   Wedemann, W. (2)
    Lang, H.   Wettstein, H.

Ach, was soll ich, Suender,
  machen (Altdorf) (cont.)

  Variant:
  Kommst du, kommst du, Licht
  der Heiden

      Luedders, P.   Soenke, H.
      Oley, J. C.

Ach wie elend ist uns're Zeit
  See: Aus tiefer Not (Strassburg)

Ach, wie fluechtig
  See: Ach, wie nichtig, ach
  wie fluechtig

Ach, wie hat des Herren Hand
  (Richter)
  See: Hjelp! ja kvar er hjelp
  aa faa

Ach, wie herrlich
  See: Sicilian Mariners

Ach, wie ist doch uns're Zeit

      Hasse, K.

Ach, wie nichtig, ach, wie
  fluechtig (Franck)
                    Z 1887b

      Bach, J. S. (2)   Karow, K.
      Boehm, G. (2)   Kropfreiter, A. F.
      Crane, R.   Rinck, J. C. H.
      Dupré, M. J. J.   Vogel, M. W.

  Variant:
  Ach, wie fluechtig

      Claussnitzer, P. (4)   Mulder, E. W.
      David, J. N.   Pepping, E.
      Distler, H.   Piutti, K.
      Franke, F. W.   Seyerlen, R.
      Kammeier, H.   Streicher, J. A.
      Kickstat, P.   Vierling, J. G.
      Krause, P.

Ach, wir armen Suender (German)
                    Z 8187c

Telemann, G. P. (2)   Weckmann, M.

Variant:
O, wir armen Suender

Bornefeld, H.   Micheelsen, H. F.   Walcha, H.
Gerke, A.   Pepping, E. (3)   Zipp, F.
Koch, J. H. E.   Telemann, G. P. (2)

Ach, wundergrosser Siegesheld
See: O wundergrosser Siegesheld

Ack bliv hos oss
See: Pax (Swedish)

Ack, kjaertans ve
See: O Traurigkeit

Ack, laer oss Gud med froejd
och flit (Waldis)

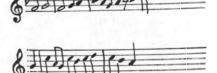

Melin, H.

Ack, vad aer dock livet haer
See: Swedish Litany

Ad Coenam Agni (Mode 9)

*Cavazzoni, G.
*Fasolo, G. B. (2)

Ad Coenam Agni (Sarum)

*Pearce, C. W.
Willan, H.

Ad Coenam Agni
See: Lucis Creator Optime
(Angers)

Ad Perennis Vitae Fontem
(French)

Peeters, F.   Sowerby, L.
Powell, R. J.

Ad Regias Agni Dapes

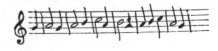

Veith, J. J.

Ad Regias Agni Dapes (Mode 8)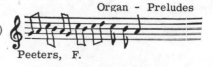

    Dupré, M. J. J.   Peeters, F.
    Lesur, D. J. Y.

Ad Te Levavi (Tone 2)

    Hulse, C. Van

Adelaide (Stebbins)

    Goode, J. C.
Variant:
Have Thine Own Way

    Lorenz, E. J. (2)

Adeste Fideles (Wade's)

Adams, T.		
Archer, J. S.		
Ashford, E. L.	Gotch, O. H.	Nordman, C.
Barrett, R.	Grace, H.	Noyon, J.
Beck, A.	Guilmant, A. (2)	Papy, N.
Becker, L. E.	Haase, K.	Peeters, F.
Bratt, C. G.	Harris, C.	Pepin, N. A.
Buck, D.	Hofland, S.	Piché, P. B.
Calver, F. L.	Hollins, A.	Plas, A. Van den
Candlyn, T. F. H. (2)	Hosmer, E. S.	Purvis, R. (2)
Cassler, G. W.	Hulse, C. Van (2)	Reading, J.
Coleman, R. H. P.	Ives, C. E.	Reuter, F.
Cronham, C. R.	Jacquet, M.	Rohlig, H. (3)
DeBrant, C.	Jimenez, M. B.	Rogers, S. E.
Deden, O.	Karg-Elert, S.	Schumacher, M. H.
Demessieux, J.	Kessel, G.	Shaw, G. T.
Dethier, G. M.	Kreckel, P. G.	Shroyens, R.
Dickey, M.	Lefebure-Wely, L. J. A.	Southgate, T. L.
Dickinson, P.	Lemare, E. H.	Stanford, C. V. (2)
Diggle, R. (2)	Lerman, J. W.	Sumsion, H. W.
Drakeford, R.	Liszt, F.	Thayer, W. E.
Dressler, J.	Loret, C.	Thiman, E. H.
Dunn, M. A.	Luard-Selby, B.	Thomas, V. C. (2)
Dupré, M. J. J.	MacLean, D.	Tridemy, A.
Edmundson, G. (2)	Markworth, H. J.	Walton, K.
Faulkes, W.	McGrath, J. J.	Weiss, C. A.
Fisher, A. C.	Meale, A.	Whitford, H. P. (2)
Fleury, A.	Melville, C. E.	Whiting, G. E.
Frazee, G. F.	Mueller, C. F.	Wilson, R. C. (2)
Gigout, E.	Murphree, C. L.	Wyton, A.
	Nicholl, H. W.	Yon, P. A.
	Nieland, J.	Zúñiga, J.

Adeste Fideles (cont.)

    Variants:
    Auf, glaeubige Seelen

        Kraft, K.   Lampart, K.
        Krieger, F.   Sister M. F.

    Herbei, O Ihr Glaeubigen

        Stehle, J. G. E.

    Komt allen tezamen

        Kousemaker, A.   Zwart, J.
        Kruijs, M. H. van'T.

    Song 18 (Dutch)

Adesto Sancta Trinitas (Mode 3)

        Evans, P. A.

Adon Olom (Gerovitch)

        Freed, I.

Adoremus in Aeternum (Gregorian)

        Perilhou, A.
        Webbe, W. Y.

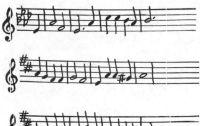

Adoro Te (Louvain)

        Schehl, J. A.

Adoro Te (Van Damme)

        Bratt, C. G.
        Kreckel, P. G.

Adoro Te Devote (Plainsong)

Bedell, R. L.	Casner, M. D.	Englert, E.
Biggs, R. K.	Cassler, G. W.	Guilmant, A.
*Boellmann, L.	Castellvi, J. C. Y.	Harwood, B.
Bont, H. de	Coleman, R. H. P.	Huijbers, B. (2)
Bratt, C. G.	DeBrant, C. (2)	Johnson, D. N.
Brun, F.	Dupré, M. J. J.	Kreckel, P. G.
Capocci, F.	Edmundson, G.	Langlais, J. F.

Adoro Te Devote (cont.)

Lefebure-Wely, L. J. A.   Shimmin, S.
Lesur, D. J. Y.   Talmadge, C. L.
Marier, T. N.   Thomas, V. C.
Peeters, F.   Titcomb, E. H.
Porter, A. B.   Togni, V.
Purvis, R.   Warner, R. L.
*Ravanello, O.   Willan, H.
Schehl, J. A.   Woolen, R.

Aeterna Christi Munera (Guid-
etti - Mode 7)

Goodhart, A. M.   Willan, H.
Peeters, F. (2)

Aeterna Christi Munera
(Rouen)

Cassler, G. W.

Aeterna Rex Altissime

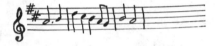

Sister M. G.

Af dybsens noed til dig, min Gud
See: Aus tiefer Not (Phrygian)

Af hoejheden oprunden er
See: Wie schoen leuchtet

Agincourt Song
See: Deo Gracias

Agnus Dei (Liturgy)

Z 58

Horn, P. M.   Poppen, H. M.
Lee, J.   Raasted, N. O.
Lenel, L.   Ravanello, O.
Markworth, H. J.
Variants:
Christe, du Lamm Gottes

Bach, J. S.   Dupré, M. J. J.
Baldamus, F.   Enckhausen, H. F.
Bausznern, W. von   Fischer, M. G.
Beck, A.   Gulbins, M. (2)
Bender, J.   Haase, K.
Blum, R.   *Hoyer, K.
Distler, H.   Karg-Elert, S. (2)

Kickstat, P.
Koch, J. H. E.
Krause, P. (2)
Merk, G.
Merkel, G.
Mueller, G.
Nagel, W.
Piutti, K.
Rabich, E.
Reichel, B. (2)
Reinbrecht, A.
Rinck, J. C. H.
Roessler, E. K.

*Ruettinger, J. C.
Rumpf, W.
Schaab, R. (2)
Schneider, J. G.
Schumacher, M. H. (3)
Schwencke, J. F. (2)
Stecher, H.
Trautner, F. W.
Vierling, J. G.
Walcha, H.
Wedemann, W.
Wenzel, E. (2)

Song 37 (Dutch)

Vogel, W.

Ainsi que la biche rée
See: Freu dich sehr

Ainsworth 97
See: Psalm 74

Ajalon
See: Redhead 76th

Ak Fader, lad dit Ord og Aand
(Lindeman)

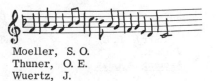

Baden, C.
*Frandsen, H. B.
Hamburger, P.
Variant:
Gud, lat din ande og ditt ord
(Lindeman)

Moeller, S. O.
Thuner, O. E.
Wuertz, J.

Nielsen, L.

Ak, Gud, fra Himlen se herned
See: Ach, Gott, vom Himmel
sieh darein (Erfurt)

Ak, vidste, du som gaar (Balle)

*Wuertz, J.

Ak, vidste du, som gaar
(Freylinghausen)
See: Mein Freund zerschmiltz

Ak vidste du, som gaar (Han-
　　nover)　　　　Z 3141
　　See: Nun jauchzt dem Herren
　　(Hannover)

Akk, visste du som gaar i syn-
　　dens lenke (Lindeman)

　　　Alnaes, E.
　　　Anderssen, F.　　　　　　Hovland, E.

Akk, visste du som gaar (Meyer)
　　See: Nun jauchzt dem Herren
　　(Hannover)

Al d'aard' en alles
　　See: Psalm 24 (Dutch)

Alas, and Did My Saviour
　　(Southern)

　　　Read, G.

Albano (Novello)

　　　Coleman, R. H. P.

Albany (Jeffery)

　　　Curry, R. D.
　　Variant:
　　Ancient of Days

Albert
　　See: Gott des Himmels

Aldri er jeg uten vaade (Linde-
　　man)

　　　Frandsen, H. B.　　　　Nielsen, L.

Aldri er jeg uten vaade
　　See: Jesus Christus, unser
　　Heiland, der von uns (Wittenburg)

Aldrig er jeg uden vaade (Berg-
　　green)

　　　*Wuertz, J.

Aldrig er jeg uden vaade (Horn)

　　　Karlsen, R.　　　Z 1390

Aleneste Gud i Himmerig
  See: Allein Gott in der Hoehe

Alford (Dykes)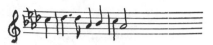

    Burdett, G. A.
    Haase, K.
    Peery, R. R.

All' Ehr' und Lob (Strassburg)

             Z 2564

    Grote, H.   Miles, G. T.
    Haase, K.   Peeters, F.
    Hulse, C. Van   Plettner, A.
    Lenel, L.

All Morgen ist ganz frisch und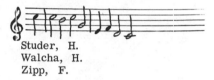
  neu (Walter)

    Bender, J.   Studer, H.
    Metzler, F.   Walcha, H.
    Roth, F.   Zipp, F.
    Variant:
    Du hoechstes Licht

All Saints
  See: Liebe, die du mich zum
  Bilde (Darmstadt)

All Saints New (Cutler)

    Crane, R.   Peeters, F.
    Haase, K.   Whitford, H. P.
    Lorenz, E. J.   Whiting, G. E.
    Matthews, H. A.   Willan, H.

All Through the Night
  See: Ar-Hyd-Y-Nos

Alle Jahre wieder (Rinck)

    Markworth, H. J.

Alle Jahre wieder (Silcher)

Alle Menschen muessen sterben
  (Mueller)

             Z 6779

Alle Menschen muessen sterben (Mueller) (cont.)

Bach, J. S.	*Lorenz, C. A.
Bender, J.	Luetzel, J. H.
*Brieger, O.	*Meibohm, D. (3)
Claussnitzer, P. (2)	Mueller, S.
*Dienel, O.	Piutti, K.
*Doles, J. F.	Reinhardt, A.
Dupré, M. J. J.	Rinck, J. C. H. (4)
Enckhausen, H. F.	Rumpf, W.
Fischer, M. G.	Schreiner, A.
*Gauss, O.	Telemann, G. P. (3)
Helmbold, C. A.	Vierling, J. G.
Herzog, J. G.	Wedemann, W. (2)
*Hesse, A. F.	*Wendt, E. A.
Kickstat, P.	Wettstein, H. (2)
Kienzl, W.	Zachau, F. W.
Krause, P. (2)	Zipp, F.
Kunze, K.	

Variants:
Du, O schoenes Weltgebaeude
Grosser Mittler

Soenke, H.

Jesu, der du meine Seele

Bach, J. C.	Rembt, J. E.
Bach, J. S.	Zachau, F. W.

Jesu, meines Lebens Leben
(Mueller)

Barner, A.	Leupold, A. W.
Faisst, I. G. F. von	Peeters, F.
Haase, K.	Schumacher, M. H.
Kaeppel, G. C. A.	Trautner, F. W.
Krebs, J. L. (2)	Zachau, F. W. (2)

Siegesfuerste, Ehrenkoenig
Song 104 (Dutch)

Wilgenburg, D. van (2)

Song 150 (Dutch)

Nauta, J.	Vogel, W.

Song 178 (Dutch)

Nauta, J.	Wilgenburg, D. van

Song 206 (Dutch)

    Wilgenburg, D. van (2)

Song 243 (Dutch)

    Wilgenburg, D. van (2)

Zween der Junger

    Oechsler, E.

Alle Menschen muessen sterben
(Wessnitzer)
                Z 6795

Variants:
Jesu er mit liv i live

    Frellsen, E.   Vaerge, A.
    Nielsen, L.   *Woeldike, M. A.
    Raasted, N. O.   Wuertz, J.

Jesus, meines Lebens Leben
(Wessnitzer)

    *Albrechtsberger, J. G.   *Matthison-Hansen, G.
    Bender, J.   Mueller, S.
    Brieger, O.   Piutti, K.
    *Claussnitzer, P.   Raphael, G.
    Drischner, M. (2)   Reichardt, B.
    Enckhausen, H. F.   Rembt, J. E.
    Franke, F. W.   Rumpf, W.
    Frenzel, H. R.   Schilling, A.
    Gebhardi, L. E.   Schmidt, F.
    Gerhardt, P.   Schweizer, R.
    *Grote, H.   Schwencke, J. F. (2)
    Grundmann, O. A.   Steinhaeuser, K.
    Haas, J.   Stolze, H. W. (2)
    Helmbold, C. A.   Streicher, J. A.
    Karow, K.   Vierling, J. G.
    Kickstat, P.   Volkmann, P.
    Koch, J. H. E.   Werner, F.
    Kuehn, K.   Wettstein, H. (2)
    Markull, F. W.   Zachau, F. W.

Song 49 (Dutch)

    Beek, W. van   Wilgenburg, D. van
    Vogel, W.

Alle Menschen muessen sterben
    (Frankfurt)
See: Jesu, der du meine Seele (Gregor)

Alle Menschen muessen sterben
    (German - Bach)
    See: Jesu, der du meine Seele
    (German - Bach)

Alle Menschen muessen sterben II
    See: Salzburg

Alle Psallite Cum Luya   Tune not found

    Dickinson, C.

Alle Welt, was lebt und webet
    (Crueger)
                    Z 3623
        *Mueller, S.

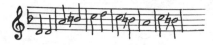

Alle Welt, was lebt und webet
    (Crueger)
                    Z 3615

    Enckhausen, H. F.

Allein Gott in der Hoehe (Plain-
    song)
                    Z 4457
                Also in 4
                        4

Abel, O.	Enckhausen, H. F.
Andersen, E.	Engelbrecht, K. F. (2)
Armsdorff, A. (2)	Eyken, J. A. Van
Bach, J. C.	Fink, C.
Bach, J. M.	Fischer, A.
Bach, J. S. (13)	Fischer, M. G.
Baldamus, F.	Fluegel, G. (6)
Barner, A. (2)	Frenzel, H. R. (3)
Bender, J.	Fricke, R.
Boehm, C.	Geist, C.
Boehm, G. (4)	Gerhardt, P.
Brede, A.	Goetze, H.
Brieger, O.	Grote, H.
Busoni, F.	Gruel, E.
Cebrian, A.	Gulbins, M. (3)
Chaix, C. (2)	Haase, K.
Claussnitzer, P. (2)	Hasse, K.
David, J. N.	Hasse, P. (2)
David, T. C.	Hassen, --
Dienel, O.	Herzog, J. G.
Doppelbauer, J. F.	Homilius, G. A.
Dupré, M. J. J.	Hovland, E.
Dueben, A. (5)	Hoyer, K.
Eckardt, A.	Kaeppel, G. C. A. (2)
Edmundson, G.	Karg-Elert, S. (2)

Karges, W. (2)
Kempter, K.
Kickstat, P. (2)
Kienzl, W.
Kimstedt, C.
Kirnberger, J. P.
Kittel, J. C.
Klauer, F. G.
Klaus, V.
Koch, M.
Koeckert, C.
Koehler-Wumbach, W.
Koetzschke, H.
Krebs, J. L.
Kuehmstedt, F. (2)
Kuehn, K.
Kuntze, C.
Leupold, A. W.
Loeffler, C. M. T.
Loewe, J. K. G.
Looks, R.
Lubrich, F. , Jr.
Luetzel, J. H.
Lux, F.
Manz, P.
Markull, F. W.
Marpurg, F. W.
Matthews, J. S.
Meibohm, D. (7)
Merk, G.
Merkel, G. (2)
Metzger, H. A.
Muehling, A.
Mueller, S. (2)
Mulder, E. W.
Oechsler, E.
Pachelbel, J. (3)
Palme, R.
Papperitz, B. R.
Peeters, F.
Piutti, K. (2)
Praetorius, J.
Praetorius, M.
Raphael, G. (2)

Reger, M. (2)
Reuter, F. (2)
Richter, E. F.
Rinck, J. C. H. (5)
Ritter, A. G.
Roeseling, K.
Rudnick, W. (5)
Rumpf, W.
Schaab, R. (2)
Scheidt, G.
Scheidt, S. (3)
Schoenfelder, E.
Schuetze, W.
Schwarz-Schilllng, R.
Schwencke, J. F. (3)
Seyerlen, R.
Spiering, G.
Stapf, O.
Stade, F. W. (2)
Steinhaeuser, W.
Stolze, H. W. (2)
Streicher, J. A.
Sweelinck, J. P. (2)
Telemann, G. P. (5)
Toepfer, J. G. (2)
Vetter, A. N.
Vierling, J. G.
Vogel, M. W.
Volckmar, F. W.
Volckmar, W. V.
Walther, J. G. (4)
Weber, H.
Wedemann, W. (2)
Wenzel, E. (2)
Wenzel, H.
Wettstein, H. (4)
Wilson, R. C.
Wolfrum, K. (3)
Zachau, F. W. (5)
Ziehr, E.
Zierau, F.
Zipp, F.
Zopff, H.

Variants:
Aleneste Gud i Himmerig

Andersen, E.   Laub, T.   Videroe, F. (2)
Frellsen, E.   Moeller, S. O.
Godske-Nielsen, H.   Raasted, N. O.
Jensen, S.   Rosenkilde-Larsen, E.
Jeppesen, K.   Vetter, A. N.

Allein Gott in der Hoehe (cont.)

Als God, mijn God

    Post, P.

Bis hierher halfst du mir

    Riedel, H.

Das Gloria

    Schwarz-Schilling, R.

Decius

    Hovdesven, E. A.

Der Herr ist mein getreuer
   Hirt

    Marpurg, F. W.

Gloria in Excelsis (German)

Song 56 (Dutch)

    Wilgenburg, D. van

Song 91 (Dutch)

    Dragt, J.   Wilgenburg, D. van

Song 201 (Dutch)

    Nauta, J.

Allein zu dir, Herr Jesu Christ
  (Wittenberg)
             Z 7292b

Armsdorff, A.	Kauffmann, G. F.	Stolze, H. W.
Bach, J. C.	Kickstat, P.	Sweelinck, J. P.
Baldamus, F.	Meibohm, D. (2)	Vierling, J. G.
Bestel, G. E. (3)	Merk, G.	Walther, J. G.
Brod, K.	Merkel, G.	Wendt, E. A.
Claussnitzer, P. (3)	Metzger, H. A.	Wettstein, H.
Erich, D.	Micheelsen, H. F.	Zachau, F. W. (3)
Franke, F. W.	Oley, J. C.	
Gerhardt, P.	Pachelbel, J. (3)	
Grote, H.	Peeters, F.	
Gulbins, M. (3)	Piutti, K.	
Haase, K.	Rumpf, W.	
Karow, K. (2)	Siedel, M.	

Variant:
Til dig alene

      Aahgren, K. E.   Thuner, O. E.
      Bergh, L.   Videroe, F. (2)
      Noergaard, P.

Alleluia

Falcinelli, R.

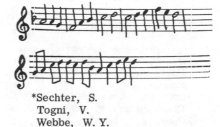

Alleluia (Latin)

      *Arnaldi, A.   *Sechter, S.
      *Jaeggi, O.   Togni, V.
      *Kreckel, P. G.   Webbe, W. Y.
      Peeters, F.

Alleluia (Wesley)

Cassler, G. W.

Alleluia-Ascendit Deus

Jaeggi, O.

Alleluia Dulce Carmen (Webbe)

      Cassler, G. W.
Variant:
Dulce Carmen

      Cassler, G. W.   Manz, P.
      Curry, R. D.

Alleluia, lasst uns singen

      Berghorn, A.
      Goller, V.

Alleluia Pascha Nostra (Gregorian)

      *Sister M. T.   Titcomb, E. H.

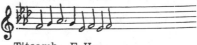

Allenthalben, wo ich gehe (Fritsch)
See: Sollt es gleich (Fritsch)

Aller Glaeub'gen Sammelplatz
(Kocher)
           Z 1243
    Lang, H.

Alles ist an Gott gelegen
See: Alles ist an Gottes Segen

Alles ist an Gottes Segen
(Koenig-Kuhnau)
          Z 3842 f

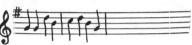

Baldamus, F.	Klotz, H. (2)
Beck, A.	Koehler-Wumbach, W.
Bender, J.	Krause, P.
Brieger, O.	Kunz, E.
Claussnitzer, P. (2)	Magnus, E.
Cook, J.	Meibohm, D. (3)
Drischner, M.	Merkel, G.
Fink, C.	Neumann, F.
Frenzel, H. R. (2)	Otto, H.
Gerke, A.	Peeters, F.
Grundmann, O. A.	Piutti, K. (2)
Haase, K. (2)	Reger, M. (2)
Hasse, K.	Rumpf, W. (2)
Hennig, W.	Schaab, R. (2)
Hering, K. E.	Streicher, J. A. (2)
Herrmann, W.	Traegner, R.
Herzog, J. G.	Tuerke, O.
Kaeppel, G. C. A.	Wolfrum, K.
Karg-Elert, S. (3)	Wettstein, H.
Kickstat, P.	Zehrfeld, O. (2)

Variants:
Alles ist an Gott gelegen

    Gruel, E.

Jesus Christus herrscht als
    Koenig

*Faehrmann, H.	Koch, J. H. E.
*Grundmann, O. A.	Pepping, E.

Jesu, der du bist alleine

    Scholz, H. G.

Song 47 (Dutch)

    Beek, W. van

Song 191 (Dutch)

    Nauta, J.

Wunderanfang, herrlich Ende

    Hasse, K.

Alles meinem Gott zu Ehren
(Compare with "Wach auf, du
Geist")

    Kraft, K.   Miggl, E.
    Kuntz, M. (2)   Romanovsky, E.

Alles was mir Gott gegeben
(Freylinghausen)
           Z 3596

    Enckhausen, H. F.

Allgegenwaertiger bin ich
  See: In dich hab' ich gehoffet,
  Herr (Nuernberg)

Allguetiger mein Preisgesang
(Weimar)
           Z 2452

    Peeters, F.
Variant:
Erfurt

    Peeters, F.

Alltid freidig naar du gaar (Weyse)
  See: Dagen gaar med raske Fjed

Alma Redemptoris Mater (Plainsong)

    Dufay, G.   Lapierre, E.
    Dupré, M. J. J.   Olsson, O. E.
    Erb, M. J. (4)   *Piechler, A.
    Kreckel, P. G.

Alma Redemptoris Mater
  See: Consolation (Webbe)

Almindelig er Kristi Kirke
  See: Psalm 118

Almsgiving (Dykes)

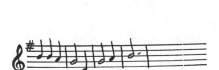

    Grote, H.
    Peeters, F.

Almsgiving (Dykes) (cont.)

Variant:
O God van Hemel

   Hanegraaf, C.

Als Christus mit seiner (Bo-
hemian)
                        Z 1179
Variant:
Dagen viger og gaar bort

   Thuner, O. E.

Als ge in nood gezeten   Tune not found

    Asma, F.   Nieland, H.

Als God mijn God
   See: Allein Gott in der Hoehe

Als ich bei meinen Schafen wacht
   See: While By Our Flocks

Als ik Hem maar kenne
   See: Wenn ich ihn nur habe

Als Jesu geboren war
   See: Der Tag der ist so freudenreich

Als Jesu jetzund sterben wollte

                        Z 5694
    Oley, J. C.

Als Jesu von seiner Mutter ging

    Doppelbauer, J. F.

Also heilig ist der Tag

       Herzog, J. G.
       *Meibohm, D.

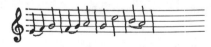

Also liebt Gott (Schwarz)

       Petzold, J.
       Pfeiffer, C. D.
       Schwarz, G.

Alt hvad som Fuglevinger   Tune not found
   (Hartman)

   Matthison-Hansen, F.   Raasted, N. O.

Alt hvad som Fuglevinger (Laub)

   Godske-Nielsen, H. (2)   Videroe, F.
   Rosenkilde-Larsen, E.   Woeldike, M. A. (2)

Alt oprejst maanen staar
   See: Der Mond ist aufgegangen

Alt staar i Guds faderhaand
   (Laub)

      *Moeller, S. O.   *Wuertz, J.
      *Vestergaard-Pedersen, C.

Alt staar i Guds faderhaand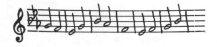
   (Rung)

      Andersen, E.
      Jeppesen, K.   *Raasted, N. O.
      *Moeller, S. O.   *Thuner, O. E.

Alt staar i Guds faderhaand
   See: Haarleg er Guds (Wideen)

Alta Trinita Beata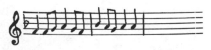

      Dickinson, C.
      Peeters, F.

Altets baerer, uten baand (Steen-
   berg)

      Karlsen, R.

Am Kreuz erblasst
   See: O Traurigkeit

Am Sabbath frueh, Marien drei
   See: Erschienen ist der herrliche Tag

Am Sonntag, eh' die Sonne

      Weber, H.

Amazing Grace (American)

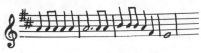

    Colvin, H.   Murphree, C. L.
    Lorenz, E. J.   Wilson, R. C.

Ambrose (Ambrose)

    Thomas, V. C.

Ambrosian Hymn of Praise
  See: Grosser Gott, wir loben dich

Amen, raabe hver en Tunge
  (Berggreen)

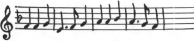

    Wuertz, J.

America (Carey)

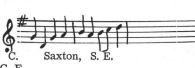

    Ashford, E. L.   Goode, J. C.
    Best, W. T. (2)   Haase, K.
    Boehner, J. L.   Ives, C. E.
    Coke-Jephcott, N.   Lange, S. de
    Dickey, M.   Langston, P. T.
    Diggle, R.   Peeters, F.
    Flagler, I. V.   Richolson, G. H.
  Variants:
  God Save the King (Queen)

    Fisher, E.   Pearce, C. W.
    Groothengel, J. G.   Reger, M.
    Gulbins, M.   Thayer, W. E.
    Hesse, A. F.   Wesley, S. S.
    Matthison-Hansen, H. Zoelner, K. H.
    Maxson, F.

  Gud sign vaar konge God

    Nielsen, L.

  Heil dir im Siegerkranz

    Gebhardi, L. E.   Ritter, A. G.

  Heil, unser'm Koenig, Heil

    Reger, M.

Amsterdam (Nares)

    Demarest, C.   McKinley, C.   Saxton, S. E.
    Matthews, H. A. Mueller, C. F.

An dir allein, an dir hab' ich
  gesuendigt (Kuhnau)

            Z 887
    Krause, P.   *Piutti, K.

An dir allein hab' ich (Becker)

            Z 770
    Vierling, J. G.

An einen Gott nur glauben wir
(Darmstadt)

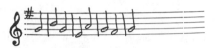

            Z 4002
    *Frenzel, H. R.
    Schaab, R. (2)

An einen Gott nur glauben wir,
Vater, Sohn (Schleinitz)
            Z 8746

    *Claussnitzer, P.   *Piutti, K.

An Wasserfluessen Babylon
(Dachstein)
            Z 7663

Ahle, J. R.	Mueller, S.
Bach, J. S. (2)	Mueller, S. W.
Baldamus, F.	Pachelbel, J. (3)
Barlow, W.	Piutti, K.
Claussnitzer, P. (5)	Raasted, N. O.
Dupré, M. J. J.	Reinbrecht, A.
Faisst, I. G. F. von	Reincken, J. A.
Fluegel, G. (2)	Riedel, H.
Forchhammer, T.	Rinck, J. C. H. (2)
Franke, F. W. (2)	Rumpf, W.
Fricke, R.	Schaab, R.
Grote, H.	Schuetze, W.
Gulbins, M.	Schwencke, J. F. (3)
Haase, K.	Traegner, R.
Karg-Elert, S.	Wettstein, H.
Kickstat, P.	Wolfrum, K.
Kuehn, K.	Wolfrum, P.
Meibohm, D. (4)	Zachau, F. W. (2)
Merkel, G.	Zehrfeld, O.

Variants:
Ein Laemmlein geht und traegt die
  Schuld

Bender, J.	*Enckhausen, H. F.
Bornefeld, H.	Fluegel, G.
Brieger, O.	*Gulbins, M.
Driessler, J.	Herrmann, C. F.

An Wasserfluessen Babylon (cont.)

Ein Laemmlein geht und traegt die Schuld (cont.)

Herrmann, W.	Reichel, B.
Hoyer, K.	Ricek, W.
Krause, P.	Rinck, J. C. H.
Micheelsen, H. F.	*Scheidt, S.
Michel, J.	*Schumann, G.
Mueller, G.	*Senftleben, G.
Mueller, W. A.	Vierling, J. G.
Pepping, E.	Walther, J. G.
Reda, S. (2)	Zipp, F.

Ein Lamm geht hin

Ebhardt, G. F.

Her ser jeg da et Lam aa gaa
(Strassburg)

Gangfloet, S.	Raasted, N. O.
Nielsen, L.	Thuner, O. E.

Lofzang van Zacharias

Kee, C.

O Koenig dessen Majestaet

Doles, J. F.	Wenzel, H.
Krebs, J. L. (2)	

Song C (Dutch)

Berg, J. J. van den	Wilgenburg, D. van

Anbetungswuerdiger Gott

*Sachs, J. G.

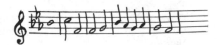

Ancient of Days (Jeffery)
See: Albany

Ande, full av naade
See: Brunnquell aller Gueter
(Crueger)

Andernach (French Psalm)

Z 2645

Willan, H.

Variants:
<u>Herr Jesu Christ, wahr Mensch</u>
<u>und Gott</u> (French Psalm)

    Zachau, F. W.

<u>Wann einer schon ein Haus aufbaut</u>

<u>Angel Gabriel</u>

    Phillips, C. G.

<u>Angel Voices</u> (Sullivan)

    Nourney, G.

<u>Angeli Archangeli</u>

    Sister M. G.

<u>Angel's Hymn</u>
  See: <u>Song 34</u> (Gibbons)

<u>Angels Song</u>
  See: <u>Song 34</u> (Gibbons)

<u>Angel's Story</u> (Mann)

    Haase, K.
    Willan, H.

<u>Angelus</u> (Joseph)

    Barlow, W.   Johnson, D. N.
    Edmundson, G.   Kreckel, P. G.
    Haase, K.   Peeters, F.
    James, F.
  Variant:
<u>Song 283</u> (Dutch)

    Westering, P. C. van

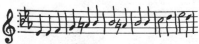

<u>Angelus Ad Virginem</u> (Folk Song)
             Also in 4
                  4
    Gray, A.   Lee, J.
    Hollins, A.   Pearce, C. W.

<u>Anglica Fortunae</u>

    Scheidt, S.

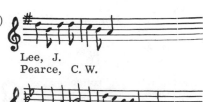

Anima Christi (American Catholic)

Schehl, J. A.

Annue Christe

Titelouze, J.

Anthes (Anthes)

Beck, A.
Haase, K.   Hildner, V.

Antioch (Handel)

Andrews, B.   Norris, H. A.
Ashford, E. L.   Pepin, N. A.
Edmundson, G.   Schumacher, M. H. (2)
Gehrke, H.   Thomas, V. C.
Haase, K.   Wehmeyer, W.
Held, W.   Whitney, M. C.
MacLean, D.   Wilson, R. C.
Marier, T. N.

Apostlene sad i Jerusalem
(Lindeman)

Alnaes, E.
Frandsen, H. B.   Karlsen, R.
Gangfloet, S.   *Wuertz, J.

Apostlene sad i Jerusalem
See: O Gud ske lov til evig tid
(Arrebo)

Ar-Hyd-Y-Nos (Welsh)

Ashford, E. L.   Groves, R.
Cronham, C. R.   Matthews, H. A.
Edmundson, G.   Rogers, S. E.
Variant:
All Through the Night

Diggle, R.   Goldsworthy, W. A.
Faulkes, W.   Wood, D.

Arbeid, ti natten kommer
(Schulz)
                    Z6249
Nielsen, L.

Variant:
Warum sind der Thraenen

Archdale (Law)

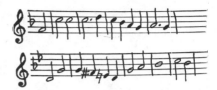

    Maganini, Q.

Arfon (French-Welsh)

    Peek, R. M.

Ariel (Mason-Mozart)

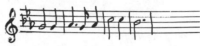

    Ashford, E. L.
    Shanko, S. W.   Stults, R. M.

Arimathea (Roper)

    Gaul, H.
    Stults, R. M.

Arise (Southern Hymn Tune)

    Bartow, N.   Murphree, C. L.
    Colvin, H.   Shaffer, J. E.

Arlington (Arne)

    Lynn, G. A.   Pool, K.

Armsel'ges Huettlein meiner
  Seelen
               Z 5950

    Rinck, J. C. H.

Arnsberg
  See: Wunderbarer Koenig (Neander)

Arthur's Seat (Goss)

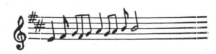

    Langston, P. T.

Ascendit Deus

    *Benoit, Dom P.
    Jaeggi, O.

Ascendit Deus (Schicht)

Ascension (Monk)

    Cassler, G. W.
    Willan, H.

Ash Grove (Welsh)

    Faulkes, W.

Asleep In Jesus (Bradbury)

    Ashford, E. L.
Variant:
Rest (Bradbury)

    Haase, K.

Asperges Me (Kyrial)

    Barnes, E. S.
    Beltjens, J.   Langlais, J. F.
    Boslet, L. (2)   Ravanello, O.
    Couper, A. B.   Sychra, J. C.
    Erb, M. J. (6)   Thomas, V. C.
    Kreckel, P. G.   Tranzillo, D.

Assumpta Est Maria   Tune not found

    Claussmann, A.

Assurance
  See: Blessed Assurance

At the Cross (Hudson)

    Thompson, V. D.

Attende Domine (Plainsong,
  Mode 5)

    DeBrant, C.
    Demessieux, J.   Kreckel, P. G. (2)

Au bien faiteur le plus tendre
  (Calvinist)

    Sowerby, L.

Auctor Beate Seculi (Mode 7)

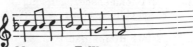

    DeKlerk, A.
    Lesur, D. J. Y.

Audi Benigni Conditor (Mode 2)

    Dupré, M. J. J.   Lesur, D. J. Y.
    *Hulse, C. Van   Peeters, F.

Auf, auf, Ihr Reichsgenossen
   (Selle)
              Z 5288
    Bender, J.
    Haase, H. H.   Luedders, P.
    Herrmann, K. H.   Weinreich, W.

Auf, auf, mein Herz, mit Freuden (Crueger)
              Z 5243
    Bender, J.   Marpurg, F. W.
    Bornefeld, H.   *Meibohm, D. (3)
    Ehmann, H.   Moser, R. (2)
    Fluegel, G.   Oley, J. C.
    Franke, F. W.   Peeters, F.
    Fromm, H.   Pepping, E.
    *Grote, H.   Poppen, H. M.
    Haase, H. H.   Reuter, F.
    Haase, K.   *Riedel, H.
    Hennig, W.   Rinck, J. C. H.
    Hoyer, K.   Rohwer, J.
    *Hulse, C. Van (2)   Rumpf, W.
    Kickstat, P.   Schumacher, M. H.
    Koch, J. H. E.   *Toepfer, J. G.
    Kousemaker, A.   Walcha, H.
    Magnus, E. (2)   Wedemann, W.
    Markworth, H. J.

Auf, auf, mein Herz, mit
   Freuden (Freylinghausen)
              Z 5245

    Piutti, K.   Vierling, J. G.
    Streicher, J. A.   Wickenhausser, R.

Auf, auf, mein Herz, und du
   mein ganzer Sinn (Leipzig)
              Z 837

    Piutti, K.   Weber, H.

Auf, auf, weil der Tag erschienen
  See: Mannheim

Auf, bleibet treu (Luther)
                    Z 7245

  Poppen, H. M.

Auf, Christen, singt festliche
  Lieder

  Sister M. F.

Auf, Christenmensch, auf, auf

                Z 2406

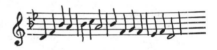

Auf, Christenmensch, auf, auf
  See: Mach's mit mir Gott (Schein)

Auf Christi Himmelfahrt
  See: Nun freut Euch, lieben
  Christen (Klug)

Auf den Nebel (Mergner)

                    Z 4823
    Franke, F. W.
    Magnus, E.   Schink, H.

Auf den Nebel (Nuernberg)

    Zahn, J.

Auf, denn, singen wir   Tune not found

    Rohwer, J.

Auf diesen Tag bedenken wir
  (Old Church)
                    Z 5771
      Bornefeld, H.
      Driessler, J.   Haase, H. H.
      Ehmann, H.   Pepping, E.
      Franke, F. W.   Schneider, M. G.

Auf, glaeubige Seelen
  See: Adeste Fideles

Auf, hinauf, zu deiner Freude
  (derived from "Morgenglanz")
                    Z 7098b
      Hasse, K.   Lorenz, C. A.   Piutti, K.

Auf, jauchzet dem Herrn
  See: Wo Gott zum Haus

Auf meinen Herren Jesum Christ
  See: Auf meinen Herrn, auf
  Jesu Christ

Auf meinen Herrn, auf Jesu
  Christ   Z 5706

    Umbreit, K. G.
Variant:
Auf meinen Herren Jesum Christ

    Vierling, J. G.

Auf meinen lieben Gott
                      Z 2145

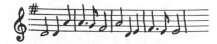

    Tunder, F.

Auf meinen lieben Gott (Regnart)

                Z 2164

Albrecht, G.	*Meibohm, D. (3)
Bach, J. C.	*Merk, G.
Bach, J. S.	Merkel, G.
Baldamus, F.	Micheelsen, H. F.
Beck, A.	Mueller-Zuerich, P. (2)
Boehm, G. (2)	Neumann, F.
*Brandt, A.	Pachaly, T. J.
*Brosig, M. (2)	Pachelbel, J.
Buxtehude, D. (4)	Piutti, K.
Carlsen, C.	Raphael, G.
Claussnitzer, P.	Reichel, B.
Doles, J. F. (2)	Reinbrecht, A.
Dupré, M. J. J.	Richter, E. F.
Enckhausen, H. F.	Ritter, A. G.
Fiebig, K.	Rinck, J. C. H. (2)
Fischer, M. G.	Rudnick, W.
Fischer, P.	Rudolph, C. F.
*Fluegel, G. (2)	Rumpf, W.
*Gradehand, F.	Schaab, R. (2)
Hanff, J. N.	Sering, F. W.
Kaeppel, G. C. A.	Vierling, J. G.
Kickstat, P.	Wedemann, W.
Kienzl, W.	Wettstein, H. (3)
Krause, P.	Zachau, F. W.
Kuhnau, J.	Zehrfeld, O. (2)

Auf meinen lieben Gott - (cont.)

Variants:
Fryd dig, du Kristi Brud

    Frellsen, E.   Rosenkilde-Larsen, E.
    Godske-Nielsen, H.   Videroe, F.
    Jeppesen, K.   Woeldike, M. A.
    Raasted, N. O. (2)

Glaed dig, du Kristi Brud

    Olson, D.

Kom foelg i aanden med

    Raasted, N. O.

Wo soll ich fliehen hin

    Bach, J. S. (2)   Michl, A.
    Dupré, M. J. J.   Palme, R.
    Fischer, M. G.   *Vierling, J. G.
    *Homilius, G. A.   Zachau, F. W.
    Krebs, J. L.

Auf, schicke dich recht feierlich
(Franck)
             Z 2058
    Seiffert, U.

Auf, Seele, sei geruest't
(Filitz)
             Z 2117
    Nawratil, K.

Aufersteh'n, ja, aufersteh'n
(K. P. E. Bach)
             Z 1991
    Piutti, K.

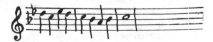

Aufersteh'n, ja, aufersteh'n
(Kittel)
             Z 1997

    Hoyer, K.   Pfaff, H.
    Kickstat, P.   Reger, M.
    Kittel, J. C.   *Rinck, J. C. H. (2)
    Michel, A.   *Vierling, J. G.

Aufersteh'n, ja, aufersteh'n
(Graun)
Z 1987
Reuter, F.

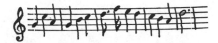

Aufersteh'n, ja, aufersteh'n
(Kocher)
Z 2005
Breuninger, K. F.
*Claussnitzer, P.   *Lux, F.
*Gruel, E.   *Zehrfeld, O.

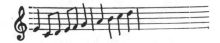

Aufersteh'n, ja, aufersteh'n
(Schicht)
Z 2003

Aughton (Bradbury)

Bingham, S.
Matthews, J. S.
Variant:
He Leadeth Me

Ashford, E. L   Stults, R. M.
Hulse, C. Van   Thomas, V. C.
Lorenz, E. J.   Thompson, V. D. (2)
Smith, H. M.   Young, G.

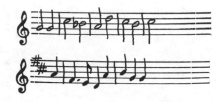

Auprès de la crèche

Chrétien, H.

Aurelia (Wesley)

Beck, A.   Reuter, F.
Bunjes, P. G.   Reynolds, W. G.
Dressler, J.   Rogers, L.
Haase, K.   Rohlig, H.
Hustad, D.   Schmutz, A.
Larson, E. R.   Stults, R. M.
Peeters, F.   Taylor, C. T.
Variants:
Een naam is onze hope

Rippen, P.

Guds menighet er grunnet

Song 112 (Dutch)

Nieland, H.

Aurora Lucis Rutilat (Sarum)

    Meek, K.
Variant:
Claro Paschali Gaudio

    Alwoode, R.

Aus, der Tiefe rufe ich (Halle)

    Walther, J. G.

Aus der Tiefe rufe ich (Herbst)

             Z 1217

Andriessen, H.	Lang, C. S.
Bach, J. S.	Milford, R. H.
Doles, J. F.	Phillips, C. G.
Groves, R.	Schoenfeld, H.
Haase, K.	Sowerby, L.

Variants:
Ach, was ist doch unser Leben

Bach, J. S.	Umbreit, K. G.

Heinlein

Archer, J. S.	Matthews, H. A.
Clokey, J. W.	Mudde, W.
Higgs, H. M.	Smith, R.
Hunt, W.	Wallace, J. E.
Lutkin, P. C.	Wyton, A. (2)

Aus diesen tiefen Grunde (Geneva)
See: Old 130th

Aus meines Herzens Grunde
(Hamburg)
             Z 5269

Bach, J. C. (2)	Forchhammer, T. (2)
Baldamus, F.	Franke, F. W. (2)
Barlow, W.	Genzmer, H.
Barner, A.	Goetze, H.
Bender, J.	Grosse-Weischede, A. (2)
Braun, C.	Grote, H.
Brieger, O. (2)	Gulbins, M. (3)
Drischner, M.	Haase, K.
Eberlin, J. E.	Hasse, K.
Enckhausen, H. F.	Hoyer, K.
Engelbrecht, K. F. (2)	Huth, A.
Fehr, R.	Kaeppel, G. C. A.
Fischer, M. G.	Karg-Elert, S. (2)
Fluegel, G.	Kickstat, P. (2)

Kienzl, W.
Klotz, H.
Kuntze, C.
Kunze, K.
Lang, H.
Lorenz, C. A.
Meibohm, D. (3)
Merkel, G.
Metzler, F.
Micheelsen, H. F. (2)
Mueller, S.
Mueller, S. W. (2)
Otto, H.
Palme, R.
Piutti, K.
Reda, S.
Reger, M.
Reinbrecht, A. (2)
Reinhardt, A.

Riedel, H.
Rinck, J. C. H.
Rudnick, W.
Rumpf, W. (2)
Schuetze, W.
Schwencke, J. F. (2)
Stolze, H. W.
Theile, A. G.
Trenkner, A. W.
Tuerke, O.
Vierling, J. G.
Volckmar, F. W.
Walther, J. G. (4)
Wedemann, W.
Wettstein, H. (2)
Wickenhausser, R.
Zehrfeld, O. (2)
Zipp, F.

Variants:
Den tro som Jesum favner

Drischner, M.
Nilsen, I. F.

Thuner, O. E.
Videroe, F. (2)

Der Heilige Christ ist kommen

Claussnitzer, P.

Des Morgens erste Stunde

Schaab, R.

Eisleben (Wolder)

Purvis, R.

I doeden Jesus blunded

Moeller, S. O.

Ich will mit Danken kommen

Doles, J. F.

Jeg vil din pris

Hamburger, P.   Jeppesen, K.

Kommt her, ihr seid geladen

Claussnitzer, P. (2)

Aus meines Herzens Grunde (cont.)

Nun jauchzet, all ihr Frommen

Bieske, W.   Micheelsen, H. F.
Haase, H. H.   Schwarz, G. von
Meyer, R.   *Vierling, J. G.

Schwingt heilige Gedanken

*Herzog, J. G.   *Theile, A. G.
*Stecher, H.

Song 4 (Dutch)

Beek, W. van   Wilgenburg, D. van
Berg, J. J. van den   Zwart, J.
Dragt, J.

Aus tiefer Not

Kunze, K.

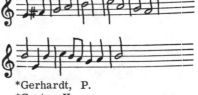

Aus tiefer Not (Phrygian)
                Z 4437

Abel, O.   *Gerhardt, P.
Anderssen, F.   *Grote, H.
Bach, J. S. (2)   *Gruel, E.
*Bauer, J.   *Gulbins, M.
*Beck, A.   *Haase, R.
Bender, J.   Hanebeck, H. R.
*Boehm, G.   Hark, F.
Brosig, M.   *Herrmann, W.
Burkhard, W.   Herzog, J. G. (2)
Busch, A. G. W. (2)   Herzogenberg, H. von
Chemin-Petit, H.   *Hesse, A. F.
Claussnitzer, P. (3)   Hoyer, K. (2)
Copley, R. E.   *Johns, D.
Crane, R.   Karg-Elert, S. (2)
David, J. N.   Karow, K. (2)
Davin, K. H. G.   Kickstat, P. (2)
*Dienel, O.   *Kittel, J. C.
Doebler, K.   Klotz, H. (2)
Driessler, J.   Krause, P. (2)
Drischner, M. (2)   Kreckel, P. G.
Dupré, M. J. J.   Lange, D. de
Enckhausen, H. F.   Langlais, J. F.
Fiebig, K.   Litzau, J. B. (2)
Fischer, J. K. F.   Lublin, J. de
Forchhammer, T. (2)   *Meibohm, D. (3)
Franke, F. W.   Mendelssohn-Bartholdy, F.
Frenzel, R.   *Merkel, G. (2)

Metzger, H. A.
Micheelsen, H. F.
*Mueller-Hartung, C.
*Naubert, F. A.
Oertzen, R. von
*Palme, R.
Peeters, F.
Pepping, E.
*Pillney, K. H.
Piutti, K. (3)
Raasted, N. O.
Ramin, G.
Raphael, G.
*Rebling, G.
Reda, S.
Reger, M. (2)
*Richter, E. F.
Rinck, J. C. H.
Ritter, A. G.
Rudnick, W.
Saffe, F.

*Schaab, R.
Scheidt, S. (4)
Schmeel, D.
Schreiber, F. C.
Schumann, G.
Stout, A. (2)
Strohofer, J.
Studer, H.
Thomas, G. A. (2)
Trautner, F. W.
Vierling, J. G.
Wagner, A.
Wagner, F.
Weigl, B.
Wendt, E. A.
Wenzel, E.
Wettstein, H.
*Wolff, C. M.
Zachau, F. W. (4)
Zipp, F.

Variants:

Af dybsens noed til dig, min Gud

Alnaes, E.
Andersen, E.
Hamburger, P. (2)
Hoegenhaven, K. J.

Raasted, N. O.
Thybo, L.
Woeldike, M. A.

Av dypest noed

Thorkildsen, J.

De Profundis

Read, G.

Aus tiefer Not (Strassburg)
Z 4438a

Armsdorff, A.
Bach, J. C.
Baldamus, F.
Bausznern, W. von (2)
Bieske, W.
Brieger, O.
Enckhausen, H. F.
Engelbrecht, K. F.
Fluegel, E. P.
Franke, F. W.
Haase, H. H.
Hasse, K.

Inderau, H.
Kickstat, P.
Klaus, V.
Koch, M.
*Koeckert, C.
Kotter, H. (2)
Kunze, C.
Lang, H.
Leupold, A. W.
Lorenz, J. F. (2)
Luetzel, J. H.
Marpurg, F. W.

Metzger, H. A.
Micheelsen, H. F.
Mueller, G.
Mueller, S.
Oley, J. C.
Pachelbel, J.
Reda, S. (2)
Reinhardt, A.
Rinck, J. C. H.
Rudnick, W.
Rumpf, W.
Schuetze, W.

Aus tiefer Not (Strassburg) (cont.)

Schwencke, J. F. (2)   Walther, J. G. (3)   Wiemer, W.
Seyerlen, R.   Weber, H.   Wolff, E. M.
Sprung, W.   Wedemann, W.   Zipp, F.
Vierling, J. G. (2)   Wettstein, H.
Variants:
Ach Gott, die armen Kinder dein

Gotha, G.

Ach, wie elend ist uns're Zeit

Pachelbel, J.

Aus tiefer Not lasst uns zu Gott

Driessler, J.

Et trofast hjerte, Herre min

Jeppesen, K.   Raasted, N. O.   *Wuertz, J.
Laub, T. (2)   Soerensen, S.
Nielsen, T. H.   Thybo, L.
Olsen, P. R.   *Videroe, F.

Herr, wie du willst

Arbatsky, Y.   Grote, H.   Piutti, K. (3)
Baldamus, F.   Gulbins, M. (2)   Reger, M.
Berthold, K. F. T.   Haase, K.   Reichardt, B.
Boehm, G.   Heinrich, J. G.   Reinbrecht, A.
Claussnitzer, P.   Karg-Elert, S.   Schaab, R. (2)
Doles, J. F.   Kunze, K.   Stiller, K.
Drischner, M.   Marpurg, F. W.   Streicher, J. A. (2)
Fluegel, G.   Merkel, G.   Tuerke, O.
Frenzel, H. R.   Muehling, A.   Wettstein, H.
Geist, C.   Pachelbel, J.   Wolff, C. M.
Geist, P.   Palme, R.   Zehrfeld, O. (2)
Gerber, E. L.   Peeters, F.

O Hellig Aand, du skatt

Bergh, L.   Skottner, F.
Drischner, M.

O Jesu Krist som mandom tog

Strassburg

Hovdesven, E. A.

Unser Zukunft, Gott, du bist

Pachelbel, J.

Wie heilig ist die Staette hier

Mendelssohn, A.

Aus tiefer Not lasst uns zu Gott
See: Aus tiefer Not (Strassburg)
- middle section of tune.

Austrian Hymn (Haydn)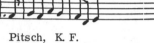

Ashford, E. L.	Gruber, J.	
Attrup, C.	Hulse, C. Van	Pitsch, K. F.
Balderston, M.	Hustad, D.	Purvis, R.
Bibl, R.	Koehler, E.	Reger, M.
Birn, M.	Larson, E. R.	Schmid, J.
Brown, A. G. Y.	Melville, H.	Sechter, S.
Conway, M. P.	Messner, J.	Stehle, J. G. E.
Diggle, R.	Paine, J. K.	Whitford, H. P.

Variants:
Deutschland ueber alles

Finzenhagen, L. H. O.

Gott erhalte Franz der Kaiser

Schmidt, F.   Sechter, S.

Autumn (Barthelemon)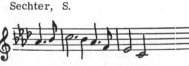

Ashford, E. L.

Autuuden ja armon sana (Finnish)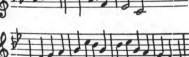

Salonen, S.

Variant:
Ordet om Guds naad

Av dypest noed
See: Aus tiefer Not (Phrygian)

Av hoeyheten opprunnen er
See: Wie schoen leuchtet

Ave Jerarchia
See: Gottes Sohn ist kommen (Weisse)

Ave Maria (Plainsong - Mode 1)

  *Hulse, C. Van
  *Karg-Elert, S.   Marier, T. N.
  *Kreckel, P. G. (3)   Peeters, F.
  Lee, J.   Togni, V.
             Tranzillo, D.

Variant:
Salutio Angelica

  *Karg-Elert, S.

Ave Maria (Narenza)
  See: Narenza (Cologne)

Ave Maria Kaiserin

  Orlinski, H.

Ave Maria klare, du leichter
  Morgenstern
See: Narenza (Cologne)

Ave Maria zart

  Ahrens, J.
  *Kutzer, E.

Ave Maria zart (Weisse 1675-
  Braun)

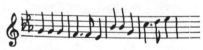

  *Brand, T.   *Miggl, E.
  Doebler, K.   Spranger, J.
  Doppelbauer, J. F.   *Weber, H.
  Lampart, K.

Ave Maris Stella

  Kreckel, P. G.

Ave Maris Stella (Arundel)

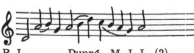

  *Grace, H.
  *Olsson, O. E.   Rowley, A.

Ave Maris Stella (Mode 1)
         Z 1065

  *Benoist, F.   Bedell, R. L.   Dupré, M. J. J. (2)
  Benoit, Dom P. Cavazzoni, G. Fasolo, G. B.
  Bermudo, J.   Coelho, M. R. *Grieg, E. H.
  *Bourdon, E.   De Klerk, A.   Guilmant, A. (2)
  Brun, F.   Doppelbauer, J. F. *Hilaire, R. F.

Jong, M. de
Kauder, H.
*Keldermans, R. A.
Lenel, L.
Lesur, D. J. Y.
*Magin, C.
Marraco-Sancho, J.
Nibelle, H.
Peeters, F. (2)
Radole, G.
Variant:
Stella Maris

Tebaldini, G.
Titcomb, E. H.
Titelouze, J. (3)
Tombelle, F. de la
Tournemire, C.
Vadon, J.
Vierne, R.
*Villermont, D. de
Willan, H.

Weitz, G.

Ave Regina

*Arnaldi, A.
Erb, M. J. (4)
*Weitz, G.

Ave Regina Caelitum

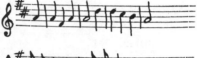

McGrath, J. J.

Ave Regina Caelorum (Solesmes-Mode 6)

*Ahrens, J.
Kropfreiter, A. F.
Woollen, R.

Ave Verum Corpus (Rouen-Mode 6)

Dupré, M. J. J.
Frey, C.
Kauder, H.
Kreckel, P. G. (2)

Lee, J.
Marier, T. N.
McGrath, J. J.
Titcomb, E. H.

Ave Virgo Speciei

Magin, C.

Tune not found

Avison

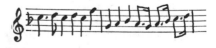

Ashford, E. L.

Avon
See: Martyrdom

Avondzang (Old Dutch)

    Kee, C.
Variants:
O groote Christus

    Rippen, P.

Song L (Dutch)

    Beek, W. van   Westering, P. C. van

Awake Thou Wintry Earth (Dutch)

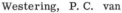

    Thomas, V. C.
Variant:
Vreuchten

Away in a Manger
See: Mueller

Ayn-kay-lo-hay-nu (Lewandow-
ski)

    Miller, R. K.

Aynhoe (Nares)

    Haase, K.

Azmon (Glaeser)

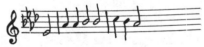

    Beck, A.
    Haase, K.
    Wyton, A.

Babe of Bethlehem (English)

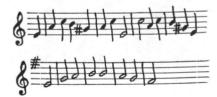

    Best, W. T.

Babylon's Streams (Campion)

        Dyson, G.
        Harris, W. H.
        Stewart, C. H.

Balerma (Barthelemon)

    Peeters, F.

Balfour, (Knowles)

    Orr, R. R. K.

Baltimore (Schumacher)

 Haase, K.

Bangor (Tans'ur)

 Noble, T. T.
 Willan, H.
 Variant:
Den kaerlek du till

 Aahgren, K. E.   Lindroth, H.

Baruch Haba (Hebrew)

 Fromm, H.

Battle Hymn of the Republic
(Steffe)

 Diggle, R.
 Kinder, R.   Wehr, D.
 Simon, B.   Wilson, R. C.

Beata Nobis Gaudia (Cherubic
Hymn)

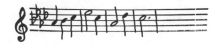

 Blackburn, J.

Batty
 See: Ringe recht (Kuhnau)

Beata Viscera

 Hulse, C. Van
 Sister M. G.

Beatitudo (Dykes)

 Beck, A.
 Haase, K.
 Hulse, C. Van

Bedenke, Mensch, das Ende
 See: Herzlich tut mich verlangen

Bedford (Wheall)

 Haase, K.
 Harwood, B.   Palmer, C. C.
 Mansfield, O. A.   Wesley, S. S.
           Willan, H.

Beecher (Zundel)

    Lorenz, E. J.
    Whitford, H. P.
Variant:
Song 300 A (Dutch)

    Nieland, H.   Westering, P. C. van

Befal du dine veje
   See: Herzlich tut mich verlangen

Befall i Herrens haender
   See: Old 130th

Befiehl du deine Wege (Gesius)

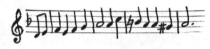

             Z 5393

André, J. O.	Hark, F.	Roth, F.
Brieger, O.	Hasse, K.	Schaab, R.
Cebrian, A.	Hempel, H.	Schneider, M. G.
Degen, H.	Karow, K.	Straumann, B.
Doles, J. F.	Kickstat, P.	Thomas, O.
Drischner, M. (2)	Magnus, E. (2)	Toepfer, J. G.
Ebhardt, G. F.	*Meibohm, D. (5)	Vierling, J. G.
Eyken, J. A. Van	Micheelsen, H. F.	Weber, H.
Franke, F. W.	Muehling, H. J.	Wettstein, H.
Gotha, G.	Mueller-Zuerich, P. (3)	Wieruszowski, L.
Grosheim, G. C.	Piel, P.	(2)
Grote, H.	Reda, S.	Zechiel, E.
		Zorn, B.

Variant:
Das Jahr geht still zu Ende

    Drischner, M. (2)   Spiering, G.
    Gulbins, M.

Befiehl du deine Wege
   See: Herzlich tut mich verlangen

't Behaag' U, Heer, naar
   See: Psalm 17

Behoed uw kerk (Bastiaans)

    Variant:
    Song 103 (Dutch)

    Dragt, J.

Behold a Mystical Rose (Haller)
(Breton)

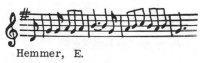

Englert, E.   Hemmer, E.
Variant:
Christmas Pastorale

Schehl, J. A.

Behold a Virgin
See: O Heiland, reiss die
Himmel auf (Rheinfels)

Behold the Great Redeemer
(Careless)

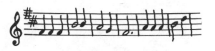

Schreiner, A.

Behoud, O Heer, wil ons
See: Psalm 12

Bei dir, Jesu, will ich bleiben
(Basel)
See: O du Liebe meiner Liebe
(Ebeling)

Bei stiller Nacht
See: In stiller Nacht

Beim fruehen Morgenlicht

Lampart, K.

Beim letzten Abendmahle
See: Ach bleib mit deiner
(Vulpius)

Belmont (Gardiner)

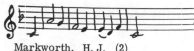

Beck, A.   Markworth, H. J. (2)
Edmundson, G.   Peeters, F.
Grote, H.   Pletner, A.
Haase, K.   Rowley, A.

Bemerton (Filitz)
                      Z 1127
Variants:

Caswall

Cassler, G. W.   Taylor, C. T.
Choveaux, N.   White, H. D.
Coleman, R. H. P.

Bemerton (Filitz) (cont.)

Wem in Leidenstagen

    Beck, A.   Hurford, P.
    Haase, K.   Powell, N. W.
    Hulse, C. Van

Benedic Anima Mea (Goss)

    Hill, L. E.
    Knight, V.
    Salter, S.
Variants:
Lauda Anima

    Adam, J. L.   Groves, R.
    Baumgartner, H. L.   Schaffer, R. J.
    Bratt, C. G.   Walter, S.

Song 147 (Dutch)

    Kousemaker, A.

Benedicamus Domine

    Erb, M. J. (8)
    Ravanello, O.
    Tod, E. A. (2)

Benedicamus Domine

    Baeuerle, H.
    Evans, E.

Benedicamus Domino

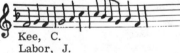

    Becker, R. L   Kee, C.
    Hoff, R.   Labor, J.

Benedicite Dominum

    Weitz, G.

Benediction
  See: Ellers (Hopkins)

Benedictus (Plainsong)
  See Also: Ite Missa Est

    Arnatt, R. K.   Boslet, L. (2)

Bentley (Hullah)

  Hulse, C. Van

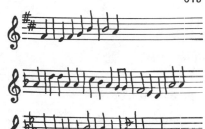

Benton Harbor (Hoffman)

  Figh, V. P.

Bera (Gould)

  Steere, W. C.

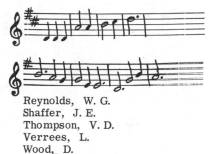

Bereden vaeg foer Herran
 See: Messiah (Swedish)

Bergers, pourquoi
 See: Les Anges dans nos

Besançon Carol (French)

  Faulkes, W.

Bethany (Mason)

  Ashford, E. L.
  Bingham, S.   Reynolds, W. G.
  Colvin, H.   Shaffer, J. E.
  Haase, K.   Thompson, V. D.
  Matthews, J. S. Verrees, L.
  Reuter, F.   Wood, D.
 Variant:
 Naeher mein Gott

  Karg-Elert, S.

Bethlehem (Ancient Christmas
 Hymn)

  Kreckel, P. G.

Bethlehem (Fink)

  Haase, K. (2)

Bevan (Goss)

  Haase, K.
  Willan, H.

Beveel gerust Uw wegen
 See: Herzlich tut mich verlangen

Bewaar, mij toch
     See: Psalm 16

Billing (Terry)

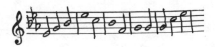

          Bratt, C. G.
          Huijbers, B.

Bis hierher halfst du mir
     See: Allein Gott in der Hoehe

Bis hierher hat mich Gott
     See: Elbing (Sohren)

Bis hierher hat mich Gott
     See: Es ist das Heil uns
     kommen her (Wittenberg)

Bis willkommen (Kittel)

                    Z 3781
          Haase, K.

Bishopthorpe (Clark)

          Willan, H.

Blaenhafren (Welsh)

          Penick, R. C.

Blaenwern (Rowlands)

          Archer, J. S.

Bleibe gut, heit'rer Muth

                    Z 3232
          Umbreit, K. G.

Blessed Assurance (Knapp)

          Thompson, V. D.
     Variant:
     Assurance

          Colvin, H.

Blessed Be God (Andriessen)

          Huijbers, B.

Blijf bij mij, Heer
    See: Eventide (Monk)

Bliv kvar hos mig

    Ahlberg, V.

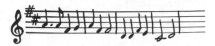

Blomstertid (Swedish)

    Peeters, F.
Variants:
Den blomstertid nu kommer
(Swedish Psalm)

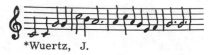

    Wikander, D.

Jeg vil mig Herren love
(Swedish Psalm)

    Nielsen, L.

Blomstre som en rosengaard
(Hartman)

    *Raasted, N. O.

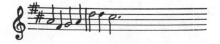

Blomstre som en rosengaard
(Laub)

    *Frandsen, H. B.   *Wuertz, J.
    Woeldike, M. A.

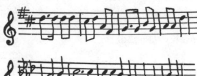

Blomstre som en rosengaard
(Steenberg)

    Karlsen, R.

Boar's Head Carol (English)

    Best, W. T.

Boenhoer mig, Gud

    Berg, G.

Bohemian Brethren
    See also: Psalm 138
                        Z 8186
    Reger, M.   Walter, S.
Variants: Wyton, A.
Mein ganzes Herz erhebet dich

    Franke, F. W.   Mueller-Zuerich, P.

Bohemian Brethren (cont.)

   Mit Freuden zart

Abel, O.	Drischner, M. (2)	Oncley, A. L.
Bender, J.	Haase, H. H. (2)	Pepping, E. (2)
Bornefeld, H.	Hennig, W.	Poppen, H. M.
Bratt, C. G.	Herrmann, K. H.	Rasley, J. W.
Candlyn, T. F. H.	Krapf, G.	Rohlig, H.
Distler, H.	Lorenz, E. J.	Walcha, H.
Driessler, J.	Micheelsen, H. F.	Withrow, S. S.

Bona Patria (Bristol)

   Haase, K.

Bortnianski
   See: St. Petersburg

Bortvend din vrede, Gud
   See: Herzliebster Jesu

Boven de Starren

   Zwart, W. H.

Boylston (Mason)

Beck, A.	Haase, K.
Bingham, S.	Lenel, L.

Bradford
   See: Messiah (Harold-Kingsley)

Braint (Welsh)

   Matthias, W.

Bramley (English)

   Variant:
   Great God of Heaven

   Faulkes, W.

Brat, Herre Jesu, blandt dine
(Laub)

   Wuertz, J.

Brattle Street (Pleyel)

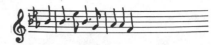

    Zeuner, C.

Bread of Heaven (Maclagen)

    Coleman, R. H. P.
    Trevor, C. H.

Bread of Life (Sherwin)

    Ashford, E. L.   Duro, J.   Miles, R. H.
    Bingham, S.   Johnson, D. N.   Shaffer, J. E.

Bremen
   See: Wer nur den lieben
   (Neumark)

Breslau (Leipzig)
               Z 533
          Also in 4
               4

    Douglas, W.   Porter, A. B.
    Graf, F.   Sumsion, C. C.
   Variants:
   Ach blein bei uns

    Walcha, H.

Ach Gott, wie manches Herzeleid
(Psalmodia Nova)

    Forchhammer, T.   Riedel, H.
    Merk, G.   Walther, J. G.
    Merkel, G.

Ach lieber Herre Jesu Christ

    Beyer, M.   Zipp, F.

Herr Jesu Christ, meins Leben's Licht

    Baldamus, F.   Manz, P.
    Fischer, M. G.   Merkel, G. (3)
  *Forchhammer, T.   Michel, A.
    Frech, J. G.   Oechsler, E.
    Haase, K.   Piutti, K.
  *Herzog, J. G.   Reinbrecht, F.
    Hiss, F.   Rinck, J. C. H. (2)
    Kauffmann, /G. F. (2) Schwencke, J. F. (2)
  *Litzau, J. B.   Stolze, H. W.

<u>Breslau</u> (cont.)

<u>Herr Jesu Christ, meins Leben's Licht</u> (cont.)

Toepfer, J. G. (2)	Walther, J. G. (2)
Vierling, J. G.	*Zehrfeld, O.
*Walcha, H.	

<u>O Herre Jesus, mit levneds lys</u>

Thuner, O. E.

<u>O Jesu Christ, meins Leben's Licht</u>

Bodenschatz, S. H.	*Mueller, S. W.
Drischner, M.	Oechsler, E.
Engelbrecht, K. F.	Piutti, K.
Franke, F. W.	Reda, S.
Frenzel, H. R.	Reger, M.
Grabner, H.	*Streicher, J. A.
Hofmeier, A.	Traegner, R.
*Hoyer, K.	Waag, G.
Kickstat, P.	Weber, H.
Leupold, A. W.	Witteborg, A.
Merkel, G.	Wolfrum, K.
Micheelsen, H. F.	

<u>O Jesu Christus, wahres Licht</u>

Magnus, E.

<u>Wir danken dir, Herr Jesu Christ</u>

Pfeiffer, C. D.	*Spiering, G.

<u>Brich an, du schoenes Morgenlicht</u>
See: <u>Ermuntere dich, mein
schwache Geist</u> (Schop)

<u>Brich an, du schoenes</u> (Leipzig)
See: <u>Kommt her zu mir</u>

<u>Brich entzwei, mein armes Herze</u>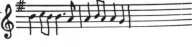

Baldamus, F.
Vierling, J. G.

<u>Brich herein, suesser Schein</u>

Franke, F. W.
Schmid, K.

Brich uns, Herr, das Brot
(Micheelsen)

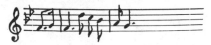

      Metzger, H. A.   Micheelsen, H. F. (3)

Brightly Beams Our Father's
    Mercy (Bliss)

      Thompson, V. D.
Variant:
Lower Lights

      Wilson, R. C.

Bring a Torch (French)

      Rogers, S. E.   Williams, D. H.
Variant:
Un Flambeau

      Bingham, S.   Hulse, C. Van

Bristol (Ravenscroft)

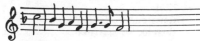

      *Cameron, G.
      Dyson, G.   Palmer, C. C.
      Groves, R.   West, J. E.
      Hunt, W.   Westrup, J. A.
      Lang, C. S.   Willan, H.

Brocklesbury (Barnard)

      Powell, R. J.

Broedre og soestre, vi skilles
(Simonson)

      Frandsen, H. B.   Wuertz, J.

Bromsgrove (Dyer)

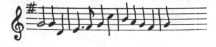

      Rowley, A.

Brorson
  See: Kender du den (Berggreen)

Brother James Air (Bain)

      Darke, H. E.
      Owens, S. B.
      Wright, M. S.
Variant:
Marosa

Brunn alles Heils
   See: Old 100th

Brunnquell aller Guter (Crueger)

           Z 6252c

   Oley, J. C.
   Variant:
   Ande, full av Naade

      Aahgren, K. E.   Olson, D.

Bryd frem, mit hjertes trang at
   lindre (Lindeman)

      Bergh, L.   Karlsen, R.
      *Frandsen, H. B.

Bryd frem, mit hjertes trang at
   lindre (Zinck)

      Godske-Nielsen, H.   Thuner, O. E.
      Nielsen, L.   *Vaerge, A.
      Raasted, N. O.   *Videroe, F.
      Rosenkilde-Larsen, E.   Woeldike, M. A.

Bryn Calfaria (Owen)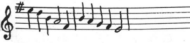

      Vaughan-Williams, R.

Buckau (Walker)

      Walker, E.

Buckland (Haynes)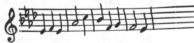

      Haase, K.

Bullinger (Bullinger)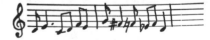

      Hokanson, M.

Buǒh Všemohúci (Czech)

      Vycpalek, L. (V.)

Burford (Purcell)

      Best, W. T.
      Bouman, P.   Haase, K.
      Edmundson, G.   Wesley, S. S.

By Babel's Streams (U. S. Southern)

 Read, G.

Byrd (Peery)

 Peeters, F.

Ça Bergers (French)

 Piché, P. B.

Caersalem (Welsh)

 Diggle, R.

Caithness (Scotch)

 Groves, R.   Stewart, C. H.
 Krapf, G.   Verrees, L.
 Peeters, F.   Willan, H.

Cambridge (Harrison)

 Haase, K.

Cambridge Gate (Walker)

 Walker, E.

Campion (Campion's Tune)

 Harris, W. H.
 Willan, H.

Canonbury (Schumann)

 Stults, R. M.
Variant:
Nachtstueck

 Edmundson, G. (2)

Canterbury
 See: Song 13 (Gibbons)

Canticum Refectionis (Williams)

 Diggle, R.
 Leitz, D.

Cantus Novus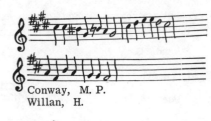

    Schwarz-Schilling, R.

Cape Town (Filitz)

    Archer, J. S.   Conway, M. P.
    Cameron, G.   Willan, H.

Capel (English)

    Sowerby, L.

Carey's
  See: Surrey (Carey)

Caritas Perfecta (Atkinson)

    Haase, K.

Carlisle (Lockhart)

    Lang, C. S.
    Peeters, F.   Willan, H.

Carol (Willis)

    Matthews, H. A.   Thomas, V. C.
    Nordman, C.   Thompson, V. D.
    Seely, J. G.   Vibbard, H.
    Stults, R. M.   Walton, K.

Carol of the Angels (Appalachian)

    Niles, J. J.

Carter (Carter)

    Baumgartner, H. L.

Caswall
  See: Bemerton

Celestia (Danish)

    Cassler, G. W.
    Rogers, S. E.   Wood, D.
  Variants:
  Dejlig er den himmel blaa (Danish)

    Moeller, S. O.   Vaerge, A.
    Nielsen, L.   Videroe, F.
    Thuner, O. E.

Lieblich ist der Himmel blau

    Raasted, N. O.

Chantons un Saint Cantique
(French)

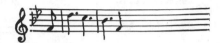

    Erb, M. J.

Chapel Royal (Purcell)

    Palmer, C. C.

Chaque jour de ma vie   Tune not found

    Hess, C. L.

Charity (Stainer)

    Noble, T. T. (2)

Charterhouse (Evans)

    Sowerby, L.

Chartres (French)

    Daquin, L. C.
    Faulkes, W.   Piché, P. B.
    Guilmant, A. (3)   Powell, R. J.
    Hastings, E. H.   Purvis, R.
    Variants:
    Nous voici dans la ville

      Bingham, S.   Borucchia, N.

    Or dites-nous, Marie

      Chauvet, C. A.   Lebègue, N.
      Franck, C.

Chatauqua (Sherwin)

    Thompson, V. D.

Chef couvert de blessures
  See: Herzlich tut mich verlangen

Cherry Tree Carol

    Reichenbach, H.

Cheshire (Este's)

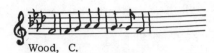

    Dyson, G.
    Slater, G. A.   Wood, C.

Chester (Billings)

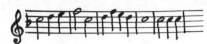

    Gaul, H.

Chesterfield
  See: Richmond

Chichester (Ravenscroft 1621)

  Variant:
  O God My Strength

    Dyson, G.

Chorus Novae Jerusalem (Sarum
  - Mode 3)

    Edmundson, G.   Peeters, F.

Christ, alles was dich kraenket
             Z 5534
    Rinck, J. C. H.

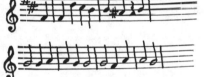

Christ Arose (Lowry)

    Shaffer, J. E.
    Wilson, R. C.

Christ der du bist der helle
  Tag (Bohemian)
            Z 384

    Bach, J. C.   Distler, H.   Karow, K.
    Bach, J. S. (2) Dupré, M. J. J. Kickstat, P.
    Bach, W. F.   Faehrmann, H. Pepping, E.
    Becker, K. F.   Goetz, H.   Piutti, K.
    Claussnitzer, P. Hark, F.   Toepfer, J. G.
  Variant:
  Christe du bist der helle Tag

    Poppen, H. M.   Zipp, F.
    Werner, F.

Christ fuhr gen Himmel
  See: Christus Resurrexit

Christ Is Born

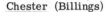

    Guilmant, A.

Christ Is Born Today (Lithuanian)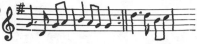

    Whitmer, T. C.

Christ ist erstanden (Folk)
    See: Christus Resurrexit

Christ lag in Todesbanden (Walther)
    See: Christus Resurrexit

Christ, the Lord, is Risen Today
    See: Victimi Paschali Laudes
    (traditional Catholic)

Christ, unser Herr, zum Jordan
    kam (Walther)
               Z 7246

Abel, O.	Franke, F. W.	Praetorius, M.
Bach, J. S. (2)	Homann, E.	Reda, S.
Bornefeld, H.	Karow, K. (2)	Seiffert, U.
Buxtehude, D. (2)	Metzger, H. A.	Vierling, J. G.
Dupré, M. J. J.	Pachelbel, J.	Weber, H.
Fiebig, K.	Pepping, E.	Wedemann, W.
Fischer, M. G.	Piutti, K.	Zachau, F. W.

Christ Was Born in Bethlehem
    (English)

    Best, W. T.

Christe, aller Welt Trost

    Bach, J. S.
    Dupré, M. J. J.   Kropfreiter, A. F.
Variant:
Christe, Trost aller Welt

    Kegel, K. C.

Christe, der du bist Tag und
    Licht (Old Church)
               Z 343

Boehm, G. (3)	Krieger, J.	Praetorius, M.
De Klerk, A.	Metzler, F.	Scheidt, S.
Dragt, J.	Micheelsen, H. F.	Weber, H.
Haase, K.	Pachelbel, J.	

Variants:
Christe Qui Lux Es (Old Church)

Lenel, L.	Scheidt, S. (2)
Redford, J.	Sweelinck, J. P. (2)
Routh, F.	

Christe, der du bist Tag und Licht (cont.)

  O Kriste, du som ljuset aer

    Berg, G.

Christe, du Beistand (Loewen-
      stern)
                        Z 993

    Bender, J.
    Fiebig, K.   Karow, K.
    Grabner, H.   Reda, S.
    Hark, F.   Schneider, M. G.

Christe, du bist der helle Tag
  See: Christ der du bist der helle Tag

Christe, du Lamm Gottes

    Raasted, N. O.

Christe, du Lamm Gottes
  See: Agnus Dei (Liturgy)

Christe, du Lamm Gottes (Decius)
  See: O Lamm Gottes, unschuldig (Decius)

Christe, du Schoepfer aller Welt
      (Koenigsberg)

    Brod, K.
    Driessler, J.   Senftleben, G.

Christe Fons Jugis (Rouen)

    Coleman, R. H. P.
    Wallbank, N.

Christe, hie merk
  See: O Christ, hie merk

Christe Qui Lux Es (Old Church)
  See: Christus, der du bist Tag und Licht

Christe Redemptor Omnium
      (Sarum)

        Cavazzoni, G. (2)
        Dupré, M. J. J.   Parry, C. H. H.
        Evans, P. A.   Peeters, F. (2)
        Fasolo, G. B.   Purvis, R.
        Hulse, C. Van   Redford, J.
        Matthews, J. S.   Willan, H.

Variant:
Jesu Redemptor Omnium

Dupré, M. J. J.   Hulse, C. Van

Christe Sanctorum (French)

   *Butcher, V.
   Healey, D.   *Sinzheimer, M.

Christe Sanctorum (Plainsong)

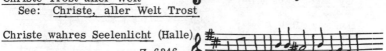

Christe Sanctorum (Sarum)

Christe Trost aller Welt
   See: Christe, aller Welt Trost

Christe wahres Seelenlicht (Halle)
              Z 6346

   Haase, K.
Variant:
Schwing dich auf (Halle)

   Reichardt, A.   Schwencke, J. F. (2)

Christe, wahres Seelenlicht
   See: Schwing dich auf (Ebeling)

Christen, schaut zum Kreuz   Tune not found
   hinan

   Brosig, M.

Christen sind ein goettlich Volk
(Elberfeld)
            Z 6376
   Franke, F. W.

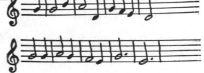

Christen singt mit frohem
   Herzen (Joseph)

   Telemann, G. P.

Christglaeubig Mensch, wach auf

   Kickstat, P.

Christi Mutter (German)
             Z 39
   *Weber, H.

Christi Mutter (cont.)

    Variants:
Corner

      Purvis, R.

Seht die Mutter dort voll Schmerzen

      Rinck, J. C. H. (2)

Christi Mutter stand mit
    Schmerzen
             Z 41
      Philipp, F.

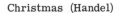
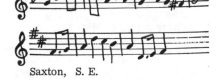

Christian Union (Knoxville)

      Donovan, R. F.

Christians, Who of Jesus Sorrows

      DeBrant, C.

Christmas (Handel)

      Barlow, W.
      Reuter, F.   Saxton, S. E.

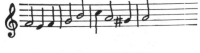

Christmas Carol (Dutch)
    See: Song 7 (Dutch)

Christmas Cradle Song (Bo-
    hemian)

      Poister, A. W.

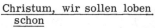

Christmas Eve

      Thomas, V. C.

Christmas Pastorale
    See: Behold a Mystical Rose (Haller)

Christo, dem Osterlaemmlein
    (Stenger)
             Z 1767
      Walther, J. G. (2)

Christum, wir sollen loben
    schon
             Z 297

Bach, J. S. (2)	Herzog, J. G.	Reuter, F.
Boehm, G.	Krapf, G.	Scheidt, S.
Dupré, M. J. J.	Krieger, J.	Walther, J. G.
Franke, F. W.	Piutti, K.	Weinreich, W.
Haase, K.	Praetorius, M.	Willan, H.

Variants:

A Solis Ortus Cardine (Plainsong- Mode 3)

De Klerk, A.	Lenel, L.	Praetorius, M. (2)
Dupré, M. J. J.	Peeters, F.	Scheidt, S.
Fleury, A.	Pepping, E.	Titelouze, J. (2)

Crudelis Herodes

Guilmant, A. (2)

Fra Himlen hoeit jeg kommer her

Karlsen, R.

Christus, Christus, Christus ist
See: Schwing dich auf zu deinem
Gott (Franck)

Christus, der ist mein Leben
See: Ach, bleib mit deiner Gnade

Christus, der uns selig macht
(Ancient German)
See also: O hilf, Christe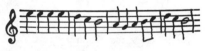

Z 6283

Bach, J. S. (2)	Dupré, M. J. J.	Krieger, J. (2)
Baldamus, F.	Enckhausen, H. F.	Pepping, E. (2)
Bender, J.	Fluegel, E. P.	Rinck, J. C. H.
Bornefeld, H.	Franke, F. W. (2)	Schwencke, J. F. (3)
Bossler, K.	Herrmann, K. H.	Telemann, G. P. (3)
Brieger, O.	Hoyer, K.	Theile, A. G.
Claussnitzer, P.	Kammeier, H.	Vierling, J. G.
Driessler, J.	Kindermann, J. E.	Walcha, H.
		Walther, J. G. (3)

Variants:
Jesu, deine Passion

*Gulbins, M.	Micheelsen, H. F. (2)
Huebner, E.	

Jesu, Kreuz, Leiden und Pein

Borngaesser, W.

Christus, der uns selig macht (cont.)

   Seele, mach dich heilig

      Abel, O.

Christus Factus Est

      Rheinberger, J.

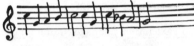

Christus ist auferstanden

      Niermann, R.

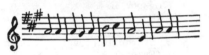

Christus ist erstanden (Bohemian)
           Z 6240c
    *Litzau, J. B.

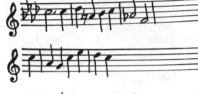

Christus ist erstanden (German
   Carol)

      Schmalz, P.
Variant:
German Carol - Easter

      Wilson, R. C.

Christus ist erstanden
  See: Christus Resurrexit

Christus ist geboren   Tune not found

      Reichenbach, H.

Christus ist heut zum Himmel g'fahr'n
  See: Til Himmels for den (Crailsheim)

Christus Pro Nobis
  See: Jesus Christus, wahr Gottes Sohn

Christus Resurrexit (Plainsong)
          Z 7012
     See also Z 8584

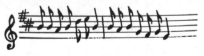

    Bingham, S.   Vogel, W.
    Sorge, E. R.
Variants:
Christ fuhr gen Himmel

    Driessler, J.   Rinck, J. C. H.
    Huth, A.   Schwarz-Schilling, R. (2)
    Piutti, K.

Christ ist erstanden (Folk)

Ahrens, J.
Albrechtsberger, J. G.
Bach, H.
Bach, J. S. (2)
Baldamus, F.
Bartmuss, R.
Bender, J.
Bibl, R.
Bornefeld, H.
Bratt, C. G. (2)
Breydert, F. M.
Brosig, M.
Buchner, J. A. (2)
Buttstedt, J. H.
Candlyn, T. F. H.
Claussnitzer, P.
Conze, J.
David, J. N.
Driessler, J.
Dupré, M. J. J.
Fischer, J. K. F. (4)
Forchhammer, T.
Gindele, C.
Gloetzner, A.
Goller, F.
Grabner, H. (2)
Haase, K.
Hanebeck, H. R.
Hark, F.
Heilmann, H.
Hennig, W.
Herzog, J. G.
Hicks, M.
Hoyer, K.
Hulse, C. Van
Kaestel, L.
Karow, K. (2)
Kickstat, P.
Klotz, H.
Koch, K.
Krohn, I. H. R.
Kuntz, M.

Kutzer, E.
Lasso, O. di
Lauterbach, L.
Lenel, L.
Leupold, A. W.
Meibohm, D. (2)
Mueller-Zuerich, P. (2)
Nieland, J.
Oechsler, E.
Oertzen, R. von
Peeters, F.
Pfeiffer, C. D.
Piutti, K.
Poppen, H. M.
Pranschke, J.
Purvis, R.
Raasted, N. O. (2)
Reger, M.
Reichardt, B.
Reutter, G.
Riemenschneider, G.
Rinck, J. C. H. (2)
Rohlig, H.
Romanovsky, E.
Rumpf, W.
Scheidt, S.
Schilling, H. L.
Schmidt, F.
Schroeder, H.
Schumacher, M. H.
Schwarz-Schilling, R.
Schweppe, J.
Spitta, H.
Thomas, B.
Traegner, R.
Unbehaun, G.
Vierling, J. G.
Vogel, W.
Walcha, H.
Weathers, K.
Willan, H.
Wilson, R. C.

Christ lag in Todesbanden

Bach, J. B.
Bach, J. S. (6)
Bausznern, W. von
Bender, J.
Boehm, G. (3)
Buckland, J.

Burkhard, W.
Buttstedt, J. H. (3)
Buxtehude, D.
Cassler, G. W. (2)
Driessler, J.
Dupré, M. J. J.

Christus Resurrexit (cont.)

Christ lag in Todesbanden   (cont.)

Grabner, H.   Pachelbel, J.
Gulbins, M. (4)   Piutti, K.
Haase, K.   Raasted, N. O.
Homilius, G. A. (2)   Rinck, J. C. H. (2)
Hopkins, J.   Scheidt, S. (7)
Horst, A. Van der   Schroeder, H.
Huebner, E.   Stout, A.
Kaeppel, G. C. A.   Telemann, G. P. (4)
Karow, K.   Vetter, A. N. (2)
Kickstat, P.   Videroe, F. (2)
Kindermann, J. E.   Vierling, J. G.
Koch, J. H. E. (2)   Volckmar, F. W.
Krapf, G.   Volckmar, T. (2)
Krebs, J. L.   Weber, H.
Litzau, J. B.   Zachau, F. W. (3)
Micheelsen, H. F.

Christus ist erstanden

Ahrens, J. (2)   *Preyer, G.
*Claussnitzer, P.   Schwencke, J. F. (2)
Fischer, J. K. F.   *Sechter, S.
*Hohn, W.   Weber, H.
Merkel, G.

I doedens baand vor Frelser laa

Andersen, E.   Nielsen, T. H.
Jeppesen, K.   Raasted, N. O.
Laub, T.   Videroe, F.

Krist stod op af Doede, i Paaskemorgenrede

Hamburger, P.   *Thuner, O. E.
Jeppesen, K.   Woeldike, M. A.
*Laub, T.   *Wuertz, J.
Maegaard, J.

Sitt oega Jesus oeppnat har

Berg, G.

Christus Urunknak
   See: Hungarian Christmas Song

Christus Vincit (Ambrosian)

Berthier, P.   Kreckel, P. G.
Bragers, A. P.

Christus Vincit (Gregorian)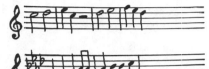

Peeters, F.

Chtic, aby spal (Czech)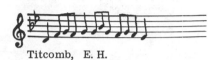

Wiedermann, B. A.

Cibavit Eos (Corpus Christi)

Plum, P. J. M.
*Stoegbauer, I.   Titcomb, E. H.

Cibavit Eos
See: Pange Lingua Gloriosa (Sarum- Mode 3)

Clairvaux (Polack)

Haase, K.

Claro Paschali Gaudio
See: Aurora Lucis Rutilat

Cleansing Fountain (Mason)

Diemer, E. L.

Clementissime Domine   Tune not found

Plum, P. J. M.

Cleveland (Burnap)

Beck, A.

Cloisters (Barnby)

Whitford, H. P.

Close to Thee (Vail)

Thompson, V. D.

Coelestis Urbs Jerusalem
(Mode 4)

Peeters, F.
Ravanello, O.   Tombelle, F. de la

Coelestis Urbs Jerusalem
(Mode 8)

    Dupré, M. J. J.
    Peeters, F.   Webbe, W. Y.

Colur tout à Dieu
  See: Psalm 1

Come All You Worthy Gentlemen
  See: Somerset Carol (English)

Come, Come, Ye Saints
(English)

    Jenkins, C.

Come Holy Ghost (Lambillotte)
  See: Veni Creator (Lambillotte)

Come Rock the Cradle (Koeln
  1619)

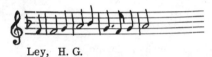

    Gotch, O. H.   Ley, H. G.

Come Shepherds Awake

    Guilmant, A.

Come Ye Disconsolate
  See: Consolation (Webbe)

Communion (Gregorian)

    Purvis, R.

Concord

    Thatcher, H. R.

Concordi Laetitia
  See: Orientis Partibus

Conditor Alme Siderum
  See: Creator Alme Siderum

Conqueror
  See: Palestrina

Consolation (Lindeman)

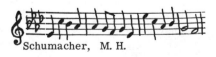

    Haase, K.   Schumacher, M. H.

Variant:
Naar mit oeie (Lindeman)

Baden, C.   Steenberg, P.
Sandvold, A.

Consolation (Webbe)

Gillette, J. R.
Lorenz, E. J.   Stults, R. M.
Variants:
Alma Redemptoris Mater

*Beck, A.   Reuter, F.
Haase, K.

Come Ye Disconsolate

Ashford, E. L.   Thomson, V.

Converse
See: What a Friend

Converted Thief

Pfautsch, L.

Copenhagen (Zinck)

Peeters, F.
Variants:
Er Gud for mig, saa traede

Christensen, B.   Hamburger, P.
Frellsen, E.   *Videroe, F.
Godske-Nielsen, H.

Jeg ved paa hvem

Jeppesen, K.   Westerlund, E.
Weinholt-Pedersen, K.

Jeg vil mig Herren love (Zinck)

Haase, K.   Lindorff-Larsen, E.
Karlsen, R.   Raasted, N. O.

Cor Jesu (Plainsong)

*Falcinelli, R.

Corde Natus
See: Divinum Mysterium

Corner
    See: Christi Mutter (German)

Coronae (Monk)

    Hulse, C. Van

Coronation (Holden)

Burdett, G. A.	Hokanson, M.	Reuter, F.
Dressler, J.	Hustad, D.	Stults, R. M.
Fleischer, H.	Langlais, J. F.	Whitford, H. P.
Groom, L. H.	Mansfield, O. A.	

Courage (Parker)

    Stults, R. M.

Covenanters Tune (Scotch)

    Bitgood, R.
    Hailing, R. G.   Peek, R. M.
    Variant:
    Pisgah

        Colvin, H.

Coventry Carol (English)

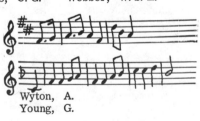

Gibbs, C. A.		
Gore, R. T.	Lenel, L.	Sumsion, H. W.
Healey, D.	Milford, R. H.	Walton, K. (2)
Hulse, C. Van (2)	Phillips, C. G.	Webber, W. S. L.

Cowper (Mason)

    Reuter, F.

Cradle Song (Kirkpatrick)

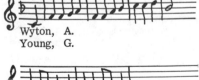

    Kirkpatrick, W. J.   Wyton, A.
    Marryott, R. E.   Young, G.

Cramer (Rousseau)

    Variant:
    Milde Jesu, du som sagde

        Sandvold, A.

Crasselius
    See: Winchester New

Creation (Billings)

    Powell, R. J.

Creation (Haydn)

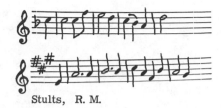

    Ashford, E. L.
    Koehler, E.   Stults, R. M.

Creator Alme Siderum (Mode 4)

              Z 339

Ahrens, J.	Kreckel, P. G. (2)	Thomas, V. C.
Brandon, G.	Oldroyd, G.	Titelouze, J.
Bratt, C. G. (2)	Peeters, F.	Tombelle, F. de la
Dupré, M. J. J.	Schehl, J. A.	Yon, P. A. (2)

Variants:
Conditor Alme Siderum

    Rowley, A.   Waters, C. F.
    Titelouze, J.

Gott, Heil'ger Schoepfer aller Stern (Meisse)

    Ahrens, J.   Titelouze, J.
    Romanovsky, E.   Weber, H.
    Schroeder, H.

Lob sei dem Allmaechtigen Gott

    Bach, J. S. (2)   Hasse, K.
    Dupré, M. J. J.   Walther, J. G.

Credo (Mode 1)

    Kreckel, P. G.

Credo (Strassburg)

    Vogel, W.

Credo In Unum Deum

    Olsson, O. E.
    *Titcomb, E. H.

Crimond (Scotch)

Archer, J. S.	Mueller, C. F.
Brydson, J. C.	Rowley, A.
Irvine, J. S.	Thiman, E. H.
Mansfield, P. J.	Titcomb, E. H.

Croft's 136th (148th)

     Blackburn, J.
     Haase, K.   Peeters, F.
     Parry, C. H. H.   Stewart, C. H.

Cromer (Lloyd)

     Cassler, G. W.

Croon Carol
   See: Joseph, lieber Joseph mein

Cross of Jesus (Stainer)

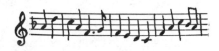

     Cassler, G. W.

Croyland (La Trobe)
   See: La Trobe

Crucifer (Smart)

     Cummins, R.

Crudelis Herodes
   See: Christum wir sollen loben

Crusader (Whitney)

     Whiting, G. E.

Crusaders Hymn
   See: Schoenster Herr Jesu (Silesian)

Crux Ave Benedicta

     Kreckel, P. G.

Culbach (Breslau)

     Haase, K.

Culrose (Scotch)

     Rimmer, F. (2)

Cunningham

     Smith, E. A.

Cwm Rhondda (Hughes)

    Langston, P. T.
    Mansfield, P. J.   Peeters, F.
    McKay, G. F.   Whitney, M. C.

Czech Christmas Carol

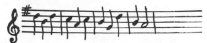

    Weinberger, J.

Czech Song

    Wiederman, B. A.

Da Christus geboren war
  (Bohemian)   Z 4816
      Also in 4
          4
    Bornefeld, H.   Kickstat, P.
    Driessler, J.   Koch, J. H. E.
    Fiebig, K.   Pepping, E.
    Franke, F. W.   Zipp, F.
  Variants:
Frygt, min Sjael, den sande Gud (Horn)

    Wuertz, J.

Frykt mitt barn

    Anderssen, F.   Raasted, N. O.
    Gangfloet, S.

In Natali Domini

    Matthison-Hansen, G.

Meine Seele, gib das Brot

    Raasted, N. O.

Singen wir aus Herzens Grund (Horn)

    Gulbins, M.   Rinck, J. C. H.
    Piutti, K.   Vierling, J. G.

Somnar jag in med blicken faest (Nuernberg)

    Nielsen, L.

Synge vi, av hjertens grund

    Alnaes, E.   Borg, O.

Da Christus geboren war (cont.)

   Treuer Wachter Israel

      Pepping, E.

   Wunderbarer Gnadenthron

      Herrmann, K. H.   Werner, F.
      Pfeiffer, C. D.

Da Jesu an dem Kreuze stund
     des Kreuzes Stamm
           Z 1706

Ahrens, J.	Humpert, H.	Pepping, E.
Bach, J. S.	Kickstat, P.	Rinck, J. C. H. (3)
David, J. N.	Kindermann, J. E.	Scheidt, S. (7)
Dupré, M. J. J.	Krieger, J.	Schwarz-Schilling, R.
Fischer, J. K. F.	Pachelbel, J. (4)	Vierling, J. G.
Hulse, C. Van	Palme, R.	

Variants:
Da Jesus hing am Kreuzesstamm

      Doebler, K.

Da Jesu hing am Kreuzesstamm
   See: Da Jesu an dem Kreuze

Da Jesu sterft aan   Tune not found

      Zwart, J.

Da Pacem Domine
   Based on Veni Redemptor

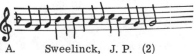

      Hennig, W.   Raison, A.   Sweelinck, J. P. (2)
      Langlais, J. F.   Schlick, A.   Werner, J. J.

Daa Jesus fraa mor (German)

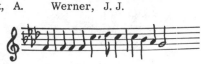

      Nielsen, L.
   Variant:
   Das Leiden des Herrn

Daar is uits werelde duistre wolken
   See: Song 10 (Dutch)

Daar juicht een Toon

      Zwart, J.

Daar ruist langs de wolken   Tune not found

     Bruin, B.   Zwart, J.
     Nieland, H.

Dagen gaar med raske Fjed
(Weyse)

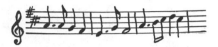

     Nielsen, E.
     Wuertz, J.
     Variant:
Alltid freidig naar du gaar

     Nielsen, L.

Dagen viger og gaar bort
   See: Als Christus mit seiner

Daily, Daily, Sing to Mary (Trier)
   See: Omni Die Dic Mariae

Dal Tuo Celeste
   See: Es blueht der Blumen eine (Gorres)

D'Almachtig is mijn herder
   See: Song 182 (Dutch)

Dank sei Gott in der Hoehe
(Crueger)
               Z 5422

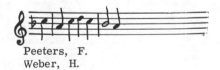

     *Herzog, J. G.   Roth, F.
     Kessler, F.

Dank sei Gott in der Hoehe
(Gesius)
               Z 5391

     Leupold, A. W.   Peeters, F.
     Variant: Weber, H.
Geduld die soll'n wir haben

     Haase, K.   Stecher, H.

Danket dem Herrn
   See: Nun danket alle Gott

Danket dem Herrn, denn er ist
   freundlich (Bohemian)
               Z 12

     Buxtehude, D.
     Koetzschke, H.   Rinck, J. C. H.
     Oley, J. C.   Walther, J. G.
     Ottenwaelder, A.   Wedemann, W.

Dans cette étable (French)
                    Also in 6
                             8

    Borucchia, N.

Darmstadt
    See: Was frag ich nach der Welt

Darwall
    See: Darwall's 148th

Darwall's 148th
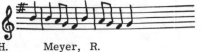

        Beck, A.   Haase, K.
        Coleman, R. H. P.   Marks, H. K.
        Darke, H. E.   Miles, G. T.
        Dressler, J.   Palmer, C. C.
        Gardner, J. L.   Peeters, F.
        Goodhart, A. M.   Rogers, S. E.
    Variant:
    Darwall

        Candlyn, T. F. H.   Thiman, E. H.
        Diggle, R. (2)   Whitlock, P.
        Rowley, A.   Willan, H.

Das alte Jahr vergangen ist
    (Steuerlein)
                    Z 381

        Bach, J. S.   Distler, H.   Meyer, R.
        Bieling, H. H.   Driessler, J.   Pepping, E.
        Bornefeld, H.   Dupré, M. J. J. Reda, S.
        Busch, A. G. W.   Hoegner, F.   Walther, J. G. (2)

Das Credo
    See: Wir glauben all an einen Gott,
    Schoepfer (Wittenberg)

Das Feld ist weiss (Koenigs-
    berg)

        Grabner, H.
        Roth, F.

Das Gloria
    See: Allein Gott in der Hoehe

Das Halleluiah (Gerold)
                    Z 7143
        *Rinck, J. C. H.
    Variant:
    Jehova, Jehova, deinem Namen

Fischer, M. G.   Unbehaun, G.
Rinck, J. C. H. (2)   Unruh, E.
Toepfer, J. G.

Das Halleluiah
                        Z 7142

**Das Heil der Welt, Herr Jesu
Christ** (Koeln)

    Doebler, K.

Das Jahr geht still zu Ende
  See: Befiehl du deine Wege (Gesius)

Das Jahr geht still zu Ende
  See: Herzlich tut mich verlangen

**Das Jesulein soll doch mein
Trost** (Helder)
                        Z 7597
                     also in 4
                             4
    Bach, J. S.   Fischer, M. G.   Rinck, J. C. H.
    Dupré, M. J. J.   Kittel, J. C.   Vierling, J. G.

Das Leiden des Herrn
  See: Daa Jesu fraa mar (German)

Das neugebor'ne Kindelein
(Vulpius)
                        Z 491
    Cassler, G. W.
    Johnson, D. N.   Peeters, F.

Das Sanctus
  See: Jesaia, dem Propheten

Das Tagwerk nun vollendet ist
(Braun)

    Schwarz-Schilling, R.

Das walt Gott, Vater (Vetter)

                        Z 673
    Haase, K.   Peeters, F.
Variant:
Vetter

    Peeters, F. (2)

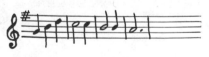

Das walt mein Gott (Vopelius)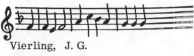

    Fischer, M. G.
    Toepfer, J. G.   Vierling, J. G.

Das walte Gott, der helfen kann

             Z 1775
    *Lang, H.

Das walte Gott, der helfen kann
    See: Dies sind die heil'gen Zehn Gebot

Das walte Gott, der uns (Sohr)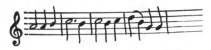

             Z 930
    Variant:
    Det koster mer, end man fra

      *Wuertz, J.

Das Wort geht von dem Vater aus
    See: Wir danker dir, Herr Jesu Christ,
    dass du (Wittenberg)

Dass Jesus siegt, bleibt ewig
    See: Es ist genug (Muehlhausen)

David's Lamentation (Billings)

     Read, G.

De dag door Uwe gunst
    See: St. Clement

De God des heils wil mij
    See: Psalm 23

De Gospel Train Is Coming
(Spiritual)

    Thomas, V. C.

De Heer is God en niemand meer
    See: Elbing (Sohren)

De Heer is Groot
    See: Psalm 48

De hellig tre konger (Stoerl)
            Z 3916

Moeller, S. O. Woeldike, M. A.
Thuner, O. E.

De Herders (Peeters)

*Zwart, J.

De herdertjes lagen bij nachte

Zwart, J.

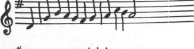

De herlige himlar som skaparen
(Lindeman)

Nielsen, L.

De herlige himlar (Wideen)

Karlsen, R.

De hoge God alleen
See: O Mensch bewein

De Lofzang van Maria
See: Lofzang van Maria

De Profundis (Latin)

Kreckel, P. G.

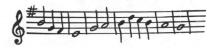

De Profundis
See: Aus tiefer Not (Phrygian)

De Profundis Clamavi

Maekelberghe, A.

Decius
See: Allein Gott in der Hoehe

Deck the Halls (Welsh)

Hulse, C. Van (2)
Pasquet, J. Thomas, V. C.

Deep River (Spiritual)

Felton, W. M.
Kemmer, G. W.

Deerhurst (Langran)

Reuter, F.

Dein Jesus rufet
   See: Wer nur den lieben Gott (Neumark)

Dein Koenig kommt in niedern

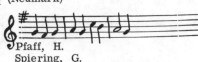

     Knab, A.   Pfaff, H.
     Luedders, P.   Spiering, G.

Dein Koenig kommt in niedern
   (Zahn)

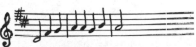

     Claussnitzer, P.
     Grabner, H.   Herrmann, K. H.

Dein Koenig kommt, O Zion

              Z 8630c
     Pfeiffer, C. D.

Dein Lob, Herr, ruft der Himmel aus

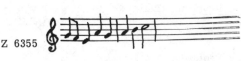

     Ahrens, J.

Dein Wort ist, Herr
   See: Elbing (Sohren)

Deines Gottes freue dich
   (Boehner)

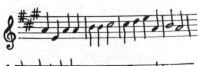

             Z 6355
     *Volckmar, F. W.

Deines Gottes freue dich (Stern)

             Z 8796

Dejlig er den himmel blaa (Laub)

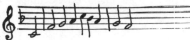

   *Jensen, S.
    Moeller, S. O.

Dejlig er den himmel blaa (Danish)
   See: Celestia

Dejlig er jorden
   See: Schoenster Herr Jesu

Den bitre doed dig traengte   Tune not found

     Thuner, O. E.

Den blomstertid nu kommer (Swedish Psalm)
   See Blomstertid

Den die Hirten lobten sehr (Latin)

Z 1380

Bender, J.
Claussnitzer, P. (2)
Driessler, J.
Drischner, M. (2)
Franke, F. W.
Grosse-Weischede, A. (2)
Haas, J.
Herrmann, K. H.

Kickstat, P.
Piutti, K.
Proeger, J.
Spiering, G.
Streicher, J. A.
Weinreich, W.
Wieruszowski, L.

Variants:

Gentle Mary Laid Her Child

Powell, R. J.

Gib mir, Gott, ein Loblied

Raasted, N. O.

Giv mig, Gud, en salmetunge

Frellsen, E.
Godske-Nielsen, H. (2)
Jeppesen, K.
Moeller, S. O.

Nielsen, O. S.
Raasted, N. O.
Woeldike, M. A.

Jesus, Creator of the World (Andernach)

Herzog, J. G.

Kommt und lasst uns Christum ehren

Bender, J.
Bornefeld, H.
Driessler, J.
*Hark, F.
*Hoyer, K.
Huth, A. (2)
Kickstat, P.

Micheelsen, H. F.
Otto, H.
Pepping, E. (2)
Poppen, H. M.
Rinck, J. C. H.
Rumpf, W.
*Zahn, J.

Komt en laet ons Christus eeren

Dalm, W.

Kee, C.

Quem Pastores

Grundmann, O. A.
Gulbins, M.
Kickstat, P.
Kousemaker, A. (2)
Kuehn, K.

Thiman, E. H.
Walcha, H.
Warner, R. L.
Willan, H.

Den die Hirten lobten sehr (cont.)

   Quempas Carol

      Krapf, G.   Lenel, L.

   Song 22 (Dutch)

      Berg, J. J. van den   Wilgenburg, D. van
      Stulp, G.

Den er slet ikke af Gud forladt

      Videroe, F.

Den Himmels Vorschmack
(Gregor)
               Z 19
      Rinck, J. C. H.

Den idraet Gud
   See: I fyrste upphav var Guds ord

Den kaerlek du till
   See: Bangor (Tans'ur)

Den lyse Dag forgangen er (Kingo)
   See: Vergangen ist der lichte Tag

Den moerke nat forgangen er
(Laub)

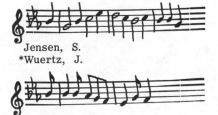

      *Frandsen, H. B.   Jensen, S.
      Godske-Nielsen, H.   *Wuertz, J.

Den moerke nat forgangen er
(Winding)

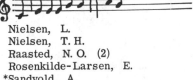

      Raasted, N. O.
      *Videroe, F.

Den signede dag med fryd (Weyse)

      Bitsch, V.
      Gangfloet, S.   Nielsen, L.
      Haase, K.   Nielsen, T. H.
      Hamburger, P.   Raasted, N. O. (2)
      Jeppesen, K.   Rosenkilde-Larsen, E.
      Laub, T.   *Sandvold, A.
      Moeller, S. O.   Wuertz, J.

Den signede dag som nu vi ser
(Thomissen)

  Bergh, L.   Nielsen, L.
  Lindberg, O. F.
Variant:
Gud Fader og Soen og Helligaand

  Woeldike, M. A.

Den sjael, som Gud i sandhed
kender (Zinck)

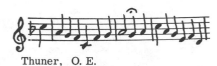

  Hamburger, P.   Thuner, O. E.
Variant:
Du hoeie fryd for rene sjele

  Nielsen, L.

Den store hvite flokk (Laub)

  Bjerre, J.
  Videroe, F. (3)   *Wuertz, J.

Den store hvite flokk (Lindeman)

  Bergh, L.
  Karlsen, R.

Den store hvite flokk (Nebelong)

  Nielsen, T. H.
  Thuner, O. E.   Vad, P.

Den store hvite flokk (Norwegian)

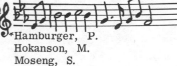

  Cappelen, C.   *Hamburger, P.
  Drischner, M.   Hokanson, M.
  *Frandsen, H. B.   Moseng, S.
  Gangfloet, S.   Nielsen, L.
Variant:
Great White Host

  Haase, K.   Hovland, E.

Den store mester kommer (Hartman)

  Bjerborg, W.   Woeldike, M. A.
  *Moeller, S. O.   *Wuertz, J.

Den store mester kommer (Hoffmann)

    Bitsch, V.   Grinsted, B.
   *Frandsen, H. B.   *Wuertz, J.

Den trange vej er bred (Freylinghausen)

    Karlsen, R.

Den tro som Jesum favner
  See: Aus meines Herzens Grunde

Den yndigste Rose
  See: Iam Moesta

Denby (Dale)

    Haase, K.

Denmark Hill (Walker)

    Walker, E.

Denne er dagen, som
  See: Lobet den Herren, ihr Heiden (Vulpius)

Dennis (Naegel)

    Ashford, E. L.   Stults, R. M.
    Manookin, R. P.   Thomas, V. C.

Dennoch bleib ich stets
  See: Meinen Jesum lass ich nicht (Ulich)

Deo Gracias (English)

    Galeotti, C.   Whitlock, P.
    Peeters, F.   Willan, H.
  Variant:
  Agincourt Song

    Dunstable, J.   Roberts, M. J.

Deo Gratias

    Biggs, R. K.

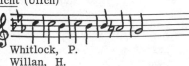

Deo Gratias (Latin)

    Brun, F.
    Kreckel, P. G.

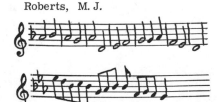

Der am Kreuz (Soehnlein)

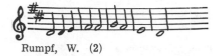

         Z 6644

   Homilius, G. A.   Rumpf, W. (2)

Der am Kreuz (Koenig)
   See: Jesu, deine tiefen Wunden

Der beste Freund (Reichhardt)

         Z 2885

   Beck, A.

Der du bist A und O
   See: Mein Friedefuerst

Der du bist Drei in Einigkeit
   (Plainsong)
   See also: O Lux Beata (Sarum)

         Z 335c

Alberti, J. F. (2)	Reuter, F.
Barbe, H.	Schweppe, J.
Praetorius, M.	Walther, J. G.

Der du das Los von meinen Tagen

         Z 3037

   Lang, H.

Der du dein Wort mir hast
   gegeben (Knecht)

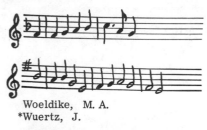

         Z 2897

   Schwencke, J. F. (3)

Der du, Herr Jesu, Ruh
   See: Nun lasst uns den Leib (Stahl)

Der du zum Heil erschienen

   Ehinger, H. R.

Der er en vej (Laub)

   Frandsen, H. B.
   Thuner, O. E.   Woeldike, M. A.
   Videroe, F.   *Wuertz, J.

Der Gerechten Seelen

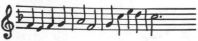

   Ricek, W.

Der goden God
  See: Psalm 50 (Dutch)

Der graue Winter   Tune not found

      Litzau, J. B.

Der grimmig Tod
  See: Durch Adams Fall

Der Heiland ist erstanden (Wen-
  ninger)

      Schehl, J. A.

Der Heiland ist erstanden
                geboren
                    Z 163
      *Sechter, S.

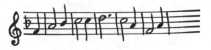

Der Heiland ist geboren

      Lampart, K.

Der Heil'gen Leben
                Z 5008
      Praetorius, M.

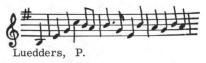

Der Heilige Christ ist kommen
  See: Aus meines Herzens Grunde

Der helle Tag vergangen ist
  See: Vergangen ist der lichte Tag

Der Herr bricht ein um Mitter-
  nacht

      Fink, C.   Luedders, P.

Der Herr ein Koenig ist (Goudimal)
  See: Psalm 97

Der Herr ist gut, in dessen
  Dienst wir steh'n (Kocher)

                    Z 3111
      Lang, H.

Der Herr ist Koenig ueberall

      Franke, F. W.

Der Herr ist mein getreuer Hirt
  (Eisleben)
               Z 1709
     Pepping, E.

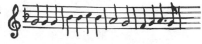

Der Herr ist mein getreuer Hirt
  See: Allein Gott in der Hoehe

Der Herr ist mein getreuer Hirt
  (Wittenberg)
  See: Psalm 23 (Bourgeois)
            Z 4466

Der Herr mein Licht
  See: Psalm 27

Der Hoelle Pforten sind
  zerstoert

    Karg-Elert, S.

Der lieben Sonne, Licht und
  Pracht (Freylinghausen)
            Z 5659
    Buehl, W.   Haase, K.

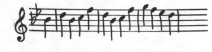

Der lieben Sonne, Licht und
  Pracht (Telemann)
            Z 5663?

Abel, O.	Franke, F. W.	
Bachem, H.	Gulbins, M.	*Stolze, G. C.
Claussnitzer, P.	Haupt, A.	Vierling, J. G.
Eyken, J. A. Van	Piutti, K.	Weinreich, W.

Der lieben Sonnen licht (Penn-
  sylvania Dutch)
  See: O dass ich Tausend
  (Dretzel)   Z 5668

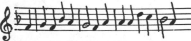

Der Mange skal komme
  See: Stockholm

Der Mond ist aufgegangen (Schulz)

           Z 2322

Fiebig, K. (2)	Riemenschneider, G.
Hessenberg, K.	Schweppe, J.
Magnus, E.	Walcha, H.
Proeger, J.	Weber, H.

Variants:
Alt oprejst maanen staar

    Joergensen, G.

Der Mond ist aufgegangen (Schulz) (cont.)

  Sig maanen langsomt haever

    Nielsen, T. H.

Der Mond ist aufgegangen
See: Nyberg

Der Morgenstern ist aufgedrungen
  (Praetorius)
                Z 808
      Drischner, M. (2)

Der sad en fisker (Nielsen)

    Frandsen, H. B.

Der Spiegel der Dreifaltigkeit

    Spranger, J.

Der Tag bricht an (Vulpius)
                Z 1765
      Franke, F. W.
      Koehler, K.   Pepping, E.
Variant:
Wach auf, wach auf, 's ist hohe Zeit

    Hark, F.

Der Tag der ist so freudenreich
  (Wittenburg)
                Z 7870

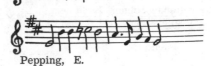

      Bach, J. S. (2)   Fischer, J. K. F.(3)   Looks, R.
      Baldamus, F.   Grote, H.   Manz, P.
      Buttstedt, J. H. (2)   Haase, K.   Moser, R.
      Buxtehude, D. (3)   Hokanson, M.   Neumann, F.
      David, T. C.   Hulse, C. Van   Pachelbel, J. (2)
      Driessler, J.   Humpert, H.   Pfeiffer, C. D.
      Drischner, M.   Karow, K.   Rinck, J. C. H.
      Dupré, M. J. J.   Koch, J. H. E.   Vierling, J. G.
                                                    Zipp, F.

Variants:
Als Jesu geboren war
Dies Est Laetitiae

    Edmundson, G.   Yon, P. A.

  Ein Kindelein so loebelich

    Ahrens, J.   Schwencke, J. F. (2)
    Enckhausen, H. F.

Et lidet Barn saa lystelig
Glaeden hun er foedt i dag

    Jensen, S. (2)   Videroe, F.
    Thybo, L.   Wuertz, J.

O lue fra Guds (Weisse)

    Drischner, M.   Gangfloet, S.

Der Tag ist hin (Stratner)

    Schaeffer, A.

Der Tag ist hin (Geneva)
See: Psalm 8

Der Tag ist seiner Hoehe nah
(Werner)

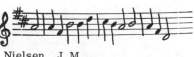

    Werner, F.

Der Tag neigt sich dem Abend zu
    See: Herr Jesu Christ, dich zu uns wend

Des Morgens erste Stunde
    See: Aus meines Herzens Grunde

Det aer en ros utsprungen
    See: Es ist ein Ros'

Det er saa yndigt aa foelges ad
(Laub)

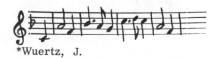

    Christensen, B.   Nielsen, J. M.
    Godske-Nielsen, H.   Woeldike, M. A.
    Hamburger, P.

Det er saa yndigt aa foelges ad
(Weyse)

    *Frandsen, H. B.   *Wuertz, J.
    Karlsen, R.

Det hellige Kors (Rudolfi)   Tune not found

    Pedersen, A.

Det hellige Kors (Thomisson)

    Hamburger, P.   Thuner, O. E.
    *Larsen, K. L.   Woeldike, M. A.

Det kimmer nu til Julefest
　　See: Emmanuel (Balle)

Det koster ej for megen strid
　　(Laub)

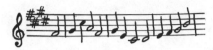

　　　*Thuner, O. E.

Det koster ej for megen strid
　　(Steenberg)

　　　Nielsen, L.

Det koster ej for megen strid
　　See: Es kostet viel (Freylinghausen)

Det koster mer enn man fra
　　foerst (Zinck)

　　　Nielsen, L.

Det koster mer end man fra foerst
　　See: Das walte Gott, der uns (Sohr)

Det koster mer enn man fra foerst
　　See: Psalm 8

Det lakker nu ad aften brat
　　See: Herr Jesu Christ, dich zu uns
　　wend (Gotha)

Det livets ord vi bygger paa
　　See: Mach's mit mir, Gott (Schein)

Dette er dagen som Herren
　　(Steenberg)

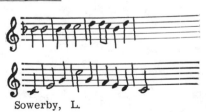

　　　Nielsen, L.

Deus Fortis
　　See: Herre Gud, ditt dyre navn og aere

Deus Qui Sedes Super Thronum

　　　Lublin, J. de

Deus Tuorum Militum (Grenoble)

　　　*Butcher, V.
　　　Krapf, G.   Sowerby, L.

Deus Tuorum Militum (Mode 3)

  Cavazzoni, G.
  *Fasolo, G. B.

Deus Tuorum Militum (Mode 8)

  Peeters, F.

Deus Tuorum Militum (Latin -
Mode 8)

  Variants:
  Exultet Caelum Laudibus

  Titelouze, J.

Jesu Corona Virginum

  Sister M. G.

Deutschland ueber Alles
 See: Austrian Hymn (Haydn)

Devant la crèche

  Wideroee, H.
 Variant:
 Foran Krybber

Diadem (Eller)

  Hustad, D.

Diademata (Elvey)

Boalt, J. E.	Loret, C.	
Curry, R. D.	Lutkin, P. C.	Rogers, S. E.
Hasse, K.	Reuter, F.	Stults, R. M.
Hemmer, E.	Rogers, L.	Wyton, A.

Dich lieb ich, O mein Gott und Herr
 See: Mach's mit mir, Gott

Dich seh' ich wieder, Morgenlicht
 See: Wie schoen leuchtet

Die Erde ist des Herren

  Reichel, B.

Die ganze Welt, Herr Jesu Christ

    Murschhauser, F. X. A.

Die ganze Welt, Herr Jesu
   Christ (Koeln)

      *Bender, J.   Lange, M.
       Driessler, J.   Pepping, E.
       Kickstat, P.   Weber, H.
    Variant:
    Hilariter

Die Gnade unser's Herrn Jesu
   Christ (Gregor)
               Z 8648

     Piutti, K.   Streicher, J. A.

Die gueld'ne Sonne voll Freud
   und Wonne (Ebeling)
               Z 8013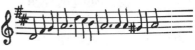

      Barner, A.   Krause, P.
      Bender, J.   Kunz, E.
      Claussnitzer, P. (3) Leupold, A. W.
      Drischner, M. (2)   Magnus, E.
     *Drwenski, W.   Meissner, H.
      Fiebig, K.   *Merk, G.
      Grosse-Weischede, A. Piutti, K.
      Hanebeck, H. R.   Ramin, G. (2)
      Hark, F. (2)   Reda, S.
     *Hasse, K.   Rumpf, W.
      Hessenberg, K.   Schink, H.
      Hoyer, K.   Straesser, E.
      Huth, A.   Weber, H.
      Kickstat, P.   Wettstein, H.
      Klotz, H.   Wolfrum, K.

Die gueld'ne Sonne voll Freud
   und Wonne (Freylinghausen)

              Z 8015

Die helle Sonn' leucht't jetzt
   herfuer (Vulpius)

            Z 504

     Bender, J.   Hark, F.   *Otto, H.
     Brod, K.   Huth, A.   Petzold, J.
     Franke, F. W. Kickstat, P.   Rumpf, W.
     Gradehand, F. Magnus, E.   Weyrauch, J.
     Haase, K.   Micheelsen, H. F. Wieruszowski, L.

Die Himmel ruehmen
            Z 1560
    Piutti, K.

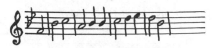

Die Himmel ruehmen des
    Ewigen Ehre (Folk)
             Z 1545a

      Fischer, M. G.
      *Vierling, J. G.   Wolfrum, K.

Die Himmel ruehmen des
    Ewigen Ehre (Hiller)

      Lapo, C. E.

Die Kirche ist ein altes Haus
   (Lindeman)

      Hokanson, M.
      Lorenz, E. J.   Nielsen, L.
Variants:
Die Kirche steht auf ew'gem Grund

      Raasted, N. O.

Gammel aer kyrkan

      Salonen, S.

Kirken den er et gammelt Hus

      Bergh, L.   Moseng, S.
      Christensen, B. (2)   Nielsen, L. (2)
      Frellsen, E.   Peeters, F. (2)
      Haase, K.   Raasted, N. O. (3)
      Held, W.   Rosenkilde-Larsen, E.
      Hoegenhaven, K. J.   Steenberg, P.
      Hoelty-Nickel, T.   Thomsen, P.
      Janáček, B.   Thuner, O. E.
      Jeppesen, K.   Videroe, F.
      Laub, T.   Walter, S.
      Matthison-Hansen, G. Woeldike, M. A.
      Moeller, S. O.   Wuertz, J.

    Song 227 (Dutch)

      Beek, W. van   Nauta, J.
      Bijster, J.

Die Kirche steht auf ew'gem Grund
   See: Die Kirche ist ein altes Haus

Die lieblichste Ros'
　　See: Iam Moesta

Die Nacht ist kommen (Bohemi-
　　an)
　　　　　　　　Z 5000

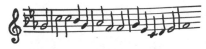

　　　Haase, K.
　　　Jacobi, M.　　　　　Weber, H.
　　　Litzau, J. B.　　　　Zahn, J.
　　　Reichel, B.　　　　　Zechiel, E.

Die Nacht ist vorgedrungen
　　(Petzold)

　　　Artmueller, K.
　　　Koch, J. H. E.　　　Petzold, J. (2)

Die Natur feiert das Pfingstfest

　　　Raasted, N. O.

Die Natur feiert das Pfingstfest
　　(Berggreen)
　　See: Naturen holder Pinsefest

Die Seele Christe heil'ge mich
　　(Seelenlust)
　　　　　　　　Z 636
　　　*Gulbins, M.

Die Seele Christe heil'ge mich
　　See: Nun lasset uns den Leib (Stahl)

Die Sonn' hat sich mit ihrem Glanz
　　See: Psalm 8

Die Stimme eines Engels ruft

　　Variant:
　　En fridens Aengel

　　　Lindberg, O. F.

Die Tugend wird durch's Kreuz
　　geuebet (Halle)
　　　　　　　　Z 6009

　　Baldamus, F.　　　Kickstat, P.　　　*Ricek, W.
　　Breuninger, K. F.　Krause, P.　　　　Riedel, H.
　　*Claussnitzer, P.　Lang, H.　　　　　Rudnick, W.
　　Fluegel, G.　　　　Looks, R.　　　　Schwencke, J. F. (2)
　　Franke, F. W.　　　*Palme, R.　　　　Seyerlen, R.
　　*Gruel, E.　　　　Penick, R. C.　　　*Streicher, J. A.
　　Hoyer, K.　　　　Piutti, K.　　　　Wettstein, H.

Variants:
Du hoeie fryd for rene sjele

    Drischner, M.

Song 52 (Dutch)

    Wilgenburg, D. van

Song 102 (Dutch)

    Wilgenburg, D. van

Song 144 (Dutch)

    Wilgenburg, D. van

Song 151 (Dutch)

    Nauta, J.   Wilgenburg, D. van

Song 224 (Dutch)

    Wilgenburg, D. van

Song 280 (Dutch)

    Hoogewoud, H.   Wilgenburg, D. van
    Stulp, G.

Wie gross ist des Allmaecht'gen (Halle)

André, J.	*Merk, G.
Bender, J.	Mueller, S.
Brosig, M.	*Spittal, W.
Drischner, M.	*Toepfer, J. G.
*Freudenberg, C. G.	*Volckmar, W. V.
Kuntze, C.	*Wenzel, H.

Die Tugend wird durch's Kreuz
geuebet (Knecht)
             Z 6031

    *Frenzel, H. R.
Variant:
Wie gross ist des Allmaecht'gen (Knecht)

    Burkhardt, C.   Weeber, J. C.
    Koch, M.

Die wir uns all hier beisamen finden
    See: Herr und Aeltster deiner
    Kreuzgemeinde

Dies Est Laetitiae
 See: Der Tag der ist so freudenreich

Dies Irae, Dies Illa (Catholic
 Melody)

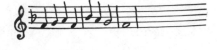

 Haase, K.

Dies Irae, Dies Illa (Plainsong)
     Z 44

Ahrens, J.	Hulse, C. Van	Simonds, B.
Dethier, G. M.	Luard-Selby, B.	Snow, F. W.
Edmundson, G.	Plum, P. J. M.	Stanford, C. V.
Erb, M. J. (2)	Purvis, R.	Woyrsch, F.

Variants:
Dommens Dag

 Karlsen, R.

Tag des Zorns

 Piutti, K.

Dies ist der Tag den Gott gemacht
 See: Lobet den Herrn, ihr Heiden all
 (Vulpius)

Dies ist der Tag den Gott gemacht
 See: Vom Himmel hoch

Dies ist der Tag zum Segen
 eingeweiht
     Z 1021

 *Forchhammer, T.   *Sechter, S. (3)
 Rinck, J. C. H.   *Volckmar, F. W.

Dies ist die Nacht, da mir
 See: O dass ich Tausend (Koenig)

Dies sind die heil'gen Zehn
 Gebot (Erfurt)
     Z 1951

Bach, J. C.	Enckhausen, H. F.	Pachelbel, J. (2)
Bach, J. M. (2)	Fiebig, K.	Piutti, K. (2)
Bach, J. S. (3)	Fromm, H.	Sweelinck, J. P.
Briegel, W. C.	Karow, K.	Toepfer, J. G.
Dupré, M. J. J.	Kuhnau, J. C.	Vierling, J. G.
		Walther, J. G.

Variants:
Das walte Gott, der helfen kann

In Gottes Namen fahren wir

Bach, J. C.   Franke, F. W.
Chemin-Petit, H.   Walcha, H.
*Fiebig, K.

Dieu donne ses lois   Tune not found

Hess, C. L.

Dieweil wir sind versammelt

Z 5355
*Hoyer, K.

Dieweil wir sind versammelt (Schuetz)
See: Ich weiss an wen ich glaube

Diffusa Est   Tune not found

Hilaire, R. F.

Dig rummer ej himle (Laub)

Thuner, O. E.

Dig skall min sjaal
See: Winchester New (Crasselius)

Dig vil jeg elske
See: Ich will dich lieben (Koenig)

Dilexisti (Gregorian)

Boslet, L.

Din dyre Ihukommelse (Gesius)
See: Lasst uns zum Kreuze (Danish)

Din godhet laat oss lova
(Finnish)

Salonen, S.

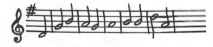

Din spira, Jesu, straeckes ut
See: Nun freut Euch, lieben (Klug)

Dir dank ich fuer mein Leben
(Stuttgart)
Z 2335

Schwencke, J. F. (2)

Dir, dir, Jehova
            Z 3075
   Schwencke, J. F.

Dir, dir, Jehova (Halle)
   See: Winchester New (Wach auf,
   du Geist) (Halle)

Dir, dir, Jehova (Hamburg)
   See: Winchester New (Crasselius)

Dir, Gott, dir will ich
   (Zuerich)
              Z 2888
   Brede, A.

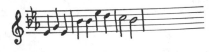

Dir, Gott, dir will ich (Crasselius)
   See: Winchester New (Crasselius)

Ditt ljuva minne, Jesu kaer
   (Finnish)

      Kuusisto, T.

Ditt ord, O Herre (Finnish)

      Kuusisto, T.

Diva Servatrix (Bayeaux
   Melody-Huet)

      Butcher, V.

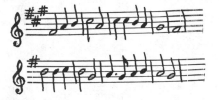

Divinum Mysterium (Plainsong)

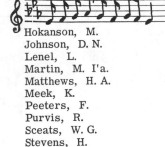

     Archer, J. S.   Hokanson, M.
     Arnatt, R. K.   Johnson, D. N.
     Barlow, W.   Lenel, L.
     Barnes, F. M.   Martin, M. I'a.
     Blackburn, J.   Matthews, H. A.
     Broughton, R.   Meek, K.
     Candlyn, T. F. H.   Peeters, F.
     Cassler, G. W.   Purvis, R.
     Cook, J.   Sceats, W. G.
     Edmundson, G.   Stevens, H.
     Groves, R.   Thomson, V.
     Haase, K.   Watkinson, J. R.
   Variant:
   Corde Natus

     Hull, A. E.   Pepping, E.
     Luard-Selby, B.

Dix (Kocher)

Z 4809

Algra, J.	Haase, K.	
Beck, A.	Harris, W. H.	Pritchard, A. T.
Bingham, S.	Herbeck, R.	Rasley, J. W.
Colvin, H.	Lutkin, P. C.	Smith, E. H.
Cowell, C. P.	Markworth, H. J.	Taylor, C. T.
Dasher, J. A.	Pearce, C. W.	Thompson, V. D.
Dressler, J.	Peeters, F. (2)	Withrow, S. S.

Variant:

Treuer Heiland, wir sind hier

    Buehl, W.   Schink, H.
    Lang, H.

Do Not I Love Thee, O My Lord
(Sacred Harp)

    Powell, R. J.   Read, G.

Doane (Doane)

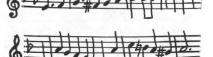

    Lorenz, E. J.

Dolgelly (Welsh)

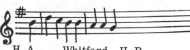

    Groves, R.

Domine Clamavi (Knecht)

    Haase, K.

Domine Jesu (Kyrial)

    Demessieux, J.

Dominus Dixit

    Lechthaler, J.
    Stoegbauer, I.

Dominus Regit Me (Dykes)

Archer, V. B.	Matthews, H. A.	Whitford, H. P.
Ashford, E. L.	McKinley, C.	Willan, H.
Coleman, R. H. P.	Noble, T. T.	Wood, F. H.
Diggle, R.	Rogers, S. E.	Young, G.
Elmore, R. H.	Thiman, E. H.	
Lang, C. S.	Vaughan-Williams, R.	

Dommens Dag
  See: Dies Irae, Dies Illa (Plainsong)

Donne Secours
  See: Psalm 12

Donnez au Seigneur
  See: Psalm 107

Dort (Mason)

     Mason, D. G.

Dover (Williams)

     Haase, K.
     Plettner, A.

Down Ampney (Vaughan-
     Williams)

     Arnatt, R. K.   Ley, H. G.
     Gardner, J. L.   Means, C.
     Gehring, P.   Sinzheimer, M.

Doxology
  See: Old 100th (Geneva)

Drag, Jesus, mig dog efter dig
     (Gebauer)

     Hamburger, P.   *Wuertz, J.

Drag, Jesus, mig dog efter dig
  See: O Traurigkeit

Dreiein'ger, heil'ger, grosser Gott
  See: Es ist das Heil

Dreifaltigkeit, urewig Licht
  See: Old 100th (Geneva)

Drop, Drop, Slow Tears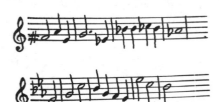
     (Persichetti)

     Persichetti, V.

Drumclog (Wilson)

     Noble, T. T.

Du bar ditt kors, O Jesu mild
See: So gehst du nun, mein Jesu, hin
(Darmstadt)

Du bester aller Menschenkinder
See: Wer weiss wie nahe (Rudolfstadt)

Du bist's, dem Ruhm und Ehre
geboren (Hiller)
Z 1538
Vierling, J. G.

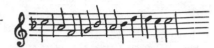

Du des sich alle Himmel freun
(Gregor)
Z 1772
Rumpf, W.

Du fort de ma détresse
See: Old 130th

Du, Frelser, har vaar barndom
(Lindeman)

Nielsen, L.

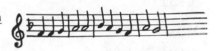

Du Friedefuerst, Herr Jesu
Christ (Gesius)
Z 4373
Bach, J. B. (2)
Proeger, J.
Rinck, J. C. H.
Rohlig, H.

Umbreit, K. G.
Weber, H.
Zipp, F.

Du gehest in den Garten beten
See: Wer nur den lieben (Neumark)

Du Gottmensch bist mit
See: O suessester der Namen

Du grosser Schmerzensmann
(Vopelius)
Z 5159
Abel, O.
Driessler, J.
Drischner, M. (2)
Genzmer, H.
Hennig, W.
Variant:
O grosser Schmerzensmann

Meyer, R.
Oertzen, R. von
Reda, S.
Walcha, H.
Weyrauch, J.

Lehmann, G.

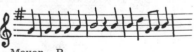

Du guet'ger Heiland   Tune not found

    Brosig, M.
Variant:
Es glueht ein Morgenrot

Du hast, O herr, dein Leben
  See: Valet

Du haver seger vunnit
  See: Praise (Swedish)

Du Herre Krist (Berggreen)

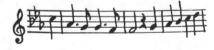

    Bitsch, V.
    Hamburger, P.   Nielsen, T. H.
    Jeppesen, K.   Raasted, N. O. (2)
    *Laub, T.   *Rosenkilde-Larsen, E.
    *Moeller, S. O.   Rung-Keller, P. S.
Variants:
Herr Christ, du bist mein Erloeser
Salvator (Danish)

Du Herre Krist (Rhau)

    *Frandsen, H. B.   *Vaerge, A.
    Holstebroe, H. J.   Woeldike, M. A.

Du Herre Krist (Mainz)
  See: Geborn ist uns ein Kindelein

Du hoechstes Licht
  See: All Morgen ist ganz

Du hoeie fryd for rene sjele
  See: Den sjael, som Gud (Zinck)

Du hoeie fryd for rene sjele
  See: Die Tugend wird durch (Halle)

Du keusche Seele, du (Ahle)

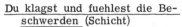

              Z 3983
    Peeters, F.

Du klagst und fuehlest die Be-
  schwerden (Schicht)
              Z 779
    Fluegel, E. P.

Du Lebensbrot, Herr Jesu Christ
   (Sohr)

    Pasquet, J.
Variant:
O Lebensbrot, Herr Jesu Christ

    Claussnitzer, P.

Du Lebensbrot, Herr Jesu Christ
   (Sohren)
See: Elbing

Du lieber, heil'ger, frommer
   Christ (Siegert)

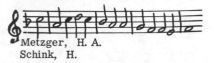

    Markworth, H. J.

Du meine Seele, singe (Ebeling)

            Z 5490

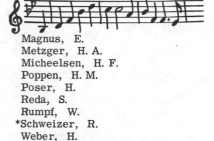

Bender, J.	Magnus, E.
*Ergenzinger, H.	Metzger, H. A.
Franke, F. W.	Micheelsen, H. F.
Hennig, W.	Poppen, H. M.
Hessenberg, K.	Poser, H.
*Hoyer, K.	Reda, S.
Huth, A.	Rumpf, W.
Kickstat, P.	*Schweizer, R.
Leupold, A. W.	Weber, H.

Du meine Seele, singe (Gesius)

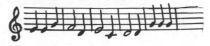

Hasse, K.	Metzger, H. A.
Lang, H.	Schink, H.

Du meiner Seelen (Hungarian-
   Joseph)
            Z 2763

    Englert, E.
Variants:
I Love Thee, O Lord, My Strength

    Kreckel, P. G.

I Love Thee, O Thou Lord Most High

    Kreckel, P. G. (2)

Ich will dich lieben

Frischmann, M.	Romanovsky, E.
Miggl, E.	Weber, H.

Du, O schoenes Weltgebaeude
(Crueger)
                    Z 6776

Caruso, F.
*Gulbins, M. (2)   Richter, E. F.
Kauffmann, G. F.   Schwencke, J. F. (2)
Oley, J. C.   *Smyth, E. M.
Variants:
Jesus, aer mitt liv, min haelsae

Parviainen, J.

Jesu, er mitt liv i live

Gangfloet, S.   Nielsen, L.

Du, O schoenes Weltgebaeude
See: Alle Menschen muessen sterben
(Mueller)

Du rocher de Jacob

Hess, C. L.

Du som gaar ud fra (Barnekow)

*Laub, T.
Lindorff-Larsen, E.   Woeldike, M. A.

Du som gaar ud fra (Lindeman)

Gangfloet, S.
Nielsen, L.   *Videroe, F.

Du som gaar ud fra (Franck)
See: Gen Himmel aufgefahren ist

Du som veien er og livet (Lindeman)

Karlsen, R.

Du vaere lovet (Walther)
See: Gelobet seist du

Du Wunderbrot
                    Z 2063

Ahrens, J.

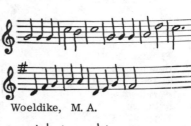

Duke Street (Hatton)

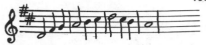

    Balderston, M.
    Colvin, H.   Lewis, J. L.
    Dean, T. W.   Matthews, H. A.
    Dickey, M.   Mead, E. G.
    Gehrke, H.   Reuter, F.
    Groom, L. H.   Sheldon, C. A.
    Haase, K.   Thompson, V. D. (2)
    Hatton, J. L.   Whitford, H. P.
    Kinder, R.   Whiting, G. E.
    Knight, V.   Wienhorst, R.

Dulce Carmen
  See: Alleluia Dulce Carmen (Webbe)

Dundee (Scotch)

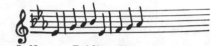

    Ashford, E. L.
    Beck, A.   Johnson, D. N.   Rohlig, H.
    Best, W. T. (2)   Lang, C. S.   Sewell, M. G.
    Buck, D.   Mackinnon, H. A. Sweeting, E. T.
    Curry, R. D.   Noble, T. T.   Thompson, V. D.
    Curry, W. L.   Palmer, C. C.   Tootell, G.
    Diggle, R.   Parry, C. H. H.   Unkel, R.
    Gardner, J. L.   Peeters, F.   Warner, R. L.
    Groves, R. (2)   Reuter, F.   Whitford, H. P.
    Haase, K.   Ridout, G.   Willan, H.

Dunfermline (Scotch)

    Bevan, G. J.

Dunstan (Barnby)

    Beck, A.
    Haase, K.   Reuter, F.

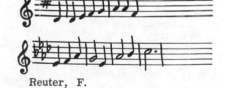

Durch Adams Fall (Klug)
          Z 7549

    Bach, J. C.
    Bach, J. S. (2)   Hoepner, C. G.   Schwencke, J. F. (2)
    Bach, W. F.   Homilius, G. A. (2) Sweelinck, J. P.
    Baldamus, F.   Karow, K. (2)   Telemann, G. P. (2)
    Buxtehude, D.   Kickstat, P.   Vierling, J. G.
    Claussnitzer, P. (2) Pachelbel, J. (4)   Walcha, H.
    Dupré, M. J. J.   Pepping, E.   Walther, J. G.
    Fiebig, K.   Piutti, K. (2)   Weyrauch, J.
    Fischer, M. G.   Reda, S.   Zachau, F. W. (3)
    Franke, F. W.   Rinck, J. C. H.   Zipp, F.

Durch Adams Fall (cont.)

   Variant:
   Der grimmig Tod

      Hark, F.   Marckhl, E.
      Kropfreiter, A. F.   Rabsch, E.

Durham (Ravenscroft)

     Willan, H.

Duše milý přesvatý (Czech)

     Michálek, F.

Dybt haelder aaret i sin

     Raasted, N. O.

Dying Christian (Harwood)

     Colvin, H.

Dyp av naade
   See: <u>Folkefrelsar, til oss kom</u> (Sletten)

Dype, stille, staerke, milde
   (Lindeman)

     Nielsen, L.
   Variant:
   Herre, jeg har handlet ille

Easter Alleluia (Latin)

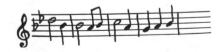

     *Albrechtsberger, J. G.   Springer, M. (2)
     Muffat, G.   *Stoegbauer, I.
     Ottenwaelder, A.   *Webbe, W. Y.

Easter Alleluia
   See: <u>Lasst uns erfreuen</u> (Cologne)

Easter Hymn
   See: <u>Lyra Davidica</u>

Easter Morrow

     McKay, G. F.

Eaton (Wyvill)

   Mansfield, O. A.

Ebeling (Bonn)
                Z 6456a
      Couper, A. B.
Variants:
Hoechster Troester

      Herrmann, K. H.

Warum sollt ich mich denn graemen

      Bach, C. F.   Pfaff, H.
      Brieger, O.   Piutti, K.
      Claussnitzer, P. (2)   Reger, M. (2)
      Erbe, K.   Reichardt, A.
      Faisst, I. G. F. von   Reichardt, B.
      Fluegel, G. (2)   Reinhardt, A.
      Franke, F. W.   Rohwer, J.
      Haase, K.   Rudnick, W.
      Hark, F.   Rumpf, W.
      Herzog, J. G. (2)   Schwencke, J. F. (2)
      Kickstat, P.   Stolze, H. W.
      Krebs, J. L.   Sutter, G. de
      Kuntze, C.   Traegner, R.
      Lang, H.   Vierling, J. G.
      Merkel, G.   Walther, J. G. (3)
      Moser, R.   Wedemann, W.
      Oley, J. C.   Wickenhausser, R.
      Otto, H.   Zipp, F.
      Pepping, E.
Ebenezer
See: Ton-Y-Botel

Ecce Advenit

      Stoegbauer, I.

Ecce Agnus (Dresden)
                Z 2072
      Haase, K.
Variants:
Ihr Christenleut

      Krebs, J. L. (2)

Wir Christenleut hab'n jetzo Freud (Fritsch)

      Bach, J. S. (2)   Dupré, M. J. J.
      Baldamus, F.   Mendelssohn, A.
      Brieger, O.   Oley, J. C. (3)

Ecce Agnus (cont.)

   Wir Christenleut hab'n jetzo Freud (cont.)

      *Otto, H.   Walther, J. G.
      Umbreit, K. G.   Zachau, F. W.

Ecce Ancilla (Mode 8)   Tune not found

   Ravanello, O.

Ecce Iam Noctis (Sarum)

   Edmundson, G.
   Willan, H.

Ecce Lignum Crucis

   Benoit, Dom P.
   Gauss, J.   Heiller, A.

Ecce Panis Angelorum (Plainsong - Mode 8)

      Ahrens, J.   Guilmant, A.   Nieland, J.
      Beltjens, J.   Kreckel, P. G.   Pepin, N. A.
      Claussmann, A.   Lee, J.   Tranzillo, D.
      Diebold, J.   Marier, T. N.

Ecce Panis Angelorum (17th
   Century)

   Kreckel, P. G.

Ecce Tempus Idoneum (Mode 3)
   See: Fons Bonitans

Echo Carol
   See: While By Our Flocks

Eden (English)

   Rowley, A.

Eden (Sacred Hymns - Boston)

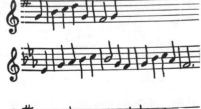

   Haase, K.
   Peeters, F.

Edina (Oakeley)

   Pearce, C. W.

Edsall (Day)

    Leitz, D.

Een naam is onze hope
  See: Aurelia

Een trouwe vriend

    Mazyk, R. van

Een vaste Burg is onze God
  See: Ein feste Burg

Eere zij aan God den Vader
  See: Regent Square

Eg hev ei tenesta stor (Karlsen)

    Karlsen, R.

Eg let att mine troeytte (Steenberg)

    Nielsen, L.

Eg veit i himmerick (Folk Tune)

Gangfloet, S.	Sandvold, A. (2)
Karlsen, R.	Solberg, L.

Eg veit meg
  See: Jeg vet mig

Ehre sei Gott (Bortniansky)

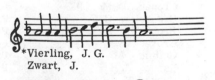

Kruijs, M. H. van'T.	*Vierling, J. G.
Lux, F.	Zwart, J.

Ein feste Burg (Luther)

           Z 7377

Arnell, R. A. S.	Besemann, I. C.
Ashford, E. L.	Boehner, J. L.
Bach, J. C.	Boehnicke, H.
Bach, J. S.	Borg, O.
Baldamus, F.	Bornefeld, H.
Barner, A.	Bossler, K.
Baumert, L.	Brede, A.
Becker, A.	Breidenstein, H. K.
Becker, O.	Brieger, O.
Beer-Walbrunn, A.	Buckland, J.
Bender, J. (2)	Burkhard, W.

Ein feste Burg (cont.)

Buxtehude, D. (5)
Chemin-Petit, H.
Claussnitzer, P.
Copley, R. E.
Curry, W. L.
David, J. N.
Davin, K. H. G.
Dienel, O.
Diggle, R.
Dragt, J.
Draht, T.
Dupré, M. J. J.
Eckardt, A.
Edmundson, G. (2)
Enckhausen, H. F.
Egidi, A. (2)
Engelbrecht, K. F. (2)
Faehrmann, H.
Faisst, I. G. F. von
Faulkes, W.
Fink, C.
Fischer, C. A.
Fischer, M. G.
Fleck, M.
Fluegel, G. (3)
Forchhammer, T. (2)
Franke, F. W.
Freudenberg, C. G.
Gerhardt, P.
Graedener, H. T. O.
Gronau, D. M. (2)
Grosheim, G. C.
Grote, H.
Groves, R.
Gulbins, M. (3)
Haase, H. H.
Haase, K.
Haase, R. (2)
Haenlein, A.
Hanff, J. N. (2)
Hasse, K. (2)
Hennig, W.
Herzog, J. G.
Hess, C. L.
Hesse, A. F. (3)
Hilty, E. J.
Hoogewoud, H.
Hoyer, K.
Johnson, D. N.
Karg-Elert, S.
Karow, K.

Kauffmann, G. F.
Kee, C.
Kickstat, P. (2)
Kienzl, W.
Kint, C.
Kittel, J. C. (2)
Klaus, V.
Koeckert, C.
Koetsier, J.
Kruijs, M. H. van'T.
Kuehmstedt, F.
Kuntze, C.
Lang, H.
Lange, S. de
Linnarz, R. (2)
Lorenz, E. J.
Lorenz, O.
Lux, F.
Markull, F. W.
Marpurg, F. W.
Merk, G.
Merkel, G. (2)
Middleschulte, W.
Mojsisovics, R. von
Mueller, S.
Mueller-Hartung, C.
Mueller-Zuerich, P. (2)
Nikolai, O.
Oley, J. C.
Pachelbel, J. (3)
Paine, J. K.
Palme, R.
Peeters, F. (2)
Piutti, K. (3)
Praetorius, M. (3)
Preston, W. J.
Pruefer, C.
Raphael, G.
Reger, M. (5)
Reuter, F. (2)
Reuter, J. F.
Riedel, H.
Riedel, L.
Rinck, J. C. H. (5)
Roberts, R. M.
Roch, F. W.
Rogers, S. E.
Rohlig, H.
Rudnick, W. (3)
Rumpf, W. (2)
Saffe, F.

Schaab, R. (2)   Trier, J.
Schaper, G.   Unbehaun, G.
Scheidt, S.   Vierling, J. G.
Schellenberg, H.   Volckmar, F. W.
Schindler, W.   Walcha, H.
Schmid, J.   Walliser, C. T.
Schreiner, A.   Walther, J. G. (4)
Schuetze, W.   Wangemann, O.
Schumann, C.   Weber, H.
Schumann, G.   Wedemann, W. (2)
Schwencke, J. F. (2)   Weidenhagen, E.
Seiffer, C. T.   Weiss, C. A.
Seiffert, U.   Wendt, E. A.
Sellars, G.   Wenzel, H. (2)
Seydler, T.   Werner, J. J. (2)
Seyerlen, R.   Wettstein, H. (4)
Stade, F. W. (2)   Whitford, H. P.
Stein, K.   Winter-Hjelm, O.
Sulze, B.   Wolfrum, K.
Thomas, G. A.   Zahn, J.
Toepfer, J. G.   Zorn, B.
Trautner, F. W.   Zwart, J. (2)

Variants:
Een vaste Burg is onze God

    Bonset, J.

Guds ord det er vort

    Raasted, N. O.

Song 96 (Dutch)

    King, H. C.   Zwart, J.

Vaar Gud han er

    Gangfloet, S.

Vor Gud han er saa fast en Borg

    Bergh, L.   Nielsen, T. H.
    Frellsen, E.   Raasted, N. O. (2)
    Jeppesen, K.   Thomsen, P.
    Moeller, S. O.   Woeldike, M. A.
    Nielsen, J. M.

Ein Haus steht wohlgegrundet

    Moosmair, A.
    Pachelbel, J.

Ein Haus voll Glorie schauet

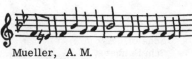

Berghorn, A.   Mueller, A. M.
Gindele, C.   Roesseling, K.
Kuntz, M.   Romanovsky, E.

Ein Kind geboren

Hulse, C. Van
Peeters, F.

Ein Kind geboren (14th Century)

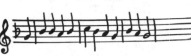

Variant:
A Child is Born in Bethlehem

Bratt, C. G.   Nieland, J.

Ein Kind geboren
    See: Puer Natus In Bethlehem

Ein Kind gebor'n
    See: A Child is Born (Pennsylvania Dutch)

Ein Kindelein so loebelich
    See: Der Tag der ist so Freudenreich

Ein Klang so suess
    See: In Dulci Jubilo

Ein Laemmlein geht und traegt
    die Schuld (Stoerl)
                       Z 7685
        Breuninger, K. F.   Burkhardt, C.

Ein Laemmlein geht und traegt die Schuld
    (Dachstein)
    See: An Wasserfluessen Babylon

Ein Lamm geht hin
    See: An Wasserfluessen Babylon

Ein neues Glaubenslied
    See: Wir glauben Gott im hoechsten
    Thron (Lahusen)

Ein neues Jahr

        Wenzel, H.

Einen guten Kampf hab ich
    See: Jesus naar eg maa faa (Schlesian)

Einer ist Koenig, Emmanuel
  sieget (Darmstadt)
                Z 3953b

Variant:
Jesu hilf siegen, du Fuerste des Lebens

Burkhardt, C.   Piutti, K.
Frenzel, H. R.   *Ricek, W.
Karg-Elert, S.   *Streicher, J. A.
Lang, H.   *Wurm, A.

Einer ist Koenig, Emmanuel
  sieget (Hille)
                Z 3960

Baldamus, F.   Kickstat, P.   *Mueller, A. E.
Hofmeier, A.   *Klotz, H.   Ricek, W. (2)
Huth, A.   Magnus, E.   Schumann, G.
                                     Wettstein, H.

Variants:
Grosser Prophete

Franke, F. W.   Obersold, H.
Inderau, H.

Jesu, hilf siegen, du Fuerste des Lebens

*Claussnitzer, P.   *Oppel, R.
*Eyken, J. A. van   Thomas, O.
Hasse, K.

Jesus ist kommen (Hille)

*Bender, J.   *Hennig, W.
Bornefeld, H.   Micheelsen, H. F.
Brod, K.   Reger, M.
Claussnitzer, P.   Senftleben, G.
Fiebig, K.   Weber, H.

Einer ist's an dem wir hangen
See: Wachet auf

Eines wuensch ich mir
                Z 6930b

Bender, J.
Weber, H.

Eins ist Not, ach Herr

Merk, G.

Eins ist Not, ach Herr, dies eine
  (Layriz)
               Z 7135
    *Beck, A.
    Haase, K.   Reuter, F.

Eins ist Not, ach Herr (Crueger)
  See: Ratisbon (Crueger)

Eirene (Havergal)

    Haase, K.

Eisenach
  See: Mach's mit mir, Gott

Eisleben (Wolder)
  See: Aus meines Herzens Grunde

Eja, min sjael ret inderlig (Ring)

    Wuertz, J.

Eja mitt hjaerta hur innerlig

    Wideen, I.

Elbing (Sohren)
             Z 4680
  Variants:
  Bis hierher hat mich Gott

    *Huebner, E.   Muench, G.
    Marx, K.   Raphael, G.

De Heer is God en niemand meer

    Groothengel, J. G.   Mudde, W.
    Kee, C.   Voogd, T. de

Dein Wort ist, Herr

    Bausznern, W. von

Du Lebensbrot, Herr Jesu Christ (Sohren)

    Bender, J.   Krause, P.
    Claussnitzer, P. (2)   Piutti, K.
    Haas, J.   Wendt, E. A.

Herr Jesu Christ, du hast bereit

Arbatsky, Y.
Haase, K.

Mudde, W.
Wienhorst, R.

Herr, lass mich deine Heiligung
Ich weiss, dass mein Erloeser lebt

Doles, J. F.

Meins Herzens Jesu, meine Lust

*Faisst, I. G. Y. von
*Franke, F. W.
Kempff, W.
Kickstat, P.
Kunz, E.
Obersold, H.
Reda, S.

Rinck, J. C. H. (3)
Ritter, A. G.
Schink, H.
Schwencke, J. F. (3)
Traegner, R.
Wolfrum, K.

Sei Lob und Ehr dem

Hasse, K.

Song 29 (Dutch)

Zwart, J.

Song 138 (Dutch)

Dragt, J.
Nauta, J. (2)

Wilgenburg, D. van

Elgin (Scotch)

Rimmer, F.

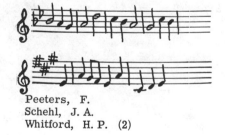

Ellacombe (Wuertemburg)

Haase, K.
Hulse, C. Van
Kreckel, P. G.
Metzger, H. A.
Variants:
God roept ons broeders

Peeters, F.
Schehl, J. A.
Whitford, H. P. (2)

Song 121 (Dutch)

Christiaansz, N. J.

Nauta, J.

Ellers (Hopkins)

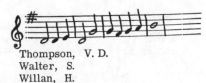

    Ashford, E. L.
    Haase, K.   Thompson, V. D.
    Pearce, C. W.   Walter, S.
    Phillips, C. G.   Willan, H.
Variant:
Benediction

    Altman, L.   DuPage, F.
    Barker, C. W.   Hopkins, E. J.

Elm (Roberts)

    Hulse, C. Van

Elton (Maker)

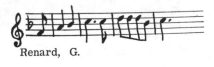

    Thompson, V. D.
Variants:
Quies

    Freeman, A.

Rest (Maker)

    Mulloy, R. E.

Whittier

    Whitford, H. P.

Emmanuel (Balle)

    Nelson, R. A.   Nystedt, K.
Variant:
Det kimmer nu til Julefest

    Jensen, S.   Kaestel, L.
    Joergensen, G.

En cette nuit d'ou vient (French
Noël)

    Alain, A.   Renard, G.

En fridens Aengel
  See: Die Stimme eines Engels

En Jungfru foedde ett barn
  Compare with Der Tag der ist

        Wikander, D.

En Rose saa jeg skyde
  See: Es ist ein Ros'

En saedemand gik ud (Laub)

        Thuner, O. E.
        Woeldike, M. A.

Energy
  See: St. Ethelwald (Monk)

Engelberg (Stanford)

        Stanford, C. V. (2)

Engelkens zingen
  See: Les Anges dans nos

England's Lane (English)

        Casner, M. D.

English Tune (Scotch)

        Parry, C. H. H.

Enhver, som tror og bliver doebt
  See: Es ist das Heil

Entre le boeuf
  See: Gevaert

Eola (Sellers)

        Robinson, W. N.

Er du modfalden
  See: Min Jesus, lad mit (Nielsen)

Er Gud for mig, saa traede
  See: Copenhagen (Zinck)

Er is een Kindeke geboren op aard
  See: A Little Child on the Earth (Flemish)

Erbarm' dich mein (Walther)

        Z 5851

Bach, H.	Hanff, J. N. (2)	
Bach, J. C.	Homilius, G. A.	Vierling, J. G.
Bach, J. S.	Krebs, J. L.	Walther, J. G. (3)
Dupré, M. J. J.	Pachelbel, J.	Werner, J. J.
Franke, F. W.	Sweelinck, J. P.	Zachau, F. W. (2)

Erde singe

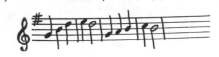

    Ahrens, J.
    Goller, F.

Erfreu dich, alle Christenheit
   See: Es ist das Heil (Wittenberg)

Erfreue dich, O Christenheit
   See: Es ist das Heil (Wittenberg)

Erfreut euch, liebe Seelen
   (Landshuter)

    Sechter, S. (2)

Erfurt (Ilse)

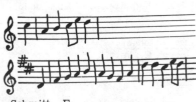

    Haase, K.

Erfurt
   See: Allguetiger mein Preisgesang

Erhabner Gott

    Rinck, J. C. H.

Erhabner Mutter uns'res Herrn

    Brand, T.
    Romanovsky, E.   Schmitt, E.

Erhalt uns, Herr, bei deinem
   Wort (Klug)
        Z 350a
     also in 3
        4

Albrechtsberger, J. G.	Buxtehude, D. (2)
Bach, J. C.	Claussnitzer, P. (3)
Barlow, W.	David, J. N.
Beck, A.	Driessler, J.
Bender, J. (2)	Fischer, M. G.
Boehm, G. (2)	Fischer, P.
Brosig, M. (2)	Fluegel, G. (2)

Gerber, E. L.
Gottschick, F. (2)
Grabner, H.
Grote, H.
Haase, H. H.
Haase, K.
Hanebeck, H. R.
Hoyer, K.
Huth, A.
Johnson, D. N.
Kempff, W.
Kickstat, P.
Krause, P.
Lang, H.
Leupold, A. W. (2)
Magnus, E.
Manz, P.
Markworth, H. J.
Merkel, G.
Metzger, H. A.
Micheelsen, H. F. (2)
Naubert, F. A.
Pachelbel, J.
Paix, J.
Papperitz, B. R.

Peeters, F.
Pepping, E.
Piutti, K. (2)
Praetorius, M.
Ramin, G.
Raphael, G.
Reda, S.
Reuter, F. (2)
Ricek, W.
Rinck, J. C. H. (2)
Roth, F.
Rumpf, W.
Scheidt, S.
Schink, H.
Schmidt, F.
Schwencke, F. G. (2)
Schwencke, J. F.
Vierling, J. G.
Walcha, H.
Walther, J. G. (3)
Wettstein, H.
Wiemer, W. (2)
Wolfrum, K. (2)
Wurm, A.

Variants:

Ach, bleib bei uns (Klug)

Luedeke, A.

Hinunter ist der Sonne Schein
Hold oppe Gud, hos oss dit ord

Gangfloet, S. (2)
Sandvold, A.

Thorkildsen, J.

Jesu Dulcedo Cordium

Cassler, G. W.

Komm, Heidenheiland

Meyer, R.

Song 9 (Old Dutch)

Beek, W. van

Song 279 (Dutch)

Wilgenburg, D. van

Erhalt uns, Herr (cont.)

   <u>Spires</u>

      Bratt, C. G.

<u>Erhalte mir, O Herr, mein Hort</u>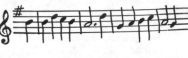

      Schaefer, K.

<u>Erhebt in vollen Choeren, Maria,
singt ihr Lob</u>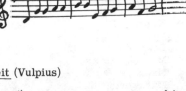

      Andlauer, E. J.

<u>Erhoer, O Schoepfer</u>
See: <u>Nun loben wir mit Innigkeit</u> (Vulpius)

<u>Erleucht mich, Herr mein Licht</u>
   (Freylinghausen)
          Z 4253

      Hasse, K.

<u>Ermunt're dich, mein schwacher
Geist</u> (Schop) 
        Z 5741
     Also in 4
        4

Baldamus, F.	Magnus, E.	Richter, E. F.
Bornefeld, H.	Marpurg, F. W.	Roth, F.
Franke, F. W.	Merkel, G.	Rumpf, W.
Gerhardt, P.	Naubert, F. A.	Schwencke, J. F. (3)
Hennig, W.	Oechsler, E.	Soenke, H.
Hering, K. E.	Oley, J. C. (2)	Vierling, J. G.
Hoyer, K. (2)	Pasquet, J.	Wetherill, E. H.
Kickstat, P.	Piutti, K.	Wieruszowski, L.
Lorenzen, J.	Preitz, F.	Zahn, J.

Variants:
<u>Brich an, du schoenes Morgenlicht</u>

Cassler, G. W.	*Hesse, A. F.
Gaul, H.	Marpurg, F. W.

<u>Har haand du lagt paa Herrens plov</u>

Karlsen, R.	Thuner, O. E.
*Laub, T.	*Wuertz, J.
*Nielsen, O. S.	

<u>Erquicke mich, du Heil der
Suender</u>

      Kuehn, K.

Erquicke mich, du Heil der
Suender (Freylinghausen)

Z 2943

Bachem, H.
Claussnitzer, P. (2)

*Piutti, K.
*Wendt, E. A.

Erquicke mich, du Heil der
Suender (Kittel)

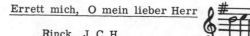

Z 2963

Wettstein, H.
Variant:
Ach, schoenster Jesu, mein Verlangen

Walther, J. G. (2)

Errett mich, O mein lieber Herr

Rinck, J. C. H.

Errett mich, O mein lieber Herr (Bourgeois)
See: Wenn wir in hoechsten Noethen

Erschienen ist der herrlich Tag
(Herman)

Z 1743

Ahrens, J.
Bach, J. S.
Baldamus, F.
Bausznern, W. von
Bender, J.
Brieger, O. (2)
Buxtehude, D. (2)
Claussnitzer, P. (3)
Diercks, J. H.
Driessler, J.
Drischner, M. (2)
Dupré, M. J. J.
Engelbrecht, K. F. (3)
Franke, F. W.
Frescobaldi, G.
Grote, H.
Hark, F.
Herrmann, K. H.
Herzogenberg, H. von (2)
Hoyer, K.
Karg-Elert, S.
Karow, K.
Kickstat, P.
Klotz, H.
Krause, P.

Kunze, K.
Kutzer, E.
Langstroth, I. S.
Merkel, G.
Micheelsen, H. F. (3)
Mudde, W.
Pepping, E. (2)
Piutti, K.
Rabich, E.
Reger, M.
Reichardt, B.
Rinck, J. C. H. (2)
Rudnick, W.
Rumpf, W.
Schaab, R.
Schmidt, F.
Schwencke, J. F. (2)
Smyth, E. M.
Stolze, H. W. (3)
Telemann, G. P. (2)
Vierling, J. G. (2)
Walther, J. G. (7)
Wenzel, H.
Werner, F.
Wolfrum, K.

Erschienen ist der herrlich Tag (cont.)

Variants:
Am Sabbath frueh Marien drei
Gott Lob, der Sonntag

 Beyer, M.

Hill dig Frelser og forsoner

 *Godske-Nielsen, H.   Karlsen, R.

Lebt Christus, was bin ich betruebt

 Toepfer, J. G.

Wir danken dir, Herr Jesu Christ, dass du vom Tod
 (Fischer)

 Buxtehude, D. (2)

Erstanden! Erstanden!
See: Walther

Erstanden ist der Heil'ge Christ
See: Surrexit Christus Hodie

Erwuenschter Brunnquell aller
 Freuden (Meyer)
     Z 2954

 Albrechtsberger, J. G.   Frescobaldi, G.

Es blueh'n drei Rosen

 Ahrens, J.

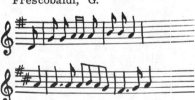

Es blueht der Blumen eine
(Gorres)

 Schehl, J. A.
Variant:
Dal tuo celeste

 Kreckel, P. G.

Es flog ein kleins Waldvoegelein
    Taeublein weisse
Compare Aus meines Herzens

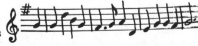

 Schroeder, H.

Variant:
Woodbird

Diercks, J. Lynn, G. A.

Es geht daher des Tages Schein
(Bohemian)
Z 322
Metzler, F.

Es glaenzet der Christen in-
wendiges Leben (Freylinghausen)
Z 6969
Bender, J.
Brod, K. Kuehmstedt, F.
Gerke, A. Piutti, K.
Krause, P. *Vogel, M. W.

Es glaenzet der Christen in-
wendiges Leben (Stoetzel)
Z 6972
Kunz, E.
*Oechsler, E. Schink, H.

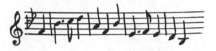

Es glueht ein Morgenrot
See: Du guet'ger Heiland

Es ist das Heil uns kommen her
(Wittenberg)
Z 4430

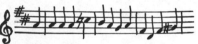

Anonymous   Fischer, M. G. (2)
Bach, J. C. (2)   Fluegel, E. P. (2)
Bach, J. S.   Gebhardi, L. E.
Bachem, H.   Grote, H.
Baldamus, F.   Gulbins, M.
Barlow, W.   Haase, K.
Becker, O.   Hahn, F.
Bender, J.   Hasse, K.
Breitenbach, C. G. J. Hesse, A. F.
Brieger, O. (2)   Hoyer, K.
Brosig, M. (2)   Huth, A.
Buxtehude, D. (3)   Karg-Elert, S. (2)
Claussnitzer, P.   Kickstat, P. (2)
David, J. N.   Kimstedt, C.
Davin, K. H. G.   Kirnberger, J. P.
Degen, H.   Kittel, J. C.
Draht, T.   Koeckert, C.
Drischner, M.   Krebs, J. L.
Dupré, M. J. J.   Leupold, A. W.
Egidi, A.   Lorenz, C. A.
Enckhausen, H. F.   Markull, F. W. (2)
Erich, D.   Marx, K.
Faisst, I. G. F. von Merkel, G.

Es ist das Heil uns kommen her (cont.)

Micheelsen, H. F. (2)   Schwencke, J. F. (3)
Mueller, G.   Stolze, H. W.
Mueller, S.   Sweelinck, J. P.
Palme, R. (3)   Theile, A. G.
Papperitz, B. R.   Toepfer, J. G.
Peeters, F.   Trier, J.
Pfaff, H.   Vierling, J. G. (3)
Piutti, K. (2)   Vogel, W.
Reda, S. (3)   Walcha, H.
Reger, M. (2)   Walther, J. G. (2)
Reinbrecht, A. (2)   Wedemann, W. (2)
Reinhardt, A.   Wenzel, E.
Ricek, W.   Wettstein, H. (2)
Rinck, J. C. H. (2)   Wieruszowski, L.
Rudnick, W. (2)   Wolff, C. M.
Rumpf, W.   Wolfrum, K.
Saffe, F.   Zachau, F. W.
Schaper, G.   Zehrfeld, O. (2)
Scherzer, O.   Zipp, F.
Schueler, H.

Variants:
Bis hierher hat mich Gott
Dreieinger, heil'ger, grosser Gott

Wenzel, H.

Enhver, som tror og bliver doebt

Raasted, N. O.   Videroe, F.

Erfreu dich, alle Christenheit

Ruedinger, G.

Erfreue dich, O Christenheit

Adler, E.   Brosig, M.

Guds Soen kom ned fra himmerig (Nuernberg)

Jeppesen, K.   Moeller, S. O.
Laub, T.   Woeldike, M. A.

O Tod wo ist dein Stachel (1523)

Knab, A.   Pfeiffer, C. D.
Koch, J. H. E.

Sei Lob und Ehr dem

Becker, O.   Bender, J.

Krebs, J. L.   Mueller, W. A.
Kreckel, P. G.   Wedemann, W.
Merk, G.
Wie Gott mich fuehrt

Hasse, K.

Wir Menschen sind zu dem, O Gott

Hasse, K.

Es ist ein Ros' entsprungen
(Praetorius)
                Z 4296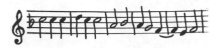

Adler, E.   Miggl, E.
Ahrens, J.   Monar, A. J.
Baumann, M.   Mueller, G.
Beck, A.   Near, G.
Bornefeld, H.   Oertzen, R. von
Brahms, J.   Pasquet, J.
Bratt, C. G.   Peeters, F.
Bush, G.   Pepin, N. A.
Cassler, G. W.   Porter, H.
Copley, R. E.   Pranschke, J.
David, J. N.   Raasted, N. O.
Davidson, R. , Jr.   Raphael, G.
DeBrant, C.   Reichel, B.
Deigendesch, K.   Reichenbach, H.
Diemer, E. L.   Roff, J.
Doebler, K.   Romanovsky, E.
Doppelbauer, J. F.   Rumpf, W.
Driessler, J.   Sattler, K.
Drischner, M. (2)   Schehl, J. A.
Erb, M. J.   Schmalz, P.
Eyken, J. A. Van   Schroeder, H.
Frischmann, M.   Soenke, H.
Geist, P.   Springer, M.
Haase, K.   Stout, A.
Hanebeck, H. R.   Strohofer, J.
Hark, F.   Thate, A.
Johnson, D. N.   Thomas, O.
Kousemaker, A. (2)   Thomas, V. C.
Kraft, K.   Vogel, W.
Krapf, G.   Volckmar, F. W.
Kreckel, P. G. (2)   Weber, H.
Lang, H. (2)   Wehmeyer, W.
Langstroth, I. S.   Wettstein, H.
Lechthaler, J.   Young, G. (3)
Lester, T. W.   Zipp, F.
Marryott, R. E.
Matthison-Hansen, G.
Micheelsen, H. F.

752 Organ - Preludes

Es ist ein Ros' entsprungen (cont.)
Variants:
Det aer en ros utsprungen

    Karlsen, R.   Olson, D.

En Rose saa jeg skyde

    Hamburger, P.   Raasted, N. O.

Praetorius

    Thiman, E. H.

Rosa Mystica

    Cassler, G. W.   Rogers, S. E.

Song 17 (Dutch)

    Berg, J. J. van den   Wolf, C. de
    Stulp, G.

Es ist ein Schnitter, heisst der
    Tod (Folksong)
               also in 3
                     4

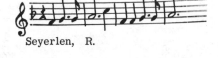

    David, J. N.   Gindele, C.
    David, T. C.   Thomas, K. G. H.

Es ist genug (Ahle)

    Franke, F. W.
    Lang, H.   Seyerlen, R.
Variant:
Ich hab' genug (Ahle)

    Luetzel, J. H.

Es ist genug, so nimm, Herr,
    meinen Geist (Muehlhausen)
              Z 7173
      Beutler, J. G. B.   *Merk, G.
      Buckland, J.   Piutti, K.
      *Claussnitzer, P. (2) *Riedel, H.
      *Fischer, M. G.   Rudnik, W.
      Haase, K.   Rumpf, W.
      *Hasse, K.   Unbehaun, G.
      Herzogenberg, H. von Vierling, J. G.
      Krause, P.   *Wendt, E. A.
    Variants:
    Dass Jesus siegt, bleibt ewig

Hennig, W.

Es ist vollbracht

*Wolfrum, K.

Ich hab' genug, so nimm, Herr

Rinck, J. C. H. (2)

Es ist gewiss ein' grosse Gnad'
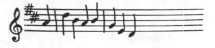
                    Z 5740
    Gulbins, M.

Es ist gewisslich an der Zeit
    See: Nun freut Euch, lieben Christen (Klug)

Es ist kein Tag (Meyer)
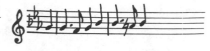
                    Z 285
    Haase, K.

Es ist vollbracht
                    Z 2692
    Oley, J. C.

Es ist vollbracht
    See: Es ist genug, so nimm, Herr (Muehlhausen)

Es jamm're wer nicht glaubt
    (Hirschberg)

    Krenkel, E.

Es kam die gnadevolle Nacht
                    Z 681
    Kraft, K.

Es kam ein Engel
    See: Vom Himmel hoch

Es kennt der Herr die Seinen
    See: Ich freu mich in dem Herren (Helder)

Es kommt ein Schiff geladen
    (Andernach)

                    Z 131
    Ahrens, J.   Fiebig, K.   Luedders, P.
    Bornefeld, H.   Franke, F. W.   Micheelsen, H. F.
    David, J. N.   Hanebeck, H. R.   Mueller, S. W.
    Driessler, J.   Koch, J. H. E.   Pepping, E.

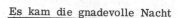

Es kommt ein Schiff geladen (cont.)

    Poppen, H. M.   Spiering, G.   Zipp, F.
    Rohlig, H.   Walcha, H.
    Schweppe, J.   Wettstein, H.
Variant:
Song 2 (Dutch)

    Hooven, N. van den   Stulp, G.

Es kostet viel ein Christ zu sein
(Freylinghausen)
         Z 2727

    Baldamus, F.
    Knecht, J. H.   Rumpf, W.
    Piutti, K.   Thomas, G. A.
    Rinck, J. C. H.   Wieruszowski, L.
Variant:
Det koster ej for megen strid

    *Wuertz, J.

Es senkt sich leiser nieder   Tune not found
(Christmas Song)

    Forchhammer, T.

Es sind doch selig alle die
    See: O Mensch, bewein (Strassburg)

Es spricht der Unweisen Mund
(Walther)
         Z 4436

    Bender, J.   Schwencke, J. F. (2) Walther, J. G.
    Buxtehude, D.   Sweelinck, J. P.   Weinreich, W.
    Oley, J. C.   Vierling, J. G.   Wurm, A.
    Pachelbel, J. (2) Volkmann, P.
Variants:
Herr, fuer dein Wort sei hoch gepreist

    Bauer, J.   Proeger, J.
    Metzger, H. A.

Wenn ich, O Schoepfer

    Adler, E.

Es steh'n fuer (vor) Gottes
    Throne (Burck)
         Z 4298
    Walther, J. G.

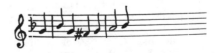

Es sungen drei Engel (Mainz)

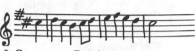

   David, J. N.
   Gindele, C.   Thate, A.
   Micheelsen, H. F.   Zehm, F.

Es wird schier der letzte Tag
  herkommen (Babst)
        Z 1423
   Gronau, D. M.

Es wolle Gott uns g'naedig sein
  wollt uns Gott (Strassburg)
        Z 7247

Bach, J. C.	Kittel, J. C.	Reinbrecht, A.
Baldamus, F.	Klaus, V.	Rinck, J. C. H. (3)
Barlow, W.	Markull, F. W. (2)	Schaab, R.
Bausznern, W. von	Merk, G.	Scheidt, S.
Boehner, J. L.	Merkel, G.	Schuetze, W.
Driessler, J.	Metzger, H. A.	Schwencke, J. F. (3)
Eberlin, J. E.	Micheelsen, H. F.	Schweppe, J.
Enckhausen, H. F.	Mueller, S.	Seiffert, U. (2)
Fischer, M. G.	Oley, J. C. (2)	Tag, C. G.
Forchhammer, T.	Pachelbel, J. (3)	Vierling, J. G.
Franke, F. W.	Palme, R.	Walther, J. G. (2)
Kammeier, H.	Piutti, K.	Wedemann, W.
Karow, K.	Reda, S. (3)	Weyrauch, J.
Kickstat, P.		

Variant:
Psalm 67

Esprits Divin (Denizot)

   Boëly, A. P. F.

Et Barn er foedt i Bethlehem
  (Berggreen)

   Christensen, B.   *Joergensen, G.   *Vaerge, A.
   Hamburger, P.   *Raasted, N. O.   Woeldike, M. A.

Et Barn er foedt i Bethlehem
  (Lindeman)

   Gangfloet, S.
   Karlsen, R.   *Moeller, S. O.

Et Barn er foedt i Bethlehem
  See: Puer Natus in Bethlehem

Et er noedig, dette ene (Folk)

   Nielsen, L.

Et Futurae (Gregorian)

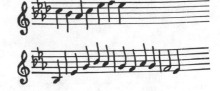

    Falcinelli, R.

Et kors, det var, det haarde,
trange (Berggreen)

    Beck, J.
    Boereh, P.   Frandsen, H. B.

Et lidet Barn saa lystelig (Balle)

    Jeppesen, K.
    *Thuner, O. E.

Et lidet Barn saa lystelig
   See: Der Tag der ist so Freudenreich

Et trofast hjerte, Herre min
(Lindeman)

    Nielsen, L.

Et trofast hjerte, Herre min
(Praetorius)
           Z 4552
    Karlsen, R.
Variant:
Herr Jesu Christ, ich weiss gar wohl

Et trofast hjerte, Herre min
   See: Aus tiefer Not (Strassburg)

Ett er noedig, dette ene (Krieger)
   See: Ratisbon (Crueger)

Eucharistia (Sullivan)

    Cassler, G. W.

Eucharistic Hymn (Hodges)

    Duro, J.
    Goode, J. C.   Walter, S.
    Mead, E. G.   Young, G.

Eudoxia (Baring-Gould)

    Edmundson, G. (2)
    Haase, K.   Pew, D.

Evan (Havergal)

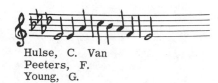

    Beck, A.
    Beebe, E. J.
    Edmundson, G.
    Haase, K.

Hulse, C. Van
Peeters, F.
Young, G.

Evelyns (Monk)

    Cassler, G. W.

Evening Hymn (Gounod)

    Haase, K.

Evening Hymn
  See: Tallis Canon

Evening Prayer (Stainer)

    Taylor, C. T.

Evening Prayer (Stebbins)

    Haase, K.

Eventide (Monk)

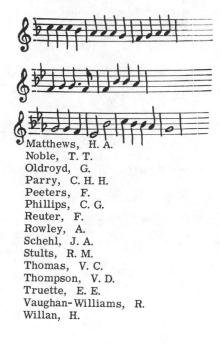

    Allen, G. P.
    Beck, A. (2)
    Bingham, S.
    Coleman, R. H. P.
    Diggle, R.
    Frazee, G. F.
    Frysinger, J. F.
    Haase, K.
    Hofland, S.
    James, F.
    Kinder, R.
    Lang, C. S.
    Larson, E. R.
    Lorenz, E. J.
    Mansfield, O. A.
Variants:
Blijf bij mij, Heer

Matthews, H. A.
Noble, T. T.
Oldroyd, G.
Parry, C. H. H.
Peeters, F.
Phillips, C. G.
Reuter, F.
Rowley, A.
Schehl, J. A.
Stults, R. M.
Thomas, V. C.
Thompson, V. D.
Truette, E. E.
Vaughan-Williams, R.
Willan, H.

    Groothengel, J. G.

O bliv hos mig

    Karlsen, R.

Eventide - (cont.)

   Song 282 (Dutch)

      Wilgenburg, D. van

Everton (Smart)

   Groves, R.
   Hulse, C. Van

Ewig sand er Herrens Tale

   *Thuner, O. E.

Ewing (Ewing)

Ashford, E. L.	Haase, K.	
Beck, A.	Knight, V.	Richolson, G. H.
Beck, T.	Lynn, G. A.	Spark, W.
Booth, O.	Nevin, G. B.	Stults, R. M.
Calver, F. L.	Peeters, F.	Whiting, G. E.

Ex More Docti Mistico

   Tallis, T.

Expectans Expectavi (Cassler)

   Cassler, G. W.

Exsultet Resurrexi

   Hulse, C. Van

Exultet Caelum Laudibus

   Cavazzoni, G.

Exultet Caelum Laudibus
   See: Deus Tuorum Militum (Latin -
   Mode 8)

Exultet Cor Praecordiis

   Variant:
   Jesu Dulcis Memoria (Mode 1)

      Peeters, F.

Exultet Orbis Gaudiis

   Peeters, F.

Fader milde
   See: Unser Vater, lass uns deine Gnade

Fager kveldsol smiler (Rinck)

   Nielsen, L.
   Variant:
   Abend wird es wieder (Rinck)

Fagert er landet (Vulpius)
   See: Lobet den Herren, ihr Heiden all

Fahre fort, fahre fort
   See: Fahre fort, Zion

Fahre fort, Zion (Schmidt-Halle)

                 Z 4791

   Blumenthal, P.   Karow, K.
   Borchers, G.   Kickstat, P.   Piutti, K. (3)
   Claussnitzer, P.   Klotz, H.   Rabich, E.
   Dienel, O.   Koetzschke, H.   Ramin, G.
   Fiebig, K.   Krause, P.   Ricek, W. (2)
   Franke, F. W.   Kuehmstedt, F.   Rinck, J. C. H.
   Frenzel, H. R.   Kuehn, K.   Rumpf, W.
   Haase, K.   Mueller-Zuerich, P.   Wolfrum, K.
   Hoyer, K.   Peters, A.
   Variants:
Fahre fort, fahre fort

   Brieger, O.   Petzold, J.   Weber, H.
   Palme, R.   Rinkens, W.   *Wettstein, H.

Skynd dig frem

   Karlsen, R.

Fairest Lord Jesus (Muenster)

                 Z 3975
   Kreckel, P. G.   Powell, R. J.
   Variant:
Schoenster Herr Jesu (Muenster)

   Weinreich, W.

Fall On Your Knees (Lithuanian)

   Whitmer, T. C.

Fang dein Werk (Franck)
   See: Schwing dich auf (Franck)

Far verden, far vel (Lindeman)

    Karlsen, R.
    Variant:
O Kristelighed (Lindeman)

    Thuner, O. E.

Far verden, far vel (Zinck)

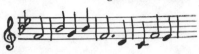

    Nielsen, L.
    Sandvold, A.

Farnaby (English)

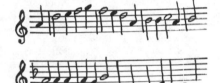

    Wallbank, N.

Farrant (Tye)

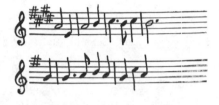

    Haase, K.
    Peeters, F.

Father Brebeuf's Carol

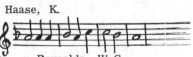

    Hulse, C. Van

Fatherland (Sullivan)

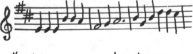

    West, J. E.
    Variant:
Heaven Is My Home

    Ashford, E. L.   Haase, K.

Federal Street (Oliver)

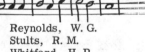

Bingham, S.	Dasher, J. A.	Reynolds, W. G.
Buck, D.	Haase, K.	Stults, R. M.
Colvin, H.	Markworth, H. J.	Whitford, H. P.
	Mead, E. G.	

Fedrane kyrkja i Noregsland
(Steenberg)

    Nielsen, L.

Fest soll mein Taufbund (Faber)

Frischmann, M.	Miggl, E.
Kraft, K.	Romanovsky, E.
Variant:	
Jesus My Lord, My God, My All	

Curry, R. D.   McGrath, J. J.
Kreckel, P. G.

Festal Song (Walter)

Bingham, S.

Fight On, My Soul (Sacred Harp)

Powell, R. J.
Read, G.

Filius Dei (Gaul)

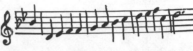

Hulse, C. Van

Finlandia (Sibelius)

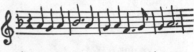

Haase, K.

Finnish Chorale #2

Raphael, G.

Finnish Chorale #3

Raphael, G.

Finnish Song (Suonen Koraal-
kirje)

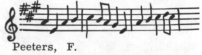

Hokanson, M.   Peeters, F.

Firm Foundation (Schumacher)

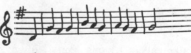

Haase, K.

Firmator Sancte

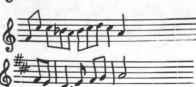

Clokey, J. W. (2)

First Nowell (English)

Balogh, L. A.   Gehrke, H.
Bingham, S.   Grace, H.
Bratt, C. G.   Gray, A.
Burdett, G. A.   Groom, L. H.
Burton, C. P. P.   Howard, J. T.
Couper, A. B.   Hulse, C. Van
DeBrant, C.   Huybrechts, L.
Diggle, R. (2)   Keldermans, R.
Faulkes, W.   Lester, T. W.
Foote, A. W.   Nieland, J.

First Nowell (cont.)

Nordman, C.   Thomas, V. C.
Phillips, C. G.   Walton, K.
Plant, A. B.   West, J. E. (2)
Reichenbach, H.   Westbrook, W. J.
Rohlig, H.   Wilson, R. C.
Thiman, E. H.   Wyton, A.

Fix Me, Jesus (Negro Spiritual)

Hancock, E. W.

Flemming (Flemming)

Dickey, M.
Variants:
Integer Vitae

Reynolds, W. G.

Maegtigste Kriste

Kaestel, L.   Wuertz, J.

Flemish Christmas Carol   Tune not found

Reichenbach, H.

Flow Gently, Sweet Afton (Hume)

Gaul, H.   Thomas, V. C.

Foerlossningen
See: Herr Christ, der einig Gott's Sohn

Folkefrelsar til oss kom (Sletten)

Gangfloet, S.   Karlsen, R.
Variants:
Dyp av naade
Jesus Come To Me

McGrath, J. J.

Folkefrelsar (1524)
See: Nun komm der Heiden Heiland

Fons Bonitans

Clokey, J. W.

Variants:
Ecce Tempus Idoneum (Mode 3)

    Tallis, T. (2)

Herre Gud Fader, du vaar store trost
   (10th Century)

    Karlsen, R.

Kyrie Fons Bonitatis

    Langlais, J. F.

Pater Noster (Liturgical)

    Grabner, H.

For dig, O Herre, som dage kun
  (Barnekow)

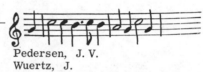

    Frandsen, H. B.   Pedersen, J. V.
    Hamburger, P.   Wuertz, J.

For You I Am Praying (Sankey)

    Marshall, P.

Foran Krybber
   See: Devant la Crèche

Forest Green (English)

    Diemer, E. L.   Groves, R.   Purvis, R.
    Diggle, R.   Phillips, C. G. Williams, R. R.

Fortunatus (Sullivan)

    Curry, R. D.

Foundation (Early American)

    Bartow, N.
    Colvin, H.
    Hamill, P.   Herbek, R. H.
                  Shaffer, J. E.

Fountain (Early American)

    Colvin, H.

Fra Himlen hoeit jeg kommer her
   See: Christum wir sollen loben

Fra Himlen hoejt kom budskab her
   See: Vom Himmel hoch

Fra Himlen kom en Engel klar (Hartmann)
   See: Jeg kommer, Herre, paa dit ord

Fra Himlen kom en Engel klar
   See: Puer Nobis Nascitur (Praetorius)

Fragrance

   Brown, A. G. Y.
Variants:
What Is This Lovely Fragrance

   Lovelace, A.

Whence Comes This Goodly Fragrance

   Oxley, T. F. H.   Webber, W. S. L.

Framingham
   See: Grosser Gott, wir loben dich

Franconia (Koenig-Havergal)
                Z 2207

   Cameron, G.
   Coleman, R. H. P.   Lang, C. S.
   Farrar, E. B.   Peeters, F.
   Haase, K.   Rowley, A.
   Head, R.   Trevor, C. H.
   Hillert, R.   Wallbank, N.

Frankfort
   See: Wie schoen leuchtet

Franzen (Tomissoen)

   Peeters, F.
Variant:
O Jesu, aan de dine

   Aahgren, K. E.

Fred til bod for bittert savn
   (Hartmenn)

      Bergh, L.   Karlsen, R.
      *Frandsen, H. B.   *Wuertz, J.

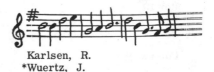

Fred til bod for bittert savn
(Lindeman)

    Cassler, G. W.
    Haase, K.   Peeters, F.

Fred til bod for bittert savn (Schop)
  See: Hilf, Herr Jesu, lass gelingen

Frederick (Kingsley)

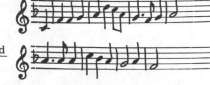

    Ashford, E. L.

Frelseren er mig en hyrde God
(Barnekow)

    Klaebel, F.
    *Thuner, O. E.

Frelseren er mig en hyrde God
(Laub)

    Jensen, S.
    *Lindorff-Larsen, E.   *Wuertz, J.

Freu dich, du Himmelskoenigin
         werte Christenleut
           Z 1979c

    Kropfreiter, A. F.   Romanovsky, E.
    Monar, A. J.   Ruedinger, G.
    Roeseling, K.   Schmalz, P.
  Variant:
  Regina Caeli Jubila (Leisentritt)

    Bratt, C. G.   *Sorge, E. R.
    Hemmer, E.

Freu dich Erd und Sternenzelt
  See: Salvator Natus (Bohemian)

Freu dich sehr, O meine Seele
(Bourgeois)

           Z 6543

André, J.	Claussnitzer, P.	Gebhardi, L. E.
Baldamus, F.	Dienel, O.	Godske-Nielsen, H.
Bender, J.	Drischner, M.	Gulbins, M.
Beutler, J. G. B. (2)	Dupré, M. J. J.	Haase, K.
Boehm, G.	Enckhausen, H. F.	Haase, R.
Boehner, J. L.	Fiebig, K.	Hamburger, P.
Brieger, O.	Fink, C.	Hasse, K.
Brosig, M.	Fluegel, E. P.	Heiller, A. (2)
Busch, A. G. W.	Fluegel, G. (2)	Heinrich, J. G.
Cassler, G. W. (2)	Forchhammer, T.	Helmbold, C. A.

Freu dich sehr, O meine Seele (cont.)

Hennig, W.	Mueller, S.	Schueler, H.
Herzog, J. G.	Nicolai, J. G. (3)	Schumacher, M. H.
Hesse, A. F. (2)	Oley, J. C. (2)	Stade, F. W. (3)
Hoepner, C. G.	Pachelbel, J.	Stecher, H. (2)
Karg-Elert, S. (2)	Pembauer, J.	Steinhaeuser, K. (2)
Kellner, J. C.	Piutti, K.	Stiller, K.
Kickstat, P.	Redecker, A. A. H.	Stolze, H. W. (2)
Kittel, J. C.	Reger, M. (3)	Streicher, J. A.
Klaus, V.	Reichardt, B.	Thomas, G. A.
Knecht, J. N.	Reinbrecht, A.	Vierling, J. G.
Kothe, B.	Reinhardt, A.	Walther, J. G.
Krause, P.	Reuter, F.	Weber, H.
Krebs, J. L.	Richter, E. F.	Wedemann, W.
Kuntze, C.	Riemenschneider, G.	Wendt, E. A.
Kunze, K.	Rinck, J. C. H. (6)	Wettstein, H. (2)
Leupold, A. W.	Roeder, E. O.	Wolfrum, K.
Lorenz, C. A.	Rudnick, W.	Wolfrum, P.
Manz, P.	Rumpf, W.	Woodward, H.
Markull, F. W.	Schaab, R.	Zehrfeld, O.
Merkel, G. (2)	Schreiber, F. C.	Zinck, G. F.

Variants:
Abermals ein Jahr

Soenke, H.

Ainsi que la biche rée

Peeters, F.

Herr, auf dich will ich fest (stets) hoffen

Doles, J. F.

Jesu dine dype vunder

Bergh, L.	Hamburger, P.	Moeller, S. O.
Drischner, M.	Jeppesen, K.	Nielsen, J. M.
Frellsen, E.	Karlsen, R.	Nielsen, T. H.
Gangfloet, S. (2)	Laub, T. (2)	Raasted, N. O.

Jesus, jeg dit kors vil holde

Raasted, N. O.

Psalm 42

Asma, F. (2)	Couper, A. B.	Weelden, J. van (4)
Beek, W. van	Hess, C. L.	Westering, P. C. van
Bijster, J.	Rippen, P.	Wieruszowski, L.
Brakman, P. C.	Speuy, H. J.	Wilgenburg, D. van (2)
Bruin, B. (2)	Titcomb, E. H.	Zwart, J. (2)

Skriv dig, Jesus, paa mit hjerte

 Raasted, N. O.

Song 50 (Dutch)

 Blekkenhorst, H.   Wilgenburg, D. van

Song 175 (Dutch)

 Wilgenburg, D. van

Treuer Gott, ich muss dir klagen

 Oley, J. C.   Pachelbel, J. (2)

Vater, krone du mit Segen

 Brosig, M.

Warum willst du draussen stehen

 Gulbins, M.

Wie der Hirsch

 Wieruszowski, L.

Wie nach einer Wasserquelle

Barner, A.	Herzog, J. G.	Palme, R.
Beutler, J. G. B.	Jehle, J.	Rinck, J. C. H. (3)
Buehl, W.	Kempff, W.	Schink, H.
Claussnitzer, P.	Knecht, J. H.	Schwencke, J. F. (2)
Franke, F. W.	Lang, H.	Wettstein, H. (2)
Gulbins, M.	Magnus, E.	Zahn, J.
Hasse, K.		

Freuet Euch der schoenen Erde
See: Ringe recht (Basel)

Freuet Euch, ihr Christen alle
(Hammerschmidt)
      Z 7880

Bachem, H.	Huebner, E.
Brod, K.	Hulse, C. Van
Claussnitzer, P. (2)	Karow, K.
Fiebig, K.	Kickstat, P.
Franke, F. W.	Pepping, E.
Grote, H.	Pfeiffer, C. D.
Haase, K.	Piutti, K. (2)
Hasse, K.	Weber, H.

Freuet Euch, ihr Christen alle
  (Hammerschmidt)
  Refrain of first tune.
                Z 7880a
     Bornefeld, H.   Droebs, J. A.
  Variant:
  Halleluia

Freut Euch des Herren (Schuetz)
  See: Op alle folk

Freut Euch, ihr lieben Christen
  all (Gesius)

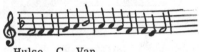

     Driessler, J.   Soenke, H.
     Fiebig, K.   Wenzel, E.

Freut Euch, ihr lieben Christen,
  freut Euch (Schroeter)
                Z 5375

     Franke, F. W.   Hulse, C. Van
     Haase, K.   Meyer, R.

Friend
  See: What A Friend (Converse)

Frisk op, min sjael (Breitendich)
  See: Min glede i min Gud (Kingo)

Froehlich soll mein Herze
  springen (Crueger)
                Z 6481

     Baldamus, F.   Haase, K.   Mueller, S. W.
     Bender, J.   Hark, F.   Oechsler, E.
     Borchers, G.   Hoyer, K.   Pepping, E. (3)
     Bornefeld, H.   Hulse, C. Van   Piutti, K.
     Bunjes, P. G.   Huth, A.   *Riedel, H.
     Claussnitzer, P. (2) Kickstat, P. (2)   Schmid, K.
     Drischner, M. (2)   Koch, J. H. E.   Schrenk, J.
     Fiebig, K.   Kunz, E.   Troetschel, H.
     Franke, F. W.   Magnus, E. (2)   Walcha, H.
     Gerhardt, P. (2)   Micheelsen, H. F.   *Wendt, E. A.
     Grabner, H.   Mueller, A. E.
  Variants:
  Hjerte loeft din glaedes vinger

     Frellsen, E.   Raasted, N. O.
     Godske-Nielsen, H.   *Rosenkilde-Larsen, E.
     Laub, T.   *Thomsen, P.

Skulle jeg dag vaere bange

    Raasted, N. O.

Froehlich soll mein Herze
   springen (Freylinghausen)
                Z 6483
    Ehinger, H. R.

Froehlich wir nun all fangen an
   (Strassburg)

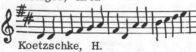

        Bornefeld, H.
        Gottschick, F.
        Hennig, W.
                          Kickstat, P.
                          Metzger, H. A.

Frueh am Morgen Jesus gehet

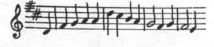

    Franke, F. W.
                        Koetzschke, H.

Fryd dig, du Kristi Brud
   See: Auf meinen lieben Gott (Regnart)

Frygt, min sjael, den sande Gud (Horn)
   See: Da Christus geboren war (Bohemian)

Frykt mitt barn
   See: Da Christus geboren war (Bohemian)

Fuenf Bruennlein sind
   2nd tune for Ach Gott und Herr

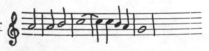

    Gulbins, M. (2)

Fuerwahr du bist, O Gott

    Eyken, J. A. van
    Luetzel, J. H.

Full of Glory (Terry)

    Variant:
    Terry

    Titcomb, E. H.

Ga niet alleen door 'tleven   Tune not found

    Nieland, H.

Gaa nu hen og grav (Berggreen)

    Johnsson, B.   *Wuertz, J.

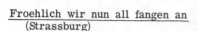

Gaa nu hen og grav (1668)
   See: Meinen Jesum lass ich nicht (Swedish)

Gaa varsamt, O sjael (Norsk)
   See: Min lodd falt mig liflig

Gaar det, Herre, som jeg vil
   (Laub)

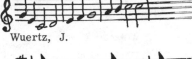

     Hamburger, P.   Wuertz, J.

Gabriel's Salutation

     Bingham, S.

Gak ud, min sjael, betragt med flid
   See: Psalm 21 (Bourgeois)

Gak under Jesu kors
   See: Lasst uns zum Kreuze

Galilean (Barnby)

     Haase, K.
     Hofland, S.   Reuter, F.

Galilee (Armes)

     Lang, C. S.
     Palmer, C. C.

Galilee (Jude)

     Conway, M. P.
     Lorenz, E. J.   Matthews, J. S.
     Matthews, H. A.   Thompson, V. D.

Gallery Carol (English)

     Campbell, S. S.

Gammal aer kyrkan
   See: Die Kirche ist ein altes Haus

Garden Hymn (White Spiritual)

     Pfautsch, L.   Shepherd, A.
     Variant:
   (The) Lord Into His Garden Comes

     Kettering, E. L.

Gardiner
  See: Germany (Beethoven)

Gaudeamus

  Titcomb, E. H.

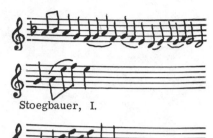

Gaudeamus (Gregorian)

  Brun, F.
  Erb, M. J. (7)   Stoegbauer, I.

Gaudeamus Omnes

  Lechthaler, J.

Gaudeamus Pariter (Horn)

                   Z 6285
  Peeters, F. (3)
  Powell, R. J.
  Variant:
  Jesus Christ Is Risen Today

Gaudens Gaudebo   Tune not found

  Stoegbauer, I.

Gebor'n ist uns ein Kindelein
  (Mainz)

  Variant:
  Du Herre Krist

  Frellsen, E.   *Wuertz, J.

Gedanke der uns Leben gibt (C.
  P. Bach)
                   Z 718
  *Helmbold, C. A.

Gedanke der uns Leben gibt
  (Schicht)
                   Z 723
  *Schwencke, J. F. (2)

Geduchte God
  See: Psalm 43

Geduld die soll'n wir haben
  See: Dank sei Gott in der Hoehe
  (Gesius)

Geest des Heeren, kom van boven
  See: Sollt ich meinem Gott (Schop)

Gegruesset seist du, Koenigin
  (Hildesheim)

      *Piechler, A.

Gegruest seist du, O Jesulein
  (Erfurt)   Maria rein

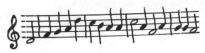

      Brosig, M.
      Goller, F.   Murschhauser, F. X. A.

Geh aus, mein Herz, und suche
  Freud (Schmidlin)
                        Z 2535
      Claussnitzer, P.   Lang, H.

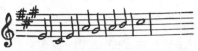

Geh aus, mein Herz, und suche
  Freud (1852)

      *Wurm, A.

Geh aus, mein Herz, und suche Freud
  See: Heut singt die liebe Christenheit
  (Herman)

Geh unter Jesu Kreuz
  See: Lasst uns zum Kreuze treten hin

Geht hin, ihr glaeubigen Gedanken
  2nd tune for Wer nur den lieben

      Variants:
      Ich bin getauft auf deinem Namen

      Wer nur den lieben Gott -2nd tune

      Karg-Elert, S.   Piutti, K.
      Lapo, C. E.   Streicher, J. A.
      Merkel, G.

Geist der Wahrheit

      Jenny, A.

Geist des Glaubens
  See: O Durchbrecher (Halle)

Geistlich Bittfahrlied
  See: Mitten wir im Leben sind (Walther)

Gelobet sei der Herr, der Gott
 Israels
See: Nun danket alle Gott

Gelobet seist du, Jesu Christ
 (Walther)
              Z 1947

Ahrens, J.

Alberti, J. F.

Bach, J. S. (5)

Baldamus, F.

Barbe, H.

Barlow, W.

Barthel, J. C.

Bausznern, W. von

Bender, J.

Boehm, G. (2)

Bornefeld, H.

Breydert, F. M.

Brieger, O.

Buttstedt, J. H.

Buxtehude, D. (3)

Chemin-Petit, H.

Claussnitzer, P. (2)

David, J. N.

David, T. C. (2)

Driessler, J.

Dupré, M. J. J.

Enckhausen, H. F.

Fischer, M. G.

Forchhammer, T.

Franke, F. W.

Geist, C.

Hanebeck, H. R.

Hark, F.

Hasse, K.

Hennig, W.

Herzog, J. G.

Huth, A.

Kaeppel, G. C. A.

Karg-Elert, S.

Karow, K.

Kauffmann, G. F.

Keller, H. M.

Kickstat, P.

Kirnberger, J. P.

Koch, J. H. E.

Krause, P.

Kuntze, C.

Kutzer, E.

Lenel, L.

Merkel, G.

Meyer, R.

Micheelsen, H. F.

Muehling, A.

Pachelbel, J. (3)

Pepping, E. (2)

Piel, P.

Piutti, K. (2)

Raphael, G.

Reinbrecht, A.

Riedel, H.

Rinck, J. C. H. (2)

Roth, F.

Rudnick, W.

Rumpf, W.

Schaab, R. (2)

Scheidt, S. (6)

Schoenfeld, H.

Schumann, G.

Schwencke, J. F. (2)

Spranger, J.

Stolze, H. W.

Thomas, G. A.

Traegner, R.

Vierling, J. G.

Volckmar, F. W.

Walcha, H.

Walther, J. G.

Weckmann, M.

Wedemann, W.

Wettstein, H. (3)

Wolfrum, K. (2)

Zoller, G.

Variants:
Du vaere lovet (Walther)

Gangfloet, S.

Lofwad ware tu Jesu Christ
Lov vaere dig, O Jesu Krist

Aahlen, W.
Berg, G.

Kullnes, A.

Lovet vaere du, Jesu Krist

Hamburger, P. (2)

Raasted, N. O. (2)

Gelobt sei Gott im hoechsten
  Thron (Vulpius)
                      Z 283

Abel, O.	Grosheim, G. C.	Peeters, F.
Ahrens, J.	Haase, K.	Pepping, E. (3)
Bausznern, W. von	Hark, F.	Poppen, H. M.
Bender, J.	Hulse, C. Van	Schneider, M. G.
Blackburn, J.	Johnson, D. N.	Schwarz-Schilling, R.
Bornefeld, H.	Karg-Elert, S.	Troetschel, H.
Driessler, J.	Kickstat, P.	Walcha, H.
Drischner, M.	Meyer, R.	Weber, H.
Fischer, P.	Miggl, E.	Wenzel, E.
Fiebig, K.	Mueller, S. W.	Willan, H.
Gerke, A.	Oechsler, E.	

Variants:
Nun lobet Gott im hohen Thron

Fromm, H.

Vulpius

  Mead, E. G.   Wyton, A.

Gelobt sei Jesu Christus

  Ahrens, J.

Gelukkig is het Land (English)

  Bijster, J.
  Zwart, J.
Variant:
Song 304 (Dutch)

Gen Himmel aufgefahren ist

                      Z 187b
  Litzau, J. B.

Gen Himmel aufgefahren ist
  (Franck)
                      Z 189
  Bender, J.
  Bornefeld, H.   Franke, F. W.   Kickstat, P. (2)
  Dallmann, W.   Hennig, W.   Pepping, E.
  Driessler, J.   Herrmann, K. H.   Weber, H.
Variant:
Du som gaar ud fra (Franke)

  *Frandsen, H. B.   *Nielsen, O. S.
   Frellsen, E.   *Vaerge, A.
   Jeppesen, K.   *Wuertz, J.

Gen Himmel fahren   Tune not found

    Rohwer, J. (2)

Geneva 86
  See: Psalm 86 (Geneva)

Geneva 118
  See: Psalm 118

Geneva 135
  See: Psalm 135 (Geneva)

Gentle Mary Laid Her Child
  See: Den die Hirten lobten sehr

Gently Raise the Sacred Strain
  (Griggs)

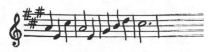

    Schreiner, A.

Georgetown (Williams)

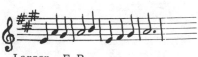

    Lacey, D. T.

German Carol
  See: Now Glad of Heart

German Carol - Easter
  See: Christus ist erstanden
  (German Carol)

Germania
  See: Germany (Beethoven)

Germany (Beethoven)

    Bingham, S.
    Edmundson, G.   Larson, E. R.
    Grote, H.   Mead, E. G.
  Variants:
  Gardiner

    Baumgartner, H. L.   Willan, H.
    Whitford, H. P.

  Germania

    Steere, W. C.

  Walton

    Peeters, F.   Sinzheimer, M.

Gerontius (Dykes)

    Cassler, G. W.
    Pearce, C. W.

Webber, W. S. L.

Geseg'n uns, Herr, die Gaben
(von Hessen)
            Z 459

    Abel, O.

Gethsemane
  See: Redhead 76th

Gevaert

    Martin, G. M.
    Mauro-Cottone, M.
  Variants:
  Entre le boeuf

Purvis, R.

    Bingham, S.

Clokey, J. W.

  Sleep of the Child Jesus
         Infant

    Marier, T. N.

Rogers, S. E.

Gezang
  See: Song (Dutch)

Giardini (Giardini)

    Dressler, J.
    Hustad, D.
  Variants:
  Italian Hymn

Whitford, H. P.

Andrews, B.	Dickey, M.	Reuter, F.
Ashford, E. L.	Haase, K.	Stellhorn, M. H.
Beck, A.	Markworth, H. J.	Thompson, V. D.
Dean, T. W.	Matthews, H. A.	Whitney, M. C.

  Moscow

    Lang, C. S.
    McKinley, C.
    Peeters, F.

Stults, R. M.
Taylor, C. T.

Gib dich zufrieden, und sei stille
(Hintze)
           Z 7415
    Also in 3
        4

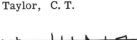

        *Claussnitzer, P.   Pfaff, H.
        Faehrmann, H. (2)   Piutti, K.
        Forchhammer, T.   Raphael, G.
        *Grundmann, O. A.   Rinck, J. C. H. (2)
        *Hark, F.   Ritter, A. G.
        Hoyer, K.   Rudnick, W.
        Kickstat, P.   Vogel, G.
        Krause, P.   Weinreich, W.
        Kuehmstedt, F.   Zechiel, E.
        Lapo, C. E.

Gib mir, Gott, ein Loblied
  See: Den die Hirten lobten sehr

Gib unser'm Fuersten und aller
  Obrigkeit

    Piutti, K.

Giv mig, Gud, en salmetunge
  See: Den die Hirten lobten sehr

Gjoer det lille du kan (Russ
  1923)
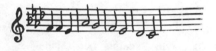

    Karlsen, R.

Gjoer doeren hoej, gjoer porten vid
  See: Old 100th

Glade jul, hellige jul (dejlige jul)
  See: Stille Nacht

Gladelig vil vi halleluja kvede
  (Lindeman)

    Karlsen, R.

Gladness (Bohemian)
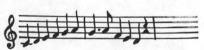

    Haase, K.

Glaed dig, Du Kristi Brud
  See: Auf meinen lieben Gott (Regnart)

Glaed dig, Sion (Zinck)

    Thuner, O. E.

Glaeden hun er foedt i dag
  See: Der Tag der ist so

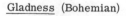

Glaeubige Seel', schau dein Herr
    und Koenig (Weisse)
                        Z 2037
        Litzau, J. B.   Pepping, E.

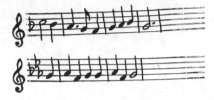

Glaub nur feste

        Volkmann, P.

Gloaming (Stainer)

        *Stainer, J.
        Thatcher, H. R.

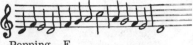

Gloria (French Noël)
    See: Les Anges dans nos

Gloria in Excelsis Deo (Mode 8)

        Kreckel, P. G.
        Reger, M.

Gloria in Excelsis (German)
    See: Allein Gott in der Hoehe

Gloria, Laus et Honor (Plainsong
    - Mode 1)

        *DeBrant, C.

Gloria Tibi Trinitas

        Tallis, T.

Glorie, Lob, Ehr und Herr-
    lichkeit

        Kaminski, H.

Glorification (Leipzig)

        Haase, K.

Glorious Name (McKinney)

        Smith, H. M.

Glorwuerd'ge Koenigin

        Miggl, E.

Go All To Joseph (Stoecklin)

 Kreckel, P. G.

Go Down Moses (Negro Spiritual)

 Sowanda, F.

Go, Tell It On the Mountains
(Negro Spiritual)

 Hancock, E. W.

God Be With You (Tomer)

 Ashford, E. L.
 Evans, O. H.

God enkel licht
 See: Song 153 (Huet)

God Father, Praise and Glory
(Mainz)

 Variant:
 O God, Eternal Father

 Peeters, F.

God is een toevlucht
 See: Psalm 46

God is goed, looft Hem tezaam Tune not found

 Vos, C.

God is mijn licht
 See: Psalm 27

God Rest Ye Merry (English)

Andrews, B.	Faulkes, W.	
Best, W. T.	Gotch, O. H.	Rogers, S. E.
Bingham, S.	Gray, A.	Thomson, V.
Blair, H.	Hull, A. E.	Walter, S.
Candlyn, T. F. H.	Hulse, C. Van	Walton, K.
Diggle, R. (2)	Kingsbury, C.	Webber, W. S. L.
Dow, M. W.	Oxley, T. F. H.	Williams, D. H.
Elmore, R. H.	Roberts, M. J.	Wilson, R. C.

God roept ons, broeders
 See: Ellacombe

God Save the King (Queen)
   See: America (Carey)

Goer
   See: Gjoer

Goer dig nu rede, kristenhed   Tune not found

      Vestergaard-Pedersen, C.

Golden Carol
   See: Merchant's Carol

Golden Harp
   See: Y-Delyn-Aur (Welsh)

Golden Mornings (English)

      Warner, R. L.

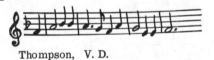

Gomotka Tune

      Breydert, F. M.

Good King Wenceslas
   See: Tempus Adest Floridum

Gordon (Gordon)

      Colvin, H.
      Goode, J. C.   Thompson, V. D.
      Variant:
      My Jesus, I Love Thee

      Porter, J. B.   Thompson, V. D.

Gordon (Smart)

      Peeters, F.

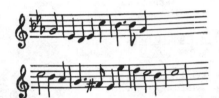

Gott, den ich als Liebe kenne
   (Freylinghausen)
                Z 6505
      Piutti, K.

Gott der Herr regiert

      Franke, F. W.

Gott der Vater wohn uns bei
   (Wittenberg)
                Z 8507

Bach, J. S.
Barlow, W.
Bieling, H. H.
Bornefeld, H. (2)
Buchner, J. A.
Buxtehude, D. (2)
Driessler, J.
Ehmann, H.
Enckhausen, H. F.

Franke, F. W.
Haase, K.
Hark, F. (3)
Karow, K.
Kempff, W.
Krebs, J. L.
Micheelsen, H. F.
Pachelbel, J. (2)
Reda, S.

Reuter, F.
Rinck, J. C. H.
Scheidt, S.
Stolze, H. W.
Telemann, G. P. (2)
Vierling, J. G.
Vogler, G. J.
Walther, J. G.

Gott des Himmels

Mueller, S. W.

Gott des Himmels und der Erden
(Alberti)

Z 3614b

Also in 3
4

Albrecht, G.
Bachem, H.
Baldamus, F.
Brieger, O. (2)
Claussnitzer, P.
Doles, J. F.
Enckhausen, H. F.
Engelbrecht, K. F.
Fluegel, G. (2)
Franke, F. W.
Fricke, R.
Fry, H. S.
Gerhardt, P.
Grote, H.
Haase, K.
Hasse, K.
Heinrich, J. G.
Helmbold, C. A.
Hesse, A. F. (3)
Hurford, P.
Karg-Elert, S.
Kickstat, P. (2)
Krause, P. (2)

Kuntze, C.
Kunze, K.
Lang, H.
Langstroth, I. S.
Ludwig, C. A.
Lux, F.
Markworth, H. J. (2)
Marpurg, F. W.
Merk, G.
Merkel, G.
Metzler, F.
Mueller, W. A.
Oley, J. C.
Peeters, F.
Piutti, K. (3)
Reger, M.
Reinbrecht, A.
Richter, E. F.
Riedel, H.
Rinck, J. C. H. (6)
Roth, F.
Rumpf, W.
Saffe, E.

Schaeffer, A.
Schneider, J.
Schrenk, J.
Schuetze, W. (2)
Schwencke, J. F. (2)
Stiller, K.
Streicher, J. A. (2)
Toepfer, J. G. (3)
Traegner, R.
Trautner, F. W. (2)
Tuerke, O.
Vierling, J. G. (2)
Volckmar, F. W.
Volckmar, W. V.
Walcha, H.
Walther, J. G. (2)
Wedemann, W.
Wendt, E. A.
Wettstein, H. (3)
Wenzel, E.
Wenzel, H.
Wolfrum, K. (6)
Zinck, G. F.

Variants:
Albert

Elmore, R. H.

Grosser Gott von alten Zeiten

Hasse, K.

Halleluia schoener Morgen

Gott des Himmels und der Erden (cont.)

   Helligaand, vor Sorg du slukke

      Jensen, S.   Woeldike, M. A.
      Thuner, O. E.

   Ordets Herre, du som givit

      Salonen, S.

   Tut auf die schoene Pforte

      Landmann, A.

   Waltham (Albert)

      Anderson, H. J.   Farrar, E. B.

Gott, du bist von Ewigkeit
   See: Liebster Jesu

Gott du bist von Ewigkeit
   See: Sollt es gleich bisweilen (Fritsch)

Gott du hast in deinem Sohn
   See: Liebster Jesu

Gott durch deine Guete
   See: Gottes Sohn ist kommen

Gott erhalte Franz, der Kaiser (Haydn)
   See: Austrian Hymn

Gott hab ich lieb, er hoerte
   See: Psalm 74

Gott hat das Evangelium (Alberus)
                         Z 1788
      Pachelbel, J.
      Reuter, F.   Walther, J. G.

Gott, Heil'ger Schoepfer aller Stern (Meisse)
   See: Creator Alme Siderum (Mode 4)

Gott ist gegenwaertig

      Kunze, K.

Gott ist gegenwaertig (Neander)
   See: Wunderbarer Koenig

Gott ist getreu
  Pfaff, H.   Z 7186
  Rinck, J. C. H.

Gott ist mein Heil, mein Huelf
  und mein Trost
          Z 4421
  Walther, J. G.

Gott ist mein Hirt

  Straumann, B.

Gott ist mein Hirt

  Inderau, H.

Gott ist mein Hirt (Bourgeois)
  See: Psalm 23 (Bourgeois)

Gott ist mein Hort (Egli)

  Fleck, M.

Gott ist mein Lied

  Pfaff, H.

Gott ist mein Lied

  Eyken, J. A. van

Gott ist mein Lied (C. P. E. Bach)
          Z 86
  Variant:
  Song 248 (Dutch)

  Vogel, W.

Gott ist mein Lied (Doles)
          Z 78
  *Stolze, H. W.

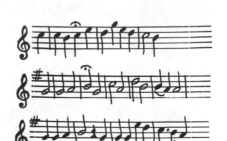

Gott ist mein Lied (Hiller)
          Z 89
  *Rinck, J. C. H. (2)

Gott ist mein Lied (Quantz)
          Z 79
  Piutti, K.

Gott ist mein Lied, er ist der
___Gott___
                          Z 8666

    *Unbehaun, G.
    Weigl, B.

Gott lebet noch (Dretzel)
                          Z 7953

    Bachem, H.
    Piutti, K.

Gott Lob, der Sonntag
    See: ___Erschienen ist der Herrlich Tag___

Gott Lob, ein Schritt
    See: ___Nun freut Euch, lieben___ (Klug)

Gott rufet noch
    See: ___Psalm 8___

Gott sei Dank durch alle Welt
(Halle)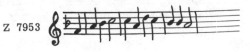
                          Z 1230

Eyken, J. A. van	Hulse, C. Van	
Fink, C.	King, O. A.	Lenel, L.
Haase, K.	Kleemeyer, H.	Peeters, F.
Haessler, J. W.	Kunze, K.	*Rumpf, W.
Herzog, J. G.	Lang, H.	Schaab, R.

Variants:
___Jesu, komm doch selbst zu mir___

    *Claussnitzer, P. (2)   *Kunze, K.
    *Krause, P.

    ___Luebeck___

    Hegedus, A.   Lynn, G. A.

    ___Triumphiere Gottes Stadt___

    Franke, F. W.   Kickstat, P.
    Hoyer, K.

Gott sei Dank durch alle Welt
    See: ___Nun komm der Heiden Heiland___

Gott sei gelobet und gebenedeiet
(Walther)
                          Z 8078

    Bach, J. C. (2)   Franke, F. W.
    Bender, J.   Haase, K.
    Fischer, M. G.   Karow, K.

Maistre, M. Le   Rinck, J. C. H.
Metzger, H. A.   Scheidemann, H. (2)
Oley, J. C.   Toepfer, J. G.
Poser, H.   Vogler, G. J.
Pranschke, J.   Weber, H.
                      Wieruszowski, L.

Variants:
Herr Jesu Christe, mein getreuer Hirte

Hennig, W.   Wenzel, E.

Herr sey gelobet

Vierling, J. G.

Gott sei uns gnaedig und barmherzig
  See: Meine Seele erhebet den Herren

Gott sorgt fuer dich
               Z 1051
  Krause, P.
  Piutti, K.

Volkmann, P.

Gott und Vater, wir erschienen   Tune not found

  Brosig, M.

Gott, Vater, der du deine Sohn
  (Herman)
               Z 380
  Pachelbel, J. (2)

Gott, Vater, Herr, wir danken dir
  See: Wir wollen singen ein Lobgesang
  (Gesius)

Gott, Vater, sende deinen Geist
  See: Kommt her zu mir (Leipzig)

Gott, Vater, Sohn und Heiliger Geist
  See: O Herre Gott, dein goettlich Wort
  (Erfurt)

Gott will's machen, dass die
  Sachen (Freylinghausen)
               Z 1286
   Erbe, K.
Variant:
Seelenweide, meine Freude

Gott will's machen, dass die
  Sachen (Steiner)
               Z 1297

Gott will's machen, dass die Sachen (cont.)

    Variant:
    Steiner

        Larkin, J.

Gott will's machen, dass die
    Sachen (Stoetzel)
                        Z 1298
        Lang, H.

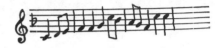

Gott will's machen, dass die Sachen
    See: Ringe recht (Kuhnau)

Gott, wir sind deine Kinder

        Rinck, J. C. H.

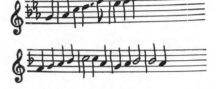

Gottes Sohn in Brodgestalten

        Sechter, S. (2)

Gottes Sohn ist kommen (Weisse)

                        Z 3294

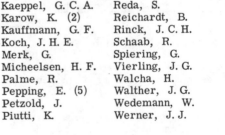

        Bach, J. S. (4)   Hoyer, K.
        Bornefeld, H.   Kaeppel, G. C. A.   Reda, S.
        Brieger, O.   Karow, K. (2)   Reichardt, B.
        Buttstedt, J. H. (2)   Kauffmann, G. F.   Rinck, J. C. H.
        Driessler, J.   Koch, J. H. E.   Schaab, R.
        Dupré, M. J. J.   Merk, G.   Spiering, G.
        Fischer, M. G.   Micheelsen, H. F.   Vierling, J. G.
        Forchhammer, T.   Palme, R.   Walcha, H.
        Goos, W.   Pepping, E. (5)   Walther, J. G.
        Hark, F.   Petzold, J.   Wedemann, W.
        Heinrich, J. G.   Piutti, K.   Werner, J. J.
    Variants:
    Ave Jerarchia

        Krakau, N. von

    Gott durch deine Guete

        Bach, J. S.

    Ravenshaw

        Lang, C. S.

Gottlob es geht nunmehr zu Ende
    (Bach)
                        Z 2855

DuPage, F.   Hulse, C. Van
Haase, K.   Kaun, H.

<u>Gottschalk</u>
  See: <u>Mercy</u>

<u>Grace Church</u> (Pleyel)

Cassler, G. W.

<u>Graefenburg</u>
  See: <u>Nun danket all und bringet Ehr</u>

<u>Grand Dieu, nous te bénissons</u>   Tune not found

Hess, C. L.

<u>Great God</u>

Guilmant, A.

<u>Great God of Heaven</u>
  See: <u>Bramley</u>

<u>Great Shepherd of Thy People</u>
  (Wetherill)

Wetherill, E. H.

<u>Great White Host</u>
  See: <u>Den store hvite Flok</u> (Norwegian)

<u>Green Hill</u> (Stebbins)

Langston, P. T.

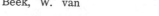

<u>Greenland</u> (Haydn)

Kreckel, P. G.
Whitford, H. P.
Variant:
<u>Song 225</u> (Dutch)

Beek, W. van

<u>Greensleeves</u> (English)

Archer, J. S.   Gehrke, H.   Vaughan-Williams, R.
Bingham, S. (2)   Lorenz, E. J.   Wolff, S. D.
Brusey, Dom J. G.   Purvis, R.   Wright, M. S.
Drummond, W.   Rohlig, H.   Young, G.
Faulkes, W.   Rowley, A.
Foote, A. W.   Thomas, V. C.

Greenville (Rousseau)

    Cowan, C. J.

Greenwood (Sweetser)

    Hulse, C. Van

Groot en eeuwig
  See: Psalm 38

Groote God, wij loven| U
  See: Grosser Gott wir loben dich

Gross ist der Herr (3rd Psalm
    Tone)

    Schindler, W.

Grosser Gott, du liebst Erbarmen
  See: Psalm 38 (Geneva)

Grosser Gott von alten Zeiten
  See: Gott des Himmels und der Erden

Grosser Gott, wir loben dich
  (Ritter-Monk)

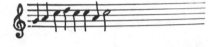

Z 3495

Burkhard, W.	Huth, A.	Poppen, H. M.
Diebold, J.	Kickstat, P.	Reger, M.
Fricke, R.	Kraft, K.	Rumpf, W.
Haase, K.	Kreckel, P. G.	Sattler, K.
Haessler, J. W.	Markworth, H. J.	Schmalz, P.
Hasse, K.	Merk, G.	Sechter, S.
Hecht, G.	Mueller-Zuerich, P.	Stehle, J. G. E.
Hulse, C. Van	Peeters, F. (2)	Zoller, G.

Variants:
Ambrosian Hymn of Praise

    Mueller, C. F.

Framingham

    Fleischer, H.

Groote God wij loven U

    Nieland, H.   Weelden, J. van

Hursley

    Ashford, E. L.   Couper, A. B.
    Bingham, S.   Curry, R. D.

Fry, H. S.
Goemanne, N.
Haase, K.
Hemmer, E.
James, F.
Lynn, G. A.

Matthews, H. A.
McGrath, J. J.
Mead, E. G.
Mehner, G.
Schaffer, J. E.
Thompson, V. D. (2)

Seele, was ermuedst du dich

Ricek, W.

Song 149 (Dutch)

Bruin, B.   Nauta, J.

Te Deum (Vienna)

Labunski, F. R.   Wyton, A.
*Latzelsberger, J.

Grosser Mittler
See: Alle Menschen (Mueller)

Grosser Prophete
See: Einer ist Koenig (Hille)

Gruss, Himmelskoenigin
See: Salve Regina

Gud efter dig jeg laenges
See: Innsbruck

Gud ei sitt tryckta barn

Lindberg, O. F.

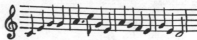

Gud er naadig (Lindeman)

Nielsen, L.

Gud Fader og Soen og Helligaand
See: Den signede dag (Thomisson)

Gud Fader udi Himmerig
See: Lad vaje hoejt vort kongeflag

Gud frede um vaart fedreland
(Grieg)

Karlsen, R.

Gud Helligaand, O kom (Laub)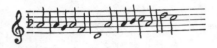

    *Frandsen, H. B.
    Frellsen, E. (2)
    *Thuner, O. E.
    *Wuertz, J.

Gud Helligaand, O kom (Winding)

    Hamburger, P.

Gud Helligaand, opfuld med lyst
    (Thomisson)

    Thuner, O. E.

Gud Helligaand, vor troestermand
    (Arrebo)

    Thuner, O. E.

Gud la oss i din kunnskap
    fremmes (Norsk)

    Karlsen, R.   Sandvold, A.

Gud laeter sina
    See: Nun freut Euch, lieben (Klug)

Gud, lat din ande og ditt ord (Lindeman)
    See: Ak, Fader, lad dit ord

Gud sign vaar konge God
    See: America

Gud signe vaart dyre Faadreland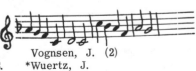

    Kjeldaas, A.
    Sandvold, A.

Gud skal allting (Crueger)
    See: Jesu, meine Freude

Gud skal alting mage (Lindemann)

    Baden, C.   Karlsen, R.
    Bjerre, J.   *Laub, T.   Vognsen, J. (2)
    Gangfloet, S.   *Nielsen, O. S.   *Wuertz, J.

Guds fred er mer end (Barnekow)

    Bangert, E.
    Frandsen, H. B.

Guds Godhed vil vi prise
　　See: Von Gott will ich nicht lassen
　　(Erfurt)

Guds igenfoedte, nylevende sjaele
　　See: Lobe den Herren, O meine Seele

Guds Menighed, syng (Berggreen)

　　　　Joergensen, G.
　　　　*Moeller, S. O.　　　　*Raasted, N. O.

Guds Menighed, syng (Folk)

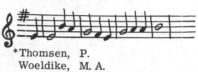

　　　　Godske-Nielsen, H.
　　　　*Jensen, S.　　　　*Thomsen, P.
　　　　Jeppesen, K.　　　　Woeldike, M. A.
　　　　*Nielsen, T. H.　　　　*Wuertz, J.

Guds Menighed, syng (Hoff)

　　　　Haase, K.
　　　　Karlsen, R.　　　　Peeters, F.

Guds Menighet er grunnet
　　See: Aurelia

Guds ord det er vort
　　See: Ein feste Burg

Guds Soen kom ned fra himmerig (Nuernberg)
　　See: Es ist das Heil

Guidance (Brackett)

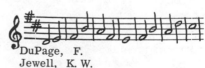

　　　　Altman, L.　　　　DuPage, F.
　　　　Brackett, L.　　　　Jewell, K. W.

Guide Me (Warren)

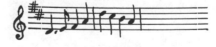

　　　　Haase, K.
　　　　Hoelty-Nickel, T.

Gunfield (Walker)

　　　　Walker, E.

Gute Baeume bringen (Sohren)
　　　　　　　　　　Z 6244
　　　　Peeters, F.
　　　　Sinzheimer, M.

Gute Maer
   See: <u>Vom Himmel hoch</u>

<u>Gwalchmai</u> (Jones)

    Purvis, R.
    Rogers, S. E.   Wetherill, E.

<u>Haarleg er Guds</u> (Wideen)

   Variant:
   <u>Alt staar i Guds faderhaand</u>

     Nielsen, L.   Rosenkilde-Larsen, E.

<u>Haec Dies</u>

    Olsson, O. E.   Weber, H.
    Piedelievre, P.   Widor, C. M.

<u>Haerlig er jorden</u>
   See: <u>Schoenster Herr Jesu</u>

<u>Hail Ye Sighing Sons</u> (U. S.
   Southern)

    Read, G.

<u>Halifax</u> (Handel)

    Best, W. T.
    Diggle, R.

<u>Halleluia</u>
   See: <u>Freuet Euch, ihr Christen alle</u>
   (Hammerschmidt) (Refrain)

<u>Halleluia, Gott sei hoch gepreist</u>
   (Hille)
              Z 7341a

    Haase, K.
   Variant:
   <u>Ich will streben nach dem Leben</u>

    Rumpf, W.

<u>Halleluia, Gott zu loben</u> (Baess-
   ler)
           Z 3678

    Gerke, A.
    Menzel, C.   Volckmar, F. W.

Halleluia, Lofgezongen
See: Sollt ich meinem Gott (Schop)

Halleluia schoener Morgen
See: Gott des Himmels und der Erden

Halleluja eeuwig dank en eere
See: Herr und Aeltster

Halleluya, jauchzt ihr Choere
See: Wachet auf

Hamburg (Mason - Plainsong)

Beck, A.	Goode, J. C.	
Bingham, S.	Haase, K.	Reynolds, W. G.
Bunjes, P. G.	McKinley, C.	Shaffer, J. E.
Colvin, H.	Miles, R. H.	Young, G.

Hampton (Wesley)

Parry, C. H. H.
Sowerbutts, J. A.

Han paa korset (Koenig)
See: Jesu, deine tiefen Wunden

Han som har hjiolpet (Winding)

Raasted, N. O.

Han som paa jorden bejler
See: Hilf Gott, dass mir's gelinge
(Thomisson)

Hankey
See: I Love to Tell the Story

Hanover (Croft)

Ashford, E. L.	Hulse, C. Van	Peeters, F.
Beck, A.	Jewell, K. W.	Rowley, A.
Best, W. T.	Knight, V.	Stam, G.
Calver, F. L.	Lang, C. S.	Stanford, C. V.
Coleman, R. H. P.	Lemare, E. H.	Steward, A. P.
Dicks, E. A.	Matthews, H. A.	Thiman, E. H.
Emery, W. J.	Mead, E. G.	Wallbank, N.
Francis, G. T.	Milford, R. H.	Wesley, S. S.
Haase, K.	Mudde, W.	Young, G.
Harris, C.	Palmer, C. C.	
Hinton, J. E. A.	Parry, C. H. H.	

Hanover (cont.)

Variants:
In Bethlehem's Stall

Hoogewoud, H.

O selige Nacht

Schmalz, P.

Psalm 104

Wesley, S. S.

Song 202 (Dutch)

Christiaansz, N. J.   Nauta, J.

Har haand du lagt paa Herrens
    plov (Glaeser)

*Frandsen, H. B.

Har haand du lagt paa Herrens plov
    (Schop)
See: Ermunt're dich (Schop)

Harewood (Wesley)

Groves, R.

Hark the Jubilee

Read, G.

Harre meine Seele (Malan)
                         Z 8427
Beck, A.   Rahn, E.
Draht, T.   Reuter, F.
Ore, A.   Wettstein, H.

Harvest Hymn (St. Gallen)

Haase, K.

Harwell (Mason)

Ashford, E. L.
Brinkley, T. F.   Elmore, R. H.

Hast du denn, Jesu
   Liebster
 See: Lobe den Herren, den

Have Thine Own Way
 See: Adelaide (Stebbins)

Haven of Rest (Moore)

  Wilson, R. C.

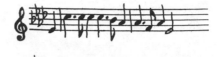

Hawkhurst (Gauntlett)

  Rowley, A.

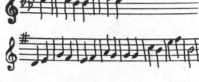

Hayling

  Alderson, A. P.

Hayn (Grimm's)
     Z 3416
  Elmore, R. H.

He Leadeth Me
 See: Aughton

He Was Crucified For Us (Pales- Tune not found
 trina)

  Brown, A. G. Y.

Head of the Church Triumphant
  (Mason)

  Colvin, H.

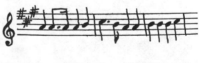

Heart of God (McAfee)

  Rand, J.

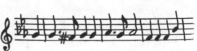

Heath
 See: Schumann (Mason & Webb)

Heathlands (Smart)

  Conway, M. P.

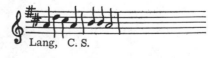

      Lang, C. S.

Heaven Is My Home
 See: Fatherland (Sullivan)

Heavenly Love (Mendelssohn)

  Hokanson, M.

'kHeb lang den Heer
    See: Psalm 40

Heer ik hoor van rijken zegen   Tune not found

      Mazyk, R. van

Heer, onze Heer, grootmachtig
    See: Psalm 8

'kHef mijn ziel, O God
    See: Psalm 25

Heil dir im Siegerkranz
    See: America

Heil, unser'm Koenig, Heil
    See: America

Heil'ger Geist, du Troester mein
    (Crueger)
                         Z 37b

      Barbe, H.   Hoeller, K.
      Bornefeld, H.   Kickstat, P.   Rowley, A.
      Driessler, J.   Meyer, R.   Soenke, H.
      Franke, F. W.   Pepping, E.   Walcha, H.

Heil'ges Kreuz, sei hoch verehret

      Miggl, E.

Heilig, heilig Herre stor (Mueller)

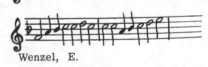

      Nielsen, L.

Heilig ist Gott der Vater
                         Z 8630b
      Kuehmstedt, F.
      Rinck, J. C. H.   Wenzel, E.

Heilige Namen

      Lampart, K.

Heilige Namen

      Ahrens, J.
      *Romanovsky, E.   *Schwammel, J.

Heiligste Nacht (Folk Tune)

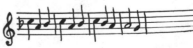

      Sister M. F.

Heinlein
 See: Aus der Tiefe rufe ich (Herbst)

Helft mir Gott's Guete preisen
 (Figulus)
     Z 5267
  Haase, K.

Helft mir Gott's Guete preisen
 (Magdeburg)

  Bach, J. S.   Fluegel, G.
  Dupré, M. J. J.   Ritter, A. G. (2)
  Variant:
  Zeuch ein zu deinen Toren

  Krebs, J. L.

Helft mir Gott's Guete preisen

  Hanff, J. N.

Helft mir Gott's Guete preisen
 (Erfurt)
 See: Von Gott will ich nicht lassen
 (Erfurt)

Helgen her og helgen hisset (Laub)

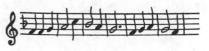

  Moeller, S. O.
  Thuner, O. E.

Helige Ande, laat nu ske

  Lindberg, O. F.

Hellig, hellig (Dykes)
 See: Nicaea

Helligaand, hoer hvad vi bede
 (Jeppesen)

  Thuner, O. E.   Videroe, F.

Helligaand, vor sorg du slukke
 See: Gott des Himmels (Albert)

Helligaanden trindt pa jord   Tune not found

  Frandsen, H. B.

Helmsley (Olivers)

     Webber, W. S. L.

Hendon (Malan)

     Laverty, J. T.

Henley (Mason)

     Bingham, S.

Her ei ties (Lindeman)

     Nielsen, L.
Variant:
Her vil ties

Her ei ties (German)
   See: O wer alles haet verloren

Her kommer, Jesus, dine smaa
   (Schulz)   dine arme

     Jensen, S.
     Nielsen, L.   Raasted, N. O.
     Nielsen, T. H.   Wuertz, J.

Her ser jeg da et lam aa gaa (Strassburg)
   See: An Wasserfluessen Babylon

Her vil ties, her vil bies
   (Berggreen)

     *Moeller, S. O.

Her vil ties, her vil bies (Laub)

     *Wuertz, J.

Her vil ties, her vil bies (Darmstadt)
   See: Sieh, hier bin ich (Darmstadt)

Her vil ties, her vil bies (Lindeman)
   See: Her ei ties (Lindeman)

Her vil ties, her vil bies (Lindeman)
   See: Paaskemorgen, slukker sorgen

Herald Angels
   See: Mendelssohn

Herbei, O ihr Glaeubigen
See: Adeste Fideles

Herr, auf dich will ich fest hoffen
                    stets
See: Freu dich sehr

Herr Christ, der einig Gottes
Sohn (Erfurt)
                    Z 4297a

Bach, J. S. (3)	Kauffmann, G. F.	Rinck, J. C. H. (2)
Bachem, H.	Kickstat, P.	Roth, F.
Baldamus, F.	Koch, J. H. E.	Rumpf, W.
Bornefeld, H.	Krieger, J. (3)	Schildt, M.
Brieger, O. (2)	Magnus, E.	Streicher, J. A.
Buxtehude, D. (3)	Markworth, H. J.	Sweelinck, J. P.
Driessler, J.	Micheelsen, H. F.	Telemann, G. P. (2)
Dupré, M. J. J.	Olsson, O. E.	Vierling, J. G.
Engelbrecht, K. F.	Pachelbel, J. (2)	Walcha, H.
Fischer, M. G.	Pepping, E.	Walther, J. G. (2)
Franke, F. W.	Piutti, K. (2)	Wettstein, H.
Frenzel, H. R.	Proeger, J.	Witte, C. F.
Hoyer, K.	Richter, E. F.	Wurm, A.
Karow, K.		

Variants:
Foerlossningen
Herr Gott, nun sei gepreiset

Palme, R.

Herr Jesu, Gnadensonne

Bach, J. C.   Fischer, M. G.
Enckhausen, H. F.   Hennig, W.

O naadens sol og sete

Gangfloet, S.

Herr Christ, du bist mein Erloeser
See: Du Herre Krist (Berggreen)

Herr Christe, treuer Heiland
                    Z 314c
    Wolfrum, K.

Herr, Dir gelob ich
                    Z 2872b
    Schmalz, P.

Herr, erhoere meine Klagen
See: Psalm 86 (Geneva)

Herr, fuer dein Wort sei hoch gepreist
See: Es spricht der Unweisen Mund

Herr Gott, der du mein Vater
bist (Nuernberg)
                    Z 309
                    Z 436
        Gulbins, M.

Herr Gott, dich loben alle wir
See: Old 100th (Genevan)

Herr Gott, dich loben wir (Babst)
                    Z 8652

Alberti, J. F. (2)	Gulbins, M.	Sulze, B.
Bach, A. W.	Karow, K.	Toepfer, J. G.
Bach, J. S.	Kittel, J. C.	Tunder, F.
Bornefeld, H.	Piutti, K.	Vierling, J. G.
Brieger, O.	Rinck, J. C. H. (2)	Walther, J. G. (2)
Buxtehude, D. (2)	Siedel, M.	Zehrfeld, O.

Variant:
Te Deum Laudamus (Babst)

Alberti, J. F.	*Gauss, O.	
Borris, S.	Grabner, H.	Lenel, L.
Buxtehude, D. (2)	*Koehler, E.	Stehle, J. G. E.

Herr Gott, dich loben wir
See: Nun danket alle Gott

Herr Gott in deinem hoechsten Thron
See: O hjelp mig Gud (Waldis)

Herr Gott, lass dich erbarmen
See: Innsbruck

Herr Gott, nach deiner Guete

        Rinck, J. C. H.

Herr Gott, nun schleuss den
Himmel auf
                    Z 7641a
               also in 4
                       4

Bach, J. S.	Rinck, J. C. H.
Dupré, M. J. J.	Vierling, J. G.
Fischer, M. G.	Walther, J. G. (2)
Franke, F. W.	

Herr Gott, nun sei gepreiset
See: Herr Christ, der einig Gott's Sohn

Herr, habe acht auf mich
        Z 2103
    Buehl, W.

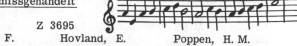

Herr, ich bekenn von Herzensgrund
    See: Mag' ich Unglueck nicht wiederstahn

Herr, ich bin dein Eigentum
    See: Mache dich, mein Geist

Herr, ich habe missgehandelt
    (Crueger)
                Z 3695

Baldamus, F.	Hovland, E.	Poppen, H. M.
Boenicke, H.	Kaeppel, G. C. A.	Richter, E. F.
Brieger, O.	Karlsen, R.	Rinck, J. C. H.
Brosig, M.	Karow, K.	Roeder, E. O.
Cassler, G. W. (2)	Krause, P.	Rumpf, W.
Claussnitzer, P.	Kuntze, C.	Schneider, J.
Dornheckler, R.	Marpurg, F. W. (3)	Schrader, H.
Engelbrecht, K. F.	Mueller, S.	Streicher, J. A.
Godske-Nielsen, H.	Nielsen, L.	Thomas, G. A.
Gulbins, M.	Oley, J. C.	Vierling, J. G.
Haase, K.	Peters, A.	Wedemann, W.
Herrmann, W.	Pisk, P. A.	Zechiel, E.
Herzog, J. G.	Piutti, K. (2)	Zopff, H. (2)

Variants:
Herre, jeg har handlet ille

Alnaes, E.	Raasted, N. O. (2)
Gangfloet, S.	Wuertz, J.
Jeppesen, K.	

Mein Gott, ich bin jetzt erschienen

    Enckhausen, H. F.

Soendag morgen fra de doede

Godske-Nielsen, H.	Moeller, S. O.
Laub, T.	Videroe, F.

Tiefe, stille, stark und milde

    Raasted, N. O.

Herr Jesu Christ, dich zu uns
    wend (Gotha)
                Z 624
            also in 4
                4

Herr Jesu Christ, dich zu uns wend (cont.)

Anonymous	Karg-Elert, S. (2)	Rabich, E.
Armsdorff, A.	Karow, K. (2)	Raphael, G.
Bach, J. C.	Kellner, J. C.	Reda, S.
Bach, J. S. (4)	Kickstat, P.	Reger, M. (2)
Baldamus, F.	Kirnberger, J. P.	Reuter, F. (2)
Bender, J.	Kirnberger, U. L.	Rinck, J. C. H. (2)
Boehm, G. (4)	Klaus, V.	Rudnick, W.
Brieger, O.	Krause, P.	Rumpf, W.
Claussnitzer, P.	Krebs, J. L.	Schaab, R.
Draht, T.	Kuehn, K.	Schuetze, W.
Drischner, M. (2)	Kuntze, C.	Schwencke, J. F. (2)
Driessler, J.	Leupold, A. W.	Stolze, H. W.
Dupré, M. J. J.	Lichey, R.	Streicher, J. A.
Enckhausen, H. F.	Litzau, J. B.	Telemann, G. P. (7)
Fischer, M. G.	Lorenz, C. A.	Theile, A. G.
Fluegel, G.	Lynn, G. A.	Tuerke, O.
Forchhammer, T. (3)	Manz, P.	Umbreit, K. G. (2)
Franke, F. W. (2)	Merk, G. (2)	Vierling, J. G.
Gradehand, F.	Merkel, G. (2)	Volckmar, F. W.
Gulbins, M.	Metzger, H. A.	Walther, J. G. (3)
Haase, K.	Micheelsen, H. F.	Weber, H.
Haase, R.	Mueller, S. W.	Wedemann, W.
Hasse, K.	Palme, R. (2)	Wettstein, H. (3)
Helmbold, C. A.	Peeters, F.	Weyhmann, J. W.
Herzog, J. G.	Petzold, J.	Winter-Hjelm, O.
Hoyer, K.	Piutti, K. (2)	Zehrfeld, O.
		Zipp, F.

Variants:
Der Tag neigt sich dem Abend zu

Raasted, N. O.

Det lakker nu ad aften brat

Godske-Nielsen, H.	Raasted, N. O.
Hamburger, P.	Videroe, F.
Nielsen, J. M.	Wuertz, J.
Noerholm, I.	

Nun jauchzt dem Herren

Hasse, K.

O Gott du hoechster Gnadenhort

Luedeke, A.

O Herre Krist dig til oss vend

Gangfloet, S.   Vestergaard-Pedersen, C.

Pensum Sacrum (Goerlitz)

  Couper, A. B.

Psalm 146

  Dragt, J.

Herr Jesu Christ, du hast bereit
See: Elbing (Sohren)

Herr Jesu Christ, du hoechstes
  Gut
                    Z 4488
  Oley, J. C.   Zachau, F. W.

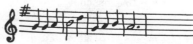

Herr Jesu Christ, du hoechstes
  Gut (Goerlitz)
                    Z 4486
  Baldamus, F.
  Bender, J.   Krause, P.   Ritter, A. G.
  Bornefeld, H.   Krebs, J. L. (2)   *Schweizer, R.
  Drischner, M.   Metzger, H. A.   Schwencke, J. F. (2)
  Hasse, K.   Pepping, E.   Vierling, J. G.
  Kaeppel, G. C. A.   Piutti, K. (2)   Walther, J. G.
  Karow, K.   Proeger, J.   Zachau, F. W.
Variants:
Herr Jesu Christ, ich weiss gar wohl

  Buxtehude, D.   Toepfer, J. G.
  Kittel, J. C.   Walther, J. G.
  Pachelbel, J.

  Herr Jesu deine Angst und Pein

  Bornefeld, H.   Haase, H. H.
  Drischner, M.   Stadlmair, H.

Herr Jesu Christ, ich weiss gar wohl
See: Herr Jesu Christ, du hoechtes Gut (Goerlitz)

Herr Jesu Christ, ich weiss gar wohl (Praetorius)
See: Et trofast hjerte

Herr Jesu Christ, meins Lebens
  Licht

  Kuntze, C.

Herr Jesu Christ, meins Lebens
  Licht (Nuernberg)
See also: Ach mein Herr Jesu,
dein Nahesein   Z 535

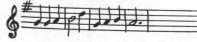

Herr Jesu Christ, meins Lebens Licht (cont.)

    Bach, J. S.   *Hoyer, K.
    Franke, F. W.
Variants:
O Jesu Christ, meins Lebens Licht (Nuernberg)

    Barlow, W.   Markworth, H. J.
    *Grote, H.   Moser, R.
    Haas, J.   Peeters, F.
    Haase, K.
O Jesu Christe, wahres Licht

    Bender, J.   Schrenk, J.
    Driessler, J.   Spiering, G.
    Haag, H.   Walcha, H.
    Hennig, W.

Herr Jesu Christ, meins Lebens Licht
  See: Breslau

Herr Jesu Christ, wahr Mensch
  und Gott (Eccard)
         Z 423
      also in 4
         4
    *Ritter, A. G.   Wedemann, W. (2)
Variant:
Wir danken dir, Herr Jesu Christ (Eccard)

    Bach, J. S.   Dupré, M. J. J.
    Bach, W. F.

Herr Jesu Christ, wahr Mensch und Gott (Vulpius)
  See: Nun loben wir mit Innigkeit

Herr Jesu Christ, wahr Mensch und Gott (French Psalm)
  See: Andernach

Herr Jesu Christ, wahr Mensch und Gott
  See: Vater Unser

Herr Jesu Christe, mein getreuer Hirte
  See: Gott sei gelobet und gebenedeiet

Herr Jesu, deine Angst und Pein
  See: Herr Jesu Christ, du hoechstes Gut

Herr Jesu, Gnadensonne
  See: Herr Christ, der einig Gott's Sohn

Herr Jesu hat ein Gaertchen
  See: Lord Jesus Hath a Garden

Herr Jesu, meines Lebens Licht

    Kunze, K.

Herr, lass mich deine Heiligung
  See: Elbing (Sohren)

Herr, lehr mich tun

    Baldamus, F.

Herr, nicht schicke deine Rache
(Wessnitzer)
           Z 6879
    Hasse, K.

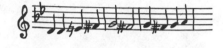

Herr nun lass' in Friede (Bohemian)
           Z 3302
    Gottschick, F.

Herr, nun selbst den Wagen halt
(Strassburg)
           Z 1570

    David, J. N.   Kickstat, P.
    Franke, F. W.   Mueller-Zuerich, P. (2)
    Heiss, H.   Reger, M. (2)

Herr, schaue auf uns nieder
  See: Wir stolzen Menschenkinder

Herr sey gelobet
  See: Gott sei gelobet

Herr, starke mich
  See: Herzliebster Jesu

Herr, straf mich nicht (Crueger)

           Z 4606a
    Werner, J. J.

Herr und Aeltster deiner Kreuzgemeinde (Moravian)
           Z 6930b

    Claussnitzer, P. Karg-Elert, S.
    Eyken, J. A. Van Kickstat, P.
    Fluegel, G.   Piutti, K.   Streicher, J. A.
    Franke, F. W.   Rudnick, W.   Traegner, R.
    Gerhardt, P.   Seyerlen, R.   Wettstein, H.
                               Wolfrum, P.

Herr und Aeltster deiner Kreuzgemeinde (cont.)

Variants:
Die wir uns all hier beisamen finden

    Meyer, R.

Halleluja eeuwig dank en eere

    Mazyk, R. van   Weyland, W.

Marter Gottes (Christi) (Jesu), wer kann dein vergessen (Gnadauer)

    Brieger, O.   Rudnick, W.
    Fluegel, G.

Song 53 (Dutch)

    Kousemaker, A. (2)   Wilgenburg, D. van (2)
    Vogel, W.

Song 94 (Dutch)

    Hoogewoud, H.   Wilgenburg, D. van
    Westering, P. C. van

Song 297 (Dutch)

    Wilgenburg, D. van

Herr, unser Gott, auf dem wir
trauen

    Franke, F. W.

Herr, wie du willst
  See: Aus tiefer Not (Strassburg)

Herr, wir stehen Hand in Hand
  See: Posen (Strattner)

Herra mull' on valo (Finnish)

    Kuusisto, T.

Herre, du et hjem oss gav (Solheim)

    Karlsen, R.

Herre Gud, ditt dyre navn og
aere (Norwegian Folk Tune)

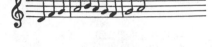

    Baden, C.   *Frandsen, H. B.   Karlsen, R.
    Bergh, L.   Gangfloet, S.   Sandvold, A. (2)
Variant:
Deus Fortis

    Peeters, F.

Herre Gud, ditt dyre navn og
aere (Norsk)

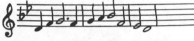

    Gangfloet, S.

Herre Gud, ditt dyre navn og
aere (Steenberg)

    Steenberg, P.

Herre Gud Fader, du vaar store
trost (Vogel)

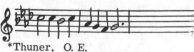

    Nielsen, L.

Herre Gud Fader, du vaar store trost (10th Century)
See: Fons Bonitans

Herre, hvor skal vi gaa hen
(Laub)

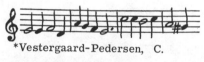

    Nielsen, L.   *Vestergaard-Pedersen, C.

Herre, hvor skal vi gaa hen
(Steenberg)

    Karlsen, R.   *Thuner, O. E.

Herre, jeg har handlet ille (Lindeman)
See: Dype, stille, starke, milde

Herre, jeg har handlet ille (Crueger)
See: Herr, ich habe missgehandelt

Herre, jeg hjertelig oensker

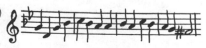

    Drischner, M.
    Kjeldaas, A.   Sandvold, A.

Herre Jesu, kom til stede (Zinck)

    Karlsen, R.

Herre Jesu, kom til stede (cont.)

 Variant:
 Medens vi i verden vandre

Herre Jesu Krist (Lindeman)

 Haase, K.
 Karlsen, R.   Peeters, F.

Herre Jesu vi er her
 See: Liebster Jesu

Herre, samla nu oss alla
 See: Trust (Mendelssohn)

Herren er mit lys og min frelse Tune not found

 Rosenkilde-Larsen, E.

Herren han har besoegt sit folk
 (Folk Tune)

 *Frandsen, H. B.

Herren han har besoegt sit folk
 (Laub)

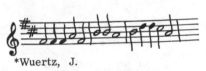

 Frellsen, E.   *Wuertz, J.
 *Hamburger, P.

Herren straekker ud sin Arm Tune not found

 Thuner, O. E.

Herrens roest, som aldrig
 See: Ringe recht (Kuhnau)

Herrnhut (Gesius)
 See: Jesu din Ihukommelse

Herrnhutters Avonlied

 Kort, J.

Herz und Herz verreint zusammen
 See: O du Liebe meiner Liebe (Ebeling)

Herzallerliebster Gott
     Z 5165
   also in 4
     4

Variant:
O Jesu, meine Lust

Walther, J. G.

Herzlich lieb habe ich dich, O
Herr (Schmid)
                    Z 8326

Alberti, J. F.	Haase, K.	Rumpf, W.
Bausznern, W. von	Hark, F.	Schaab, R.
Bender, J.	Henrich, J. G.	Scheidt, S.
Brieger, O.	Karg-Elert, S. (2)	Schumann, G.
Claussnitzer, P.	Kickstat, P.	Schwencke, J. F. (3)
David, J. N.	Kittel, J. C.	Stolze, H. W.
Doles, J. F.	Krause, P.	Umbreit, K. G.
Enckhausen, H. F.	Krebs, J. L. (5)	Vierling, J. G.
Fluegel, G.	Lubrich, F., Jr.	Wagner, A. (2)
Franke, F. W. (2)	Markull, F. W. (2)	Walther, J. G.
Freudenberg, C. G.	Merkel, G.	Wedemann, W.
Gore, R. T.	Moser, R.	Weyrauch, J.
Grabner, H.	Piutti, K. (3)	Wolfrum, K.
Grote, H.	Rinck, J. C. H.	Zoellner, K. H.

Herzlich tut mich erfreuen (German)
                    Z 5361a

Bender, J.
Bonitz, E.
Bossler, K.   Franke, F. W.
Brahms, J.   Rumpf, W.
Variants: Weber, H.
Lobt Gott in allen

Ziegler, K. M.

Min stoerste hjertens glaede

Thuner, O. E.

Herzlich tut mich verlangen
(Hassler)
                    Z 5385a
              also in 3
                    4

Bach, J. S.	Cebrian, A.	Frenzel, H. R.
Baldamus, F.	Claussnitzer, P. (9)	Grundmann, O. A.
Beck, A.	DeBrant, C.	Haase, K.
Bender, J.	Douglass, W.	Hasse, K.
Boeringer, J.	Dupré, M. J. J.	Hulse, C. Van
Bonitz, E.	Enckhausen, H. F.	Karg-Elert, S.
Brahms, J. (2)	Engelbrecht, K. F. (2)	Karow, K. (2)
Brosig, M.	Fluegel, E. P. (2)	Kellner, J. P.
Burkhard, W.	Forchhammer, T. (2)	Kickstat, P. (2)

Herzlich tut mich verlangen (cont.)

Kienzl, W.	Mueller, S.	Schreiner, A.
Kirnberger, J. P.	Pachelbel, J. (4)	Schrenk, J.
Kittel, J. C.	Palme, R.	Schuetze, W. (2)
Klaus, V.	Papperitz, B. R. (2)	Schumacher, M. H. (3)
Koch, M.	Peeters, F.	Schumann, G.
Koeckert, C.	Peters, A.	Schwencke, J. F. (3)
Koehler-Wumbach, W.	Piutti, K. (2)	Seiffert, U.
Kuehmstedt, F. (3)	Poppen, H. M.	Seyerlen, R. (2)
Landmann, A.	Reger, M. (2)	Stolze, H. W.
Langlais, J. F.	Reichardt, A.	Stout, A.
Lichey, R.	Reinhardt, A.	Streicher, J. A.
Lorenz, C. A.	Reuter, F. (2)	Strungk, D. (2)
Markull, F. W.	Rheinberger, J.	Telemann, G. P. (3)
Merk, G.	Rinck, J. C. H. (3)	Toepfer, J. G.
Merkel, G.	Rudnick, W.	Trautner, F. W.
Michálek, F.	Rumpf, W. (2)	Umbreit, K. G.
Micheelsen, H. F.	Saffe, F.	Walther, J. G. (3)
Michel, A.	Schaub, H. F.	Weber, H.
Miles, R. H.	Scheidt, S.	Wedemann, W. (2)
Muehling, A.	Schrader, H.	Wendt, E. A.
		Wettstein, H. (4)
		Wolfrum, K. (2)

Variants:
Ach herr, mich armen Suender

André, J.	Buxtehude, D. (4)	Pachelbel, J. (2)
Bach, J. C.	Fischer, M. G.	Reinbrecht, A.
Bach, J. S.	Fluegel, G.	Rinck, J. C. H.
Boehner, J. L.	Franke, F. W.	Telemann, G. P. (2)
Brosig, M.	Homilius, G. A.	Vierling, J. G.
	Kuhnau, J. (2)	Zachau, F. W. (2)

Bedenke, Mensch, das Ende

Wedemann, W.

Befal du dine veje

Jeppesen, K.	Raasted, N. O.

Befiehl du deine Wege

Hoepner, C. G.	Lange, S. de
Krause, P.	Wedemann, W. (2)
Kuntze, C.	

Beveel gerust Uw wegen

Bruin, B.

Chef couvert de blessures

Hess, C. L.

Das Jahr geht still zu Ende

Pfeiffer, C. D.   Wenzel, H.

Lass mich dein sein und bleiben

Strungk, D.

Mig hjaertelig nu laenges

Godske-Nielsen, H.   Rosenkilde-Larsen, E.
Laub, T.   Woeldike, M. A.
Noergaard, P.   Wuertz, J.

Nu hjertelig jeg lenges
O Haupt voll Blut

Abel, O.   Marpurg, F. W.
Ahrens, J.   Merk, G.
Albrecht, G.   Meyer, R.
Anacker, A. F.   Micheelsen, H. F.
Blum de Hyrth, C. E.   Mojsisovics, R. von
Bornefeld, H.   Mueller-Zuerich, P. (2)
Braehmig, B.   Pachelbel, J.
Brieger, O.   Palme, R.
Brosig, M.   Pepping, E. (5)
Busch, A. G. W.   Pfannschmidt, H.
Cassler, G. W.   Piutti, K.
Doppelbauer, J. F.   Pranschke, J.
Eckardt, A.   Raphael, G.
Faisst, C.   Rauch, J.
Faisst, I. G. F. von   Reger, M.
Fluegel, G.   Richter, E. F.
Forchhammer, T.   Riemenschneider, G.
Goetze, H.   Romanovsky, E.
Gulbins, M. (5)   Rudnick, W.
Haase, H. H.   Schaab, R.
Hesse, A. F.   Schehl, J. A.
Hoernig, O.   Schmalz, P.
Hohn, W.   Schmid, J.
Homilius, G. A.   Schwarz-Schilling, R.
Kickstat, P.   Stapf, O.
Klaus, V.   Straumann, B.
Klotz, H.   Thomas, G. A. (3)
Knab, A.   Wagenaar, J.
Koegler, W.   Walther, J. G.
Koehler, E.   Weigl, B.
Kousemaker, A.   Zwart, J. (2)
Kraft, K.

Herzlich tut mich verlangen (cont.)

O hoved, hoejt forhaanet

    Raasted, N. O.

O huvud blodigt, saarat

    Berg, G.

O Sacred Head

Andriessen, H.	Henning, E.	Phillips, C. G.
Beall, J.	Hustad, D.	Sowerby, L.
DeBrant, C.	Kaeppel, G. C. A.	Wetherill, E. H.
Edmundson, G. (3)	Milford, R. H.	Willing, D.
Englert, E.	Peeters, F. (4)	

Passion Chorale

Beck, A.	Groves, R.	Rohlig, H.
Bedell, R. L.	Helm, E.	Schehl, J. A.
Bender, J.	Kee, P.	Webber, W. S. L.
Bratt, C. G.	Kitson, C. H.	Westrup, J. A.
Copley, R. E. (2)	Martin, M. I'a.	Wiederman, B. A.
	Ratcliffe, D.	

Song 32 (Dutch)

    Wilgenburg, D. van   Zwart, J.

Song 43 (Dutch)

    Wilgenburg, D. van

Wenn ich einmal soll scheiden

Antalffy-Zsiross, D. von	Reinecke, C. H.
Daninger, H.	Rheinberger, J.
Glaus, A.	Wickenhausser, R.
Gulbins, M.	

Wie soll ich dich empfangen

    Pachelbel, J.   Walther, J. G.

Herzliebster Jesu (Crueger)
Z 983

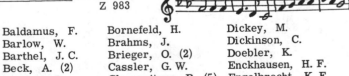

Baldamus, F.	Bornefeld, H.	Dickey, M.
Barlow, W.	Brahms, J.	Dickinson, C.
Barthel, J. C.	Brieger, O. (2)	Doebler, K.
Beck, A. (2)	Cassler, G. W.	Enckhausen, H. F.
Bender, J.	Claussnitzer, P. (5)	Engelbrecht, K. F.

Fischer, M. G.   Knecht, J. II.   Routh, F.
Fluegel, G. (2)   Koehler-Wumbach, W. Rudnick, W.
Forchhammer, T.   Krause, P.   Rumpf, W. (2)
Franke, F. W.   Kuntze, C.   Schaab, R. (2)
Frenzel, H. R.   Kunze, K.   Schehl, J. A. (2)
Gerok, K.   Landmann, A.   Schink, H.
Goode, J. C.   Lapo, C. E.   Schroeder, H.
Grote, H.   Leupold, A. W.   Schumacher, M. H.
Gulbins, M.   Merkel, G.   Schumann, C.
Haase, K.   Micheelsen, H. F.   Schwarz-Schilling,
Haase, R.   Miles, R. H.   R. (2)
Hanebeck, H. R.   Moore, M.   Seelmann, A.
Hasse, K.   Nagel, W.   Slater, G. A.
Held, W.   Nelson, R. A.   Soenke, H.
Helm, E.   Oley, J. C. (3)   Streicher, J. A.
Hennig, W.   Oncley, A. L.   Thomas, O.
Herrmann, W.   Papperitz, B. R.   Vierling, J. G.
Herzog, J. G.   Peeters, F.   Vogel, W.
Hoeller, K.   Pepping, E. (2)   Walcha, H.
Hoyer, K.   Post, P.   Walter, S.
Hulse, C. Van   Raphael, G.   Wedemann, W.
Huth, A.   Reda, S.   Weinreich, W.
Johns, D.   Reger, M.   Wettstein, H.
Kaeppel, G. C. A.   Reichardt, B.   Weyrauch, J.
Karg-Elert, S. (2) Reichel, B. (2)   Wolff, C. M.
Kauffmann, G. F.   Rinck, J. C. H. (3)   Wolfrum, K. (2)
Kickstat, P.   Ritter, A. G. (2)   Wyton, A.
Kittel, J. C.   Rohlig, H.   Young, G.
Klaus, V.   Romanovsky, E.   Zechiel, E.
                                             Zehrfeld, O. (2)

Variants:
<u>Bortvend din vrede, Gud</u>

  Woeldike, M. A.

<u>Herr, starke mich</u>

  Haase, H. H.

<u>Leer mij, O Heer</u>

  Post, P.

<u>Song 34</u> (Dutch)

  Storm, A.   Wilgenburg, D. van

<u>Song 42</u> (Dutch)

  Wilgenburg, D. van   Zwart, J.

Herzliebster Jesu (cont.)

  Vreden din avvend (Crueger)

       Gangfloet, S.   Skottner, F.
       Nielsen, L.

Hesperus
   See: Quebec (Baker)

Het ruime hemelrond
   See: Psalm 19

Heut singt die liebe Christenheit
   (Herman)
                     Z 2498a
       Beyer, M.   Kickstat, P.   Pepping, E.
       Bornefeld, H.   Metzler, F.   Rumpf, W.
       Bossler, K.   Micheelsen, H. F.   Weber, H.
   Variant:
   Geh aus, mein Herz, und suche Freud

       Bender, J.

Heut triumphieret Gottes Sohn
   (Gesius)
                     Z 2585
       Adler, E.   *Grote, H.   Reichardt, B.
       Bach, J. S.   Haase, K.   *Ritter, A. G.
       *Beyer, M.   Hark, F.   Spiering, G.
       Driessler, J.   Hennig, W.   Wedemann, W.
       Dupré, M. J. J. Looks, R.   Zahn, J.
       *Faehrmann, H.   Piutti, K. (2)
   Variant:
   Nun triumphieret Gottes Sohn

Heut triumphirt mit Freuden
   (Erfurt)
                     Z 284
       Kittel, J. C. (2)

Hic Breve Vivitur (Pettet)

       Harwood, B.

Hier ist mein Herz, O Seel'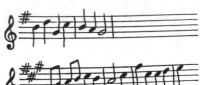
                     Z 3163
       Vogler, G. J.

Hier legt mein Geist sich vor dir
  nieder (Weimar)
                        Z 799
     Bach, A. W.
     *Baldamus, F.

                              *Sechter, S.

Hier legt mein Sinn sich vor dir
  nieder (Rosenroth)
                        Z 788
     Franke, F. W.
     *Karow, K.
     Kickstat, P.

                              Oley, J. C.
                              Pfaff, H.

Hier liegt vor deiner (Haydn)

                        Z 5607
     Schehl, J. A.

Hilariter
  See: Die ganze Welt (Koeln)

Hilf Gott, dass mir's gelinge
  (Dresden)
                        Z 4329f

     Bach, J. S.
     Dupré, M. J. J.
     Fiebig, K.
  Variant:
  Wenn meine Suend' mich kraenken (Leipzig)

     Abel, O.   *Gulbins, M.
     Baldamus, F.   *Herzog, J. G.
     Claussnitzer, P. (2)   *Oechsler, E.
     *Driessler, J.   Schweppe, J.
     Enckhausen, H. F.   Spiering, G.
     Franke, F. W.   Vierling, J. G.

                              *Piutti, K.
                              Walther, J. G.
                              Zachau, F. W.

Hilf Gott, dass mir's gelinge
  (Thomisson)
                        Z 4330
  Variants:
  Han som paa jorden bejler

     Thuner, O. E. (2)   Woeldike, M. A.
     Vestergaard-Pedersen, C.

  Naar mig min synd vil krenke

     Gangfloet, S.

                              Nielsen, L.

Hilf, Herr Jesu, lass gelingen
(Schop)
                    Z 3687a

     Driessler, J.
     Jacobi, M.   Meyer, R.
Variants:
Fred til bod (Schop)
Stille er min sjael (Schop)

     Karlsen, R.

Werde Licht, du Stadt der Heiden

     Soenke, H.

Hilf, Herr Jesu, lass gelingen
    See: Unser Herrscher (Neander)

Hill dig, Frelser og forsoner
(Laub)

     *Frandsen, H. B.   Woeldike, M. A.
     Laub, T.   *Wuertz, J.

Hill dig, Frelser og forsoner (Herman)
    See: Erschienen ist der herrlich Tag

Himlen aabnes, moerket svinder
(Berggreen)

     Wuertz, J.

Himmel, Erde, Luft und Meer
    See: Posen

Himmelan, nur Himmelan (Frei-
berg)
                    Z 7084
     *Rinck, J. C. H.   Wieruszowski, L.

Himmelan, nur Himmelan (Stoetzel)
    See: Ruhe ist das beste Gut

Himmelskapar, hoeyr (Norsk)

     Nielsen, L.

Himmelske Fader (Sande)

     Gangfloet, S.
     Karlsen, R.

Hinunter ist der Sonne Schein
(Vulpius)
            Z 506

Abel, O.	*Hanebeck, H. R.	Poppen, H. M.
Bender, J.	Hark, F.	Stadlmair, H.
Fiebig, K.	Huth, A.	Traegner, R.
Franke, F. W.	Kickstat, P.	Weber, H.

Hinunter ist der Sonne Schein
  See: Erhalt uns Herr, bei deinem Wort

Hirten, er ist geboren

    Peeters, F.

Hit, O Jesu, samloms vi

    Wikander, D.

Hjaelp mig, O Jesus (Finnish)

    Kuusisto, T.

Hjelp! ja kvar er hjelp aa faa
(Richter)
           Z 3528
    Nielsen, L.
Variant:
Ach wie hat des Herren Hand

Hjem jeg lenges (Lindeman)

    Karlsen, R.

Hjerte, loeft din gledes vinger
(Steenberg)

    Gangfloet, S.   Nielsen, L. (2)

Hjerte, loeft din glaedes vinger
  See: Froehlich soll mein Herze (Crueger)

Hlas přisný (Czech)

    Wiedermann, B. A.

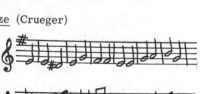

Hobed, O Hilion (Welsh)

    Middleton, J. R.

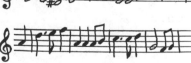

Hochheilige Dreieinigkeit (Freylinghausen)
              Z 5783

    Hasse, K.

Hodie Christus Natus Est

    *Luard-Selby, B.   Peek, R. M.

Hodie Nomen Tuum

    Sister M. G.

Hoechster Koenig, Jesu Christ

    Grote, H.

Hoechster Priester, der du mich
(Basel)
              Z 1256

    *Gulbins, M.   Haase, K.
Variants:

Jesu, komm doch selbst zu mir (Basel)

    Piutti, K.   *Vierling, J. G.

    Muede bin ich (Basel)

      Krause, P.

Savannah

      Bouman, P.

Hoechster Priester, der du mich
(Freylinghausen)
              Z 1254

Variant:
Meine Hoffnung steht auf Gott

    Piutti, K.

Hoechster Priester, der du mich
(Gregor)
              Z 1259
Variant:
Komm, O fromme Christenschaar

    Sechter, S. (2)

Hoechster Troester
  See: Ebeling (Bonn)

Hoeit fra det himmelske hoeie
   (A. Lindeman)

    Karlsen, R.

Hoer vor hellig-aftens boen (Laub)

    Rosenkilde-Larsen, E.   Vestergaard-Pedersen, C.
    Thuner, O. E.   Woeldike, M. A.

Hoeren I, vor Herre kalder   Tune not found

    Thuner, O. E.

Hoerer, I som graede
  See: Jesu, meine Freude

Hoert auf mit Trauern und
   Klagen (Uettingen)
                Z 678
    Rinck, J. C. H. (2)

Hoeyr kor Kyrkjeklokka (Norse
   Folk Tune)

    Baden, C.   Sandvold, A.
  Variant:
  Kjaerlighet er lysets kilde

    Karlsen, R.

Holcomb (McKinney)

    Smith, H. M.

Hold oppe Gud, hos oss dit ord
  See: Erhalt uns, Herr (Klug)

Holland (Verspoet's)

    Englert, E.

Holland (1539)

    Bratt, C. G.
    Nieland, J.

Holley (Hews)

    Hulse, C. Van

Hollingside (Dykes)

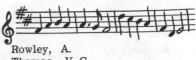

    Allen, G. P.
    Burdett, G. A.   Rowley, A.
    Conway, M. P.   Thomas, V. C.

Holly and the Ivy (English)

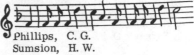

    Buck, P. C.   Phillips, C. G.
    Gotch, O. H.   Sumsion, H. W.
    Milford, R. H.   Webber, W. S. L.

Holy, Holy (Sirenes)

    Kreckel, P. G.

Holy, Holy, Holy

    Curry, R. D.

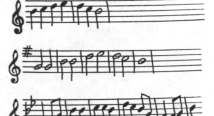

Holy Manna (Moore)

    Shaffer, J. E.

Holy Name
    See: Psalm 136

Holy Night
    See: Stille Nacht

Holy Spirit, Faithful Guide (Wells)

    Thompson, V. D.

Holy Well (English)

    Milford, R. H.

Holyrood (Watson)

    Webber, W. S. L.

Holywood
    See: St. Thomas (Wade)

Homeland (Sullivan)

    Reuter, F.

Horbury (Dykes)

    Goodhart, A. M.
    Rowley, A.

Horsley (Horsley)

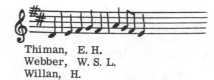

    Groves, R.
    Haase, K.   Thiman, E. H.
    Hulse, C. Van   Webber, W. S. L.
    Lang, C. S.   Willan, H.

Hos Gud er idel glede (Norse
  Folk Tune)

    Baden, C.   Nielsen, L.
    Moseng, S.   Sandvold, A.

Hosanna (Dykes)

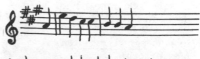

    Dickey, M.

Hosanna Filio David

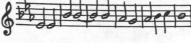

    Demessieux, J.

Hosanna In Excelsis

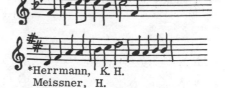

    Thomas, V. C.

Hosianna David's Sohn
           Z 6406
    Eckardt, A.
    Franke, F. W.

    *Herrmann, K. H.
    Meissner, H.

Hosianna David's Sohne (Koenig)

          Z 3600
    *Obersold, H.
    Piutti, K.

    *Rinck, J. C. H.

Hostis Herodes (Plainsong)

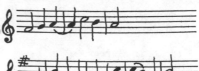

    Cavazzoni, G.

How Great the Wisdom (Mc-
  Intyre)

    Schreiner, A.

How Happy Are the Souls (U. S.
  Southern)

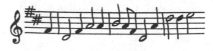

    Read, G.

Hueter, wird die Nacht (Geneva)
  See: Ach, was bin ich, mein Erretter (Geneva)

Hueter, wird die Nacht
  See: Psalm 38 (Marot)

Hungarian Christmas Song

    Sulyok, I.
  Variant:
  Christus Urunknak

Hursley
  See: Grosser Gott, wir loben dich

Hvad kan os komme til for noed
  See: Nun freut Euch, lieben (Klug)

Hvad lyus oefver groeften
  (Jespersoen)
                    also in 3
                             4
    Olsson, O. E.

Hvad vinnes paa verdens det
  (Steenberg)

    Karlsen, R.

Hvem skal jeg klage mit (Laub)

    Thuner, O. E.

Hvil ut, min sjel (Steenberg)

    Nielsen, L.

Hvilestunden er i vente (Laub)

    Thuner, O. E.
    Vestergaard-Pedersen, C.   Woeldike, M. A.

Hvo ene later Herren
  See: Wer nur den lieben Gott
  (Neumark)

Hvo ikkun lader Herren
  See: Wer nur den lieben Gott
  (Neumark)

Hvo lange skal mit
  See: Schmuecke dich

Hvo tranes lampa
  See: Vigil

Hvor er det godt aa lande (Norsk)

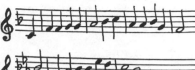

    Nielsen, L.

Hvor er det godt, i Jesu arme
(Laub)

    Thuner, O. E.

Hvor er det godt ved Herrens
(Lindeman)

    Karlsen, R.

Hvor salig er den lille flokk
(Lindeman)

    Karlsen, R.
    Variant:
Wie selig ist die kleine Schaar

    Matthison-Hansen, H.

Hvorledes skal jeg moede

    *Christensen, B.

Hvorledes skal jeg moede
  See: Valet

Hyfrydol (Pritchard)

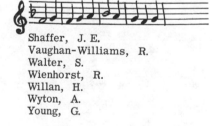

    Barnes, F. M.
    Candlyn, T. F. H.
    Coleman, R. H. P. (2)   Shaffer, J. E.
    Haase, K.   Vaughan-Williams, R.
    Hegedus, A.   Walter, S.
    Hill, L. E.   Wienhorst, R.
    Lloyd, L. S.   Willan, H.
    Manz, P.   Wyton, A.
    Near, G.   Young, G.

Hyggelig, rolig, Gud (Gether)

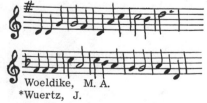

    *Thuner, O. E.

Hyggelig, rolig, Gud (Lindeman)

    Nielsen, J. M.
    *Videroe, F.   Woeldike, M. A.
                *Wuertz, J.

Hyggelig, rolig, Gud (Steenberg)

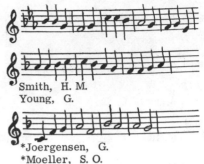

    Nielsen, L.

Hymn to Joy (Beethoven)

    Dasher, J. A.   Smith, H. M.
    Hughes, R. J.   Young, G.

I al sin glans (Rung)

    *Jensen, S.   *Joergensen, G.
    Jeppesen, K.   *Moeller, S. O.

I al sin glans
    See: Psalm 105

I Am Coming to the Cross
    (Fischer)

    Thompson, V. D.

I bygge skal huset paa (Hart-
    mann)

    Karlsen, R.

I dag er naadens tid
    See: Nun danket alle Gott

I dag er naadens tid
    See: O Gott du frommer Gott (Hannover)

I dag om Herrens roest (Swedish Psalm - Haeffner)
    See: I denne verdens sorger

I dag paa apostolisk (Weisse)
    See: Nun loben wir mit Innigkeit (Vulpius)

I dag skal allting sjung (Geneva)
    See: Psalm 6

I denna ljuva sommertid

    Berg, G.   Wikander, D.

I denne verdens sorger (Swedish
    Psalm - Haeffner)

    *Borg, O.
    Variant:
    I dag om Herrens roest
        Nielsen, L.

I denne verdens sorger (Crueger)
   See: In dieser Welt (Crueger)

I doeden Jesus blunded
   See: Aus meines Herzens Grunde

I doeden Jesus blundet
   See: Von Gott will ich nicht (Erfurt)

I doedens baand vor Frelser laa
   See: Christus Resurrexit

I fyrste upphav var Guds ord
   (Franck)

               also in 6
                     4

    Karlsen, R.
Variant:
Den idraet Gud

    Thuner, O. E.

I Hear Thy Welcome Voice (Hartsough)

    Miller, H. A.

I Herrens utvalgte (Norsk)

    Nielsen, L.

I Herrens vingaards-svenner
   (Steenberg)

    Karlsen, R.

I himmelen (Lindeman)

    Nielsen, L.

I himmelen (Norwegian)

    Gangfloet, S.   Karlsen, R.
    Hokanson, M.   Rogers, S. E.

I himmelen, I himmelen (Swedish)
   See: Laurinus

I Jesu namn (Winter-Hjelm)

    Nielsen, L.

I Jesu navn (Kingo)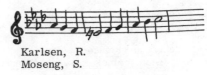

    Alnaes, E.
    Borg, O.   Karlsen, R.
    Hamburger, P.   Moseng, S.

I Jesu soeker jeg min fred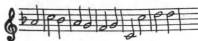
   (Lindeman)

    Gangfloet, S.

I Kristne som toer trede (Geneva)
   See: Psalm 6

I lemmer, hvis hoved har Himlen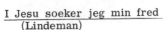
   (Laub)

    Laub, T.

I Love Thee, O Lord, My Strength
   See: Du meiner Seelen (Hungarian-
   Joseph)

I Love Thee, (O Thou) Lord Most High
   See: Du meiner Seelen (Hungarian-
   Joseph)

I Love To Tell the Story (Fischer)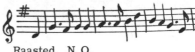

    Ashford, E. L. Hulse, C. Van Stults, R. M.
    Felton, W. M. Rogers, L.   Thompson, V. D.
  Variant:
  Hankey

    Bingham, S.   Larson, E. R.
    Elmore, R. H.   Lynn, G. A.

I Need Thee Every Hour
   See: Need

I oesten stiger solen op (Weyse)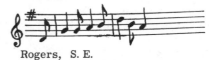

    Frandsen, H. B.
    Frellsen, E.   Raasted, N. O.
    Hamburger, P.   Vaerge, A.

I Saw Three Ships

    Brusey, Dom J. G.
    Duro, J.   Rogers, S. E.

I syndbetyngda (Finnish)

    Kuusisto, T.

I Wonder As I Wander (Appalachian)

    Niles, J. J.

Iam Lucis Orto Sidere (Bene-
dictine - Mode 6)

    Brandon, G.

Iam Lucis Orto Sidere (Mode 8)

    Peeters, F.

Iam Lucis Orto Sidere (Tallis)

    Tallis, T. (2)

Iam Moesta (Luther)
                Z 1454
    Variants:
    Den yndigste Ros'

       Andersen, E.   Moeller, S. O.
       Christensen, B.   Nielsen, T. H.
       Frandsen, H. B.   Raasted, N. O. (2)
       Frellsen, E.   Weinholt-Pedersen, K.
       Godske-Nielsen, H.   Woeldike, M. A.
       Hamburger, P.   Wuertz, J.

    Die lieblichste Ros'

       Godske-Nielsen, H.   Raasted, N. O.
       Hamburger, P.

    Med sorgen og klagen (Wittenburg)

       Bergh, L.   Nielsen, L.

Iam Sol Recedit Igneus (Mode 8)

    Peeters, F.
    Simonds, B.

Iam Sol Recedit Igneus
    See: Schon weicht der Sonne

Ich armer Mensch, ich armer
Suender
                    Z 2815b
     Wolfrum, K.

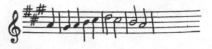

Ich bete an die Macht der Liebe
     See: St. Petersburg (Bortnianski)

Ich bin getauft auf deinem Namen
     See: Geht hin, ihr glaeubigen Gedanken

Ich bin getauft auf deinem Namen
     See: O dass ich tausend (Koenig)

Ich bin, ja, Herr, in deiner Macht
     See: O Gott, der du ein Herrfuerst bist

Ich dank dir, lieber Herre (Bohemian)
                    Z 5354b

     Bach, J. C.   Piutti, K. (3)
     Buxtehude, D.   Reger, M. (2)
     Claussnitzer, P. (2)   Schaab, R.
     Haase, K.   Schwencke, J. F.
     Herzog, J. G.   Stiller, K.
     Karg-Elert, S.   Stolze, H. W.
     Mendelssohn, A.   Streicher, J. A.
     Peeters, F.   Vierling, J. G.
Variants:
Lob Gott getrost mit Singen

     Bausznern, W. von   Huth, A.
     Bender, J.   Kickstat, P. (2)
     Franke, F. W.   Magnus, E.
     Hanebeck, H. R.   Micheelsen, H. F.
     Hennig, W. (2)   Poppen, H. M.
     Hofmeier, A.   Sprung, W.
     Hoyer, K. (2)   Traegner, R.

Nun kommt die Bluetenzeit

     Raasted, N. O.

O komm, du Geist der Wahrheit

     Spiering, G.

Ich dank dir schon durch deinen
     Sohn (Praetorius)
                    Z 247
          also in 4
                  4

Bach, J. C.
Baldamus, F.
Brieger, O.
Claussnitzer, P.
Dienel, O.
Eyken, J. A. van
Fischer, M. G.
Franke, F. W. (2)
Haase, K.
Karg-Elert, S.

Kickstat, P.
Kittel, J. C.
Kuehn, K.
Kuntze, C.
Merkel, G. (2)
Oley, J. C.
Piutti, K.
Reichardt, B.
Reinbrecht, A. (2)
Rinck, J. C. H.

Rumpf, W.
Schaab, R. (2)
Schuetze, W.
Schurig, V.
Schwencke, J. F.
Stolze, G. C.
Strungk, N. A.
Vierling, J. G.
Wettstein, H.
Zipp, F.

Variants:

Ach Herre Gott, mich treibt die Not
Ich danke dir durch deinen Sohn
Mein erst Geschaeft sei Preis
          Gefuehl

Rinck, J. C. H. (2)   Walcha, H.

Ich danke dir durch deinen Sohn
    See: Ich dank dir schon durch deinen Sohn

Ich danke dir, Herr Gott, in
    deinem Throne (1664)
                      Z 3203
    Weber, H.

Ich erhebe mein Gemuete
    See: Psalm 25

Ich folge dir nach Golgotha

    Chaix, C. (2)

Ich freu' mich in dem Herren
    (Helder)
                      Z 5427
    Franke, F. W.   Hofmeier, A.
    Hark, F.   Sprung, W.

Variants:
Es kennt der Herr die Seinen

    Hasse, K.

Ich trau' mich in dem Herren

    Hoyer, K.

O Koenig aller Ehren

    Koch, J. H. E.   Weber, H.
    Otto, H.   Zipp, F.
    Pfeiffer, C. D.

Ich freu' mich wenn man zu mir spricht

Franke, F. W.

Ich freue mich in dir (Koenig)
Z 5187
*Hulse, C. Van

Ich freue mich in dir
See: O Gott, du frommer Gott (Hannover)

Ich freue mich, mein Gott, in dir
Z 2478
Vierling, J. G.

Ich geh' zu deinem Grabe
See: Ich weiss an wen ich glaube
(Schuetz)

Ich glaub' an einen Gott

Baldamus, F.

Ich glaub' an Gott in aller Not

Kreckel, P. G.
Romanovsky, E.

Ich g'nuge mich an meinem Stande (Bach)

Papperitz, B. R. (4)

Ich hab' genug (Ahle)
See: Es ist genug (Ahle)

Ich hab' genug (Muehlhausen)
See: Es ist genug (Muehlhausen)

Ich hab' in Gottes Herz und Sinn
See: Was mein Gott will

Ich hab' mein Sach Gott heimgestellt (Cassel)
Z 1679

Bach, J. S. (3)	*Gulbins, M.	Rinck, J. C. H. (2)
*Baldamus, F.	Krause, P.	Rinkens, W.
*Barlow, M.	Muehling, A.	Strungk, D.
Dupré, M. J. J.	Pachelbel, J.	Toepfer, J. G.
Fischer, M. G.	Pepping, E.	*Vierling, J. G.
Franke, F. W.	Piutti, K.	Zipp, F.

Ich hab' mein Sach Gott heim-
    gestellt (Stuttgart)
                    Z 1738
Variant:
Wohlauf, wohlauf, zum letzten Gang

    Claussnitzer, P.   Schaeffer, A.
    Rumpf, W.

Ich hab' mein Sach Gott heimgestellt (Bourgeois)
    See: Psalm 21

Ich habe nun den Grund gefunden
    See: O dass ich tausend (Koenig)

Ich halte treulich still
    See: Was frag ich nach der Welt (Fritsch)

Ich hatt' einen Kamaraden (Folk
    Tune)

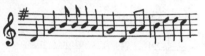

    Gulbins, M.

Ich klag' dir, lieber Herre Gott

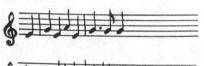

    Franke, F. W.

Ich komm' zu deinem Abend-
    mahle (Leipzig)
                    Z 2869
    Beck, A.   Grote, H.
Variant:
Ich sterbe taeglich

    Arbatsky, Y.   Haase, K.
    Canning, T.   Kretzschmar, P.

Ich komme vor dein Angesicht
    See: Wo Gott zu Haus nicht gibt sein Gunst

Ich lass' dich nicht (Schemelli)
                    Z 7455

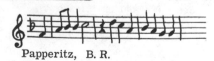

    Franke, F. W.   Papperitz, B. R.

Ich moechte mich nun troesten

    Peeters, F.

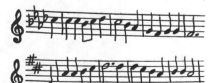

Ich ruehm den Herrn allein
    (Baessler)   Z 5231
    Gerke, A.
    Grosse-Weischede, A. (2)

Ich ruf' zu dir, Herr Jesu Christ
(Klug)
                    Z 7400

Ahle, J. R.	Karow, K.	Schaab, R.
Bach, J. C.	Kickstat, P.	Scheidt, S. (4)
Bach, J. S.	Kittel, J. C.	Schrader, H.
Baldamus, F.	Krebs, J. L. (2)	Seyerlen, R.
Bausznern, W. von	Merkel, G.	Sweelinck, J. P.
Borngaesser, W.	Noetel, K. F.	Telemann, G. P. (2)
Buxtehude, D. (2)	Pachelbel, J. (2)	Vierling, J. G.
Claussnitzer, P.	Pfaff, H.	Walcha, H.
Couper, A. B.	Piutti, K. (2)	Wieruszowski, L.
Dupré, M. J. J.	Reichel, B.	Zachau, F. W.
Grote, H.	Rinck, J. C. H.	Zipp, F.
Kaminski, H.	Ross, C.	

Variants:
O Gud, fornuften fatter ej

   Thuner, O. E.

O Jesu, som har elsket mig

   Gangfloet, S.

Til dig jeg raaber, Herre Krist

   Matthison-Hansen, F.

Ich schau' nach jenen Bergen
(Elberfeld)
                    Z 2352
      Franke, F. W.
      Grosheim, G. C.   Meissner, H.

Ich sehe dich, O Jesu, schweigen

   Philipp, F.

Ich sing' in Ewigkeit
   See: Nun danket all und

Ich singe dir mit Herz und Mund

   Oley, J. C.

Ich singe dir mit Herz und Mund
(Frankfurt)
                    Z 214
      Haase, K.   *Reinbrecht, A.
      Hofland, S.   Zopff, H.

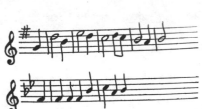

Ich singe dir mit Herz und Mund
   See: Nun danket all und

Ich steh' an deiner Krippen hier
(Bach)

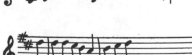

Z 4663

Abel, O.	Hofmeier, A.	Pepping, E.
*Burkhard, W.	Kickstat, P.	Thate, A.
Franke, F. W.	Luedders, P.	Walcha, H.
Herrmann, K. H.	Neuman, A.	Weber, H.

Ich steh' an deiner Krippen hier
    See: Nun freut Euch, lieben Christen (Klug)

Ich steh' in meines Herren Hand
    See: Nun freut Euch, lieben Christen (Klug)

Ich sterbe taeglich (Leipzig)
    See: Ich komm' zu deinem Abendmahle

Ich trau' mich in dem Herren
    See: Ich freu' mich in dem Herren

Ich und mein Haus
    See: Wie schoen leuchtet

Ich weiss' an wen ich glaube
(Schuetz)

    Hasse, K.
    Kickstat, P.   Magnus, E.
Variants:
Dieweil wir sind versammelt
Ich geh' zu deinem Grabe

    Meyer, R.

    Ich weiss' woran ich glaube

    Hennig, W. (2)   Siedel, M.
    Hiltscher, W.

Ich weiss', dass mein Erloeser lebt
    See: Elbing (Sohren)

Ich weiss' ein lieblich Engelspiel
(Strassburg)
                Z 1676
    Weyrauch, J.

Ich weiss', mein Gott, dass all
    mein Thun (Schein)
                Z 1712
    *Claussnitzer, P.
    Petzold, J.   Vierling, J. G.
    Piutti, K.   Zipp, F.

Ich weiss' woran ich glaube
    See: Ich weiss' an wen ich glaube

Ich will dich lieben, meine
    Staerke (Koenig)
                            Z 2767

Bauer, J.	*Grundmann, O. A. (2)	Raasted, N. O. (2)
Beck, A.	Haase, K.	*Rebling, G.
Brieger, O.	*Haase, R.	Reda, S.
Claussnitzer, P. (2)	Hessenberg, K.	Reger, M.
Degen, H.	Hoyer, K. (2)	*Rumpf, W.
Drischner, M.	Kickstat, P.	Saffe, F.
Faehrmann, H.	*Knecht, J. H.	Schmohl, G.
Fiebig, K.	Krause, P.	Schneider, F. C.
*Fink, C.	*Lehmann, B.	*Schwencke, J. F. (3)
Fischer, M. G.	Lubrich, F., Jr.	Streicher, J. A. (2)
Fluegel, G.	Mueller-Zuerich, P.	Weber, H.
Forchhammer, T.	Nelson, R. A.	Wettstein, H. (5)
*Franke, F. W.	Peeters, F.	*Wolfrum, K.
*Frenzel, H. R.	Piutti, K.	Zierau, F.
*Goetze, H.		

Variants:
Dig vil jeg elske

    Frandsen, H. B.   Wuertz, J.

    Song 218 (Dutch)

    Koppenol, J.   Wilgenburg, D. van

Ich will dich lieben, meine Staerke
    See: Du meiner Seelen (Hungarian-Joseph)

Ich will mein Gott, du Koenig
    See: In dieser Morgenstund

Ich will mit Danken kommen
    See: Aus meines Herzens Grunde

Ich will so lang ich lebe (Schuetz)

    Variants:
    Komm her mit Fleiss zu schauen

    Barbe, H.   Raphael, G.

    Kommt Kinder, lasst uns gehen

    Abel, O.   Otto, H.

Ich will streben nach dem Leben
    See: Halleluia, Gott sei hoch gepreist

Ich wollt, dass ich daheime waer
(Strassburg)
                                   Z 1

 Beyer, M.   Schoff, A.
 Kropfreiter, A. F.   Weinreich, W.
Variant:
Jeg venter dig, Herre Jesus

 *Godske-Nielsen, H.   *Thuner, O. E.
 *Rosenkilde-Larsen, E.

Ihr Christen hoch erfreuet Euch

 Ruedinger, G.

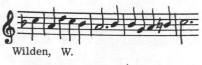

Ihr Christenleut
 See: Ecce Agnus

Ihr Engel allzumal
     also in 3
        4
 Doebler, K.   Wilden, W.

Ihr Freunde Gottes

 Biener, G.
 Romanovsky, E.

Ihr Hirten erwacht (Paderborn)

 *Kraft, K.

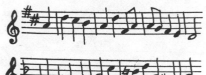

Ihr Hirten erwacht (Salzburg)

 Monar, A. J.

Ihr Hirten erwacht

 Sister M. F.

Ihr Kinder des Hoechsten (Freylinghausen)
     Z 4927
 Baldamus, F.

Ihr Kinderlein kommet (Schulz)

 Kessel, G.
 Schmutz, A.   Wettstein, H.

Ihr lieben Christen, freut Euch nun
 See: O Heilige Dreifaltigkeit (Herman)

Ik loof den Heer
  See: Psalm 34

Ik roep tot U
  See: Psalm 28

Ik wens te zijn als Jesus   Tune not found

    Asma, F.

Ik zal met al mijn hart
  See: Psalm 9

Ik zal met hart
  See: Psalm 30

Ik zie een Poort

    Mazyk, R. van

Il est né, le divin enfant (French)

    Bedell, R. L.   Erb, M. J.   Paponaud, M.
    Borucchia, N.   Hulse, C. Van   Pepin, N. A.
    Busser, H.   Linglin, M.   Philip, A.

I'm a Pilgrim (Social Harp)

    Ashford, E. L.

Im Flugschritt eilt mein Lebenszeit

    Leifs, J. T.

Im Frieden dein, O Herre mein
(Dachstein)
                          Z 7168
    Borris, S.   Franke, F. W.   Weber, H.
    Fiebig, K.   Metzger, H. A.   Werner, F.

Im Himmel und auf Erden, Herr
  See: Ist Gott fuer mich (Augsburg)

I'm Troubled (Negro Spiritual)

    Hancock, E. W.

Im Walde faellt das Laub

  Variants:
  Nu falmer skoven trindt om land

Raasted, N. O.

Nun welkt im Wald ringsum das Laub

Raasted, N. O.

In Adventus

Clokey, J. W.

In allen meinen Taten
See: Innsbruck

In Babilone (Dutch)

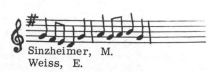

Peeters, F.   Sinzheimer, M.
Purvis, R.   Weiss, E.

In Bethlehem's Stall (Dutch)

Berg, J. J. van den
Kousemaker, A.

In Bethlehem's Stall
See: Hanover (Croft)

In de Hemel is het Schoon

Mazyk, R. van

In dem Leben hier auf Erden
(Crueger)
                    Z 3626
Rinck, J. C. H.

In des ewigen Namen

Rohwer, J.

Tune not found

In dich hab' ich gehoffet, Herr
(Leipzig)
                    Z 2461b

Bach, J. C. (2)	*Fluegel, E. P.	Pachelbel, J.
Bach, J. M.	*Franke, F. W.	Respighi, O.
Bach, J. S.	Hofmeier, A.	Thorne, E. H.
Dupré, M. J. J.	Huth, A.	Walther, J. G. (2)
Enckhausen, H. F.	*Krieger, J.	Zachau, F. W. (2)
*Finkbeiner, R.	Nicolai, J. G.	

Variants:
Mein schoenste Zier (Leipzig)

Bausznern, W. von   Mueller-Zuerich, P. Weinreich, W.
Micheelsen, H. F.   *Walcha, H.   Werner, F.

In dich hab' ich gehoffet, Herr (cont.)

Mit meinem Gott geh ich zur Ruh'

Abel, O.
Bach, J. C.
Bender, J.

Schink, H.
Walther, J. G. (2)

In dich hab' ich gehoffet, Herr
(Nuernberg)
                    Z 2459

*Bach, J. M.
Bach, J. S.
Baldamus, F.
Brieger, O.
*Claussnitzer, P.
*David, J. N.
*Doles, J. F.
Dupré, M. J. J.
Fiebig, K. (2)
Hennig, W.
*Hoyer, K.
Kaminski, H.
Kammeier, H.
Kickstat, P.

Koch, J. H. E.
Kuehn, K.
Lechthaler, J.
Metzger, H. A.
Reda, S.
*Rinck, J. C. H. (2)
Rinkens, W.
Schwarz-Schilling, R.
Schwencke, J. F. (2)
Tunder, F.
Vierling, J. G.
Weber, H.
Wedemann, W.
Wenzel, E.

Variants:
Allgegenwaertiger bin ich

Rinck, J. C. H.

In Te Domini Speravi

Scheidt, S.

Paa dig jeg hoppas, Herre kaer

Olson, D.

In dich hab' ich gehoffet, Herr
(Zuerich)
                    Z 2461d

Barthel, J. C.
*Brieger, O.
Forchhammer, T.
Haase, K.

Karow, K.
Piutti, K.
Reichardt, B.
Scheidemann, H.

Variant:
Mein schoenste Zier (Zuerich)

Hark, F.

In dieser Morgenstund
          Z 987

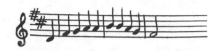

    Fischer, M. G.
Variant:
Ich will, mein Gott, du Koenig

    Gall, H.

In dieser Nacht

    Romanovsky, E.
    Weber, H.

In dieser Welt voll Sorgen
(Crueger)
          Z 5814
    Raasted, N. O.
Variant:
I denne verdens sorger

    *Videroe, F.

In dir ist Freude (Gastoldi)
          Z 8537

Bach, J. S.	Franke, F. W.	Rumpf, W.
Bender, J.	Hark, F.	Schultz, R.
Borngaesser, W.	Hempel, H.	Studer, H.
Drischner, M. (2)	Kickstat, P.	Weber, H.
Dupré, M. J. J.	Micheelsen, H. F.	

In Dulci Jubilo
          Z 4947

Ahrens, J.	Gray, A.	Peeters, F.
Andriessen, H.	Greener, J. H.	Phillips, C. G.
Anonymous	Grundmann, O. A.	Piutti, K. (2)
Bach, J. S. (4)	Hokanson, M.	Plant, A. B.
Beck, A.	Karg-Elert, S.	Raasted, N. O.
Bottenberg, W.	Kayser, L.	Rohlig, H. (3)
Buck, P. C.	Koch, P. E.	Rowley, A.
Burkhard, W.	Kousemaker, A.	Sassmannshausen, W.
Buttstedt, J. H.	Langlais, J. F.	Saxton, S. E.
Buxtehude, D. (6)	Liszt, F. (2)	Scheidt, S.
Calver, F. L.	Luebeck, V.	Schroeder, H.
Candlyn, T. F. H.	MacDonald, P. W.	Schumacher, M. H. (3)
Copley, R. E.	Marier, T. N.	Shaffer, J. E.
Couper, A. B.	Markworth, H. J.	Sicher, F.
Diggle, R.	Martin, G. M.	Sorge, E. R.
Drischner, M.	Matthews, H. A.	Sowerby, L.
Dupré, M. J. J.	Matthews, J.	Stade, F. W.
Edmundson, G. (3)	Milford, R. H. (2)	Thomas, V. C.
Faulkes, W.	Monar, A. J.	Timmermans, J.
Gotch, O. H.	Pearsall, R. L. de	Walther, J. G. (2)

In Dulci Jubilo (cont.)

  Wehmeyer, W.   Wyton, A.
  Whitford, H. P.   Zachau, F. W. (5)

Variants:
Ein Klang so suess
Jeg synger julekvad

  Karlsen, R.   Thorkildsen, J.

Lob Gott, du werte Christenheit

  Kittel, J. C.

Mit suessem Freudenschal

  Kraft, K.   Piechler, A.

Nun singet und seid froh

Bender, J.	Krenkel, E.	Pfeiffer, C. D.
Claussnitzer, P.	Lang, H. (2)	Piutti, K.
Drischner, M. (2)	Meibohm, D. (3)	Reichel, B.
Franke, F. W.	Micheelsen, H. F.	Rumpf, W.
Herzog, J. G.	Mueller, S. W.	Spiering, G.
Kickstat, P.	Pepping, E.	Weber, H.

In Dulci Jubilo (14th Century)

  Young, G.

In einem Kripplein lag ein Kind
 (Laufenburg)

  Peeters, F.

In Gott des Vaters und des
Sohnes

  Sechter, S. (2)

In Gottes Namen fahren wir

  Doebler, K.

In Gottes Namen fahren wir (Erfurt)
 See: **Dies sind die heil'gen Zehn Gebot**

In Manus Tuos (Plainsong -
 Mode 6)
  Demessieux, J.
  Peeters, F.   Villermont, de

In Memorium (Maker)

    Duro, J.

In Natali Domini
  See: Da Christus geboren war (Bohemian)

In Nomine (Plainsong)

    Alwoode, R.
    Arnatt, R. K.   Taverner, J.

In Paradisum

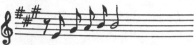

    Kreckel, P. G.
    Peeters, F.   Plum, P. J. M.

In stiller Nacht (Latin-German)

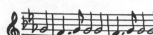

    Ahrens, J.
    Berghorn, A.   Schroeder, H.
Variant:
Bei stiller Nacht

    Stottenwerk, W.

In Te Domini Speravi
  See: In dich hab' ich gehoffet, Herr
(Nuernberg)

In the Shadow of His Wings
(Excell)

    Lorenz, E. J.

In the Sweet Bye and Bye
  See: Sweet Bye and Bye

In Vernali Tempore (Piae Cantiones)

    Elmore, R. H.

Induant Justitiam   Tune not found

    Guilmant, A.

Infant King
  See: Noël Angevin

Ingen er saa tryg i fare
  See: Tryggare kan ingen vara

Ingen kann naa fram til den
   (Steenberg)

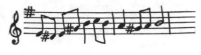

   Nielsen, L.

Ingen kann naa fram til den (Norse)
See: Ingen vinner frem til den

Ingen Vinner frem til den (Norse
   Folk Tune)

   Baden, C.
Variant:
Ingen kann naa fram til den (Norse)

   Karlsen, R.

Innocents (Smith)
           also in 3
                4

   Arnatt, R. K.
   Gehring, P.   Lutkin, P. C.
   Haase, K.   Pool, K.
   Hulse, C. Van   Stanford, C. V.

Innsbruck (Isaac)
               Z 2293

   Bedell, R. L.   Peek, R. M.
   David, J. N.   Peeters, F.
   Hovdesven, E. A.   Porter, H.
   Johnson, D. N.   Rufty, H.
   Kitson, C. H.   Schreiner, A.
Variants:
Gud efter dig jeg laenges

   Jensen, S.   Thuner, O. E.
   Jeppesen, K.   Weinholt-Pedersen, K.

Herr Gott, lass dich erbarmen

   Isaac, H.

In allen meinen Taten

   Abel, O.   *Lorenz, C. A.
   Baldamus, F.   Seifert, C. T.
   *Doles, J. F.   Walther, J. G. (2)
   *Hoyer, K.

Nu hviler mark og enge

   Alnaes, E.   Moeller, S. O.
   Andersen, E.   Raasted, N. O. (4)
   Karlsen, R.   Wuertz, J.

Nun ruhen alle Waelder

Bender, J.
Brieger, O. (2)
Chemin-Petit, H.
Dienel, O.
Drischner, M. (2)
Edmundson, G. (2)
Egidi, A.
Engelbrecht, K. F.
Eyken, J. A. van
Fluegel, E. P.
Forchhammer, T.
Franke, F. W.
Gerhardt, P.
Hoepner, C. G.
Hokanson, M.
Kaeppel, G. C. A.
Karg-Elert, S.
Knab, A.
Kuehn, K.
Kuntze, C.
Lubrich, F. , Jr.
Markull, F. W. (2)
Matthison-Hansen, G.
McCollin, F.
Merkel, G.

Micheelsen, H. F.
Mueller, S.
Palme, R.
Peeters, F.
Pfretzschner, C. R. (3)
Piutti, K. (2)
Raasted, N. O.
Riemenschneider, G.
Rinck, J. C. H. (5)
Ritter, A. G. (3)
Roeder, E. O.
Rudnick, W.
Sachs, J. G.
Schaab, R. (2)
Schwarwenka, W.
Schindler, W.
Schneider, F. C.
Stolze, H. W.
Stout, A.
Thomas, G. A.
Vierling, J. G.
Wedemann, W.
Weigl, B.
Woyrsch, F. (2)

O Esca Viatorum

Kreckel, P. G.

*Stark, L.

O heil'ge Seelenspeise

Ahrens, J.
Doebler, K. (2)
Eham, M.
Goller, F.
Kraft, K.

Kreckel, P. G.
Miggl, E.
Romanovsky, E.
Schroeder, H.

O Welt, ich muss dich lassen

Ammerbach, E. N.
Bachem, H.
Beck, A.
Bossler, K.
Brahms, J. (2)
Chaix, C.
Claussnitzer, P. (3)
David, J. N.
Davis, W. R.
Drischner, M.
Enckhausen, H. F.

Eyken, J. A. van (2)
Fink, F.
Fluegel, E. P.
Fluegel, G.
Franke, F. W. (2)
Genzmer, H.
Grundmann, O. A.
Haase, K.
Hanebeck, H. R.
Hark, F.
Hasse, K.

Herzog, J. G.
Hessenberg, K.
Huth, A.
Karg-Elert, S. (2)
Karow, K.
Kickstat, P. (2)
Krause, P. (2)
Kunze, K.
Leupold, A. W.
Looks, R.
Merkel, G.

Innsbruck (cont.)

O Welt, ich muss dich lassen (cont.)

Micheelsen, H. F.	Reuther, F.	Straumann, B.
Mueller, S. W.	Roth, G.	Streicher, J. A.
Noermiger, A.	Rumpf, W. (2)	Tuerke, O.
Ochsenkuhn, S.	Saffe, F.	Walther, J. G. (3)
Oechsler, E.	Schaper, G.	Wettstein, H. (3)
Pfretzschner, C. R.	Schrenk, J.	Wolff, L.
Piutti, K.	Schwencke, J. F. (3)	Wurm, A.
Raphael, G.	Schweppe, J.	Zehrfeld, O.
Reda, S.	Seyerlen, R.	Zipp, F.
Reger, M. (2)	Stolze, H. W.	

O Welt, sieh hier dein Leben

Bredack, W.	Oley, J. C.
Chaix, C.	Pfeiffer, C. D.
Ehmann, H.	*Rinck, J. C. H.
Herrmann, K. H.	Unruh, E.
Herrmann, W.	

Song 39 (Dutch)

Dragt, J.	Zwart, J.

Song 241 (Dutch)

Kool, B. Jr.

Integer Vitae
See: Flemming

Intercessor (Parry)

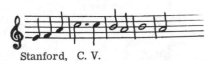

Fenstermaker, J.
Rhea, A.   Stanford, C. V.

Introibo Ad Altare Dei (Gregorian)

Webbe, W. Y.

Invicte Martyr Unicum (Mode 5)

DeKlerk, A.

Inviolata

Peeters, F.
Ravanello, O.

Invitation (Maker)

Smith, H. M.

Ipse Invocabit Me (Gregorian)

Webbe, W. Y.

Irby (Gauntlett)

Candlyn, T. F. H.   Spier, LaS.
Cowell, C. P.   Whitehead, A. E.

Irene (Scholefield)

Hulse, C. Van

Irish (Dublin)

Archer, J. S.
Coleman, R. H. P.   Peeters, F.
Harwood, B. (2)   Sowerbutts, J. A.
Kitson, C. H.   Wesley, S. S.
Lang, C. S.   Willan, H.
Palmer, C. C.   Wood, D.

Irons
See: St. Colomba (Irons)

Island
See: Min sjael og aand (Thomisson)

Isleworth (Howard)

Haase, K.   Peeters, F.

Ist das der Leib
See: O Jesulein suess (Cologne)

Ist Gott fuer mich (Augsburg)

Artmueller, K.
Bender, J.   Hennig, W.   Mueller, S. W.
Fiebig, K.   Hoeller, K.   Schneider, M. G.
Franke, F. W.   Kickstat, P.   Traegner, R.
Hark, F.   Magnus, E.   Weber, H.
Hasse, K.   Micheelsen, H. F. (2) Zipp, F.
Variant:
Im Himmel und auf Erden, Herr

Poppen, H. M.

Iste Confessor

    Guilmant, A.

Iste Confessor

    Titelouze, J.

Iste Confessor (Angers)

    Harker, C.

Iste Confessor (Mode 8)

    Cavazzoni, G.
    Dupré, M. J. J.   Lange, S. de
    Fasolo, G. B.   Olsson, O. E.
    Kreckel, P. G. (2)   Peeters, F. (2)

Iste Confessor (Rouen)
  See: Rouen (Poitiers)

Iste Confessor Domini (Plainsong)

    *Redford, J.
    *Rouher, M.   *Tallis, T.

It Is Well With My Soul (Bliss)
  See: Ville de Havre

Italian Hymn
  See: Giardini

Ite Missa Est

    Erb, M. J.   Thiel, K.

Ite Missa Est

    Montani, N. A.   Schmid, J.   Tranzillo, D.
    Nesvera, J.   Skop, V. F.   Woollen, R.
    Ponten, A.   Springer, M. Zoller, G. (2)

Ite Missa Est

    Erb, M. J.
    Keldermans, R. A.   Labor, J.

Ite Missa Est

    Barnes, E. S.   *Benoit, Dom P.
    Baeuerle, H.   *Breitenbach, C. G. J.
    *Becker, R. L.   *Goemanne, N.

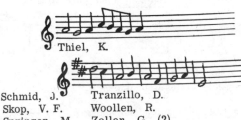
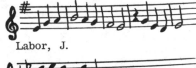

Goller, F.
Habert, J. E.
*Huber, P.
*Lemmens, N. J.
*Preyer, G.
*Quef, C.

*Sechter, S.
Sowerby, L.
Strohofer, J.
*Tournemire, C.
Trexler, G.
Verhaar, A.

<u>Ivory Palaces</u> (Barraclough)

Hustad, D.

<u>Ja, Tag des Herrn</u> (Silcher)
Z 6104
Buehl, W.

Kunz, E.

<u>Ja vi elsker dette landet</u> (Nor-
wegian)

Forwald, R. M.

Nielsen, L.

<u>Jabez</u> (Welsh)

Parrish, C.

<u>Jacob's Ladder</u> (Spiritual)

Hancock, E. W.

<u>Jauchz' Erd', und Himmel juble</u>
See: <u>O Mensch, bewein dein Suende gross</u>

<u>Jauchzet ihr Himmell</u>
See: <u>Lobe den Herren, den</u>

<u>Jauchzt alle, Gott sei hoch</u>

Franke, F. W.

<u>Jauchzt alle Lande, Gott zu Ehren</u>
See: <u>Psalm 118</u> (Geneva)

<u>Je chanterai, Seigneur, tes oeuvres</u>   Tune not found

Hess, C. L.

<u>Je sais, Vierge</u> (Noël)

Bingham, S.

<u>Je suis à tois</u>

Hess, C. L.

Je te salue, O Saint' aurore

Hess, C. L.

Tune not found

Jeg arme synder (Thomisson)
See: Mit haab og troest

Jeg er en seiler paa livets hav
(Steenberg)

Karlsen, R.

Jeg er rede til aa bede (Darmstadt)
See: Sieh hier bin ich (Darmstadt)

Jeg er saa glad hver julekveld
(Knudson)

Nielsen, L.

Jeg er traet og gaar til ro
(Malling)

Frandsen, H. B.
Rosenkilde-Larsen, E.   Wuertz, J.

Jeg gaar i fare (Zinck)

*Thomsen, P.
Wuertz, J.

Jeg gaar i fare (Lindeman)
See: Se solens skjoenne (Lindeman)

Jeg har min sak til Herren satt
(Lindeman)

Karlsen, R.

Jeg kommer, Herre, paa dit ord
(Hartmann)

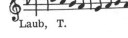

Frandsen, H. B.   Laub, T.
Variant:
Fra Himlen kom en engel klar

Jeg lever-og ved hvor (Berggreen)

Bjerre, J.
Jeppesen, K.   *Wuertz, J.

Jeg lever-og ved hvor (Sachsen)

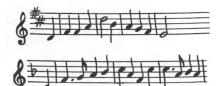

    Karlsen, R.

Jeg loefter opp til Gud (Folk
Tune)

    Gangfloet, S.

Jeg raaber fast, O Herre
See: Old 130th

Jeg raaber Herre Jesu Krist
(Wittenberg)

    Borg, O.

Jeg ser dig, O Guds Lam (Norsk
Folk)

    Karlsen, R.   Moseng, S.

Jeg synger, Julekvad
See: In Dulci Jubilo

Jeg ved en urt baade dejlig
(Netherlands)

    Godske-Nielsen, H.   Madsen, A.

Jeg ved et evigt Himmerig (German Folk Tune)
        lille
See: Op al den ting (Freiburg)

Jeg ved paa hvem (Zinck)
See: Copenhagen

Jeg venter dig, Herre Jesus

    Andersen, E.

Jeg venter dig, Herre Jesus
See: Ich wollt, dass ich daheime waer

Jeg venter dig, Herre Jesus (Crueger)
See: Ratisbon

Jeg vet mig en soevn i Jesu navn
(Fugl)

    Hovland, E.

Jeg vet mig en soevn i Jesu navn
  (Sletten)

    Nielsen, L.

Jeg vet mig en soevn i Jesu navn
  See: Mach's mit mir, Gott (Schein)

Jeg vil din pris (Folk Tune)
  See: Aus meines Herzens Grunde

Jeg vil mig Herren love (Barnekow)

Jeg vil mig Herren love (Dutch
  Psalm - Thomisson)
                Z 5254c
    Karlsen, R.   Woeldike, M. A.
    Thuner, O. E.   *Wuertz, J.

Jeg vil mig Herren love (Swedish Psalm)
  See: Blomstertid

Jeg vil mig Herren love (Norse Folk)
  See: Mitt hjerte alltid vanker

Jeg vil mig Herren love (Zinck)
  See: Copenhagen (Zinck)

Jeg ville love och prisa

    Wikander, D.

Jehova, (Jehova,) deinem Namen
  See: Das Hallelujah (Gerold)

Jenny Jones (Welsh)

    Faulkes, W.

Jerusalem, du hoch gebaute
  Stadt (Franck)
                Z 6141
    Breydert, F. M.   Fluegel, E. P.   Hesse, A. F.
    Claussnitzer, P. (3) Fluegel, G.   Hoernig, O.
    David, J. N.   Franke, F. W. (2)   Hoyer, K.
    Davin, K. H. G.   Frenzel, H. R.   Karg-Elert, S.
    Dienel, O.   Glaus, A.   Karow, K.
    Drischner, M. (2)   Haase, K.   Kempff, W.
    Engel, J.   Haase, R.   Kickstat, P.
    Fiebig, K.   Hasse, K.   Klaus, V.
    Fischer, M. G. (2)   Hennig, W.   Krause, P.

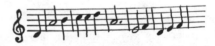

Leupold, A. W.   Reuter, J. F.   Stiller, K.
Merk, G.   Ricek, W.   Thomas, K. G. H.
Merkel, G. (2)   Rinck, J. C. H. (2)   Thomas, O.
Micheelsen, H. F.   Ritter, A. G.   Umbreit, K. G.
Papperitz, B. R.   Roth, F.   Volckmar, F. W.
Peters, M.   Rudnick, W.   Weeber, J. C.
Piutti, K. (2)   Rumpf, W.   Wenzel, E.
Poppen, H. M.   Schmid, J.   Wettstein, H.
Reger, M. (2)   Sering, F. W.   Wolfrum, K.
Reuter, F. (3)   Zipp, F.
Variant:
Song 127 (Dutch)

Beek, W. van

Jervaulx Abbey (French)
                    Z 5868
     Peeters, F.
Variants:
Mein Leben ist ein Pilgrimstand

Franke, F. W.   Schwager, J.
Rinck, J. C. H.   Walcha, H.

O Gott, der du ein Herrfuerst bist

Franke, F. W. (2)   *Rinck, J. C. H.

Psalm 84 (Geneva)

Beek, W. van   King, H. C.   Wieruszowski, L.
Drischner, M.   Post, P.   Wilgenburg, D. van
Hoogewoud, H. (2)   Rippen, P.   Zwart, J.
Kee, C.   Weelden, J. van

Wie lieblich ist das Haus

Studer, H.   Wieruszowski, L.

Wie lieblich schoen, Herr Zabaoth

Drischner, M.   Weber, H.
Hennig, W.   Wenzel, E.
Metzger, H. A.

Jesse Virga   Tune not found

Magin, C.

Jesaia, dem Propheten das
     geschah (Luther)
                    Z 8534

Jessia, dem Propheten das geschah (cont.)

    Grote, H.   Metzler, F.   Scheidt, S.
    Haase, K.   Reuter, F.   Wenzel, E.
    Karow, K.   Rinck, J. C. H.   Zachau, F. W. (2)
   Variant:
Das Sanctus

    Werner, F.

Jesu, Jesum, Jesus, Jezus all interfiled.

Jesu aar min haegrad
   See: Jesu, mein Freude

Jesu, aer mitt liv, min haelsae
   See: Du, O schoenes Weltgebaeude

Jesus, all mein Leben bist du   Tune not found

    Kraft, K.

Jesu allt mitt goda aer

    Lindberg, O. F.

Jesus, As Though Thyself Wert
Here

    DeBrant, C.

Jesus Christ Is Born of Mary

    Bratt, C. G.   Nieland, J.

Jesus Christ Is Risen Today
   See: Gaudeamus Pariter

Jesus Christus herrscht als Koenig
   See: Alles ist an Gottes Segen (Koenig)

Jesus Christus herrscht als Koenig (Layriz)
   See: Lauda Sion (Layriz)

Jesus Christus ist erstanden
   See: O Durchbrecher (Halle)

Jesus Christus, unser Heiland,
   der den Tod (Erfurt)
              Z 1977

    *Soenke, H.   *Spiering, G.

Jesus Christus, unser Heiland, der den Tod (Klug)
Z 1978

Bach, J. S.
Barbe, H.
Bornefeld, H.
*Buxtehude, D. (2)
Driessler, J.
Dupré, M. J. J.
*Franke, F. W.
Kittel, J. C.
Pachelbel, J. (2)
Pepping, E.

*Radeck, M.
Reda, S.
*Rinck, J. C. H.
*Rudnick, W. (2)
Vetter, A. N.
Vierling, J. G.
Walcha, H.
Walther, J. G.
Weber, H.
Zachau, F. W.

Jesus Christus, unser Heiland, der von uns (Erfurt)
Z 1576

Bach, J. C.
Bach, J. S. (4)
Bornefeld, H.
Distler, H. (2)
Dupré, M. J. J.
Hennig, W.
Kammeier, H.
Koch, J. H. E.
Metzger, H. A.
Pachelbel, J.

Pepping, E.
Reda, S.
*Rinck, J. C. H.
Schneidt, H. M.
Schuetz, A.
Tunder, F. (2)
Weber, H.
Wiemer, W.
Zachau, F. W. (3)

Jesus Christus, unser Heiland, der von uns (Wittenberg)
Z 1979

Arbatsky, Y.   Haase, K.
Barlow, W.   Peeters, F.
Variant:
Aldri er jeg uten vaade (Wittenberg)

Scheidt, S. (2)
Volckmar, F. W.

Jesus Christus, wahr Gottes Sohn
Z 2580

Tunder, F.
Variant:
Christus Pro Nobis

Jesus Come To Me
See: Folkefrelsar til oss kom (Sletten)

Jesu Corona Virginum

Cavazzoni, G.
Fasolo, G. B.

Peeters, F.

Jesu Corona Virginum (Mode 5)

    DeKlerk, A.

Jesu Corona Virginum
    See: Deus Tuorum Militum (Latin-Mode 8)

Jesus, Creator of the World (Andernach)
    See: Den die Hirten lobten sehr

Jesus Crucifixus (Read)
    See: Windham

Jesu deine Passion
    See: Christus, der uns selig macht (Bohemian)

Jesu, deine Passion
    See: Jesu, Leiden, Pein und Tod (Vulpius)

Jesu, deine tiefen Wunden
    (Koenig)
                Z 6641
      Gulbins, M.   Hasse, K.
    Variant:
    Der am Kreuz (Koenig)

      Ehmann, H.   Inderau, H.   Obersold, H.
     *Fluegel, G.   Kaeppel, G. C. A. *Rinck, J. C. H.
     *Gulbins, M. (3) Kickstat, P.   Schumacher, M. H.
     Haase, K.   Miles, G. T.

    Han paa korset (Koenig)

    Nielsen, L.

    Sei mir Tausendmal gegruesset

    Gulbins, M.   Pasquet, J.

Jesu, der du bist alleine
    See: Alles ist an Gottes Segen

Jesu, der du meine Seele

    Schwencke, J. F. (3)

Jesu, der du meine Seele

    Baldamus, F.

Jesu, der du meine Seele (Bach)
                 Z 6783
    *Wolfrum, K.

Variant:
Alle Menschen muessen sterben (German)

    Walther, J. G.

Jesu, der du meine Seele (Gregor)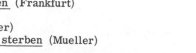
                  Z 6804
    Claussnitzer, P. (2)
    *Herzog, J. G.   Piutti, K. (2)
    Merkel, G.   Schwarz-Schilling, R.
    Variant:
Alle Menschen muessen sterben (Frankfurt)

Jesu, der du meine Seele (Mueller)
  See: Alle Menschen muessen sterben (Mueller)

Jesu, der du wollen buessen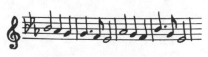
(1662)
                Z 6804
    Weber, H.

Jesu, det eneste (Sinding)

    Nielsen, L.

Jesu, det eneste (Soerlie)

    Karlsen, R.

Jesu, din Ihukommelse (German
1605)

    Hokanson, M.
Variant:
Herrnhut (Gesius)

    Peeters, F.

Jesu, din soede forening (Koenig)
  See: Sollt mich die Liebe (Koenig)

Jesu din soete forening (Norse
Folk)

    Baden, C.
    Moseng, S.   Nielsen, L. (2)

Jesu dine dype vunder (Lindeman)

    Nielsen, L.

Jesu dine dype vunder (cont.)

    Variant:
    Over Kedron

Jesu dine dype vunder
    See: Freu dich sehr

Jesu, du min fryd

      Aahgren, K. E.

Jesu, du min glaede

    *Borg, O.

Jesu, du min glaede
    See: Jesu, meine Freude

Jesu Dulcedo Cordium (Mode 2)

      Peeters, F.

Jesu Dulcedo Cordium
    See: Erhalt uns, Herr

Jesu Dulcis Memoria

      Kreckel, P. G.

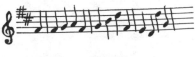

Jesu Dulcis Memoria (Andernach)
                 Z 553

    *Diggle, R.

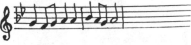

Jesu Dulcis Memoria (Peoples
Hymnal)

      Schehl, J. A.

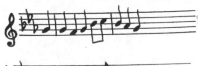

Jesu Dulcis Memoria (Sarum)

      Davies, H. W.   Togni, V.

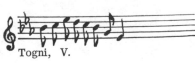

Jesu Dulcis Memoria (Mode 1)
    See: Exultet Cor Praecordiis

Jesu er mit liv i live
    See: Alle Menschen muessen sterben
    (Wessnitzer)

Jesu er mitt liv i live (Crueger
    See: Du, o schoenes Weltgebaeude

Jesus er nav net mageloest   Tune not found
 (Barnekow)

      Hamburger, P.

Jesus fraan Nasaret

    *Wikander, D.

Jesus, Frelser, Saliggoerer
 (Berggreen)

      Wuertz, J.

Jesu, Frelser, vi er her
  See: Liebster Jesu (Ahle)

Jesu geh voran
  See: Seelenbraeutigam (Drese)

Jesu, grosser Wunderstern
  See: Meinen Jesum lass ich nicht (Ulich)

Jesu han er syndres ven
  See: Jesu, meine Zuversicht (Crueger)

Jesu hilf siegen, du Fuerste des Lebens
  See: Einer ist Koenig (Darmstadt)

Jesu hilf siegen, du Fuerste des Lebens
  See: Einer ist Koenig (Hille)

Jesus i det hoeie troner (Lindeman)

      Karlsen, R.

Jesus Is All the World To Me
 (Thompson)

      Hustad, D.

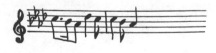

Jesus ist das schoenste Licht
            Z 6415a

      Rinck, J. C. H.

Jesus ist kommen (Hille)
  See: Einer ist Koenig (Hille)

Jesus ist mein Aufenthalt
  See: Meinen Jesum lass ich nicht,
  Jesus (Lueneberg)

Jesus, jeg dit kors vil holde
  See: Freu dich sehr

Jesus, Jesus, Come to Me
  (Scheffler)

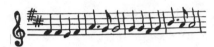

  Variant:
  Jesu, Jesu, komm zu mir

    Doebler, K.

Jesus, Jesus, Jesus sigter
  (Kalhauge)

    Frandsen, H. B.

Jesu, Jesu, komm zu mir
  See: Jesus, Jesus, Come to Me

Jesus, Jesus, Nichts als Jesus
  (Hamburg)
                        Z 3658a
    Haase, K.   Wettstein, H. (2)
  Variant:
  Weicht, ihr Berge

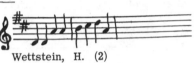

    Kuehn, K.

Jesus, Jesus, Rest Your Head
  (Appalachian)

    Niles, J. J.

Jesu komm doch selbst zu mir
  See: Gott sei Dank durch alle Welt (Halle)

Jesu komm doch selbst zu mir
  See: Hoechster Priester (Basel)

Jesu, Kreuz, Leiden und Pein
  (Bohemian)
                        Z 6287a
    Pepping, E.   Soenke, H.

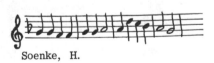

Jesu, Kreuz, Leiden und Pein
  See: Christus, der uns selig macht

Jesu, Kreuz, Leiden und Pein (Vulpius)
  See: Jesu, Leiden, Pein und Tod (Vulpius)

Jesu Kriste, ščedrý kněže (Czech)

    Vycpalek, L. (V.)

Jesus Kristus, Frelsermanden   Tune not found

    Wuertz, J.

Jesus lebt, mit ihm auch ich
  See: Jesu, meine Zuversicht

Jezus leeft, en wij met Hem
  See: Jesu, meine Zuversicht

Jesu, Leiden, Pein und Tod
(Vulpius)

              Z 6288

Birn, M.	Piutti, K.
Bratt, C. G.	Reger, M.
Claussnitzer, P. (3)	Reichardt, B.
Heinrich, J. G.	Vierling, J. G.
Kittel, J. C.	Vogler, J. C.
Merkel, G. (2)	Walther, J. G.

Variants:
Jesu, deine Passion

    Wedemann, W.   Weyrauch, J.

  Jesu, Kreuz, Leiden und Pein (Vulpius)

Beck, A.	Huth, A.
Haase, K.	Litzau, J. B.
Helm, W.	Peeters, F.
Hulse, C. Van	

  Weimar (Vulpius)

    Peeters, F.

Jesu Leiden unsere Seligkeit

    Rohwer, J.

Jesum lieb' ich ewiglich
  See: Meinen Jesum lass ich nicht, Jesus
(Darmstadt)

Jesus livets sol og glaede
  See: Schmuecke dich (Crueger)

Jesus Loves Me (Bradbury)

    Bingham, S.   Rogers, L.

Jesu, meine Freude (Crueger)
              Z 8032

Jesu, meine Freude (cont.)

Ahrens, J. (2)	Herzog, J. G.	Reichardt, B.
Bach, J. S. (3)	Hesse, A. F.	Reinbrecht, A.
Bach, W. F. (2)	Hoeller, K.	Reinhardt, A.
Baldamus, F.	Hokanson, M.	Rembt, J. E.
Barlow, W. (2)	Hoyer, K.	Richter, E. F.
Bartmuss, R. (2)	Johns, D.	Riedel, H.
Bastiaans, J. G.	Karg-Elert, S. (2)	Rinck, J. C. H. (4)
Beck, A.	Karow, K.	Rinkens, W.
Bender, J.	Kickstat, P. (2)	Ritter, A. G.
Beyer, M.	Kittel, J. C.	Rogers, S. E.
Brieger, O.	Koch, H. E.	Rudnick, W.
Bruin, B.	Koetzschke, H.	Rumpf, W.
Cassler, G. W.	Krause, P.	Schaab, R. (3)
Claussnitzer, P. (2)	Kuntze, C.	Schuetze, W.
Conrad, J. C. (2)	Leupold, A. W. (2)	Schwarz-Schilling, R.
Doles, J. F.	Lundquist, M. N.	Schwencke, J. F. (2)
Drischner, M.	Marpurg, F. W. (2)	Stade, F. W. (2)
Dupré, M. J. J.	Merkel, G.	Stapf, O.
Edmundson, G.	Miles, R. H.	Steinhaeuser, K.
Enckhausen, H. F. (2)	Muehling, A.	Stout, A.
Engelbrecht, K. F.	Mueller, S.	Streicher, J. A.
Faehrmann, H.	Oley, J. C.	Telemann, G. P. (2)
Fiebig, K.	Osterholdt, -	Toepfer, J. G. (2)
Fink, C.	Palme, R.	Umbreit, K. G. (3)
Fischer, I.	Papperitz, B. R.	Vierling, J. G. (2)
Fischer, M. G.	Peeters, F.	Voigtmann, R. J.
Fluegel, G. (3)	Pepping, E.	Volckmar, F. W.
Forchhammer, T.	Piutti, K. (2)	Walther, J. G. (6)
Franke, F. W.	Raphael, G.	Wedemann, W.
Gradehand, F.	Read, G.	Wettstein, H. (2)
Grote, H.	Reda, S.	Wolfrum, K.
Hasse, K. (3)	Reger, M.	Zachau, F. W. (2)

Variants:
Gud skal allting (Crueger)

Drischner, M.	*Videroe, F.
Nielsen, T. H.	Woeldike, M. A.

Hoerer, I, som graede

Raasted, N. O.

Jesu aar min haegrad

Kullnes, A.	Nordquist, G.

Jesu du min glaede
Schmueckt das Fest mit Maien

Herrmann, K. H.

Song 113 (Dutch)

Koppenel, J.   Wilgenburg, D. van

Jesu, meine Liebe
See: Wort aus Gottes Mund (Witt)

Jesu, meine Zuversicht
(Crueger)
                    Z 3432

André, J.   Koetzsche, H.
Arbatsky, Y.   Krause, P. (2)
Bach, J. S.   Kuehn, K. (2)
Bachem, H.   Kuntze, C.
Baldamus, F.   Landmann, A.
Barth, G. A. H.   Leupold, A. W.
Blumenthal, P.   Lorenz, C. A.
Boenicke, H.   Luetzel, J. H.
Brieger, O. (2)   Markull, F. W. (2)
Claussnitzer, P. (6)   Mergner, F.
Couper, A. B.   Merk, G.
Dienel, O. (2)   Merkel, G. (2)
Dupré, M. J. J.   Micheelsen, H. F.
Enckhausen, H. F.   Michel, A. (2)
Fink, C. (2)   Mueller, J. L.
Fischer, M. G. (2)   Mueller, S.
Fluegel, G. (3)   Mueller, S. W.
Forchhammer, T.   Nagel, W.
Franke, F. W.   Nicolai, J. G.
Frenzel, H. R.   Oley, J. C. (2)
Geierhaas, G.   Palme, R. (3)
Grote, H.   Papperitz, B. R.
Grueters, A.   Paulstich, D.
Gulbins, M. (4)   Petrich, R. T.
Haase, K.   Petzold, J.
Hark, F.   Pfretzschner, C. R. (2)
Hasse, K.   Piutti, K. (2)
Helmbold, C. A.   Raasted, N. O.
Hennig, W.   Reda, S.
Herzog, J. G. (2)   Reger, M. (2)
Hesse, A. F.   Reichardt, A.
Hoernig, O.   Reinhardt, A.
Hoyer, K. (3)   Reuter, F.
Karg-Elert, S. (2)   Rheinberger, J.
Kaun, H.   Richter, E. F.
Kee, C.   Rinck, J. C. H. (8)
Kegel, K. C.   Ritter, A. G.
Kempff, W.   Rudnick, W. (3)
Kickstat, P.   Rumpf, W.
Klaus, V.   Schaab, R. (2)
Koch, J. H. E.   Schilling, A. (2)
Koehler-Wumbach, W.   Schreck, G.

Jesu, meine Zuversicht (cont.)

Schumacher, M. H.
Schumann, C.
Schwencke, J. F. (3)
Sechter, S.
Stapf, O.
Stecher, H.
Stout, A.
Streicher, J. A. (2)
Theile, A. G.
Thoerner, H.
Toepfer, J. G. (2)
Tuerke, C.
Tuerke, O.
Varients:

Umbreit, K. G.
Vierling, J. G. (2)
Vogel, P. (2)
Volckmar, F. W.
Wagner, F.
Walther, J. G. (3)
Weber, H.
Wedemann, W. (2)
Wendt, E. A.
Wettstein, H. (3)
Winter-Hjelm, O.
Wolfrum, K. (3)
Zier, E.

Jesu han er syndres ven

Jeppesen, K.   Raasted, N. O. (2)

Jesus lebt, mit ihm auch ich

Gulbins, M.   Spiering, G.
Koch, J. H. E.   Zoellner, K. H.
Schwencke, J. F. (3)

Jezus leeft, en wij met Hem

Kee, C.

Jesus neemt de zondaars aan

Mudde, W.

Luise

Sowerby, L.

Meine Lebenszeit verstreicht

Wenzel, H.

Seele, geh nach Golgotha

Gulbins, M.   Riemenschneider, G.

Soerger du endnu, min sjael

Laub, T.   Raasted, N. O.
Maegaard, J.

Song 62 (Dutch)

    Tromp, A.   Wilgenburg, D. van
    Vogel, W.

Song 168 (Dutch)

    Asma, F.

Song 189 (Dutch)

    Wilgenburg, D. van

Song 234 (Dutch)

    Asma, F. (2)

Song 252 (Dutch)

    Vogel, W.

Jesu, meiner Seelen Wonne
  See: Werde munter, mein Gemuete

Jesu, meines Herzens Freud
(Ahle)
            Z 4797
    *Doles, J. F.   Piutti, K.

Jesu, meines Herzens Freud
  See: Lueneburg

Jesu, meines Lebens Leben

    Oley, J. C.

Jesu, meines Lebens Leben (Mueller)
  See: Alle Menschen muessen sterben (Mueller)

Jesu, meines Lebens Leben (Wessnitzer)
  See: Alle Menschen muessen sterben (Wessnitzer)

Jesu, meines Lebensbrot   Tune not found

    Kittel, J. C.

Jesus My Heart's Delight (Pennsylvania Dutch)

    Johnson, A. H.

Jesus My Lord, My God, My All
  See: Fest soll mein Taufbund (Faber)

Jesus, naar eg maa faa (Schles-
   ian, 1742)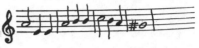
                Z 6304
    Nielsen, L.
    Variant:
    Einen guten Kampf hab' ich

Jesus neemt de zondaars aan
    See: Jesu, meine Zuversicht

Jesu nimmt die Suender an
    See: Meinen Jesum lass ich nicht, weil
    (Ulich)

Jesu, Nostra Redemptio (Tone 3)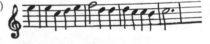

    *Botazzi, Fra B.   Fasolo, G. B.

Jesu, Nostra Redemptio (Mode 4)

    Cavazzoni, G.   Peeters, F.

Jesu, notre Maître

    Erb, M. J.

Jesu, nun sei gepreiset (Dresden)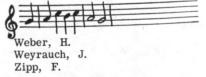
             Z 8477
    Barlow, W.

Jesu, nun sei gepreiset (Vulpius)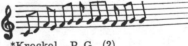
             Z 8478
    Bornefeld, H.
    Driessler, J.   Weber, H.
    Herrmann, K. H.   Weyrauch, J.
    *Litzau, J. B.   Zipp, F.

Jesu Redemptor Omnium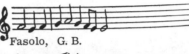

    *Blithman, W.
    *Boulfart, C.   *Kreckel, P. G. (2)
    *Cavazzoni, G.   *Nivers, G. G.

Jesu Redemptor Omnium

    Clokey, J. W.

Jesu Redemptor Omnium
    See: Christe Redemptor (Sarum-Mode 1)

Jesus soll die Loesung sein
    See: Meinen Jesum lass ich nicht, weil (Ulich)

Jesus the Christ Is Born (Appa-
    lachian)

    Niles, J. J.

Jesus Thy Name Hath Power to Bless
    See: Wenn wir in hoechsten Noethen

Jesus, Trost der armen Seelen
    See: Morgenglanz

Jesus, unser Trost und Leben
    (Bach)
            Z 4918
    Nieland, H.

Jesu, zu dir rufen wir

    Philipp, F.

Jewells (Root)

    Bitgood, R.

Jewett (von Weber)

    Blake, G.

Jingle Bells

    Thomas, V. C.

J'irai la voir un jour

    Erb, M. J.

Magin, C.

Joanna (Welsh)

    Langston, P.
    Penick, R. C.
    Variant:
St. Denio

Powell, R. J.
Williams, R. R.

    Cameron, G.   Parrish, C.
    Cassler, G. W.   Rohlig, H. (2)
    Groves, R.   Whitlock, P.
    Jones, R. W.

Jordan (Billings)

    Colvin, H.

Joseph est bien marié (French
    Noël)

    Balbastre, C. (2)

Joseph, lieber Joseph mein
(Klug)

              Z 8573
    Barlow, W.   Means, C.
    Drakeford, R.   Nagle, W. S.
    Hulse, C. Van   Raasted, N. O.
    Lechthaler, J.
Variants:
Croon Carol

    Whitehead, A. E.

Lad det klinge soedt i sky

    Laub, T.   Raasted, N. O.
    Moeller, S. O.   Vestergaard-Pedersen, C.

Resonet in Laudibus

    Anonymous (1500)   Lundquist, M. N.
    Anonymous   Marier, T. N.
    Hoegner, F.   Purvis, R.
    Hulse, C. Van   Salem, B. von
    Jaques, R.   Schaffer, R. J.
    *Karg-Elert, S.   Sicher, F.
    Kreckel, P. G.   Tranzillo, D.

Singet frisch und

    Weyrauch, J.

Joshua Fit the Battle of Jericho
(Negro Spiritual)

    Hancock, E. W.

Jour de Seigneur
    See: Ach Gott und Herr (Schein)

Jubilate (Parker)

    Warner, F. H.

Judah's Lion (Bohemian)

    Haase, K.

Judas Maccabaeus (Handel)

Variant:
Seht, er kommt

Weidenhagen, E.

Juicht, O volken
See: Psalm 47

Julen har bragt velsignet Bud
(Weyse)

*Jensen, S.   Jeppesen, K.

Julen har englelyd (Berggreen)

*Wuertz, J.

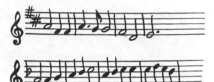

Julen har englelyd (Thomisson)

*Thuner, O. E.

Just As I Am (Bradbury)
See: Woodworth

Kaerlek av hoejden
See: Lobet den Herren, alle die ihn ehren
(Crueger)

Kaerlighed fra Gud (Hartmann)

Moeller, S. O.

Kaerligheds og sandheds aand
(Barnekow)

Hamburger, P.

Kaertner Heimatlied

Keldorfer, R.

Kas, yoellae paimenille (Finnish)

Parviainen, J.

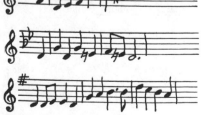

Keble (Dykes)

Ireland, J.
Whitford, H. P.

Kee hinay kachomer
    See: To Thee We Give Ourselves (Hebrew)

Kehre wieder

    Krause, P.

Piutti, K.

Kehre wieder (Frauenfels)
            Z 6765
            Z 7938
        *Claussnitzer, P. (2)
        Rumpf, W.

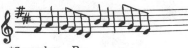

*Seyerlen, R.

Kein Stuendlein geht dahin (Franck)
            Z 4243a
        Rinck, J. C. H.

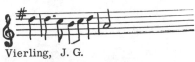

Vierling, J. G.

Keinen hat Gott verlassen
    (Crueger)
            Z 5395
        Brieger, O.

Vierling, J. G.

Keller's American Hymn (Keller)

    Ryder, A. H.

Kemath (Union Harmony)

    Kettering, E. L.

Kender du den (Berggreen)

        Hamburger, P.
        Jeppesen, K.
    Variant:
    Brorson

Kilmarnock (Dougall)

    Floyd, A. E.

Kimmer, I klokker (Rung)

        Jeppesen, K.
        Thuner, O. E.

Kindelein zart

        Lampart, K.

King's Lynn (English)

Coleman, R. H. P.   Whitlock, P.
Grace, H.   Wood, D.

King's Majesty (George)

George, G.
Sowerby, L.

King's Weston (Vaughan-Williams)

Dow, M. W.
Sandford, G.

Kirkasta, oi Kristus, meille
(Finnish)

Parviainen, J.

Kirkeklokke! ej til hovedstaeder (Rung)
See: Kirkeklokke! mellem aedle malme

Kirkeklokke! mellem aedle malme
(Rung)

Bitsch, V.
Kaestel, L.   Rung-Keller, P. S.
Variant:
Kirkeklokke! ej til hovedstaeder

Wuertz, J.

Kirkelieder (Church Song)

Matthison-Hansen, G.

Kirken den er et gammelt hus
See: Die Kirche ist ein altes Haus

Kirken er som Himmerige (Gade)

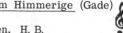

Frandsen, H. B.
Variant:
Lover Gud, I barndoms stille

Wuertz, J.

Kjaere Guds barn
See: Lovet vaere du (Folk Tune)

Kjaerlighet er lysets kilde
(Lindeman)

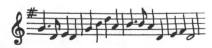

870   Organ - Preludes

Kjaerlighet er lysets kilde (cont.)

  *Drischner, M.   Sandvold, A.
  Nielsen, L.

Kjaerlighet er lysets kilde (Norse Folk)
  See: Hoeyr kor Kyrkjeklokka (Norse Folk)

Kjaerlighet fra Gud (Steenberg)

  Nielsen, L.

Kjemp alvorlig, nu Guds naade
  See: O wer alles haet verloren

Kjemp alvorlig, nu Guds naade
  See: Ringe recht (Kuhnau)

Klynke og klage (Crueger)
  See: Lobet den Herren, alle die (Crueger)

Koenig ist der Herr

  Mueller-Zuerich, P.

Kom Christenschaar (Praetorius)

  Reijden, W. van der
  Rippen, P.
  Variants:
  Song 28 (Dutch)

    Wilgenburg, D. van

  Song 41 (Dutch)

    Rippen, P.   Wilgenburg, D. van

  Song 254 (Dutch)

    Wilgenburg, D. van

Kom foelg i aanden med
  See: Auf meinen lieben Gott (Regnart)

Kom, Gud Helligaand, kom brat
(Barnekow)

  Jensen, S.   *Thuner, O. E.

Kom, Gud Helligaand, kom brat
  See: Veni Sancte Spiritus (Dublin - Mode 1)

Kom, Helge Ande, Herre God
   See: Komm Heiliger Geist, Herre Gott

Kom, Helge Ande, till mig in
   See: Kommt her zu mir

Kom, Helligaand, Gud Herre from
   See: Komm Heiliger Geist, Herre Gott

Kom Hellig Aand med skapermakt
   See: Veni Creator Spiritus (Sarum Mode 8)

Kom Hellige Aand, Herre Gud
   See: Komm Heiliger Geist, Herre Gott

Kom hit til mig (Folk Tune)
   See: Kommt her zu mir (Leipzig)

Kom hjerte, ta ditt regnebrett
(Sletten)

     Gangfloet, S.   Nielsen, L.

Kom hjerte, ta ditt regnebrett
   See: Mein Seel erhebt den Herren (Strassburg)

Kom, regn af det hoeje (Laub)

     Godske-Nielsen, H.
     Wuertz, J.

Kom, regn fra det hoeie (Steenberg)

     Karlsen, R.

Kom tot Uw Heiland

     Zwart, W. H.

Komm, ach komm, O Troester
mein

     Miggl, E.

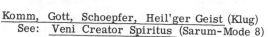

Komm, Gott, Schoepfer, Heil'ger Geist (Klug)
   See: Veni Creator Spiritus (Sarum-Mode 8)

Komm, Heidenheiland
   See: Erhalt uns, Herr

Komm, Heil'ger Geist
   See: Veni Creator Spiritus (Sarum-Mode 8)

Komm, Heiliger Geist, auf uns
   herab

   Jenny, A.

Komm, Heiliger Geist, erfuell die
   Herzen (Old Church)

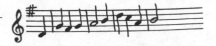

     Grabner, H.
     Marx, K.   Thomas, G. A. (2)
     *Piutti, K.   *Wedemann, W.

Komm, Heiliger Geist, erfuell
   die Herzen

     Metzger, H. A.

Komm, Heiliger Geist, ganz
   gnadenreich

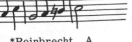

     Jenny, A.
     Plag, J.   Ruedinger, G.

Komm, Heiliger Geist, Herre
   Gott (Walther)
            Z 7445b

Ahrens, J.	Karow, K.	*Reinbrecht, A.
Armsdorff, A. (2)	Kauffmann, G. F. (2)	Reuter, F.
Bach, J. S. (2)	Kickstat, P. (2)	Reuter, J. F.
Bausznern, W. von	*Kleber, L.	Rinck, J. C. H. (2)
Beck, A.	*Koch, K.	Rogers, S. E.
Beck, C.	Krapf, G.	Scheidt, S.
Bender, J. (2)	Krebs, J. L.	Schwencke, J. F. (3)
Bornefeld, H.	Kutzer, E.	Sering, F. W.
Brieger, O.	Leupold, A. W.	Sorge, G. A. (2)
Buxtehude, D. (3)	Litzau, J. B.	Telemann, G. P. (5)
David, J. N.	Markworth, H. J.	Tunder, F. (2)
Driessler, J.	Merkel, G.	Vetter, A. N. (2)
Dupré, M. J. J.	Micheelsen, H. F. (2)	Vierling, J. G.
Eckardt, A.	Mueller, S.	Walther, J. G. (2)
Enckhausen, H. F.	Pachelbel, J. (2)	Weckmann, M.
*Fischer, M. G.	Peeters, F.	Wedemann, W.
*Gulbins, M.	Pepping, E.	Wenzel, E.
Haase, K.	Pfaff, H.	*Weyhmann, J. W.
Hasse, K.	Pfeiffer, C. D.	Winter-Hjelm, O.
Hoyer, K.	Piutti, K.	Wyton, A.
Karg-Elert, S.	Reger, M.	Zachau, F. W. (8)

Variants:
Kom, Helge Ande, Herre God

     Wikander, D.

Kom, Helligaand, Gud Herre from

    Raasted, N. O.

Kom Hellige Aand, Herre Gud

    Alnaes, E.

Komm Heiliger Geist mit deiner Gnade
See: O Jesulein suess (Cologne)

Komm her mit Fleiss zu schauen (Schuetz)
See: Ich will so lang ich lebe

Komm, O fromme Christenschaar
See: Hoechster Priester (Gregor)

Komm, O Geist der Heiligkeit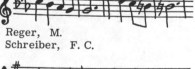

    Hoene, K. H.

Komm, O Gott, Schoepfer
See: Veni Creator Spiritus (Sarum - Mode 8)

Komm, O komm, du Geist des Lebens (J. C. Bach)
See: St. Leonard (Meiningen)

Komm, Schoepfer, Geist

    Jenny, A.

Komm, Schoepfer, Geist
See: Veni Creator Spiritus (Sarum - Mode 8)

Komm suesser Tod (Bach)
                  Z 4400
    Beck, A.
    Diggle, R.
    Peeters, F.   Reger, M.
                   Schreiber, F. C.

Komm, Suender, komm

    Neuss, H.

Kommer, sjaele dyrekoebte
(Hartman)

    *Grinsted, B.

Kommer, sjaele dyrekoebte (Laub)

    *Wuertz, J.

Kommet, ihr Hirten (Bohemian)

Birn, M. (2)
Degen, H.
Held, W.   Rogers, S. E.
Krieger, F.   Warner, R. L.
                            Wettstein, H.

Kommet, lobet ohne End

Doebler, K.

Kommst du, kommst du, Licht der Heiden
(Altdorf)
See: Ach, was soll ich, Suender, machen

Kommst du nun, Jesu
See: Lobe den Herren, den

Kommt her, des Koenigs Auf-
gebot (Schuetz)

Bieske, W.
Driessler, J.
Mueller-Zuerich, P. (2)   Weber, H.
                            Zipp, F.

Kommt her, ihr Cherubinen

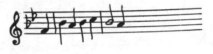

Gansloser, K. L.

Kommt her, ihr seid geladen
See: Aus meines Herzens Grunde

Kommt her, ihr seid geladen
See: Zeuch ein zu deinen Toren (Crueger)

Kommt her zu mir, spricht
Gottes Sohn (Leipzig)
                Z 2496c
                Z 7377

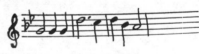

Bach, J. C.   Karow, K.   Schwencke, J. F. (2)
Baldamus, F.   Merk, G.   Siedel, M.
Buxtehude, D.   Merkel, G.   Stolze, H. W.
Fluegel, E. P.   Nicolai, J. G.   Tuerke, O.
Franke, F. W.   Oley, J. C.   Vierling, J. G.
Gulbins, M.   Pachelbel, J. (2)   Walther, J. G.
Haase, K.   Peeters, F. (2)   Wedemann, W.
Hennig, W.   Piutti, K. (2)   Weyrauch, J. (2)
Herzogenberg, H. von Rinck, J. C. H.   Wolff, C. M.
Kammeier, H.   Schmidt, F.
Variants:
Brich an, du schoenes (Leipzig)

Pfeiffer, C. D.   Soenke, H.

Gott Vater, sende deinen Geist

    Wieruszowski, L.

Kom, Helge Ande, till mig in

    Wikander, D.

Kom hit til mig (Folk Tune)

    Baden, C.   Hovland, E.
    Gangfloet, S.

O Herre god og Frelser from

    Jensen, S.   Moeller, S. O.
    Laub, T.   Thuner, O. E.

Verzage nicht, du Haeuflein klein (Leipzig)

    Abel, O.   *Oley, J. C.
    *Bausznern, W. von   Weigl, B.

Kommt Kinder, lasst uns gehen (Crueger)
  See: Von Gott will ich nicht lassen

Kommt Kinder, lasst uns gehen (Schuetz)
  See: Ich will so lang ich lebe (Schuetz)

Kommt Menschenkinder, ruehmt und preisst
  See: Old 100th

Kommt Seelen, dieser Tag (Bach)

              Z 5185

Variant:
Komt Zielen, dieze Dag

    Post, P.

Kommt und lasst uns Christum ehren
  See: Den die Hirten lobten sehr

Komt allen tezamen
  See: Adeste Fideles

Komt als kindren van het licht   Tune not found

    Asma, F.

Komt en laet ons Christus eeren
  See: Den die Hirten lobten sehr

Komt, laat ons voortgaan (Bastiaans)
See: Song 217 (Dutch)

Komt nu met zang (French)
See: Song 146 (Dutch)

Komt verwondert u hier, Mensen
(Dutch Carol)

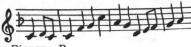

    Hoogewoud, H.   Rippen, P.
Variant:
Song 15 (Dutch)

    Dragt, J.

Komt, willt u spoeden
See: Old Netherlands Song

Kont Zielen, dieze Dag
See: Kommt Seelen, diese Tag (Bach)

Konge er du visst (Steenberg)

    Gangfloet, S.
    Nielsen, L.

Kongerne Konge (Horneman)

    Joergensen, G.   Matthison-Hansen, F.

Koraal (Chorale)

    Vranken, J.

Korset vil jeg aldrig (Folk Tune)

    Baden, C.
    Karlsen, R.   Nielsen, L.

Kremser
See: Netherlands (Valerius)

Krist have lov   Tune not found

    Thuner, O. E.

Krist stod op af doede, i paaskemorgenrede (Lindeman)

    Nielsen, L.

Krist stod op af doede, i paaskemorgenrede (Berggreen)

    Lindorff-Larsen, E.

Krist stod op af doede, i paaskemorgenrede
  See: Christus Resurrexit

Kummer und Freud', sie wandeln
  zusammen

    Raasted, N. O.

Kun Herra vain (Finnish)

    Parviainen, J.

Kvar helst eg vankar i verdi
  vida (Folk Tune)

    Karlsen, R.

Kvi skjelv kvart lauvsblad (1648)

    Nielsen, L.

Kvindelil (Horn)
            Z 1177
    Hamburger, P.
    Thuner, O. E.
  Variant:
  O liebster Herr Jesu Christ

Kyrie
  See also: Ite Missa Est

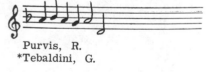

    Boslet, L.   Purvis, R.
    *Habert, J. E.   *Tebaldini, G.

Kyrie (Die Litanei)
  See: Litanei (Kyrie)

Kyrie Fons Bonitatis
  See: Fons Bonitans

Kyrie Gott, Heiliger Geist

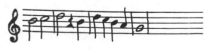

    Bach, J. S.   Kegel, K. C.
    Dupré, M. J. J.   Kropfreiter, A. F.

Kyrie Gott, Vater in Ewigkeit
  Based on <u>Kyrie Fons Bonitatis</u>

    Bach, J. S. (2)   Kaeppel, G. C. A.   Reichardt, B.
    Dupré, M. J. J.   Karg-Elert, S.   Rinck, J. C. H.
    Engel, J.   Karow, K.   Volckmar, F. W.
    Frech, J. G.   Kegel, K. C.   Volckmar, T.
    Grote, H.   Kropfreiter, A. F. Weber, H.
    Hessenberg, K.   Piutti, K.

Kyrie Magnae Deus

    Buchner, J. A.   Clokey, J. W.
Variant:
<u>O Vater, allmaechtiger Gott</u>

    Bach, J. S.

Kyrie Orbis Factor
  See also: <u>Ite Missa Est</u>

    Benoist, F.
    Jaeggi, O.   Pollen, A. H.
Variant:
<u>Orbis Factor</u>

    Clokey, J. W.

Kyrie Rex Genitor

    Kreckel, P. G.

Kyrkja stand fast (Sletten)

    Nielsen, L.

La Nativité (French Noël)

    Young, G.

Laban (Mason)

    Bingham, S.

Lad det klinge soedt i sky
  See: <u>Joseph, lieber Joseph mein</u> (Klug)

Lad vaje hoejt vort kongeflag
  (Danish)

    Godske-Nielsen, H.
Variant:
<u>Gud Fader udi himmerig</u>

Laer mig, O skov (Bull)

    Rung-Keller, P. S.
    Wuertz, J.

Laer mig, O skov (Berggreen)
  See: O Gud, ske lov (Berggreen)

Laet ons met herten reijne
  (Flemish)

    Bull, J.

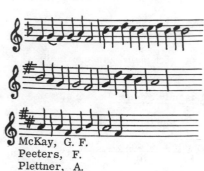

Peeters, F.

Laetabundus (Plainsong)

    Harwood, B.

Lammas (Brown)

    Reuter, F.

Lancashire (Smart)

    Arnatt, R. K.
    Gehring, P.
    Haase, K.
    Matthews, J.

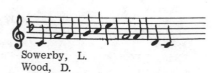

McKay, G. F.
Peeters, F.
Plettner, A.
Whitford, H. P.

Land of Pure Delight
  See: Varina (Root)

Land of Rest (Early American)

    Donovan, R. F.
    Near, G.
    Powell, R. J.

Sowerby, L.
Wood, D.

Landskron
  See: O suesser Herre, Jesu Christe
  (Bohemian)

Langran (Langran)

    Bingham, S.

Lanier (Lutkin)

    Crane, R.
    Duro, J.

Laramie (Bode)

    Diggle, R.

Lass dich Gott

    Taeger, A.

Lass dich Gott (Koenig)

        Z 3241
    Wieruszowski, L.

Lass mich dein sein und bleiben
    See: Herzlich tut mich verlangen

Lass mich dein sein und bleiben
    See: Valet

Lass mich deine Leiden singen

    Sechter, S. (2)

Lasset uns den Herren preisen
    See: Sollt ich meinem Gott nicht singen
(Schop)

Lasset uns mit Jesu ziehen (Bolze)

        Z 7916

Barlow, W.	Hillert, R.
Beck, A.	Kretzschmar, P.
Cassler, G. W.	Markworth, H. J.
*Grote, H.	Peeters, F.
Haase, K. (2)	Reuter, F.

Variant:
Sollt ich meinem Gott nicht singen (Bolze)

    Schwencke, J. F. (2)

Lasset uns mit Jesu ziehen (Schop)
    See: Sollt ich meinem Gott nicht singen (Schop)

Lasst mich gehen (Voigtlander)
          Z 1842
      *Claussnitzer, P.
      *Reuter, F.

Wettstein, H.

Lasst mich geh'n (Wermann)
          Z 1844

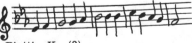

      *Finzenhagen, L. H. O.   Piutti, K. (2)
      *Fluegel, E. P.   *Streicher, J. A.

Lasst uns alle froehlich sein
   (Dresden)
                      Z 1161

  Gebhardi, L. E. Markworth, H. J. Schaab, R.
  Haase, K.   Meibohm, D. (3) Schumacher, M. H.
  Kaeppel, G. C. A. Metzger, H. A. Willan, H.

Lasst uns das Kindlein gruessen

  Monar, A. J.

Lasst uns das Kind'lein wiegen
   (Folk Tune)

  Murschhauser, F. X. A. (2)

Lasst uns erfreuen (Cologne)

Bratt, C. G.	James, P.
Choveaux, N.	Johnson, D. N.
Clausing, F.	Keldermans, R. A.
Copley, R. E.	Moser, R.
Diercks, J. H.	Peeters, F. (2)
Diggle, R.	Reichel, B.
Doppelbauer, J. F.	Rohlig, H.
Dressler, J.	Romanovsky, E.
Faulkes, W.	Schwarz-Schilling, R. (2)
Gaul, H.	Shaffer, J. E.
Gore, R. T.	Slater, G. A.
Groves, R. (2)	Staley, R. B.
Haase, K.	Vermulst, J.
Hokanson, M.	

Variants:
Easter Alleluia

  *Dittrich, R.   *Schoefmann, K. P. F.
  Rowley, A.

Lasst uns freuen herzlich sehr

  Schroeder, H.

O Splendour of God's Glory Bright (Short Form)

  Edmundson, G.

Vigiles et Sancti

  Diggle, R.   Peeters, F.
  Goldsworthy, W. A. Snow, F. W.

Lasst uns erfreuen (cont.)

  Ye Watchers and Ye Holy Ones

      Martin, M. I'a.   Nieland, J.
      Mead, E. G.

Lasst uns freuen herzlich sehr
      See: Lasst uns erfreuen (Cologne)

Lasst uns mit geruehrtem Herzen   Tune not found

      Brosig, M.

Lasst uns nun gehen zur
      See: Old Netherlands Song

Lasst uns zum Kreuze treten hin
(Gesius - Danish)
                    Z 467
      Variants:
Din dyre Ihukommelse (Gesius)

      Gangfloet, S.   Karlsen, R.

  Gak under Jesu kors

      Laub, T.   Thuner, O. E.
      Raasted, N. O. (2)

  Geh unter Jesu Kreuz

      Raasted, N. O.

  Mein' Seel', O Herr, muss loben dich

      Bossler, K.   Schweppe, J.
      Metzger, H. A.

  Vor Herre Jesu mindefest

      Moeller, S. O. (3)   Woeldike, M. A. (2)
      Videroe, F. (2)

  LaTrobe (La Trobe)

      Purvis, R.
      Variant:
  Croyland

      Cassler, G. W.

Lauda Anima
  See: Benedic Anima Mea (Goss)

Lauda Sion

  Monar, A. J.

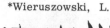

Lauda Sion (Layriz)
              Z 3880
  Variant:
Jesus Christus herrscht als Koenig (Layriz)

  Piutti, K.   *Wieruszowski, L.

Lauda Sion (Plainsong - Mode 7)

  Ahrens, J.
  *Barnes, E. S.   *Kreckel, P. G.
  Beltjens, J.   Langlais, J. F.
  Boslet, L.   *Lemmens, N. J.
  *Dupré, M. J. J.   *Magin, C.
  *Folville, J.   Plum, P. J. M. (2)
  *Karg-Elert, S.   Quingnard, R.

Lauda Zion

  Kreckel, P. G.

Laudate Dominum (Gregorian)

  Lemmens, N. J.
  *Peeters, F.   *Ravanello, O.

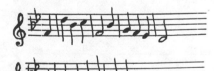

Laudate Dominum (Parry)

  *Matthews, E.

Laudes Domini (Barnby)

  Ashford, E. L.
  Baumgartner, H. L.   Lutkin, P. C.
  Feibel, F.   Matthews, H. A.
  Kingsbury, C.   Saxton, S. E.

Laurinus (Swedish)

  Variant:
  I himmelen, I himmelen

  Nordquist, G.

Laus Deo
  See: Redhead 46

Laus Regis (Moravian)

    Cassler, G. W.

Laus Tibi Christe (German)
               Z 8187d
    Bratt, C. G.
    Hegedus, A.

Lazarus (Old English)

    Rootham, C. B.

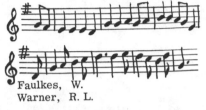

Le Fils du Roi (French Noël)

    Alain, A.   Faulkes, W.
    Borucchia, N.   Warner, R. L.

Le Paradis (French Noël)

    Borucchia, N.

Le Seigneur nous benisse et nous   Tune not found
  garde

    Hess, C. L.

Le Vermeil du Soleil (Marot-
  Denizot)

    Boëly, A. P. F. (2)

Leander

    Read, G.

Leaning On the Everlasting Arms
  (Showalter)

    Thompson, V. D.

Lebt Christus, was bin ich betruebt
  See: Erschienen ist der herrlich Tag (Herman)

Leer mij, O Heer
  See: Herzliebster Jesu

Legg ut paa djupet (Kingo)

    Karlsen, R.

Leicester (Bishop)

    Coleman, R. H. P.

Leid, milde ljos (Purday)
  See: Sandon

Leid, milde ljos (Solheim)

    Karlsen, R.

Lenox (Edson)

    Ashford, E. L.

Leohymne (Katschthaler)

    Gruber, J.

Leoni (Hebrew)

Bingham, S.	Faulkes, W.	Musgrove, T.
Calver, F. L.	Hokanson, M.	Noble, T. T.
Cassler, G. W.	Lang, C. S.	Proulx, R.
Diggle, R.	Lubrich, F. , Sr.	Whitford, H. P.

Variant:
Yigdal

Ashford, E. L.	Haase, K.	Peeters, F.
Bingham, S.	Kohs, E. B.	Stone, D. M.
Diemer, E. L.	Mueller, C. F.	Wehmeyer, W.
Freed, I.		

Les Anges dans nos (French
  Carol)

Borucchia, N.	Gigout, E.	Schehl, J. A.
DeBrant, C.	Paponaud, M.	Thomas, B.
Erb, M. J.	Papy, N.	Walton, K.

Variants:
Bergers, pourquois
Engelkens zingen

    Hoogewoud, H.

Gloria (French Noël)

Alain, A.	Rohlig, H.
Gehrke, H.	Smilde, B.
Langston, P. T.	

Les Anges dans nos (cont.)

Westminster Carol

Cronham, C. R.   Lorenz, E. J.
Feibel, F.   Wyton, A.
James, A.

Les Commandemens
See: Wenn wir in hoechsten Noethen
(Bourgeois)

Let Us Sing Loudly (Christmas
Carol)

Guilmant, A.

L'Eternel seul est Seigneur
(Benevento-Webbe)

Hess, C. L.

Letmathe (Walker)

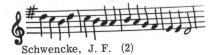

Walker, E.

Licht vom Licht, erleuchte mich (Ulich)
See: Meinen Jesum lass ich nicht (Ulich)

Liebe, die du mich zum Bilde
(Darmstadt)
                    Z 3749
Variants:
All Saints

Peeters, F.

Zeuch mich, zeuch mich

Barner, A.   Oechsler, E.

Liebe, die du mich zum Bilde
(Dretzel)
                    Z 3616
Palme, R.

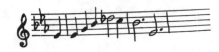

Schwencke, J. F. (2)

Liebe, die du mich zum Bilde (Meiningen)
See: St. Leonard

Lieblich ist der Himmel blau
See: Celestia

Liebster Immanuel
See: Schoenster Immanuel

Liebster Jesu, wir sind hier
(Ahle)
Z 3498b

Albrecht, G.
Bach, A. W.
Bach, J. C.
Bach, J. S. (3)
Baldamus, F.
Beck, A.
Bender, J.
Birck, W.
Bossler, K.
Brandt, A.
Brieger, O.
Brosig, M. (2)
Claussnitzer, P.
Clokey, J. W.
Coleman, R. H. P.
Davin, K. H. G.
Dienel, O.
Drischner, M.
Dupré, M. J. J.
Edmundson, G.
Enckhausen, H. F.
Fiebig, K.
Fischer, I.
Fischer, M. G. (3)
Fluegel, G.
Forchhammer, T.
Gerber, E. L. (2)
Grabner, H. (2)
Grote, H.
Grundmann, O. A.

Gulbins, M.
Haase, K.
Hasse, K.
Hennig, W.
Herzog, J. G.
Hesse, A. F.
Hofmeier, A.
Hoyer, K. (2)
Huth, A.
Karg-Elert, S. (2)
Karow, K.
Kickstat, P.
Koehler-Wumbach, W.
Koerner, G. W.
Krebs, J. L.
Kruspe, G.
Kuntze, C.
Landahl, C. W.
Leupold, A. W.
Meibohm, D. (6)
Merk, G.
Merkel, G.
Metzger, H. A.
Micheelsen, H. F.
Michel, A.
Mueller, S.
Palme, R.
Peeters, F.
Piutti, K. (2)
Post, P.

Purvis, R.
Raphael, G. (2)
Reger, M.
Reuter, F.
Rinck, J. C. H. (7)
Ritter, A. G.
Rohlig, H.
Rumpf, W. (2)
Sachs, J. G.
Schaab, R. (2)
Schaeffer, A.
Schaper, G.
Scherzer, O.
Schmidt, W.
Schwencke, J. F. (3)
Stecher, H.
Streicher, J. A. (2)
Thomas, G. A.
Umbreit, K. G.
Vierling, J. G.
Walter, S.
Walther, J. G. (7)
Wedemann, W.
Wendt, E. A.
Wettstein, H. (3)
Willing, D.
Wolfrum, K. (3)
Zipp, F.

Variants:
Gott du bist von Ewigkeit

*Rabich, E.

Gott du hast in deinem Sohn

Doles, J. F.   Toepfer, J. G.

Herre Jesu, vi er her

Jeppesen, K.   Woeldike, M. A.

Jesu, Frelser, vi er her

Drischner, M.   Gangfloet, S.

Liebster Jesu (Ahle) (cont.)

   Lover Herren, han er naer

      Raasted, N. O. (3)

   Nuremberg

      Cutler, H. S.   Thayer, W. E.

   O Herr Jesu, gib

      Brosig, M.

   Soede Jesu, vi er her

      Frellsen, E.   Thomsen, P.
      Hamburger, P.   Videroe, F.
      Rosenkilde-Larsen, E.

Liebster Jesu (Crueger?)

      Lundquist, M. N.

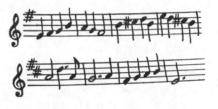

Lift High the Cross (Nicholson)

   Variant:
   Nicholson

      Arnatt, R. K.

Light (Christian Lyre)

      Powell, R. J.

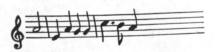

Light Divine
   See: Song 13 (Gibbons)

Lincoln (Ravenscroft)

      Wood, C.

Listen Lordlings (Gascon)

      Foote, A. W.
      Gotch, O. H.

Litanei (Luther)

      Bender, J.   Weiss, E.
      Variant:
      Kyrie (Die Litanei)

Weber, H.   Wenzel, E.

Little Jesus, Sweetly Sleep
(Czech)

Wyton, A.
Variant:
Rocking Carol

Liverpool (Wainwright)

Wesley, S. S.

Ljoset yver landet (Olav's Fest)

Baden, C.
Hovland, E.   Kvandal, J.
Variants:
Naglet til et kors (Nideros)

Karlsen, R.

Llanfair (Williams)

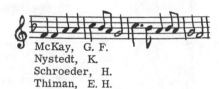

Diggle, R.   McKay, G. F.
Groves, R.   Nystedt, K.
Haase, K.   Schroeder, H.
Larkin, J.   Thiman, E. H.

Llangollen (Welsh)

Peeters, F.

Llansannan (Welsh)

Groves, R.
Parrish, C.

Lob Gott, du werte Christenheit
See: In Dulci Jubilo

Lob Gott getrost mit singen
See: Ich dank dir, lieber Herre (Bohemian)

Lob sei dem Allmaechtigen Gott
(Crueger)
                    Z 313
Peeters, F.

Lob sei dem Allmaechtigen Gott
See: Creator Alme Siderum (Mode 4)

Lob sei Gott in des Himmels
Thron (Erfurt)
Z 1748
Pachelbel, J.

Lobe den Herren, den maechtigen
Koenig (Stralsund)

Z 1912d

Ahrens, J.	Hesse, A. F.
Baldamus, F.	Hoyer, K.
Barlow, W.	Kaeppel, G. C. A. (2)
Barner, A.	Karg-Elert, S.
Beebe, E. J.	Karow, K.
Bender, J. (2)	Kickstat, P.
Bieske, W.	Kleemeyer, H.
Blackburn, J.	Klotz, H.
Bottenberg, W.	Knab, A.
Bratt, C. G.	Koch, M.
Breuker, C.	Kousemaker, A. (2)
Brieger, O.	Krapf, G.
Butcher, V.	Kuehn, K.
Cebrian, A.	Kuntze, C.
Claussnitzer, P.	Kunze, K.
Copley, R. E.	Landmann, A.
David, J. N.	Lang, H.
Diemer, E. L.	Leupold, A. W.
Dienel, O.	Luetzel, J. H.
Draht, T. (2)	Manz, P.
Dressler, J.	Markull, F. W. (2)
Drischner, M. (2)	Matthison-Hansen, H.
Eckardt, A.	Meibohm, D. (4)
Edmundson, G.	Merk, G.
Engel, D. H.	Merkel, G.
Engelbrecht, K. F. (3)	Micheelsen, H. F. (2)
Faehrmann, H.	Michl, A.
Finzenhagen, L. H. O.	Miller, A.
Fluegel, G. (4)	Mojsisovics, R. von
Franke, F. W.	Mudde, W.
Frischmann, M.	Mueller-Zuerich, P.
Freund, W.	Orlinski, H.
Fricke, R.	Palme, R. (2)
Gade, N. W.	Peeters, F.
George, G.	Piechler, A.
Grabner, H.	Piutti, K.
Grote, H.	Radecke, R.
Gruel, E.	Rebling, G.
Gulbins, M.	Reda, S.
Haas, J.	Reger, M. (3)
Haase, R.	Reichardt, B.
Hasse, K. (2)	Reinbrecht, F.
Hennig, W.	Reinhardt, A.
Herzog, J. G.	Reuter, F.

Riemenschneider, G. (2)
Rinck, J. C. H. (5)
Rinkens, W.
Rohlig, H.
Romanovsky, E.
Roth, F.
Rudnick, W.
Rumpf, W. (2)
Saffe, F.
Schaab, R. (2)
Schaper, G.
Schehl, J. A.
Schmalz, P.
Schumacher, M. H.
Schumann, C.
Schwencke, J. F. (2)
Sechter, S.
Seiffert, U.
Shaffer, R.

Shaw, M.
Stolze, H. W.
Trenkner, W.
Unbehaun, G.
Vehmeier, T.
Walcha, H.
Walther, J. G. (6)
Webber, W. G.
Wendt, E. A.
Wenzel, E.
Westering, P. C. van
Wettstein, H. (3)
Wickenhausser, R.
Wolff, L.
Young, G.
Zierau, F.
Zipp, F.

Variants:
Hast du denn, Jesu (Liebster)

Kennaway, L.

Pisk, P. A.

Jauchzet ihr Himmel

Franke, F. W.
Herrmann, K. H.

Koch, J. H. E.

Kommst du nun, Jesu

Bach, J. S.
Dupré, M. J. J.

Vierling, J. G.

Lover den Herre

Bergh, L.
Cappelen, C.
Frandsen, H. B.
Frellsen, E.
Gade, N. W.
Gangfloet, S.
Jeppesen, K.
Karlsen, R.
Laub, T.

Laub-Woeldike,
Nielsen, L.
Nielsen, T. H. (2)
Raasted, N. O.
Rosenkilde-Larsen, E.
Sandvold, A.
Thomsen, P.
Woeldike, M. A.

Song 136 (Dutch)

Mudde, W.
Nauta, J. (2)

Wilgenburg, D. van

Lobe den Herren, den maechtigen Koenig (cont.)

  Song 152 (Dutch)

    Wilgenburg, D. van

Lobe den Herren, O meine Seele
  (Freylinghausen)
                    Z 4995

Abel, O.	Metzger, H. A.
Baldamus, F.	Micheelsen, H. F.
Barner, A.	Mueller, A. E.
Bender, J. (2)	Mueller-Zuerich, P.
Borchers, G.	Peeters, F.
Claussnitzer, P. (2)	Piutti, K.
Drischner, M. (2)	Ramin, G.
Faehrmann, H.	Reda, S.
Fluegel, G.	Reichardt, B.
Forchhammer, T.	Reinbrecht, F.
Franke, F. W.	Riedel, H.
Grote, H.	Rumpf, W.
Grundmann, O. A.	Saffe, F. (2)
Haase, K.	Schaeffer, A.
Hessenberg, K.	Schmidt, F.
Kaeppel, G. C. A.	Schwencke, J. F.
Karg-Elert, S.	Seyerlen, R.
Karow, K. (2)	Wenzel, H.
Kickstat, P.	Werner, F.
Meibohm, D. (2)	Wettstein, H. (3)

Variant:
Guds igenfoedte, nylevende sjaele

Jeppesen, K.	Videroe, F.
Thomsen, P.	Wuertz, J.

Lobet den Herren, alle die Ihn
  ehren (Crueger)
                    Z 996

Bender, J.	Kickstat, P. (2)
Bossler, K. (2)	Piutti, K. (2)
Claussnitzer, P.	Rinck, J. C. H.
Franke, F. W.	Schink, H.
Haase, H. H.	Schwarz-Schilling, R.
Hoyer, K.	Weber, H.

Variants:
Kaerlek av hoejden

    Olson, D.

  Klynke og klage

Frandsen, H. B.	Wuertz, J.
Woeldike, M. A.	

Lobet den Herren, denn Er ist sehr freundlich
(Crueger)

Hennig, W.   *Meibohm, D.

Oblation

Johnson, D. N.

Lobet den Herren, denn Er ist
sehr freundlich (Scandelli)

Z 975

Walther, J. G.

Lobet den Herren, denn Er ist sehr freundlich
(Crueger)
See: Lobet den Herren, alle die Ihn ehren (Crueger)

Lobet den Herrn, ihr Heiden all
(Vulpius)
Z 4533

Anonymous   Haase, K.
Chemin-Petit, H.   Hennig, W.
Driessler, J.   Hofmeier, A.
Fischer, M. G.   Schaper, G.
Franke, F. W.   Wurm, A.
Variants:
Denne er dagen, som

Frandsen, H. B.   Moeller, S. O. (2)
Frellsen, E.   Nielsen, O. S.
Jeppesen, K.   Videroe, F. (5)
Laub, T.   Wuertz, J.

Dies ist der Tag den Gott gemacht

Raasted, N. O.

Fagert er landet (Vulpius)

Sandvold, A.

Lobt Gott, den Herrn, ihr Heiden all

Godske-Nielsen, H. (2)   Reda, S.
Hoegner, F.   Walcha, H.
Marx, K.   Weber, H.
Metzger, H. A.   Zipp, F.
Micheelsen, H. F.

Lobet den Herrn, ihr Heiden all (cont.)

   Sjaa, han gjeng inn til (Vulpius)

      Karlsen, R.

   Such wer da will

      Wieruszowski, L.

   Zeuch an die Macht

      Hark, F.   Pepping, E.
      Mueller, S. W.   Poppen, H. M.
      Mueller-Zuerich, P. (2)

Lobet den Herrn und dankt Ihm
   (Crueger)
          Z 991
      Borngaesser, W.   Roth, F.

Lobsinget, Christen Zungen   Tune not found

      Adler, E.

Lobt den Herrn, die Morgensonne
   (Halle)
          Z 1317
      Haase, K.

Lobt Gott den Herrn, ihr Heiden all
See: Lobet den Herrn, ihr Heiden all

Lobt Gott, ihr Christen, alle
   gleich (Herman)
          Z 198

Bach, A. W.	Franke, F. W.	Kuntze, C.
Bach, J. S. (3)	Godske-Nielsen, H.	Luebeck, V.
Baldamus, F.	Grabert, M. (2)	Markull, F. W.
*Becker, K. F.	Haase, K.	Markworth, H. J.
Beckmann, G.	Hegedus, A.	Meibohm, D. (3)
Bender, J.	Heinrich, J. G.	Merk, G.
Bleier, P.	Hennig, W.	Micheelsen, H. F.
Bornefeld, H.	Herrmann, K. H.	Mueller, S. W.
*Brieger, O. (2)	Herzog, J. G.	Oechsler, E.
Buxtehude, D. (5)	Hoyer, K.	Pach, W.
Claussnitzer, P. (3)	Huth, A.	Palme, R.
Driessler, J.	Karg-Elert, S. (2)	Papperitz, B. R.
Dupré, M. J. J.	Kickstat, P. (2)	Piutti, K. (2)
*Engels, A.	Kittel, J. C.	Proeger, J.
Fischer, M. G.	Klotz, H.	Rabich, E.
Fluegel, G.	Krause, P. (2)	Reger, M.
Forchhammer, T.	Kuehn, K. (2)	Reichel, B.

Rinck, J. C. H. (3)   Schumacher, M. H. (2)   Vierling, J. G.
Rudnick, W.   Schwencke, J. F. (3)   *Walcha, H.
Rumpf, W.   Sering, F. W.   Walther, J. G. (6)
Schaab, R.   Stapf, O.   Wedemann, W.
Schaper, G.   Steinhaeuser, K.   Wendt, E. A.
Scheidt, S. (2)   Thomas, G. A.   Wettstein, H.
Schrenk, J.   Toepfer, J. G.   Willan, H.
Schueler, H. (2)   Umbreit, K. G. (2)   Zehrfeld, O.
Schuetze, W. (2)   Vetter, A. N.
Variants:
Lobt Gott, ihr Christen, freuet euch

Schaab, R.

Op alle, som paa jorden bor

Frellsen, E.   Videroe, F.
Godske-Nielsen, H.

St. George (Herman)

*Morland, A.

Lobt Gott, ihr Christen - II
                    Z 199
Franke, F. W.

Lobt Gott, ihr Christen, freuet euch
See: Lobt Gott, ihr Christen, alle gleich (Herman)

Lobt Gott, ihr frommen Christen
(Old German)
                    Z 5356
David, J. N.
Koehler, K.   Zipp, F.

Lobt Gott in allen
See: Herzlich tut mich erfreuen

Lobt Gott in Seinem Heiligtum
(Schuetz)
                    Z 546a
Walther, J. G.

Loewen, lasst euch wiederfinden
(Klein)
                    Z 6521
Anonymous   Hasse, K.
Haase, K.   Meibohm, D.

Lofwad ware tu Jesu Christ
See: Gelobet seist du, Jesus Christ (Walther)

Lofzang van Maria

    Blekkenhorst, H.
    Kee, C.   Speuy, H. J.
    Post, P.   Zwart, J.
    Variants:
De Lofzang van Maria
Song B (Dutch)

    Wilgenburg, D. van

Lofzang van Simeon
    See: Song of Symeon

Lofzang van Zacharias
    See: An Wasserfluessen Babylon

London New (Scotch)

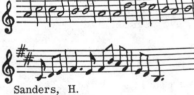

    Dyson, G.   Peeters, F.
    Grace, H.   Smart, H.
    Groves, R.   Smith, E. H.
    Lang, C. S.   Wesley, S. S.
    Palmer, C. C.   Willan, H.
    Variant:
Newtoun

    Wood, C.

London Old (Southwell)

    Best, W. T.

Londonderry (Irish)

    Archer, J. S.
    Coke-Jephcott, N.   Sanders, H.
    Felton, W. M.   Stanford, C. V.
    Pullein, J.   Whitford, H. P.

Looft nu de Here, O mijne Ziele   Tune not found

    Mazyk, R. van

Look Down To Us, St. Joseph (Flemish)
    See: Old Netherlands Song

Look Down, O Mother (Richardson)

    Kreckel, P. G.

(The) Lord At First Had Adam Made (Christmas Carol)

Faulkes, W.

Lord Bless Us All (O'Connell)

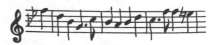

Kreckel, P. G.

Lord Into His Garden Comes
See: Garden Hymn

Lord Jesus Hath A Garden (Dutch)

Variant:
Herr Jesu hat ein Gaertchen

Peeters, F.

Lord Thee I'll Praise   Tune not found

Farrar, E. B.

Lourdes Pilgrim Hymn (French)

Benoit, Dom P.
Curry, R. D.   McGrath, J. J.
Kreckel, P. G.   Peloquin, C. A.
Larkin, J.   Raffy, L.

Lov Jesu Namn
See: Miles Lane (Shrubsole)

Lov vaere dig, O Jesu Krist
See: Gelobet seist du, Jesu Christ (Walther)

Lova Herren Gud, min Sjael (Finnish)

Parviainen, J.

Love Divine (LeJeune)

Peeters, F.   Stults, R. M.

Love Divine (Stainer)

Variants:
Song 116 (Dutch)

Kool, B., Jr.   Wilgenburg, D. van

Love Divine (cont.)

   Song 169 (Dutch)

      Wilgenburg, D. van

Love Divine

      Ponsonby, N. E.

Love Is Come Again
   See: Noël nouvelet

Lovely Infant

      Kreckel, P. G.
Variant:
Schoenstes Kindlein

Lover den Herre
   See: Lobe den Herren, den maechtigen

Lover Gud, I barndoms stille
   See: Kirken er som Himmerige (Gade)

Lover Gud I himmelshoejd

      Aahlen, W.

Lover Herren, han er naer
   See: Liebster Jesu

Love's Offering (Parker)

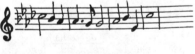

      Blake, G.

Lovet vaere du, Jesu Krist
   (Folk Tune)

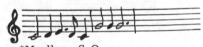

Andersen, E.	*Moeller, S. O.
Christensen, B.	*Nielsen, O. S.
*Frandsen, H. B.	Nielsen, T. H.
Frellsen, E.	*Rosenkilde-Larsen, E.
Godske-Nielsen, H.	Woeldike, M. A.

Variant:
Kjaere Guds barn

      Nielsen, L.

Lovet vaere du, Jesu Krist (Walther)
   See: Gelobet seist du, Jesu Christ (Walther)

Lovingkindness (Caldwell)

Herbek, R. H.

Lower Lights (Bliss)
See: Brightly Beams Our Father's Mercy

Lucis Creator Optime (Angers)

Z 365

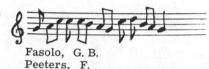

*Erbach, C.
Variant:
Ad Coenam Agni

Titelouze, J.

Lucis Creator Optime (Mode 8)

*Bedell, R. L.
*Cavazzoni, G.   Fasolo, G. B.
Dupré, M. J. J.   Peeters, F.

Lucis Creator Optime (Sarum - Mode 8)

*Kreckel, P. G.
Variant:
Salutis Aeterne Dator

Sister M. G.

Luebeck
See: Gott sei Dank durch alle Welt (Halle)

Lueneburg

Z 4799

Variant:
Jesu, meines Herzens Freud

Reuter, F. (2)

Luise
See: Jesu, meine Zuversicht

Lulajze Jezuniu (Polish Carol)

Labunski, F. R.

Luther Seminary (Dahle)

Peeters, F.

Luther's Hymn
See: <u>Nun freut Euch, lieben Christen</u> (Klug)

<u>Lux Aeterna</u> (Kyrial)

    *Erb, M. J.

<u>Lux Beata</u> (Peace)

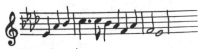

    Stults, R. M.

<u>Lux Benigna</u> (Dykes)

    Ashford, E. L.
    Hegedus, A.   Schmutz, A.
    King, H. C.   Stults, R. M.
    Reuter, F.   Thompson, V. D.
    Schehl, J. A.   West, J. A.
   Variant:
<u>Song 230</u> (Dutch)

    Asma, F.

<u>Lux Et Origo</u>

    Clokey, J. W. (2)   Kreckel, P. G.

<u>Lux Illuxit</u>

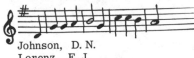

    Baden, C.

<u>Lyksalig, lyksalig, hver sjael</u>
(Berggreen)

    Gyldmark, O.   Nielsen, L.
    Moeller, S. O.   Rosenkilde-Larsen, E.

<u>Lyksalig, lyksalig, hver sjael</u>
(Danish Folk Tune)

    *Nielsen, J. M.

<u>Lyons</u> (Haydn)

    Dickey, M.   Johnson, D. N.
    Herbek, R. H. (2)   Lorenz, E. J.

<u>Lyra Davidica</u>

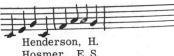

    Bratt, C. G.   Englert, E.   Henderson, H.
    Campbell, E. M. Fletcher, P. Hosmer, E. S.
    DeBrant, C.   Gray, A.   Koch, J. H. E.
    Diggle, R.   Harris, C.   Lemare, E. H.

Matthews, H. A.   Pearce, C. W.   Thomas, V. C.
McRae, W. D.   Snow, F. W.   Vause, G.
Morrison, R. S.   Thiman, E. H.   Young, G.
Norman, E. W.
Variants:
Easter Hymn

Archer, J. S.   Hodson, W.   Porter, A. P.
Ashford, E. L.   Laney, H.   Stanford, C. V. (3)
Coleman, R. H. P.   Morrison, R. S.   Thorne, E. H. (2)
Gray, A.   Mueller, C. F.   Westrup, J. A.
Haase, K.   Peeters, F.   Willan, H.
Harris, W. H.

Song 61 (Dutch)

Post, P.

Worgan

Andrews, M.   Nelson, R. A.
Diggle, R.   Nieland, J.
Fleischer, H.   Saxton, S. E.
Lutkin, P. C.   Willan, H.

Lyre ce n'est pas (Denizot)

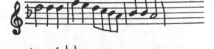

Boëly, A. P. F.

Mache dich, mein Geist, bereit
(Dresden)
                    Z 6274a
Boehner, J. L.   Koeckert, C.   Sachs, J. G.
Doles, J. F.   Luetzel, J. H.   Schaab, R.
Eckardt, A.   Magnus, E.   Toepfer, J. G.
Fluegel, E. P.   Mettner, C.   Umbreit, K. G. (2)
Franke, F. W.   Rinck, J. C. H. (2) Vierling, J. G.
Gruel, E.   Ritter, A. G.   Walther, J. G. (4)
Kittel, J. C.   Rudnick, W. (2)   Wedemann, W.
Variants:
Herr, ich bin dein Eigentum

Hesse, A. F.   Romanovsky, E.

Nassau

Edmundson, G.

Song 296 (Dutch)

Groothengel, J. G.

Mache dich, mein Geist, bereit (cont.)

Straf mich nicht

Albrecht, G.	Mueller, S.
Baldamus, F.	Palme, R.
Brede, A.	Piutti, K.
Brieger, O.	Ramin, G.
Brosig, M. (2)	Reda, S.
Claussnitzer, P. (4)	Reger, M. (2)
Enckhausen, H. F.	Reichardt, B.
Engelbrecht, K. F. (2)	Ricek, W. (2)
Fischer, M. G.	Richter, E. F.
Fluegel, G. (2)	Rinck, J. C. H. (4)
Franke, F. W.	Rudnick, W.
Gaebler, E. F.	Rumpf, W.
Haase, K.	Schneider, F. C.
Heinrich, J. G.	Schuetze, W. (2)
Hennig, W.	Schwencke, J. F. (3)
Herzog, J. G. (2)	Seiffer, C. T.
Hoepner, C. G.	Seiffert, U.
Homilius, G. A.	Stade, F. W.
Huth, A.	Stolze, H. W.
Karg-Elert, S.	Streicher, J. A.
Karow, K.	Telemann, G. P. (3)
Kempff, W.	Thomas, G. A.
Kickstat, P.	Volckmar, F. W.
Kimstedt, C.	Walther, J. G.
Kittel, J. C.	Wedemann, W.
Krause, P. (2)	Wettstein, H. (2)
Kuntze, C.	Wolff, C. M. (2)
Leupold, A. W.	Wolffin, E. M.
Marx, K. (2)	Wolfrum, K.
Merkel, G.	Zipp, F.
Metzger, H. A.	

Treder op til Herrens bord

　　Karlsen, R.

Wuertemburg

Lang, C. S.	Ratcliffe, D.

Mach's mit mir, Gott (Schein)

Z 2383

Baldamus, F.	Ergenzinger, H.	Forchhammer, T.
Bender, J.	Fehr, R.	Franke, F. W.
Boehner, J. L.	Fiebig, K.	Gradehand, F.
Bratt, C. G.	Fink, C.	Grundmann, O. A.
Claussnitzer, P. (2)	Fischer, M. G. (2)	Haase, K.
Draht, T.	Fluegel, E. P.	Heinrich, J. G.
Enckhausen, H. F.	Fluegel, G. (2)	Hering, J. C.

Karg-Elert, S. (3)
Karow, K.
Kickstat, P. (2)
Kittel, J. C.
Klaus, V. (2)
Krause, P.
Krebs, J. L.
Kuntze, C.
Kunze, K.
Leupold, A. W.
Merkel, G. (2)
Mueller, S.
Nicolai, J. G.
Oley, J. C. (2)
Peeters, F.

Petzold, J.
Piutti, K.
Raasted, N. O.
Reda, S.
Reger, M.
Reichardt, B.
Rembt, J. E.
Richter, E. F.
Rinck, J. C. H. (2)
Ritter, A. G.
Rudnick, W.
Sachs, J. G.
Saffe, F.
Schaeffer, A.
Schrenk, J.

Schwencke, J. F. (2)
Seyerlen, R.
Stolze, H. W. (3)
Streicher, J. A.
Thomas, O.
Toepfer, J. G.
Vierling, J. G.
Walther, J. G. (5)
Wedemann, W.
Weinreich, W.
Wettstein, H. (2)
Wolfrum, K.
Zehrfeld, O. (4)
Zopff, H. (2)

Variants:

Auf, Chri stenmensch, auf, auf

*Gulbins, M.   Rinck, J. C. H. (3)

Det livets ord vi bygger paa

Thuner, O. E.

Dich lieb ich, O mein Gott und Herr

Blum de Hyrth, C. E.

Eisenach

Near, G.   Rowley, A.
Powell, R. J.

Jeg vet mig en soevn i Jesu navn
Mir nach, spricht Christus

Boenicke, H.
Brieger, O.
Doles, J. F.
Fluegel, G.
Grote, H.
Haase, H. H.
Hark, F. (2)
Hasse, K.
Hesse, A. F.
Kittel, J. C.
Koehler-Wumbach, W.
Lorenz, C. A.
Markull, F. W.
Meibohm, D. (2)

Mueller-Zuerich, P.
Oley, J. C.
Rinck, J. C. H.
Roeder, E. O.
Rumpf, W.
Schaab, R. (2)
Schuetze, W.
Sechter, S.
Thomas, G. A.
Toepfer, J. G.
Umbreit, K. G.
Wedemann, W.
Wolf, E. F. (2)
Zipp, F.

Mach's mit mir, Gott (Schein) (cont.)

   Sei Mutter der Barmherzigkeit

      Doebler, K.

Till haerlighetens

      Aahgren, K. E.

Wie soll ich doch die Guete dein

      Umbreit, K. G.   Vierling, J. G.

Macht hoch die Tuer

      Kunze, K. (2)

Macht hoch die Tuer (Freyling-
    hausen)
            Z 5846
        also in 4
              4

Abel, O.	Kuehn, K.
*Ahrens, J.	Lampart, K.
Barner, A.	Leupold, A. W.
Bender, J.	*Meibohm, D. (3)
Birn, M.	Micheelsen, H. F.
Bornefeld, H.	Mueller, S. W.
Busch, A. G. W.	Mueller-Zuerich, P. (2)
*Claussnitzer, P.	*Oechsler, E.
*David, J. N.	Peeters, F.
Doebler, K.	Pepping, E. (2)
*Driessler, J.	Pickerott, A.
Drischner, M. (2)	Piutti, K. (2)
Fluegel, G. (3)	*Preitz, F.
*Forchhammer, T.	Reger, M.
*Franke, F. W.	*Rinck, J. C. H.
Gerhardt, P.	Rumpf, W.
*Goller, F.	*Schneider, M.
Haase, K.	*Schumann, G.
*Hanebeck, H. R.	*Schartz, G. von
Hasse, K.	*Soenke, H.
Heiss, H.	*Unbehaun, G.
Hessenberg, K.	Walcha, H.
Hoyer, K.	Weidenhagen, E.
Huebner, E.	Wettstein, H. (3)
Karg-Elert, S.	Wieruszowski, L.
Karow, K. (2)	Zierau, F.
Kickstat, P.	

  Variant:
Song 3 (Dutch)

Stulp, G.
Vogel, W.

Wilgenburg, D. van

<u>Macht hoch die Tuer</u> (Lemke)

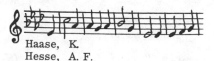

Beck, A.
*Birn, M.

Haase, K.
Hesse, A. F.

<u>Macht hoch die Tuer</u> (Stobaeus)

Z 5845a
Haase, K.

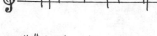

<u>Madrid</u> (Carr)

Variants:
<u>Song 174</u> (Dutch)

Bijster, J.

<u>Spanish Hymn</u>

Ashford, E. L.   Dickey, M.   Haase, K.
Bunjes, P. G.   Edmundson, G.   Taylor, C. T.

<u>Mae elaen laupeudesta</u> (Finnish)

Parviainen, J.

<u>Mae kauniin tiedaeaen</u> (Finnish)

Salonen, S.

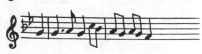

<u>Maegtigste Kriste</u>
See: <u>Flemming</u>

<u>Mag' ich Unglueck nicht wieder-
stahn</u> (Klug)

Z 8133
Pachelbel, J. (2)
Variant:
<u>Herr, ich bekenn von Herzensgrund</u>

Haessler, J. W.

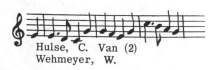

<u>Magdalen</u> (Stainer)

Beck, A.
Haase, K.

Hulse, C. Van (2)
Wehmeyer, W.

<u>Magnificat</u> - (one on each Tone)

Speth, J.

Magnificat (Tone 1 and Tone 6)
    See: Z 7372

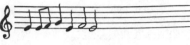

        Buxtehude, D.
        Titelouze, J.

Magnificat (Tone 4)

        Carissimi, G.

Magnificat (Mode 7)
    See also: Olmutz

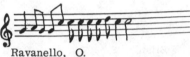

        Keldermans, R. A.   Olsson, O. E.

Magnificat (Tone 8)

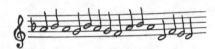

        Bas, G.
        Kreckel, P. G.   Ravanello, O.

Magnificat (Tone 9)
    See also: Magnificat (Tonus
Peregrinus)

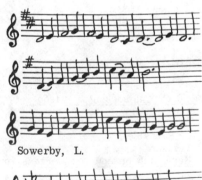

        Buxtehude, D.

Magnificat (Tonus Peregrinus)
    See: Meine Seele erhebet den Herren

Magnum Nomen Domini

        Lundquist, M. N.

Maidstone (Gilbert)

        Williams, C. à B.

Malabar (Williams)

        Arnatt, R. K.
        Gehring, P.   Sowerby, L.

Maldwyn (Welsh)

        Haase, K.

Malvern (Mason)

        Cassler, G. W.

Man betet, Herr, in Zions Stille (Bourgeois)
    See: Psalm 65

Manchester (Lampe)

 Wesley, S. S.

Manchester (Wainwright)

 Coutts, G.
 Palmer, C. C.

Manchester New (Turle)

 Palmer, C. C.

Manna
 See: Mercy (Gottschalk)

Mannheim (Filitz)
     Z 4921
 Conway, M. P.
 Lang, C. S.   Schwarz, G.
 Variant:
Auf, auf, weil der Tag erschienen

Manoah (Rossini)

 Ashford, E. L.
 Edmundson, G. Pool, K.

March of Turenne (French)

 Gaul, H.

Maria breit den Mantel aus

 Brand, T.
 Hoene, K. H.

Maria durch den Dornenwald ging
    ein
 Ahrens, J.
 David, J. N. Kropfreiter, A. F.

Maria hun er en jomfru ren
 (Lindeman)

 Alnaes, E.   Nielsen, L.

Maria hun er en jomfru ren

     Z 165
 Vestergaard-Pedersen, C.

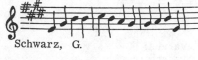

Maria sey gegruesst

    Sechter, S. (2)

Maria sollt nach Bethlehem geh'n

    Peeters, F.

Maria zart, von edler Art (Bo-
   hemian Brethren)
           Z 8552
    Schlick, A.
Variant:
O Jesu zart, in neuer Art

Maria zu lieben (Paderborn)

     Boslet, L.
     Griffiths, V. T.   Schmalz, P.
Variant:
Paderborn

     Hurford, P.

Marion (Messiter)

     Diggle, R.   Peeters, F.   Sowerby, L.
     Mead, E. G.   Sinzheimer, M. Wetherill, E. H.

Marlee (Sateren)

     Johnson, D. N.

Marosa
   See: Brother James Air (Bain)

Marter Gottes (Christi, Jesu) wer kann dein vergessen
   (Gnadauer)
   See: Herr und Aeltster

Martyn (Marsh)

     Ashford, E. L.   Lorenz, E. J. (2) Oley, H. M.
     Beck, A.   Markworth, H. J. Reuter, F.
     Bingham, S.   Matthews, H. A. Rogers, S. E.
     Haase, K.   Matthews, J. S. Stults, R. M.
     Larson, E. R.   Mueller, C. F.

Martyrdom (Wilson)

     Cameron, G.   Haase, K.   Lang, C. S.
     Conway, M. P.   Jewell, K. W.   Marchant, A. W.
     Groves, R.   Kroeger, W.   Miles, R. H.

Palmer C. C.   Powell, N. W.   Tootell, G. (2)
  Parry, C. H. H.   Rogers, S. E.   Willan, H.
Variant:
Avon

Bartow, N.   Edmundson, G.

Martyrs (Wesley)

Johnson, D. N.   Ridout, G.
Orr, R. R. K.   Sowerbutts, J. A.

Maryland, My Maryland
  See: O Tannenbaum

Maryton (Smith)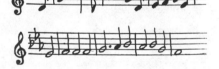

Herbek, R. H.
Peeters, F.   Rogers, L.

Mater Dolorosa
  See: Stabat Mater (Mainz)

Materna (Ward)

Beck, A.   Diggle, R.
Calver, F. L.   Hokanson, M.
Cushman, D. S.   Martin, R.
Demarest, C.   Whitford, H. P.

McComb (Sims)

Herbek, R. H.

Me ynskjer vaar brudgom
  (Swedish Psalm)

Karlsen, R.

Mear (Southern Harmony)

Buck, D.

Med fred og fryd jeg farer hen
  See: Mit Fried und Freud (Wittenberg)

Med Jesus vil jeg fara (Norse
  Folk)

Baden, C.
Bergh, L.   Karlsen, R.

Med Sorgen og Klagen (Wittenberg)
  See: Iam Moesta

Med straalekrans om tinde
  (Lindeman)

      Nielsen, L.   Skottner, F.
      Variant:
      No livnar det

      Baden, C.   Sandvold, A.

Med straalekrans om tinde (Vulpius)
  See: Ach bleib mit deiner

Medens vi i verden vandre

      Alnaes, E.

Medens vi i verden vandre (Zinck)
  See: Herre Jesu, kom til stede

Media Vita In Morte Sumus

      *Bonnal, J. E.
      Grabner, H. (2)   Lohet, S.

Meditation (Gower)

      Edmundson, G.
      Sowerby, L.   Taylor, C. T.

Meerstern, Ich dich gruesse

      Ahrens, J.

Meerstern, ich dich gruesse

      Frischmann, M.

Mein Auge wacht (Solingen)
                          Z 5040b
      Franke, F. W.
      Roth, F.

Mein banges Herz sei still   Tune not found

      Gulbins, M.

Mein erst Geschaeft (Gefuehl) sei Preis
  See: Ich dank dir schon (Praetorius)

Mein Freund zerschmilzt (Freylinghausen)
            Z 3138

    Krause, P.
    Piutti, K.
                           Rinck, J. C. H.
Variants:
Ak vidste du, som gaar (Freylinghausen)
Wie herrlich ist's ein Schaeflein

Mein Friedefuerst, dein freund-
liches Regieren

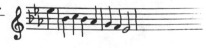

    Bachem, H.
    Knab, A.
                       Oechsler, E.
Variant:
Der du bist A und O

    Hasse, K.

Mein ganzes Herz erhebet dich
  See: Bohemian Brethren

Mein ganzes Herz erhebet dich
  See: Psalm 138 (Bourgeois)

Mein Glaub ist meines Lebens
Ruh (Knecht)
            Z 5829
    Burkhardt, C.

                       Reichardt, T.

Mein Gott, das Herze bring ich dir (Darmstadt)
                 Herz ich bringe
  See: Nun sich der Tag (Krieger)

Mein Gott, ich bin jetzt erschienen
  See: Herr, ich habe missgehandelt (Crueger)

Mein Gott, ich danke herzlich dir
  See: Wo Gott zum Haus nicht gibt sein Gunst
(Klug)

Mein Heiland nimmt die Suender
an (Churpfaelz)
            Z 7776
    Gerke, A.

Mein Heiland nimmt die Suender
an (Stoetzel)
            Z 7775
    Hasse, K.

Mein Heiland nimmt die Suender
an (Thommen)
　　　　　　　　　　Z 7766

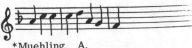

　　　Haase, K.　　　　　　　　*Muehling, A.
　　*Meibohm, D.　　　　　　　　*Rinck, J. C. H.

Mein Herz ermunt're dich
　　(Schulz)
　　　　　　　　　　Z 2886

　　　Rumpf, W.

Mein Herz und Seel' den Herrn
　　(Sohren)
　　　　　　　　　　Z 931

　　*Peters, A.

Mein Herze allzeit wandelt
　　(Nielsen)

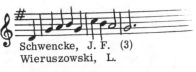

　　　Raasted, N. O.
　　Variant:
　　Mit hjerte altid vanker

Mein Jesu, dem die Seraphinen

　　　Baldamus, F.　　　　Schwencke, J. F. (3)
　　　Fluegel, G.　　　　　Wieruszowski, L.

Mein Jesu, der du mich
　　　　　　　　Z 2103
　　　Brahms, J.
　　　Claussnitzer, P. (2)　　　Piutti, K.

Mein Jesus ist mein Leben　　　Tune not found

　　　Muehling, A.　　　　Rinck, J. C. H.
　　　Ritter, A. G.

Mein Jesus, lass mein Herz empfoh'n
　　See: Nun danket all und (Crueger)

Mein Jesus lebt (Halle)
　　　　　　　　Z 2835

　　　Buehl, W.
　　　Graf, J.　　　　　　Lang, H.
　　　Kempff, W.　　　　Schwencke, J. F. (3)

Mein junges Leben hat ein End
　　(Folk Tune)

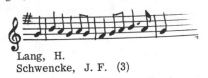

　　　Sweelinck, J. P.

Mein Leben ist ein Pilgrimstand
   See: Jervaulx Abbey

Mein schoenste Zier (Leipzig)
   See: In dich hab' ich gehoffet, Herr (Leipzig)

Mein schoenste Zier (Zuerich)
   See: In dich hab' ich gehoffet, Herr (Zuerich)

Mein Schoepfer steh mir bei
  (Meyer)
               Z 7479

Beck, A.	Haase, K.	Magnus, E.
Enckhausen, H. F.	Inderau, H.	Schwencke, J. F. (2)
Franke, F. W.	Kickstat, P.	Stolze, H. W.

Mein' Seel' erhebt den Herren
  (Strassburg)
               Z 7550
  Variants:
  Kom hjerte, ta ditt regnebrett

    Karlsen, R.   Raasted, N. O.

  O store Gud, din kaerlighed (Strassburg)

    Godske-Nielsen, H.   Moeller, S. O.

Mein' Seel', O Herr, muss loben dich
   See: Lasst uns zum Kreuze (Danish)

Mein Testament soll sein am End

    *Kunkel, F. J.

Mein Zufluckt alleine
   See also: My Refuge Alone

    Ahrens, J.   Brand, T.

Meine Hoffnung stehet feste
  (Neander)
               Z 4870

Baldamus, F.	Oley, J. C.
Claussnitzer, P.	Rinck, J. C. H.
Hasse, K.	Rudnick, W.
Kuehn, K.	*Schaab, R.

  Variants:
  Meine Seele lass es gehen (Darmstadt)

    Pachelbel, W. H.   Umbreit, K. G.

Meine Hoffnung stehet feste (cont.)

Op, I kristne, ruster eder

    Nielsen, L.

Meine Hoffnung steht auf Gott
(Dresden)
                Z 1876
    Claussnitzer, P. (2)   Krause, P.

Meine Hoffnung steht auf Gott (Freylinghausen)
    See: Hoechster Priester (Freylinghausen)

Meine Lebenszeit verstreicht
    See: Jesu, meine Zuversicht

Meine Liebe haengt am Kreuz
(Witt)
                Z 1866
    Fischer, M. G.
    Rinck, J. C. H.   Umbreit, K. G.
    Variant:
Song 45 (Dutch)

    Bijster, J.

Meine Seele erhebet den Herren
(Klug) (Magnificat, Tonus
Peregrinus)
    Bach, J. C.   Rheinberger, J.
    Bach, J. S. (2)   Scheidt, S. (2)
    Dupré, M. J. J.   Schiefferdecker, J. C.
    Moe, D.   Stolze, H. W.
    Pachelbel, J.   Strungk, D. (2)
    Piutti, K.   Walther, J. G. (3)
Variants:
Gott sei uns gnaedig und barmherzig

    Piutti, K.   Rinck, J. C. H.

    Magnificat (Tonus Peregrinus)

    Pachelbel, J.

Meine Seele gib das Brot
    See: Da Christus geboren war (Bohemian)

Meine Seele ist still zu Gott
    See: Psalm 24 (Geneva)

Meine Seele lass es gehen (Darmstadt)
    See: Meine Hoffnung stehet feste (Neander)

Meine Seele, wach auf (Finnish   Tune not found
Folk Tune)

    Krohn, I. H. R.

Meinen Jesum lass ich nicht
(Kuehnau)
           Z 3460
    Hasse, K.

Meinen Jesum lass ich nicht

    Kunze, K.

Meinen Jesum lass ich nicht
(Swedish)
           Z 3450
    Palme, R.
    Rumpf, W.
Variant:
Gaa nu hen og grav (1668)

    Nielsen, L.

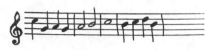

Wettstein, H. (2)

Meinen Jesum lass ich nicht,
Jesus (Lueneberg)
           Z 3448a
    *Bach, A. W.
Variant:
Jesus ist mein Aufenthalt

    Luard-Selby, B.

Meinen Jesum lass ich nicht,
Jesus (Darmstadt)
           Z 3455

Doebler, K.	Hulse, C. Van	Reuter, F. (2)
*Engelbrecht, K. F.	Kaeppel, G. C. A.	Stecher, H.
Fischer, M. G.	Lenel, L.	Stolze, H. W.
*Fluegel, G.	Marpurg, F. W.	Umbreit, K. G. (2)
Franke, F. W.	*Papperitz, B. R.	Wedemann, W.
Haase, K.	Reger, M.	Wendel, H. C.
Herzog, J. G. (2)	Reinbrecht, F.	Wettstein, H. (2)

Variant:
Jesum lieb ich ewiglich

    Sachs, J. G.

Meinen Jesum lass ich nicht,
weil (Hammerschmidt)
           Z 3449

Meinen Jesum lass ich nicht, weil (cont.)

Herzogenberg, H. von   Trautner, F. W.
Krebs, J. L. (2)   Walther, J. G. (3)
Kuntze, C.   Wolfrum, K.
Reuter, F.
Variant:
Seele, was ermuedst du dich (Hammerschmidt)

Weinreich, W.

Meinen Jesum lass ich nicht,
weil (Ulich)
                    Z 3451
Bender, J. (2)   *Oechsler, E.
*Boehner, J. L.   Otto, H.
Claussnitzer, P. (2)   *Oversold, H.
Drischner, M. (2)   Piutti, K. (2)
Eckardt, A. (2)   Raphael, G.
*Erbe, K.   Reda, S.
Ergenzinger, H.   Reger, M.
Franke, F. W.   Ricek, W.
Hennig, W.   Schaab, R. (2)
Hoyer, K.   *Schilling, A.
Karg-Elert, S.   Schmidt, F.
Kickstat, P.   *Schueler, H.
Klaus, V.   Schwencke, J. F. (3)
*Krause, P.   *Stapf, O.
*Meibohm, D. (4)   *Stiller, K.
Merkel, G. (2)   Streicher, J. A.
*Muehling, A.   Traegner, R.
Mueller, S. W.   Weber, H.
Mueller, W. A.   Wettstein, H.
Variants:
Dennoch bleib ich stets

Looks, R.

Jesu, grosser Wunderstern

Meyer, R.

Jesu nimmt die Suender an

Abel, O.

Jesus soll die Loesung sein

Koch, J. H. E.   Pfeiffer, C. D.

Licht vom Licht, erleuchte mich

Hasse, K.

Seele, was ermuedst du dich (Ulich)

    Hasse, K.

Meins Herzens Jesu, meine Lust
   (Halle)
            Z 8766
    *Rumpf, W.

Meins Herzens Jesu, meine Lust
   See: Elbing (Sohren)

Melcombe (Webbe)

Best, W. T.	Mansfield, O. A.	Parry, C. H. H.
Canning, T.	Matthews, H. A.	Peeters, F.
Conway, M. P.	McKinley, C.	Rowley, A.
Haase, K.	Noble, T. T. (2)	Willan, H.
Lang, C. S.	Palmer, C. C.	

Melita (Dykes)

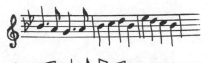

    Calver, F. L.
    Frost, C. J.   Peeters, F.
    Gaul, H.   Vergolet, P.

Men of Harlech (Welsh)

    Faulkes, W.

Mendebras (German)

    Ashford, E. L.

Mendelssohn

    Ashford, E. L.   Lutkin, P. C.
    Clark, L. S.   MacLean, D.   Schumacher, M. H.
    Conway, M. P. Marier, T. N.   Stults, R. M. (2)
    Gehrke, H.   Nordman, C.   Walton, K.
    Haase, K.   Purvis, R.   Wyton, A.
   Variant:
   Herald Angels

    Dinelli, G.   James, F.
    Frysinger, J. F.   Rogers, S. E.

Mendon (German)

    Dickey, M.   Hulse, C. Van
    Gehrke, H.   McKinley, C.
    Haase, K.   Peeters, F.

Mens Impletur (Gregorian)

    Falcinelli, R.

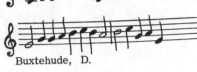

Mensch, willst du leben seliglich
(Walther)
                Z 1956

    Ahle, J. R.

Buxtehude, D.

Menschen die ihr wahrt verloren

    Sister M. F.

Mentzer
  See: O dass ich tausend Zungen haette (Koenig)

Merchant's Carol (English)

    Thomas, V. C.
  Variant:
  Golden Carol

Merck toch hoe sterck

    Kee, C.
    Zwart, W. H.

Mercy (Gottschalk)

    Frick, B.
    Gottschalk, L. M.
    Mueller, C. F.
    Reuter, F.
    Reynolds, W. G.
  Variants:
  Gottschalk

    Dasher, J. A.

Manna

    Coleman, R. H. P.

Saul, T.
Thompson, V. D.
Walton, K.
Young, G.

Purvis, R.

Mercy, O Thou Son of David
(U. S. Southern)

    Read, G.

Meribah (Mason)

    Beck, A.
    Haase, K.

Merrial (Barnby)

  Davis, C. M.
  Larson, E. R.   Taylor, C. T. (2)
  Stults, R. M.   Thompson, V. D.

Merton (Monk)

  Cassler, G. W.   Kitson, C. H.
  Groves, R.   Lang, C. S.

Messiah (Harold-Kingsley)

 Variant:
 Bradford

  *Reuter, F.

Messiah (Swedish)

  Cassler, G. W.
 Variant:
 Bereden vaeg foer Herran

  Aahgren, K. E.   Dickey, M.

Middelpunt van ons verlangen
 See: O du Liebe meiner Liebe (Basel)

Midt i livet
 See: Mitten wir im Leben sind

Midt igennen noed og fare (Laub)

  Thuner, O. E.

Mig hjaertelig nu laenges
 See: Herzlich tut mich verlangen

Mijn God, mijn God, waarom verlaut
 See: Psalm 22

Mijn hart, vervuld
 See: Psalm 45

Milde Jesu, du som sagde
 See: Cramer (Rousseau)

Miles Lane (Shrubsole)

Miles Lane (cont.)

    Attwater, J. P.   Rowley, A.
    Hustad, D.   Stults, R. M.
    McKay, G. F.   Webber, W. G.
    Mueller, C. F.   Whitney, M. C.
    Peeters, F.   Willan, H.
Variant:
Lov Jesu namn

    Gangfloet, S.   Sandvold, A.
    Nielsen, L.

Min doed er mig (Vulpius)
   See: Ach bleib mit deiner

Min glede i min Gud (Kingo)

    Nielsen, L.
Variants:
Frisk op min sjael (Breitendich)

    Thuner, O. E.

  Naar jeg betaenker tid og stund

    Frellsen, E.   Thuner, O. E.
    Moeller, S. O.   Videroe, F.

Min Gud, jeg gammel (Thomissoen)

    Godske-Nielsen, H.
    Hamburger, P.   Videroe, F.

Min hoegste skatt
   See: O Jesu Christ, du hoechstes Gut (Crueger)

Min Jesus, han er mig   Tune not found

    Thuner, O. E.

Min Jesus, lad mit hjerte faa
  (Nielsen)

    *Jensen, S.
Variant:
Er du modfalden

    Frandsen, H. B.

Min Jesus, lad mit hjerte faa
   See: Nun danket all und (Crueger)

Min lodd falt mig liflig (Cappelen)

　　　Nielsen, L.
　　　Skottner, F.

Min lodd falt mig liflig (Norsk
　Folk Tune)

　　　　Karlsen, R.
　　　Variant:
　　Gaa varsamt, O sjael

　　　　Baden, C.

Min mund og mit hjerte (Linde-
　man)

　　　Frandsen, H. B.
　　　Godske-Nielsen, H.　　　Videroe, F.
　　　Thuner, O. E.　　　　　Wuertz, J.

Min sjael, du Herren love (Kugelman)
　See: Nun lob mein Seel den Herren

Min sjael, du maaste, nu gloem-
　ma

　　　Berg, G.　　　　　　Lindroth, H.

Min sjael, min sjael, lov Herren
　(Lindeman)

　　　Karlsen, R.　　　　Lindeman, K.

Min sjael, min sjael, lov Herren (Kugelman)
　See: Nun lob mein Seel (Kugelman)

Min sjael och sinne
　See: Wer nur den lieben Gott (Neumark)

Min sjael og aand (Thomissoen)

　　　Haase, K.
　　　Nielsen, L.　　　　Peeters, F.
　　Variants:
　　Island
　　Om himmerigs rige

　　　Jeppesen, K.　　　Woeldike, M. A.
　　　Thuner, O. E.

Min stoerste hjertens glaede
　See: Herzlich tut mich erfreuen

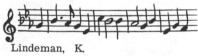

Mindes vi en fuldtro ven (Hartmann)

    Frandsen, H. B.   Moeller, S. O.

Mir ist Erbarmung widerfahren
  See: O dass ich tausend (Koenig)

Mir ist Erbarmung widerfahren
  See: Wer nur den lieben Gott (Neumark)

Mir nach, spricht Christus
  See: Mach's mit mir Gott

Missionary Hymn (Mason)

    Ashford, E. L.   Haase, K.   Stelzer, T. G.
    Beck, A.   Peeters, F.   Stults, R. M.
    Bingham, S.   Reuter, F.   West, J. A.

Mit dem Herrn fang alles an
(Grobe)

    Unbehaun, G.   Vogel, P.

Mit diesem neuen Jahre

    Peeters, F.

Mit Ernst, O Menschenkinder
  See: Von Gott will ich nicht lassen (Erfurt)

Mit Freuden zart
  See: Bohemian Brethren

Mit Fried' und Freud' fahr ich
dahin (Wittenberg)
              Z 3986

Bach, J. C.	Hark, F.	Peeters, F.
Bach, J. S.	Hennig, W.	Pepping, E. (2)
Bausznern, W. von	Herzog, J. G. (2)	Piutti, K.
Bornefeld, H.	Hoyer, K.	Raasted, N. O.
Buxtehude, D. (2)	Kaeppel, G. C. A.	Ramin, G. (2)
Claussnitzer, P.	Karow, K.	Reger, M. (2)
David, J. N.	Kickstat, P.	Rinck, J. C. H.
Dupré, M. J. J.	Krause, P.	Roth, H.
Egidi, A.	Krieger, J.	Vierling, J. G.
Fischer, M. G.	Looks, R.	Walcha, H.
Gesius, B.	Meibohm, D.	Weber, H.
Haas, J.	Othmayr, K.	Willan, H.
		Zachau, F. W. (2)

Variants:
Med fred og fryd jeg farer hen

    Godske-Nielsen, H.

Nunc Dimittis

    Johns, D.

Mit haab og troest (Thomissoen)

    Alnaes, E.
Variants:
Jeg arme synder

    Karlsen, R.

    Vor Gud er idel

Mit hjerte alltid vanker (Norse
Folk Tune)

    Baden, C.   Moseng, S.
Variant:
Jeg vil mig Herren love (Norse Folk Tune)

    Gangfloet, S.   Nielsen, L.

Mit hjerte altid vanker
  See: Mein Herze allzeit wandelt (Nielsen)

Mit hjerte goeres mig bange
  (Moeller)

    Moeller, S. O. (2)

Mit meinem Gott geh ich zur Ruh'
  See: In dich hab' ich gehoffet, Herr (Leipzig)

Mit singen dich zu loben (Boehner)

Z 5341
    Claussnitzer, P. (2)

Mit suessem Freudenschal
  See: In Dulci Jubilo

Mitt hjerte sig fryder (Lindeman)

    Bergh, L.
    Karlsen, R.

Mitten wir im Leben sind
    in dem (Walther)
                    Z 8502

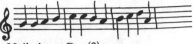

Blausznern, W. von	Meibohm, D. (2)
Clausing, F.	Micheelsen, H. F.
David, J. N.	Oechsler, E.
Driessler, J.	Oertzen, R. von
Faehrmann, H.	Peeters, F.
Fischer, M. G.	Pepping, E.
Franke, F. W.	Piutti, K.
Geierhaas, G.	Raphael, G.
Grabner, H.	Rinck, J. C. H.
Gronau, D. M.	Scheidt, S. (3)
Haase, K.	Schiske, K.
Hark, F.	Schmalz, P.
Jobst, M.	Stiller, K. (2)
Karow, K.	Vierling, J. G.
Kickstat, P.	Walcha, H.
Krause, P.	Walther, J. G.
Lenel, L.	Weber, H.

Variants:
Geistlich Bittfahrlied
Midt i livet

Moab (Roberts)

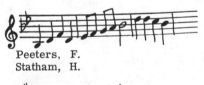

    Schmutz, A.

Mon bonheur vient de toi   Tune not found

    Hess, C. L.

Monkland (Antes)

    Cassler, G. W.
    Haase, K.   Peeters, F.
    Lang, C. S.   Statham, H.

Monksgate (English)

    Harris, W. H.

Monroe Place

    Beck, A.

Moon Shines Bright

    Faulkes, W.
    Milford, R.

Mooz Tsur
  See: Rock of Ages

More Love to Thee (Doane)

    Andrews, B.
    Edmundson, G.   Thompson, V. D. (2)
    Lawrence, M. F.   Wilson, R. C.
  Variant:
  Proprior Deo

    Goode, J. C.

Morecambe (Atkinson)

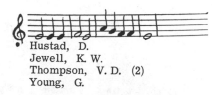

    Couper, A. B.
    Diggle, R.   Hustad, D.
    France, W. E.   Jewell, K. W.
    Hulse, C. Van   Thompson, V. D. (2)
                     Young, G.

Morewellham (Steggall)

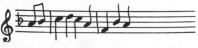

    Bingham, S.

Morgenglanz der Ewigkeit (Freylinghausen)
         Z 3427

Baldamus, F.	Hoyer, K.	Palme, R. (2)
Bender, J.	Hulse, C. Van	Peeters, F.
Beyer, M.	Huth, A.	Petzold, J.
Brieger, O.	Kaminski, H.	Pfaff, H.
Claussnitzer, P.	Kaun, H.	Piutti, K.
Doebler, K.	Kerst, S.	Reda, S.
Egidi, A.	Kickstat, P.	Reger, M.
Ehinger, H. R.	Krause, P.	Ricek, W.
Fiebig, K.	Kuehmstedt, F.	Rumpf, W.
Forchhammer, T.	Kuehn, K.	Schneider, F. C.
Franke, F. W. (3)	Kunze, K.	Schueler, H.
Grabner, H.	Leupold, A. W.	Seyerlen, R.
Grundmann, O. A.	Lubrich, F., Jr.	Streicher, J. A. (2)
Haase, K.	Mendelssohn, A.	Walcha, H.
Hark, F.	Merk, G.	Wettstein, H. (3)
Hennig, W.	Mueller, S. W.	Weyhmann, J. W.
Hoeller, K.	Oley, J. C.	Wolfrum, K. (3)

  Variants:
  Jesu, Trost der armen Seelen

    Enckhausen, H. F.

  Oremus

    Edmundson, G.

Morgenglanz der Ewigkeit (cont.)

Seele, was ist schoeneres wohl

    Schneider, F. C.   Umbreit, K. G.
    Schwencke, J. F. (2)

Song 128 (Dutch)

    Wilgenburg, D. van

Morgenstern
  See: Wie schoen leuchtet

Morgenstern der finstern Nacht

           Z 1852
    Doebler, K.   *Eham, M.

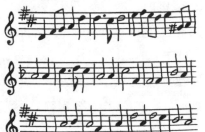

Morgenstern der finstern Nacht
  (Freylinghausen)
           Z 1853

Morgenstund har guld (Barnekow)

    Raasted, N. O.

Morgenstund har guld (Laub)

    Karlsen, R.
    *Wuertz, J.

Morgenzang
  See: Psalm 100

Morning Hymn (Barthelemon)

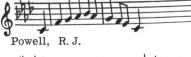

    Beebe, E. J.
    Haase, K.   Peeters, F.
    Lynn, G. A.   Thiman, E. H.

Morning Song (Wyeth- Union
  Harmony)

    Lynn, G. A.   Powell, R. J.

Morning Star (Harding)

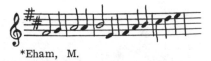

    Bender, J.   Frank, R.   Markworth, H. J.
    Cassler, G. W.   Haase, K.   Pinkham, D.
    Curry, R. D.   Hansen, C. B.   Reuter, F.

Moscow
   See: Giardini

Moultrie (Cobb)

    Hegedus, A.

Mount Olives   Tune not found

    Mansfield, O. A.

Muede bin ich (Fliedner)
              Z 1245
    Haase, K.

Muede bin ich (Basel)
   See: Hoechster Priester (Basel)

Mueller (Murray)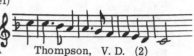

    Diemer, E. L.   Schmutz, A   Thompson, V. D. (2)
    Rogers, S. E.   Shaffer, J. E.   Vibbard, H.
    Variant:
    Away in a Manger

Muenster

    Larkin, J.
    Variant:
    Star Upon the Ocean

Mun sydaemeni temppelin (Fin-
   nish)

    Parviainen, J.

Mun tutkit, Herra (Finnish)

    Parviainen, J.
    Salonen, S.

Munich
   See: O Gott, du frommer Gott (Stoerl)

Muses soeurs de la (Denizot)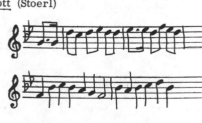

    Boëly, A. P. F.

My Gospel (Pennsylvania Dutch)

    Johnson, A. H.
    Variant:
    Wer Ohren hat zu hoeren

My Jesus, I Love Thee
   See: Gordon

My Jesus, Say What Wretch

    DeBrant, C.

My Lord, What a Morning
   (Negro Spiritual)

    Hancock, E. W.

My Redeemer (McGranahan)

    Colvin, H.

My Refuge Alone
   See also: Mein Zufluckt
   alleine

    Kreckel, P. G.

My Shepherd will Supply (Early
   American)

    Owens, S. B.   Young, G.

Naar i den stoerste (Lyons)
   See: Wenn wir in hoechsten Noethen (Bourgeois)

Naar jeg betaenker tid og stund
   See: Min glede i min Gud (Kingo)

Naar mig min synd vil krenke
   See: Hilf Gott, dass mir's gelinge (Thomissoen)

Naar mit oeje, traet af moeje
   (Laub)

    *Borg, O.   Thuner, O. E.

Naar mit oeie (Lindeman)
   See: Consolation (Lindeman)

Naar mit oeyle (Folk Tune)

    Baden, C.

Naar vi i stoerste (Lyons)
   See: Wenn wir in hoechsten Noethen

Nach einer Pruefung kurzer Tage
(Schickt)

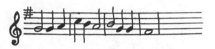

Z 2893

Brandt, A.
Claussnitzer, P. (2)
Forchhammer, T. (2)
Hoyer, K.
Karg-Elert, S. (2)
Krause, P.
Kuntze, C.
Lorenz, C. A.

Merkel, G.
Pfretzschner, C. R.
Piutti, K.
Sachs, J. G.
Schaab, R.
Steinhaeuser, K.
Stiller, K.
Streicher, J. A.

Nachtstueck
See: Canonbury (Schumann)

Naeher mein Gott
See: Bethany

Naermere dig, min Gud (R.
Karlsen)

Karlsen, R.

Naglet til et kors paa jorden
(Norse Folk)

Karlsen, R.

Naglet til et kors paa jorden
(Zinck)

Bergh, L.
Gangfloet, S.
Moseng, S.

Nielsen, L.
Skottner, F.

Naglet til et kors paa jorden (Nideros)
See: Ljoset yver landet (St. Olav's Fest)

Name of Jesus (Strom)

Cassler, G. W.
Lorenz, E. J.

Naomi (Naegeli)

Peeters, F.

Narenza (Cologne)

Macpherson, C.
Variant:
Ave Maria (Narenza)

Narenza (cont.)

   Ave Maria klare, du leichter Morgenstern

      Fischer, J. K. F. (3)   Spranger, J.

Nassau
  See: Mache dich, mein Geist, bereit

National Hymn (Warren)

     Bingham, S.
     Nordman, C.   Peeters, F.

Nativity (Lahee)

     Conway, M. P.

Naturen holder Pinsefest (Berg-
     green)

     Raasted, N. O.   Wuertz, J.
     Variant:
     Die Natur feiert das Pfingstfest

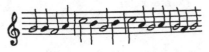

Natus est Nobis

     Tallis, T.

Navarre
  See: Psalm 118

Ne craignez pas (French Noël)   Tune not found

     Alain, A.

Ne te désole point
  See: Nun danket alle Gott

Neander
  See: Unser Herrscher (Neander)

Neapolitan Carol

     Warner, R. L.

Near the Cross (Doane)

     Colvin, H.   Porter, J. B.
     Hustad, D.   Thompson, V. D.

Nearer the Cross (Knapp)

Nolte, R. E.

Need (Lowry)

Bingham, S.
Hulse, C. Van
Larson, E. R.
Variant:
I Need Thee Every Hour

Miller, H. A.

Lorenz, E. J.
Rogers, S. E.
Thompson, V. D.

Neem, Heer, mijn bange
See: Psalm 5

Netherlands (Valerius)

Eyken, J. A. van
Fisk, B. H.
Floyd, H. A.
Hokanson, M.
Lange, R.
Lorenz, E. J.
Variants:
Kremser

McKay, G. F.
Nordman, C.
Whitford, H. P.
Zagwijn, H.
Zwart, J. (2)

Beck, A.
Bender, J.
Bingham, S.
Cassler, G. W.
Copes, V. E.
Gipe, R. A.

Haase, K.
Peeters, F.
Rohlig, H.
Steere, W. C.
Willan, H.

Wir treten zum beten

Beckman, G. W.
Hecht, G.
Hoyer, K.

Unbehaun, G.
Zwart, J.

Nettleton (Wyeth)

Ashford, E. L.
Thompson, V. D.

Young, G.

Neumark
See: Wer nur den lieben Gott (Neumark)

New Orleans (Sellers)

Herbek, R. H.

New Ulm (Reuter)

    Haase, K.

Newbury (English)

    Willan, H.

Newington (Maclagen)

    Hulse, C. Van

Newtoun
    See: London New

Nicaea (Dykes)

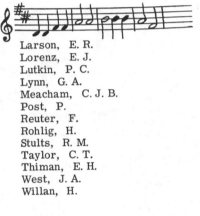

        Andrews, B.   Larson, E. R.
        Ashford, E. L.   Lorenz, E. J.
        Beck, A.   Lutkin, P. C.
        Bielawa, H.   Lynn, G. A.
        Calver, F. L.   Meacham, C. J. B.
        Canning, T.   Post, P.
        Diggle, R.   Reuter, F.
        Gangfloet, S.   Rohlig, H.
        Goemanne, N.   Stults, R. M.
        Griffiths, V. T.   Taylor, C. T.
        Groves, R.   Thiman, E. H.
        Haase, K.   West, J. A.
        Jackson, B.   Willan, H.
      Variant:
      Hellig, hellig (Dykes)

        Karlsen, R.   Sandvold, A.

Nicholson
    See: Lift High the Cross

Nicht eine Welt, die (Kocher)
    See: Aa du som kjenner all

Nicht Jerusalem (Pennsylvania
    Dutch)

    Johnson, A. H.

Nicht so traurig, nicht so sehr

    Piutti, K.

Nicht so traurig, nicht so sehr
 (Bach)
                    Z 3355
        Wordsworth, W. B.

Nicht so traurig, nicht so sehr
 (Pressburg)
                    Z 3342
        Coleman, R. H. P.   *Stolze, G. C.
        Oley, J. C.   Toepfer, J. G.

Nicht um Reichtum, nicht (Rinck)
                    Z 6752
        *Vierling, J. G.

Nimm von uns, Herr, du treuer Gott
    See: Vater unser

Nina, Nana

        Marier, T. N.

Ninety and Nine (Bridge)

        Lorenz, E. J.

No koma Guds englar (Norsk)

        Nielsen, L. (2)

No livnar det (Lindeman)
    See: Med straalekrans om tinde (Lindeman)

Nobody Knows (Negro Spiritual)

        Archer, J. S.   Thomas, V. C.

Nocte Surgens (Sarum)

        Groves, R.
        Variant: Shaw, G. T.
        Trinity Office Hymn

Noël

        Barbier, R. A. E.

Noël - A la venue de Noël
    See: A la venue de Noël

Noël - Ah ma Voisine es tu
   fachée

    Balbastre, C.

Noël Alsacien

   Variant:
   Sleep Well, Child of Heaven

    Guilmant, A. (2)

Noël ancien
   See: Noël - Ile de France

Noël Angevin

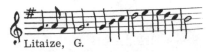

    Franck, C.   Litaize, G.
   Variant:
   Infant King

    Ratcliffe, D.

Noel - Appelons Nau (Poitevin)

    Villard, J. A.

Noël - Au ciel d'hiver
   See: Noël pour l'amour de Marie

Noël - Au jô deu de pubelle

    Balbastre, C.

Noël Basque

    Benoit, Dom P.

Noël - Carol of the Birds
   See: A la venue de Noël

Noël - Cei-ci le moître De tô
   l'univar

    Balbastre, C.

Noël - Cette journée

    Daquin, L. C.
    Lebègue, N. A.

Noël - Chantons je vous prie

    Daquin, L. C.

Noël - Chrétien

    Daquin, L. C.

Noël - Dans cette étable
  See: Dans cette étable

Noël - Dans la nuit
  See: Noël Étranger

Noël d'Arnais   Tune not found

    Reichenbach, H.

Noël de Chartres
  See: Chartres

Noël en Carillon
  See: Noël nouvelet

Noël - Entre le boeuf
  See: Gevaert

Noël Étranger

    Daquin, L. C.
    Variant:
    Noël - Dans la nuit

    Daquin, L. C.

Noël flamand

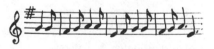

    Joulain, J.

Noël - Grand dei, ribon ribeine

    Balbastre, C.

Noël - Il est né
  See: Il est né

Noël - Il est un petit L'ange
  See: Noël suisse

Noël - Ile de France

    Huré, J.

Noël - Ile de France (cont.)

   Variant:
   Noël ancien

      Doyen, H.

Noël - Je me suis levé

      Daquin, L. C.

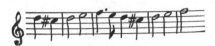

Noël - Joseph est bien marié
   See: Joseph est bien marié

Noël - Joseph revenant un jour

      Balbastre, C.

Noël-Languedocien

      Guilmant, A.

Noël - Lei plus sage (Saboly
   #33)

      Bourdon, E.

Noël - Les anges dans nos
   See: Les anges dans nos

Noël - Lor qu'en la saison
   (Bourguignon)

      Fleury, A.

Noel! Noel! (French-English)

      Gotch, O. H.

Noël - Nous sommes trois

      Borucchia, N.

Noël - Nous voici dans la ville
   See: Chartres

Noël nouvelet

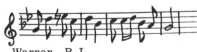

      Banks, H.
      Couper, A. B.   Warner, R. L.
      Dupré, M. J. J.   Webber, W. S. L.
      Harker, F. F.   Wilson, R. C.

Variants:
Love Is Come Again

Thomas, V. C.

Noël en Carillon

Noël - O Dieu de clémence
See: Noël suisse

Noël - Or dites-nous Marie
See: Chartres

Noël - Où s'en vont ces gais
bergers

Balbastre, C.

Noël pour l'amour de Marie

Daquin, L. C.
Variant:
Noël - Au ciel d'hiver

Daquin, L. C.

Noël pour l'amour de Marie
(Troubadours)

Borucchia, N.

Noël - Qu' Adam fut

Daquin, L. C.

Noël - Quand Dieu naquit
Jésus

Balbastre, C.
Bingham, S.   Daquin, L. C.

Noël - Quittez, pasteurs
See: Quittez, pasteurs

Noël - Quoique soyez Petit encore
See: Quoique soyez Petit encore

Noël suisse

Daquin, L. C.

Noël suisse (cont.)

Variants:
Noël - Il est un petit L'ange

Balbastre, C.

Noël - O Dieu de clémence

Franck, C.

Noël - Tous les Bourgeois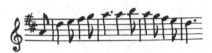

Balbastre, C.

Noël - Un flambeau
See: Bring a Torch

Noël - Une bergère jolie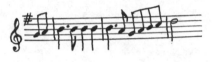

Daquin, L. C.

Noël - Une jeune pucelle
                vièrge
See: Von Gott will ich nicht (Erfurt)

Noël - Voici le Noël
See: Voici le Noël

Noël Vosgien

Bouvard, J.

Noël - Votre bonté grand Dieu

Balbastre, C.

Noël Wallon

Plum, P. J. M. (2)

Nog juicht ons toe die zaalige   Tune not found
Nacht

Zwart, J.

Non Nobis Domini (Williams)

Sowerby, L.

Nordstern (1671)
    Based on Zu Bethlehem gebo-
    ren

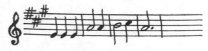

        Peeters, F.

Norham (Walker)

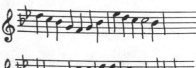

        Walker, E.

Norrland (Swedish)

        Haase, K.

Nos Autem (Mode 4)

        Woollen, R.

Nous voici dans la ville
    See: Chartres

Novello
    See: St. Thomas (Wade)

Now Glad of Heart

    Variant:
    German Carol

        Peek, R. M.

Nu bede vi den Helligaand
    See: Soldau (Wittenberg)

Nu er frelsens dag (Lindeman)

        Nielsen, L.
        Sandvold, A.
    Variant:
    Som den gylne sol frembryter (Lindeman)

        Baden, C.   Gangfloet, S.

Nu falmer skoven trindt om land
    See: Im Walde faellt das Laub

Nu fryde sig hver kristen mand
    (Hartmann)

        Thuner, O. E.

Nu fryde sig hver kristen mand (Nuernberg)
    See: Nun freut Euch, lieben (Nuernberg)

Nu hjertelig jeg lenges
  See: Herzlich tut mich verlangen

Nu hviler mark og enge
  See: Innsbruck

Nu kjaere menige kristenhet
  See: Nun freut Euch, lieben (Nuernberg)

Nu kom der bud fra engelkor (Zinck)
  See: Nun Botschaft kam vom Engelchor

Nu la oss takke Gud
  See: Nun danket Alle Gott (Crueger)

Nu rinder solen op (Kingo)
  rinner

    *Frandsen, H. B.   Pasquet, J.

Nu rinder solen op (Schop)
  rinner

    Godske-Nielsen, H.   *Laub, T.

Nu rinder solen op (Zinck)
  rinner

    Frellsen, E.
    Haase, K.   Raasted, N. O. (2)
    Karlsen, R.   Thuner, O. E.
    Moeller, S. O.   Woeldike, M. A.
    Variants:
    Nun geht die Sonne
    Staa fast, min sjael, staa fast

    Hamburger, P.   Vaerge, A.

Nu ringer alle klokker

    Joergensen, G.

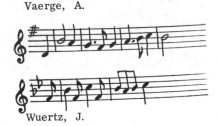

Nu ringer alle klokker (Weyse)

    Jeppesen, K.
    *Moeller, S. O.   Wuertz, J.

Nu sijt willekomme (Netherlands)
  See: Nun sei uns willkommen

Nu takker alle Gud
  See: Nun danket Alle Gott

Nu titte til hinanden (Weyse)

    Bitsch, V.
    Joergensen, G.   Lindorff-Larsen, E.

Nu vaagne alle Guds fugle smaa
(Weyse)

    Bitsch, V.   Lindorff-Larsen, E.

Nu velan, vaer frisk til mode
  See: Werde munter (Schop)

Nu vil vi sjunge (Laub)
  See: Nun woll'n wir singen

Nun bitten wir (Walther)
  See: Soldau (Wittenberg)

Nun Botschaft kam vom Engelchor (Zinck)

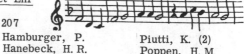

    Variant:
Nu kom der bud fra engelkor (Zinck)

    Godske-Nielsen, H.   Raasted, N. O.
    Hamburger, P. (2)   Rosenkilde-Larsen, E.
    Jensen, S.   Videroe, F.
    Matthison-Hansen, F.   Woeldike, M. A.

Nun danket all und bringet Ehr
  (Crueger)

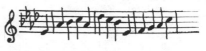

              Z 207

Barner, A.	Hamburger, P.	Piutti, K. (2)
Beck, A.	Hanebeck, H. R.	Poppen, H. M.
Biener, G.	Hark, F. (4)	Reda, S.
Buehl, W.	Herzog, J. N.	Reinbrecht, A.
Cabezon, A. de	Hoyer, K.	Rinck, J. C. H.
Cassler, G. W.	Hulse, C. Van	Rinkens, W.
Chemin-Petit, H.	Kickstat, P.	Rumpf, W.
Drischner, M. (2)	Kienzl, W.	Schrenk, J.
Eyken, J. A. van (3)	Klotz, H.	Schwarz, G.
Franke, F. W. (2)	Lang, H.	Schwencke, J. F. (2)
Gerhardt, C.	Leupold, A. W.	Vierling, J. G.
Godske-Nielsen, H.	Meibohm, D. (2)	Walcha, H.
Goller, F.	Micheelsen, H. F. (3)	Weinreich, W.
Graap, L.	Mueller-Zuerich, P. (2)	Wettstein, H.
Haase, K.	Peeters, F.	

Variants:
Graefenburg

    Rohlig, H.

Nun danket all und bringe Ehr (cont.)

  Ich sing' in Ewigkeit

    Franke, F. W.

  Ich singe dir mit Herz und Mund

Abel, O.	Fiebig, K.
Bender, J.	*Huebner, E.
*Doles, J. F.	Wieruszowski, L.

  Mein Jesus, lass mein Herz empfoh'n

    Raasted, N. O.

  Min Jesus, lad mit hjerte faa

Frandsen, H. B.	Nielsen, T. H.
Frellsen, E.	Raasted, N. O.
Jeppesen, K.	Soerensen, S.
Laub, T.	Weinholt-Pedersen, K.
Moeller, S. O.	Woeldike, M. A.

  Op alle som paa jorden bor

    Nielsen, L.

Nun danket alle Gott (Crueger)

Z 5142

Archer, J. S.	Fluegel, G.	Kauffman, G. F. (2)
Ashford, E. L. (2)	Fort, R. E.	Kee, C.
Asma, F.	Froberger, J. J.	Kempff, W.
Bach, J. S.	Gerhardt, P.	Kickstat, P.
Baldamus, F.	Grote, H.	Knab, A.
Barner, A. (2)	Gulbins, M. (2)	Knight, V.
Bender, J. (2)	Haag, H.	Koeckert, C.
Beyer, M.	Haase, H. H.	Kuntze, C.
Boehner, J. L.	Haase, K.	Lang, H.
Brieger, O. (2)	Haase, R.	Leupold, A. W.
Buckland, J.	Hark, F.	Linnarz, R.
Claussnitzer, P.	Hasse, K. (3)	Liszt, F.
Conway, M. P.	Hegedus, A.	Manz, P.
Copley, R. E. (2)	Herzogenberg, H. von (2)	
Dicks, E. A.	Hess, C.	Markull, F. W.
Diemer, E. L. (2)	Hesse, A. F.	Meibohm, D. (5)
Diggle, R.	Hoepner, C. G.	Merkel, G. (2)
Draht, T.	Hoyer, K.	Moser, R.
Drischner, M.	Hulse, C. van	Mueller, C. F.
Dupré, M. J. J.	Jackson, F. A.	Mueller, S.
Edmundson, G.	Karg-Elert, S.	Mueller-Zuerich, P.
Enckhausen, H. F.	Karow, K. (3)	Oldroyd, G.

Oley, J. C. (3)
Palme, R.
Peery, R. R.
Peeters, F. (2)
Peters, A.
Piutti, K. (2)
Post, P.
Purvis, R.
Pye, J. T.
Raphael, G.
Rebling, G.
Reger, M. (4)
Rembt, J. E. (2)
Reuter, F.
Rinck, J. C. H. (3)
Roeder, E. O.
Rohlig, H. (2)
Rowley, A.
Rudnick, W. (2)

Rumpf, W.
Saxton, S. E.
Schaab, R. (2)
Schehl, J. A.
Schmeel, D.
Schmidt, F.
Schneider, J. G.
Schuetze, W.
Schwencke, J. F. (4)
Sewell, M. G.
Steenberg, P.
Steinhaeuser, K.
Stolze, H. W. (2)
Tauscher, A. W.
Telemann, G. P. (2)
Teschner, W.
Thiman, E. H.
Toepfer, J. G.

Vierling, J. G.
Vogel, P. (2)
Voigtmann, R. J.
Volckmar, F. W. (2)
Volckmar, W. V.
Wagner, A.
Waters, C. F.
Wedemann, W.
Weelden, J. van
Weiss, C. A.
Werner, J. J.
Wettstein, H. (3)
Whitford, H. P.
Whitney, M. C.
Woyrsch, F. (2)
Wurm, A.
Yates, J. H.
Zehrfeld, O.

Variants:
Danket dem Herrn

Rudnick, W.

Gelobet sei der Herr, der Gott Israels

Koch, J. H. E.
Meyer, R.

Piutti, K.
Wieruszowski, L.

Herr Gott dich loben wir

Hessenberg, K.

I dag er naadens tid

Raasted, N. O.

Ne te désole point

Hess, C. L.

Nu la oss takke Gud
Nu takker alle Gud

Bergh, L.
Christensen, B.
Frellsen, E.
Haarklou, J.

Hamburger, P. (3)
Noerholm, I.
Raasted, N. O.
Videroe, F.

Song 135 (Dutch)

Beek, W. van
Rippen, P.

Westering, P. C. Van
Wilgenburg, D. van

Nun freut Euch Gottes Kinder all

Z 364

Walther, J. G.

Nun freut Euch Gottes Kinder all
See: Was fuercht'st du, Feind Herodes (Franck)

Nun freut Euch hier und ueberall
See: Wach auf, mein Herz, die Nacht ist hin

Nun freut Euch in Gott

Heer, E.
Wieruszowski, L.

Nun freut Euch, lieben Christen
g'mein (Klug)

Z 4429

Bach, J. B. (2)	Kunze, K.	*Schaab, R.
Bach, J. C.	Merkel, G.	Scheidt, S.
*Bach, J. M.	Oley, J. C. (2)	Telemann, G. P. (2)
Bach, J. S. (2)	Pachelbel, J.	Umbreit, K. G.
Dupré, M. J. J.	Piutti, K.	Weckmann, M.
Gerber, H. N.	Reger, M.	
Krebs, J. L. (3)	Rinck, J. C. H. (2)	

Variants:
Auf Christi Himmelfahrt

Hoyer, K.   Pfeiffer, C. D.
Pfannschmidt, H.   Wenzel, H.

Din spira, Jesu, straeckes ut

Berg, G.

Es ist gewisslich an der Zeit

Baldamus, F.	Haase, K.
Bender, J.	Hamburger, P.
Brieger, O.	Hasse, K. (2)
Claussnitzer, P.	Heinrich, J. G.
Driessler, J.	Huebner, E.
Drischner, M. (2)	Inderau, H.
Enckhausen, H. F. (2)	Karow, K.
Engelbrecht, K. F.	Kickstat, P.
Fiebig, K.	Klotz, H.
Fluegel, E. P.	Krebs, J. L. (2)
Forchhammer, T.	Kuntze, C.
Fricke, R.	Merk, G.
Gerber, H. N.	Mueller, S.
Godske-Nielsen, H. (2)	Nagel, W.
Grote, H.	Oechsler, E.

Poppen, H. M.
Praetorius, M.
Reger, M.
Reincken, J. A.
Ricek, W.
Rinck, J. C. H. (4)
Rudnick, W.
Rumpf, W.
Stolze, H. W. (4)

Telemann, G. P.
Toepfer, J. G.
Vierling, J. G.
Wedemann, W.
Wettstein, H.
Wolfrum, K. (3)
Wurm, A.
Zahn, J.
Zipp, F.

Gott Lob, ein Schritt

Spiering, G.

Gud laeter sina

Aahgren, K. E.

Hvad kan os komme til for noed

Bergh, L.
Borg, O.
Frellsen, E.
Godske-Nielsen, H.

Jeppesen, K.
Laub, T.
Raasted, N. O.
Rosenkilde-Larsen, E.

Ich steh' an deiner Krippen hier

Krebs, J. L.

Ich steh' in meines Herren Hand

Hasse, K.

Luther's Hymn

Cutler, H. S.

Rohlig, H.

Schon ist der Tag von Gott bestimmt

Rinck, J. C. H.

Was kann uns kommen an

Tunder, F.

Nun freut Euch, lieben Christen
g'mein (Nuernberg)
Z 4427

Arfken, E.
*Bausznern, W. von
Bender, J. (2)
Bieske, W.
*Claussnitzer, P.
*David, J. N.

Doles, J. F.
Drischner, M.
Enckhausen, H. F.
Faulkes, W.
Fluegel, G.

Haase, K.
Herzog, J. G.
*Hoyer, K.
Karow, K. (2)
Kempff, W.

Nun freut Euch, lieben Christen g'mein (cont.)

Kickstat, P.	Rembt, J. E.	Sweelinck, J. P.
Leupold, A. W.	Reuter, F.	Trautner, F. W. (2)
Magnus, E.	Rinck, J. C. H.	Vierling, J. G.
Meibohm, D. (5)	Rudnick, W.	Volckmar, F. W.
Micheelsen, H. F. (2)	Rumpf, W.	Walcha, H.
Mueller, S.	Schneider, M.	Weckmann, M. (2)
Mueller, S. W.	Schuetze, W.	Wettstein, H.
Oechsler, E.	Schwencke, J. F. (2)	Wiemer, W.
Pepping, E.	Seiffert, U. (2)	Wolff, E. M.
Praetorius, M.	Stiller, K.	Wolfrum, K.
Quehl, H. F.	Stolze, H. W. (2)	Zipp, F. (2)
Reda, S.	Strebel, A.	

Variants:
Nu fryde sig hver kristen mand

Woeldike, M. A.

Nu kjaere menige kristenhet

Karlsen, R.

Var man maa nu

Berg, G.

Nun geht die Sonne
See: Nu rinder solen op (Zinck)

Nun geht mein Leib dem
See: Sjaa aakrane dei gulnar alt (Reimann)

Nun Hosianna Davids Sohn
(Koenig)
               Z 2544

Franke, F. W.   Haas, J.

Nun ist Ruh'   Tune not found

Rohwer, J.

Nun ist vorbei die finst're Nacht
(Burkhard)

Wieruszowski, L.

Nun jauchzet, all ihr Frommen
See: Aus meines Herzens Grunde

Nun jauchzt dem Herren (Han-
    nover)
    See also: Puer Nobis Nascitur
            Z 4490

Lorenzen, J.	Reda, S.
Metzger, H. A.	Wagner, A.
Micheelsen, H. F.	Weber, H.
Oertzen, R. von	Zipp, F. (2)
Raphael, G.	

Variant:
Ak vidste du, som gaar (Hannover)
Akk visste du, som gaar (Meyer)

Karlsen, R.

Nun jauchzt dem Herren
    See: Herr Jesu Christ, dich zu uns

Nun komm der Heiden Heiland

        Z 1174

Aahgren, K. E.	Haase, K.	Piutti, K.
Abel, O.	Heiss, H.	Reger, M.
Artmueller, K.	Hering, K. E.	Rinck, J. C. H.
Bach, J. S. (4)	Herzogenberg, H. von	Rudnick, W.
Bach, W. F. (2)	Homilius, G. A.	Schaab, R.
Baldamus, F.	Hulse, C. Van	Scheidt, S. (2)
Barlow, W.	Karow, K.	Schumacher, M. H.
Beck, A.	Kauffmann, G. F. (2)	Schwencke, J. F.
Bender, J.	Kickstat, P. (2)	Seiffert, U.
Bornefeld, H. (2)	Klotz, H.	Sivert, P.
Brosig, M. (2)	Kniller, A.	Stade, F. W.
Bruhns, N.	Krapf, G.	Stiller, K.
Buttstedt, J. H. (2)	Krebs, J. L.	Sweelinck, J. P.
Buxtehude, D. (2)	Krieger, J.	Telemann, G. P.
Crane, R.	Langstroth, I. S.	Tauscher, A. W.
David, J. N.	Luedders, P.	Vetter, A. N. (2)
David, T. C.	Magnus, E.	Vierling, J. G.
Diercks, J. H.	Markworth, H. J.	Villermont, de
Distler, H.	Meibohm, D. (2)	Volckmar, F. W.
Driessler, J.	Micheelsen, H. F.	Walcha, H.
Dupré, M. J. J.	Mueller, G.	Walther, J. G.
Enckhausen, H. F.	Oechsler, E.	Wiemer, W.
Fluegel, G.	Pachelbel, J. (2)	Wolfrum, K. (2)
Grundmann, O. A.	Palme, R.	Zachau, F. W. (6)
Gulbins, M.	Pfeiffer, C. D.	Zipp, F.

Variants:
Folkefrelsar (1524)

    Haugene, R. B.   Steenberg, P.

Nun komm der Heiden Heiland (cont.)

Gott sei Dank durch alle Welt

Haase, H. H.   Mueller, G.
Mendelssohn, A.   Schwartz, G. von

Op dog, Sion, ser du ej

*Wuertz, J.

Veni Redemptor Gentium

Egidi, A.   Pepping, E.
Herzog, J. G.   Scheidt, S.
Manz, P.

Nun kommt die Bluetenzeit
See: Ich dank dir, lieber Herre (Bohemian)

Nun lasst uns all mit Innigkeit
(Bohemian)
                Z 358

Peeters, F.

Nun lasst uns den Leib begraben
(Stahl)
                Z 352

Baldamus, F.   Kickstat, P.   Roeder, E. O.
Bieske, W.   Kuntze, C.   Rudnick, W.
Brieger, O.   Litzau, J. B.   Schaab, R.
Franke, F. W.   Meibohm, D. (3)   Vierling, J. G.
Fromm, H.   Metzger, H. A.   Walter, J.
Haase, K.   Pepping, E.   Weber, H.
Hoyer, K.   Piutti, K. (2)   Wedemann, W.
Karow, K.   Rinck, J. C. H. (3) Zipp, F.
Variants:
Der du, Herr Jesu, Ruh'

Meyer, R.

Die Seele Christe heil'ge mich

Nun lasst uns geh'n und treten (Selnecker)
See: Nun lasst uns Gott dem Herren Dank sagen

Nun lasst uns Gott dem Herren
Dank sagen (Selnecker)
                Z 159
        also in 4
               4

Bach, J. C.
Bachem, H.
Barner, A.
Buttstedt, J. H.
Doles, J. F.
Drischner, M. (2)
Faisst, I. G. F. von
Fleck, M.
Franke, F. W.
Freund, W.
Fromm, H.
Haase, K.
Hasse, K.
Hessenberg, K.
Huth, A.

Karg-Elert, S.
Kuntze, C.
Kunze, K.
Luebeck, V. (2)
Magnus, E.
Meibohm, D. (7)
Merkel, G.
Micheelsen, H. F.
Mueller, S.
Pachelbel, J. (2)
Piutti, K. (2)
Raphael, G.
Rembt, J. E.
Reuter, F.
Rudnick, W.

Rumpf, W.
Sachs, J. G.
Schaab, R. (2)
Scheidt, S.
Schrenk, J.
Schueler, H.
Schwencke, J. F. (2)
Umbreit, K. G.
Vierling, J. G.
Wedemann, W.
Wenzel, E.
Wettstein, H.
Willan, H.
Zachau, F. W. (4)
Zehrfeld, O. (2)

Variants:

Nun lasst uns geh'n und treten

Barbe, H.
Bender, J.
Gulbins, M.
Hennig, W.
Herrmann, K. H.

Hoyer, K.
Koch, J. H. E.
Micheelsen, H. F.
Mueller, G.
Wenzel, E.

O Jesu, meine Wonne

Reda, S.

Walther, J. G.

Wach auf, mein Herz, und singe (Selnecker)

*Baldamus, F.
 Brieger, O.
 Claussnitzer, P.
*Dienel, O. (2)
 Doebler, K.
 Fluegel, E. P.
*Gulbins, M.
 Hasse, K.
*Hoepner, C. G.
 Kickstat, P.

Krause, P.
Markull, F. W.
Marpurg, F. W.
Muehling, A.
Oley, J. C.
Saemann, K. H.
Thomas, G. A.
Toepfer, J. G.
Walther, J. G.

Nun lob den Herrn   Tune not found

Sechter, S.

Nun lob', mein Seel, den Herren
(Kugelman)
                    Z 8245
            Also in 4
                    4

Abel, O.
Arbatsky, Y.
Bach, J. C.

Baldamus, F.
Beck, A.
Bender, J. (2)

Brosig, M. (2)
Burkhardt, C.
Buxtehude, D. (4)

Nun lob', mein Seel, den Herren (cont.)

Claussnitzer, P.	Kauffmann, G. F. (2)	Rumpf, W.
Diercks, J. H.	Kempff, W.	Schaab, R.
Drischner, M.	Kickstat, P.	Scheidt, S.
Enckhausen, H. F.	Krause, P.	Schmidt, W.
Fiebig, K.	Lorenzen, J.	Schrader, H.
Fischer, M. G.	Markull, F. W.	Schueler, H.
Fluegel, G. (2)	Metzger, H. A.	Schwencke, J. F. (3)
Forchhammer, T.	Nicolai, J. G.	Steinhaeuser, K.
Franke, F. W.	Oley, J. C.	Stiller, K. (3)
Guilmant, A.	Olson, D.	Stolze, H. W. (2)
Gulbins, M.	Pachelbel, J. (2)	Traegner, R.
Haase, K.	Piutti, K. (2)	Vierling, J. G.
Haessler, J. W.	Praetorius, M. (2)	Walther, J. G. (3)
Hasse, K. (2)	Raasted, N. O.	Weber, H.
Herrmann, W.	Reda, S.	Wedemann, W.
Herzog, J. G.	Reichardt, B.	Zipp, F. (2)
Hessenberg, K.	Rinck, J. C. H. (2)	
Huth, A.	Rinkens, W.	

Variants:
Min sjael, du Herren love (Kugelman)

Jeppesen, K.	Thuner, O. E.
Raasted, N. O. (2)	Videroe, F.
Rosenkilde-Larsen, E.	Wuertz, J.

Min sjael, min sjael, lov Herren (Kugelman)

Nun loben wir mit Innigkeit
(Vulpius)   Z 340c

Pasquet, J.
Variants:
Erhoer, O Schoepfer

Walther, J. G.

Herr Jesu Christ, wahr Mensch und Gott (Vulpius)

Vierling, J. G.   Walther, J. G. (2)

I dag paa apostolisk (Weisse)

Hovland, E.   Nielsen, L.

Nun lobet Gott im hohen Thron
   See: Psalm 9

Nun lobet Gott im hohen Thron (Vulpius)
   See: Gelobt sei Gott (Vulpius)

Nun preiset alle Gottes Barmherzigkeit (Loewenstern)
Z 4089

Brieger, O.   Kickstat, P.
Claussnitzer, P.   Kuehn, K.
Drischner, M. (2)   Kunze, K.
Faehrmann, H.   Palme, R. (2)
Fiebig, K. (2)   Pfaff, H.
Forchhammer, T.   Piutti, K.
Grosse-Weischede, A.   Poppen, H. M.
Grundmann, O. A.   Streicher, J. A.
Haase, K.   Weber, H.
Hennig, W. (2)   Wettstein, H.
Hesse, A. F.   Willan, H.
Hoyer, K.   Wolfrum, K. (2)

Nun ruest dich, Held
See: Rueste dich, Held von Golgotha

Nun rueste dich, O Christenheit
(1566)

Weber, H.

Nun ruhen alle Waelder
See: Innsbruck

Nun sei uns willkommen (Dutch)

Bratt, C. G.   Roeseling, K.
Variants:
Nu sijt willekomme

Bonset, J.   Mens, L. J.
Dalm, W.   Nuenen, J. van
Dragt, J.   Vermulst, J.
Hoogewoud, H.   Westering, P. C. Van
Kee, C.

Nun sei willkommen, Jesu

Peeters, F.

Song 14 (Dutch)

Berg, J. J. van den   Stulp, G.

Welcome, Son of Mary

Nieland, J.

Nun sei willkommen, Jesu
See: Nun sei uns willkommen

Nun sich der Tag geendet hat

    Gulbins, M.

Nun sich der Tag geendet hat
  (Krieger)
              Z 212b

*Baldamus, F.	Muehling, A.
*Boenicke, H.	Muehling, H. J.
*Braehmig, B.	Muench, G.
*Brosig, M. (2)	Oley, J. C.
*Claussnitzer, P. (2)	Papperitz, B. R.
Enckhausen, H. F.	Piutti, K.
Fiebig, K.	Raphael, G.
Franke, F. W.	Rinck, J. C. H. (2)
Gore, R. T.	Sandloff, P.
Hass, J.	Schneider, F. C.
Haase, K.	Schwencke, J. F. (3)
Hofmeier, A.	Sorge, G. A. (2)
Huth, A.	Stade, F. W.
Kaeppel, G. C. A.	Steinhaeuser, K.
Karg-Elert, S.	*Thomas, O.
Kickstat, P.	Umbreit, K. G.
Krause, P. (3)	Vierling, J. G. (2)
Kuehn, K.	Walcha, H.
Kunze, K.	Walter, P. (2)
Meibohm, D. (2)	Wedemann, W. (2)
Merkel, G.	Wickenhausser, R.
Michl, A.	

Variant:
Mein Gott, das Herze bring ich dir (Darmstadt)

    Doles, J. F.   Rinck, J. C. H.
    Homilius, G. A.

Nun singet und seid froh
  See: In Dulci Jubilo

Nun triumphieret Gottes Sohn
  See: Heut triumphieret Gottes Sohn

Nun welkt im Wald ringsum das Laub
  See: Im Walde faellt das Laub

Nun will sich scheiden Nacht und
  Tag (Schuetz)

    Kraft, W. W.   Weber, H.

Nun wolle Gott, dass unser Sang
  See: Wo Gott zum Haus nicht gibt (Klug)

Nun woll'n wir singen und froehlich sein (Laub)

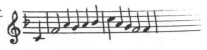

    Raasted, N. O.
Variant:
Nu vil vi sjunge

    Thuner, O. E.

Nunc Dimittis (Sternhold and
  Hopkins)

    Wood, C.

Nunc Dimittis
  See: Mit Fried' und Freud'

Nunc Dimittis (Genevan)
  See: Song of Symeon (Genevan)

Nunc Sancte Nobis Spiritus (Mode 4)

    Peeters, F.

Nunc Sancte Nobis Spiritus

    Sister M. G.

Nur frisch hinein (Darmstadt)

            Z 2090
    Claussnitzer, P.   Hasse, K.
    Fricke, R.   Piutti, K.

Nuremberg
  See: Liebster Jesu

Nutfield (Monk)

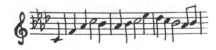

    Conway, M. P.
    Crawford, T. J.

Nyberg (Nyberg)

    Cassler, G. W.
Variant:
Der Mond ist aufgegangen

Nyland (Finnish)

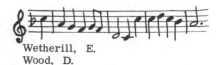

    Cummins, R.
    Hayton, R.   Wetherill, E.
    Peeters, F.   Wood, D.

Nyland (cont.)

 Variant:
 Som daggens paerlor glimma

  Kuusisto, T.

O Bethlehem, hoe blinkt (Old
Dutch Carol)

  Rippen, P.
 Variant:
 Song 16 (Dutch)

  Asma, F.

O bliv hos mig (Steenberg)

  Nielsen, L.

O bliv hos mig (Monk)
 See: Eventide

O Bone Jesu (Palestrina)

  DeBrant, C.

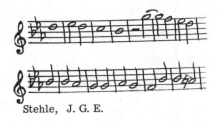

O Christ, hie merk

  Breitenbach, C. G. J.
  Ruedinger, G.   Stehle, J. G. E.
 Variant:
 Christe, hie merk

  Tod, E. A.

O Christ, j'ai vu ton agonie
 (Freylinghausen)

  Hess, C. L.

O Christe, Morgensterne
 (Gesius-Leipzig)
        Z 1661b
  Hark, F.   Proeger, J.
  Hasse, K.   Weber, H.

O Christenheit, sei hoch erfreut
 (Micheelsen)

  Micheelsen, H. F. (2)

O Come and Mourn
  See: Waer Gott nicht mit uns (Slovak)

O Come, O Come, Emmanuel
  (17th Century)

        Kreckel, P. G.

O Crux, Ave, Spes Unica
  See: Vexilla Regis Prodeunt (Sarum-Mode 1)

O dass doch bald
  See: Wenn wir in hoechsten Noethen (Bourgeois)

O dass ich tausend Zungen haette
(Dretzel)
                    Z 2858

     Haase, K.
     Manz, P.   Reuter, F.
  Variant:
  Der lieben Sonnen Licht (Pennsylvania Dutch)

     Johnson, A. H.

O dass ich tausend Zungen haette
(Gregor)
                    Z 2861b
     Brieger, O.   Hesse, A. F.

O dass ich tausend Zungen haette
(Koenig)
                    Z 2806
     Baldamus, F.   Hasse, K.
     Barner, A.   Hennig, W. (2)
    *Beck, A.   Hesse, A. F.
     Beckmann, G.   Karg-Elert, S.
     Bender, J.   Karow, K. (2)
     Bossler, K.   Kickstat, P.
     Bredack, W.   Klaus, V.
     Brieger, O.   Klotz, H.
     Claussnitzer, P. (3)   *Krause, P.
    *Dienel, O.   Kuehn, K.
     Enckhausen, H. F.   Kuntze, C.
     Fiebig, K.   Lorenzen, J.
     Fluegel, E. P.   Mendelssohn, A.
     Fluegel, G. (4)   Merk, G. (2)
    *Forchhammer, T. (2)   *Merkel, G.
     Franke, F. W. (2)   Micheelsen, H. F. (2)
    *Fricke, R.   Mueller, S. W.
     Gerhardt, P.   Nagel, W.
    *Grote, H. (2)   Oechsler, E.
    *Gruel, E.   Palme, R. (2)
     Haase, K.   Peeters, F.

O dass ich tausend Zungen haette (Koenig) (cont.)

    Pepping, E.   Rudnick, W.
   *Peters, A.   Rumpf, W. (2)
    Piutti, K. (2)   Schmidt, H.
    Ramin, G.   Schneider, M. G.
   *Rebling, G.   *Schumann, C.
    Reda, S. (2)   Streicher, J. A.
    Reger, M.   Trautner, F. W.
    Reinbrecht, A. (2)   *Volckmar, F. W. (2)
    Rembt, J. E.   Volkmann, P.
    Reuter, F.   Weber, H.
    Ricek, W.   Wettstein, H. (3)
    Rinck, J. C. H. (3)   Wolfrum, K. (2)
   *Roeder, E. O.   Zehrfeld, O. (2)
Variants:
Ach, sagt mir nichts

    Hasse, K.

Dies ist die Nacht, da mir

    Herrmann, K. H.   Meyer, R.

Ich bin getauft auf deinem Namen

   Brod, K.

Ich habe nun den Grund

    Hasse, K.

Mentzer
Mir ist Erbarmung widerfahren

    Hasse, K.

O Gott, von dem wir alles haben

    Wenzel, H.

O havde jeg dog tusind tunger

    Raasted, N. O.

Song 105 (Dutch)

    Koppenol, J.   Nauta, J.

O der alles haet verloren
   See: O wer alles haet verloren

O Dieu de clémence
 See: Noël Suisse

O du allersuesste Freude
 See: Werde munter

O du Froehliche
 See: Sicilian Mariners

O du Guds Lam (Laub)

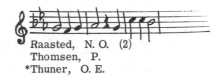

 Godske-Nielsen, H. Raasted, N. O. (2)
 Jeppesen, K.   Thomsen, P.
 *Moeller, S. O.   *Thuner, O. E.

O du Guds Lam uskyldig
 See: O Lamm Gottes, unschuldig

O du Helge Ande, kom till oss in

 Wikander, D.

O du hochheilig Kreuze (Koeln)

 Berghorn, A.
 Schwarz-Schilling, R. (2)

O du Liebe meiner Liebe (Darmstadt)
     Z 6693

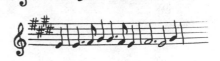

 Baldamus, F.   *Roeder, E. O.
 Franke, F. W.   Rudnick, W.
 Hoyer, K.   Spiering, G.
 Piutti, K.   Thomas, G. A.
 Rinck, J. C. H.

O du Liebe meiner Liebe (Herrn-
 hag - Ebeling)
 Minor mode   Z 6699
    also in 4
       4

 Bach, J. C.   Kickstat, P.
 Brieger, O.   Klaus, V.
 Buehl, W.   Klotz, H.
 Chaix, C.   *Koetzschke, H. (2)
 *Claussnitzer, P. *Krause, P.
 Drischner, M.   Meissner, H.
 Eyken, J. A. van *Oechsler, E.
 Faisst, I. G. F. von Pfaff, H.
 Fluegel, G.   Schink, H.
 Franke, F. W.   Schrenk, J.
 Hoyer, K.   Walter, K.
 Karg-Elert, S.

O du Liebe meiner Liebe (Herrnhag-Ebeling) (cont.)

Variants:
Bei dir, Jesu, will ich bleiben (Basel)

    Hasse, K.

Herz und Herz verreint zusammen (Basel)

    Abel, O.   Fiebig, K.
    Bender, J.   Klotz, H. (2)
    Brod, K.   Micheelsen, H. F.
    Drischner, M.   Mueller-Zuerich, P.
    Ehinger, H. R.   Otto, H.
    Ergenzinger, H.

Middelpunt van ons verlangen (Basel)

    Mazyk, R. van

O du Liebe meiner Liebe
(Basel)
Major mode

    Bodenschatz, S. H.   Rumpf, W.
    Fink, C.   *Seitz, J. A.
    Haase, K.   *Stiller, K.
    *Kleemeyer, H.   *Streicher, J. A.
    Peeters, F.   Taylor, C. T.
    Plettner, A.   Wettstein, H.
    *Poppen, H. M.   *Wolfrum, K.
    Ricek, W.

O du liebes Jesukind (Ebeling)

    Adler, E.

O Durchbrecher alle Bande (Basel)

    Wieruszowski, L. (2)

O gesegnete Regierung (Ebeling)
Singt dem Koenig Freudenpsalmen (Basel)

    Hoene, K. H.

Song 51 (Dutch)
Song 292 (Dutch)
Uren, dagen, maanden (Basel)

    Bouman, C. A.

O du liebes Jesukind
  See: O du Liebe meiner Liebe (Ebeling)

O du min aedle skatt
  See: O Gott du frommer Gott (Hannover)

O du min Immanuel (Winding)

    *Lindorff-Larsen, E.
    *Thuner, O. E.   *Wuertz, J.

O du min Immanuel (Crueger)
  See: Schwing dich auf (Crueger)

O du Selige
  See: Sicilian Mariners

O du vaar Herre, Jesu Krist
  See: Vater unser

O Durchbrecher alle Bande
  (Halle-Freylinghausen)
            Z 6709

    Abel, O.   Leupold, A. W.
    Claussnitzer, P.   Magnus, E.
    Ergenzinger, H.   Piutti, K.
    Fiebig, K.   Raasted, N. O.
    Franke, F. W.   Reda, S. (2)
    Godske-Nielsen, H.   Reger, M.
    Haase, K.   Ricek, W.
    Hasse, K.   Schmidt, W.
    Hofmeier, A.   Schmohl, G.
    Karg-Elert, S.   Schwencke, J. F. (2)
    Kickstat, P.   Seitz, J. A.
    Koetzschke, H.   Streicher, J. A.
    Kunze, K.   Thomas, O.
  Variants:
  Ach, erkennet, liebste Seelen (Freylinghausen)

    Enckhausen, H. F.   Stolze, H. W.

  Geist des Glaubens

    Koch, J. H. E.

  Jesus Christus ist erstanden

    Koehler-Wumbach, W.

  Op, min sjael, thi sol er oppe

    Rosenkilde-Larsen, E.   Thuner, O. E.

O Durchbrecher alle Bande (Halle-Freylinghausen) (cont.)

Overmaade fuldt av naade (Freylinghausen)

Bergh, L.   Karlsen, R.
Gangfloet, S.

Sehet, sehet, welche Liebe

Wenzel, H.

O Durchbrecher alle Bande (Basel)
See: O du Liebe meiner Liebe (Ebeling)

O Engel Gottes

Sechter, S. (2)

O Esca Viatorum (Haydn)
See: When Morning Gilds

O Esca Viatorum (Isaac)
See: Innsbruck

O Ewigkeit, du Donnerwort
(Schop)
                        Z 5820

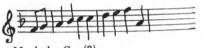

Baldamus, F.   Merkel, G. (2)
Burgstaller, A.   Metzler, F.
Claussnitzer, P.   Michl, A.
Enckhausen, H. F.   Muehling, A.
Eyken, J. A. van   Mueller, S.
Fischer, M. G.   Mulder, E. W.
Fluegel, G. (2)   Oley, J. C.
Franke, F. W.   Palme, R.
Gebhardi, L. E.   Piutti, K. (2)
Gerhardt, P.   Rinck, J. C. H.
Heger, R.   Rudnick, W.
Helmbold, C. A.   Scheel, G. R.
Hessenberg, K.   Schmidt, F.
Karg-Elert, S.   Schreck, G.
Karow, K.   Schwencke, J. F. (2)
Kickstat, P.   Stolze, H. W.
Kittel, J. C.   Vierling, J. G.
Koetzschke, H.   Volckmar, W. V.
Krauss, T.   Walther, J. G.
Krebs, J. L. (3)   Weber, H.
Marpurg, F. W.   Wolfrum, K. (2)
Merk, G.

O Fader vaar i himmerik
See: Vater unser

O Fairest Church (Sachs)

    Schreiner, A.

O Faithful Cross (Fortunatus)

    McGrath, J. J.

O Filii Et Filiae (French)

Amelsvoort, J. Van	Hulse, C. Van
Andrews, M.	Koch, J. H. E.
Andriessen, H. (2)	Kreckel, P. G.
Argenti, G.	Langlais, J. F.
Balogh, L. A.	Larkin, J.
Biggs, R. K.	Lemmens, N. J.
Boëly, A. P. F.	Loret, C.
Bratt, C. G.	Matthews, H. A.
Candlyn, T. F. H.	Milford, R. H.
Couper, A. B.	Pearce, C. W.
Dallier, H.	Peeters, F.
Dandrieu, J. F. (2)	Phillips, C. G.
DeBrant, C.	Planchet, D. C.
Demessieux, J.	Schehl, J. A.
Deshayes, H.	Sowerby, L.
Downes, R. W.	Stanford, C. V.
Dubois, F. C. T.	Tridemy, A.
Egerton, A. H.	Vadon, J.
Farnam, L.	Verrees, L.
Gibon, J. de	Walczynski, F.
Gray, A.	West, J. E.
Guilmant, A.	Willan, H.
Held, W.	Wyton, A.

O gesegnete Regierung
    See: O du Liebe (Ebeling)

O glaeubig Herz (Praetorius)
               Z 4540
    Kickstat, P.
    Otto, H.   Sandloff, P.
    Reda, S.   Zipp, F. (2)

O Gloriosa Virginum (Mode 2)

    Peeters, F.   Weegenhuise, J.
    Variant:
Te Lucis Ante Terminum (Mode 2)

    DeKlerk, A.   *Dupré, M. J. J.

O God, Eternal Father
    See: God Father, Praise and Glory (Mainz)

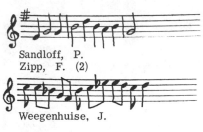

O God My Strength (Ravenscroft 1621)
　　See: Chichester

O God van hemel
　　See: Almsgiving (Dykes)

O gode Aande, led du mig
　　See: O Jesus Christ, du hoechstes Gut (Crueger)

O gode Gud, jeg takker dig

　　　　Raasted, N. O.

O Gott, der du ein Herrfuerst
bist
　　　　　　　　Z 5869

Variant:
Ich bin ja, Herr, in deiner Macht

　　　Gulbins, M.　　　　　Rinck, J. C. H.
　　　Piutti, K.　　　　　　Wedemann, W.

O Gott, der du ein herrfuerst bist
　　See: Jervaulx Abbey

O Gott, du frommer Gott

　　　Claussnitzer, P. (2)　　Kunze, K.

O Gott, du frommer Gott

　　　Kauffmann, G. F.

O Gott, du frommer Gott (Graup-
ner)
　　　　　　　　Z 5150
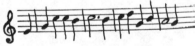
　　　Enckhausen, H. F.

O Gott, du frommer Gott (Hannover)
　　　　　　　　Z 5138

　　　Bach, J. S.　　　　　Gerber, H. N.　　　　Raphael, G.
　　　Baldamus, F.　　　　*Gerlach, G.　　　　Rudnick, W.
　　　Bieske, W.　　　　　Hoyer, K.　　　　　Schuetze, W.
　　　Borg, O.　　　　　　Kickstat, P.　　　　Schwencke, J. F. (3)
　　　Brahms, J.　　　　　Klaus, V.　　　　　*Stiller, K.
　　　Doles, J. F.　　　　　Kuntze, C.　　　　　Toepfer, J. G.
　　　Drischner, M. (2)　　Markull, F. W.　　　Trenkner, W.
　　　Dupré, M. J. J.　　　Meissner, H.　　　　Triplett, R. F.
　　　Enckhausen, H. F.　　Mueller, S.　　　　Vierling, J. G.
　　　Engelbrecht, K. F.　　*Muffat, G.　　　　Walter, S.
　　　Fiebig, K.　　　　　Oley, J. C.　　　　　Weber, H.
　　　Fluegel, G. (3)　　　Palme, R.　　　　　*Wenzel, H.

Werner, F.   *Zierau, F.
Wettstein, H. (2)   Zipp, F. (2)
Variants:
Ach Gott, verlass mich nicht

Reger, M.

Ach Jesu, dessen Treue
I dag er naadens tid

*Vaerge, A.

Ich freue mich in dir
O du min aedle skatt

Nordquist, G.

O Gud, du fromme Gud

Alnaes, E.

O Gud, du gode Gud

Karlsen, R.   Moseng, S.

Seht welch ein Mensch, seh, seh

Vierling, J. G.

O Gott, du frommer Gott (Stoerl)

Z 5148

*Beck, A.   Kickstat, P.   Rinkens, W.
Bender, J.   Krause, P.   Sachs, J. G.
Engel, J.   Landmann, A.   Schink, H.
*Faehrmann, H.   Leupold, A. W.   Schuetze, W.
Faisst, I. G. F. von Mauersberger, E.   Siebenbrodt, R.
Fischer, M. G. (2)   Oechsler, E.   Smyth, E. M.
*Forchhammer, T.   Peeters, F.   Stolze, H. W.
Franke, F. W. (2)   Piutti, K. (2)   Toepfer, J. G. (2)
Geist, P. (2)   Reda, S. (2)   Trautner, F. W.
Haase, K.   Reger, M.   Vierling, J. G.
Hasse, K.   Reinbrecht, A.   Walther, J. G.
Herzog, J. G. (2)   Reuter, F. (2)   Weber, H.
Karg-Elert, S. (3)   Ricek, W.   Wedemann, W.
Karow, K.   Rinck, J. C. H. (3)   Wolfrum, K. (2)
Variants:
Munich

Frank, R.   Lynn, G. A.   Peeters, F.
Haase, K.   McKinley, C.   Wyton, A.

O Gott, du frommer Gott (Stoerl) (cont.)

   O Seigneur Eternel

        Hess, C. L.

O Gott, du frommer Gott (Darmstadt)
   See: Was frag ich nach der Welt

O Gott, du hoechster Gnadenhort
   See: Herr Jesu Christ, dich zu uns wend

O Gott, du unser Vater bist
                        Z 8488
        Rinck, J. C. H.

O Gott im Himmel, sieh darein
   See: Ach Gott vom Himmel sieh darein

O Gott, O Geist, O Licht des
   Lebens (1714)

        Weinreich, W.

O Gott, von dem wir alles haben
   See: O dass ich tausend Zungen haette (Koenig)

O Gott, wie soll ich danken dir (Klein)
   See: Vaar Gud han held vaar fromtid loeynd

O Gottes Geist
   See: Old 100th

O Gottes Sohn, du Licht und
   Leben (Weller)
                        Z 7815
        Lang, H.

O groote Christus
   See: Avondzang

O grosser Gott (Stuttgart)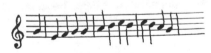

        Haase, K.

O grosser Gott, du reines Wesen

                        Z 2895
        Scheibner, G.

O grosser Gott von Macht (Franck)
                        Z 5105b
        Walther, J. G.

O grosser Schmerzensmann
   See: <u>Du grosser Schmerzensmann</u>

O Gud, det aer min glaedje
   See: <u>Ach bleib mit deiner</u>

O Gud, du fromme Gud
   See: <u>O Gott, du frommer Gott</u> (Hannover)

O Gud, du gode Gud
   See: <u>O Gott, du frommer Gott</u> (Hannover)

O Gud, fornuften fatter ej
   See: <u>Ich ruf' zu dir</u>

O Gud ske lov, det hjem ad gaar
(Berggreen)

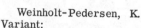

   Weinholt-Pedersen, K.
Variant:
<u>Laer mig, O skov</u>

   Wuertz, J.

O Gud ske lov til evig tid
(Arrebo)

   Raasted, N. O.
Variant:
<u>Apostlene sad i Jerusalem</u>

   Hamburger, P.   Laub, T.

O Gud, som tiden vender
   See: <u>Von Gott will ich nicht</u> (Erfurt)

O Haupt voll Blut und Wunden
   See: <u>Herzlich tut mich verlangen</u>

O havde jeg dog tusind tunger
   See: <u>O dass ich tausend Zungen haette</u> (Koenig)

O Hear the Joyful Tidings
(Schreiner)

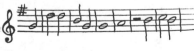

   Schreiner, A.

O Heart of Jesus (Latin)

   McGrath, J. J.

O Heer die daar
   See: <u>Valerius</u>

O Heer, doe dij gij recht
    See: Psalm 26

O Heer, mijn God, volzalig Wezen
    See: Psalm 7

O Heiland, reiss die Himmel auf
    (Rheinfels)

Ahrens, J.	Pfeiffer, C. D.
Bornefeld, H.	Poppen, H. M.
Clausing, F.	Pranschke, J.
David, J. N.	Rippen, P.
Doebler, K.	Romanovsky, E.
Driessler, J.	Ruedinger, G.
Eder, H.	Rumpf, W.
Gore, R. T.	Schwarz-Schilling, R.
Hollfelder, W.	Schweizer, R.
Kickstat, P. (3)	Spitta, H.
Luedders, P.	Walcha, H.
Matthes, R.	Weber, H.
Metzler, F.	Weyrauch, J.
Mueller, S. W.	Wurm, A.
Pepping, E.	Zipp, F.

Variant:
Behold a Virgin

    Bratt, C. G.

O heil'ge Seelenspeise
    See: Innsbruck

O Heil'ger Geist, kehr bei uns ein
    See: Wie schoen leuchtet

O Heilige Dreifaltigkeit (Hermann)

    Bender, J.
    Haase, K.   Peeters, F.

Variants:
Ihr lieben Christen, freut Euch nun

Haase, H. H.	Walcha, H.
Hennig, W.	Zipp, F.
Meyer, R.	

Steht auf, ihr lieben Kinderlein

Barbe, H.	Pepping, E.
Fiebig, K.	Rohwer, J.
Hark, F.	Weber, H.
Kickstat, P.	Wurm, A.

O Heiliger Geist, O Heiliger Gott
See: O Jesulein suess (Cologne)

O heiliges Kind
See: O Jesulein suess (Cologne)

O Heiligste Dreifaltigkeit

Schroeder, H.

O Hellig Aand, du skatt
See: Aus tiefer Not (Strassburg)

O Helligaand, mit hjerte (Laub)

Nielsen, L.

*Thuner, O. E.

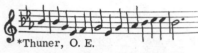

O Helligaand, mit hjerte (Swed-ish)

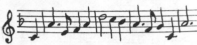

O Herr, aus tiefer Klage

Ahrens, J.

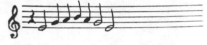

O Herr, gib Kraft und Frieden mir

Daninger, H.

O Herr Jesu, gib
See: Liebster Jesu

O Herr, mein Gott, durch den ich (Hiller)
Z 912
*Vierling, J. G.

O Herre Christus, du aufer-standner Christ

Rohwer, J.

Tune not found

O Herre god og frelser from
See: Kommt her zu mir (Leipzig)

O Herre Gott, begnade mich

Z 8451

Rinck, J. C. H.

O Herre Gott, dein goettlich Wort
(Erfurt)
Z 5690

Bach, J. C.
Bach, J. S.
Beyer, M.
Claussnitzer, P. (2)
Driessler, J.
Grote, H.
Haase, K.

Micheelsen, H. F.
Peeters, F.
Piutti, K.
Reinbrecht, A.
Schwencke, J. F.
Vierling, J. G.
Walther, J. G. (2)

Variant:
Gott, Vater, Sohn und Heiliger Geist

Driessler, J.

O Herre Jesus, mit levneds lys
See: Breslau

O Herre Krist, dig til oss vend
See: Herr Jesu Christ, dich zu uns wend (Gotha)

O hilf, Christe, Gottes Sohn
See also: Christus der uns
selig macht

Micheelsen, H. F.   Stade, F. W.

O hjelp mig, Gud (Waldis)
Z 7737

Karlsen, R.
Variant:
Herr Gott in deinem hoechsten Thron

O hjertekaere Jesus Krist
See: Vater unser

O Hoechster, deine Guetigkeit
See: O Mensch, bewein dein Suende

O hoechster Gott
See: Psalm 8

O Holy Name (O'Connell)

Kreckel, P. G.

O Holy Night (Adam)

DeBrant, C.

O hoved, hoejt forhaanet
See: Herzlich tut mich verlangen

O huvud blodigt, saarat
See: Herzlich tut mich verlangen

O Jerusalem, du schoene (Stoerl)
Z 3655

Breuninger, K. F.
Graf, J.

Haase, K.
Peeters, F.

O Jesu, aan de dine
See: Franzen

O Jesu, all mein Leben

Frischmann, M.

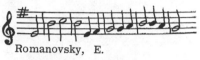

O Jesu, all mein Leben

Ahrens, J.
Roeseling, K.

Romanovsky, E.

O Jesu Christ, dein Krippelein
(Crueger)
Z 2074

Fluegel, G.
Haase, K.
Hasse, K.
Hulse, C. Van
Variant:
Wir Christenleut (Crueger)

Kaeppel, G. C. A.
Sassmannshausen, W.
Schumacher, M. H.

Borngaesser, W.
Driessler, J.
Drischner, M. (2)
Kickstat, P.

Meyer, R.
Piutti, K. (2)
*Rinck, J. C. H.
*Vierling, J. G.

O Jesu Christ, du hoechstes Gut
(Crueger)
Z 4545

Variants:
Min hoegste skatt

Aahgren, K. E.

O gode Aande, led du mig

Berg, G.

O Jesu Christ, du hoechstes Gut
See: Herr Jesu Christ, du hoechstes Gut

O Jesu Christ, meins Lebens Licht
See: Breslau

O Jesu Christ, meins Lebens Licht (Nuernberg)
   See: Herr Jesu Christ, meins Lebens Licht

O Jesu Christe, wahres Licht
   See: Herr Jesu Christ, meins Lebens Licht (Nuernberg)

O Jesu Christus, wahres Licht
   See: Breslau

O Jesu, du edle Gabe
                        Z 3889a(?)
      Walther, J. G.

O Jesu, du er min (Neusz)

      Nielsen, L.

O Jesu, du er min (Schuetz)
                         Z 4305

      Alnaes, E.   Nielsen, L.

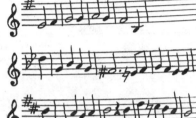
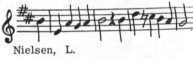

O Jesu, du mein Braeutigam

      *Oley, J. C.

O Jesu, einig wahres Haupt
   (Reuter)

      Reuter, F.
   Variant:
   Reuter

      Haase, K.   Reuter, F.

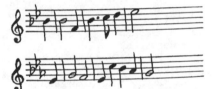

O Jesu for din pine (Kingo)
                 also in 4
                          4
   Variants:
   Se hvor nu Jesus traeder (Kingo-Arrebo)

      Gangfloet, S.   Karlsen, R.
      Godske-Nielsen, H.

   Se, vi gaa upp till Jerusalem

      Lindroth, H.

O Jesu, Jesu, Gottes Sohn
   See: Wie schoen leuchtet

O Jesu Krist, dig till oss
   See: Wenn wir in hoechsten

O Jesu Krist, du naadens brun
(Nystad)

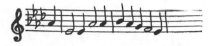

    Janáček, B.

O Jesu Krist som mandom tog
  See: Aus tiefer Not (Strassburg)

O Jesu, liebster Jesu

    Doebler, K.

O Jesu, meine Lust
  See: Herzallerliebster Gott

O Jesu, meine Wonne
  See: Nun lasst uns Gott dem Herrn

O Jesu, paa din alterfad
  See: O Jesu zu deinen Fuessen

O Jesu soet, verleent mi doch
confort

    DeKlerk, A.   Peeters, F.

O Jesu, som har elsket mig
  See: Ich ruf' zu dir

O Jesu, warum legst du mir
(Reimann)
        Z 2368
    Haase, K.

O Jesu zart, in neuer Art
  See: Maria zart, von edler Art

O Jesu, zu deinen Fuessen

    Raasted, N. O.
Variants:
O Jesu, paa din Alterfad

    Raasted, N. O.

O Jesulein suess (Cologne)
      zart
          Z 2016a

    Clausing, F.   Hoogewoud, H.
    Coutts, G.   Kauffmann, G. F.
    Fischer, M. G.   Milford, R. H.
    Hark, F.   Peeters, F.
    Hokanson, M.   Wettstein, H.

O Jesulein suess (Cologne) (cont.)

    Variants:
Ach, lieber Herre Jesu Christ

      *Goos, W.

Ist das der Leib

      Ahrens, J.

Komm Heiliger Geist mit deiner Gnade

      Fischer, J. K. F. (3)   Sechter, S. (2)
      Miggl, E.

O Heiliger Geist, O Heiliger Gott

      Becker, O.   Meissner, H.
      Brod, K.   Pfannschmidt, K. H. P.
      Driessler, J.   Pfeiffer, C. D.
      Drischner, M.   Rinck, J. C. H.
      Franke, F. W.   Tauscher, A. W.
      Kauffmann, G. F.   Vierling, J. G.
      Kickstat, P.   Weber, H.
      Kuehn, K.   Wurm, A.

O Heiliges Kind
Song 80 (Dutch)

      Dragt, J.   Wilgenburg, D. van

O Koenig aller Ehren
   See: Ich freu mich in dem Herren

O Koenig dessen Majestaet

      Wedemann, W.

O Koenig dessen Majestaet
   See: An Wasserfluessen Babylon

O Koenig, Jesu Christe (13th
   Century)

      Bender, J.
      Micheelsen, H. F.   Weber, H.

O komm, du Geist der Wahrheit
   See: Ich dank dir, lieber Herre (Bohemian)

O komm, O komm, Emmanuel
   See: Veni, O Sapientia (Plainsong)

O Kriste, du som ljuset aer
See: Christe, der du bist Tag und Licht

O Kristelighed (Laub)

   *Wuertz, J.

O Kristelighed (Lindeman)
See: Far verden, far vel (Lindeman)

O lad din aand (Lindeman)

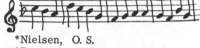

   Nielsen, L.
   Sandvold, A.

O lad din aand nu med oss vaere
(Rung)

   *Frandsen, H. B.   *Nielsen, O. S.
   Karlsen, R.   *Raasted, N. O.

O Lamm Gottes, der du trugest
                Z 59

   Rinck, J. C. H.

O Lamm Gottes, unschuldig
(Decius)
            Z 4360

Abel, O.	Karow, K.
Ahrens, J.	Kauffmann, G. F.
Bach, J. S. (2)	Kickstat, P. (2)
Baldamus, F.	Landmann, A.
Barner, A.	Lang, H. (2)
Beck, C.	Leupold, A. W.
Bender, J.	Markworth, H. J.
Bornefeld, H.	Merkel, G.
Brieger, O.	Micheelsen, H. F. (2)
Cebrian, A.	Mueller-Zuerich, P.
Claussnitzer, P. (2)	Naubert, F. A.
Copley, R. E.	Near, G.
David, J. N.	Orlinski, H.
Driessler, J.	Otto, H.
Dupré, M. J. J.	Pachelbel, J. (5)
Eckardt, A.	Pachelbel, W. H.
Enckhausen, H. F.	Peeters, F.
Eyken, J. A. Van	Pfiffner, E.
Fluegel, G. (2)	Piutti, K. (2)
Forchhammer, T.	Raasted, N. O.
Franke, F. W. (2)	Reger, M.
Grosheim, G. C. (2)	Reichardt, B.
Haase, K.	Rinck, J. C. H. (3)
Kaeppel, G. C. A.	Rudnick, W.
Karg-Elert, S.	Rumpf, W. (2)

O Lamm Gottes, unschuldig (Decius) (cont.)

Schaab, R. (2)	Telemann, G. P. (4)
Schauss-Flake, M.	Thomas, A. G.
Scherzer, O.	Unruh, E. (2)
Schink, H.	Vierling, J. G.
Schumacher, M. H. (3)	Walcha, H.
Schwencke, J. F. (2)	Wettstein, H.
Soenke, H.	Wolfrum, K.
Spiering, G.	Zachau, F. W.
Streicher, J. A.	Zwart, J.

Variants:
Christe, du Lamm Gottes (Decius)
O du Guds Lam uskyldig

Nielsen, L.

Song 38 (Dutch)

Beek, W. van   Zwart, J.

O laufet, ihr Hirten

Drischner, M.

O Lebensbrot, Herr Jesu Christ
See: Du Lebensbrot, Herr Jesu Christ

O Lebensbruennlein (Goerlitz)
               Z 7305
    Hessenberg, K.

O Leib gebrochen mir zu gut
(Vogel)

Wieruszowski, L.

O Licht geboren aus dem Lichte
See: Psalm 33

O Liebe, die den Himmel hat
zerrissen (Schicht)
               Z 3147
   *Eyken, J. A. Van
   Grosse-Weischede, A. (2)   Inderau, H.

O liebster Herr Jesu Christ
See: Kvindelil (Horn)

O liv som blev taant

Olsson, L.

O Lord of Hosts (Careless)

    Schreiner, A.

O Lord With Wondrous (Andriessen)

    Englert, E.

O lue fra Guds (Weisse)
See: Der tag der ist so (Wittenberg)

O Lux Beata
(compare with Sarum-Mode 8)

    Knecht, J. H.

O Lux Beata Trinitas (Sarum -
   Mode 8)
See also: Der du bist drei

Anonymous	Peeters, F.
*Cassler, G. W.	Pepping, E.
*Fasolo, G. B.	Praetorius, M. (4)
Hulse, C. Van	Scheidt, S.
Marriott, F. L.	Sweelinck, J. P. (2)
Meek, K.	Weckmann, M.
*Nelson, R. A.	

O Magnum Mysterium

    Davies, P. M.

O Magnum Mysterium

    Hulse, C. Van

O Maria, Mater Pia

    Magin, C.

O Mater Providentiae

    Tranzillo, D.

O mein Jesu, ich muss sterben
(Paderborn)
               Z 6762
    Haase, K.
    Markworth, H. J.

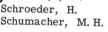

Schroeder, H.
Schumacher, M. H.

O Mensch, bewein dein Suende
gross (Strassburg)
         Z 8303
         Z 2502

Bach, J. S.
Bornefeld, H.
Burkhard, W.
Driessler, J.
Dupré, M. J. J.
Eyken, J. A. Van
Franke, F. W.
Hark, F. (2)
Hennig, W.
Herrmann, K. H.

Karges, W.
Pachelbel, J.
Pepping, E. (2)
Pfaff, H.
Reda, S.
Rumpf, W.
Sweelinck, J. P.
Walcha, H.
Weyrauch, J.

Variants:
De hoge God alleen

King, H. C.

Es sind doch selig alle die

Hoyer, K.
Mueller, S. W.

Weber, H.

Jauchz' Erd', und Himmel juble

Ehmann, H.
Grabner, H.

Reger, M.

O Hoechster, deine Guetigkeit

Wieruszowski, L.

Old 113th

Near, G.
Palmer, C. C.
Pfautsch, L.

Rohlig, H.
Wood, C.

Psalm 36 (Geneva)

Bijster, J.
Gagnebin, H.
Rippen, P.

Wieruszowski, L.
Zwart, J.

Psalm 68 (Geneva)

Bijster, J.
Bonset, J.
Bruin, B.

King, H. C.
Weelden, J. van (3)

Que Dieu se montre

    Hess, C. L.

Steh, auf in deiner Macht

    Mueller-Zuerich, P. (2)

O naadens sol og sete (Erfurt)
See: Herr Christ, der einig Gottes Sohn

O Nata Lux De Lumine (Mode 8)
See: Verbum Supernum (Plainsong - Mode 8)

O Pater Excelse

    Clokey, J. W.

O Perfect Love
See: Sandringham

O Peter Go Ring Dem Bells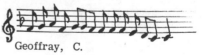
(Spiritual)

    Thomas, V. C.

O Prince of Peace (Gibbons)

    Gotch, O. L.

O Quam Amabilis

    Weegenhuise, J.

O Quam Metuendus Est   Tune not found

    Ravanello, O.

O Quam Suavis Est (Gregorian)

    Couper, A. B.   Geoffray, C.

O Quanta Qualia

    Cranmer, P.
    Dickey, M.
    Dickinson, C.   Hillert, R.
    Edmundson, G.   Hunt, R. H.
    Haase, K.   Matthews, H. A.
    Healey, D.   Pearce, C. W.
Variant: Peeters, F.
Regnator Orbis
    Lloyd, L. S.

O Queen of Peerless Majesty
(Benz)
    Kreckel, P. G. (2)

O Sacred Head
   See: Herzlich tut mich verlangen

O Sacrum Convivium

    Falcinelli, R.
    Lee, J.   Marier, T. N.

O Sacrum Convivium (Sarum)

    Olsson, O. E.
    Piel, P.   Sister M. G.

O Safe to the Rock
   See: Safe to the Rock

O Saint Esprit, descendez
(French)

    Erb, M. J.

O Salutaris Hostia (Duquet)

    Bratt, C. G.   Schehl, J. A.
    Guilmant, A.   Verhaar, A.
    Perilhou, A.   Weegenhuise, J.

O Sanctissima
   See: Sicilian Mariners

O Seigneur Eternel
   See: O Gott, du frommer Gott (Stoerl)

O selig Haus, wo man dich auf-
genommen (Lyon)
              Z 6207
    Franke, F. W.   *Papperitz, B. R.

O selig Haus, wo man dich auf-
genommen (Niemeyer)
              Z 6212
    Haase, K.

O selig sind die in Aufrechtigkeit
   See: Psalm 119 (Geneva)

O selige Nacht

    Ottenwaelder, A.

O selige Nacht
    See: Hanover

O soede Gud
    See: O store Gud

O Splendour of God's Glory Bright
    See: Lasst uns erfreuen (short form)

O store Gud (Swedish)

     *Lorenz, E. J.
     Shaffer, J. E.

O store Gud, din kaerlighed (Strassburg)
    See: Mein Seel erhebt den Herren (Strassburg)

O store konge David's Soenn
(Vogel)

     Drischner, M.

Nielsen, L.

O suesser Herre, Jesu Christe
(Bohemian)
            Z 1515
     Bossler, K.
     Degen, H.
     Driessler, J.
     Kammeier, H.
   Variant:
   Landskron

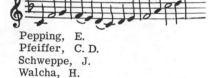

     Pepping, E.
     Pfeiffer, C. D.
     Schweppe, J.
     Walcha, H.

O suessester der Namen all

     Dalm, W.

O suessester der Namen all

     Doebler, K.
   Variant:
   Du Gottmensch bist mit

     Doebler, K.

O Tannenbaum

     Thomas, V. C.
   Variant:
   Maryland, My Maryland

     Allen, N. H.

O Thou Kind and Gracious Father
(Careless)

    Schreiner, A.

O Tod, wo ist dein Stachel (1523)
See: Es ist das Heil

O Traurigkeit, O Herzeleid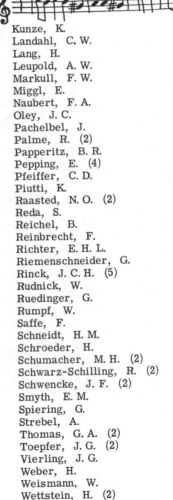
(Mainz)

                Z 1915

Abel, O.
Ahrens, J.
Albrecht, G.
Beck, A.
Bender, J.
Bibl, R.
Bornefeld, H.
Brahms, J.
Brandt, A.
Brosig, M. (2)
Cassler, G. W.
Chaix, C. (2)
Clausing, F.
Claussnitzer, P. (3)
David, J. N.
Doppelbauer, J. F.
Driessler, J.
Drischner, M. (2)
Eckardt, A.
Enckhausen, H. F.
Eyken, J. A. Van (2)
Fischer, M. G. (2)
Fluegel, G.
Forchhammer, T.
Freudenberg, C. G.
Fromm, H.
Grabner, H.
Gradehand, F.
Grote, H.
Gulbins, M.
Haas, J.
Hark, F.
Hasse, K.
Held, W.
Hohn, W.
Hulse, C. Van
Kaeppel, G. C. A.
Karow, K.
Kickstat, P.
Krause, E.
Krause, P.
Kuehn, K.

Kunze, K.
Landahl, C. W.
Lang, H.
Leupold, A. W.
Markull, F. W.
Miggl, E.
Naubert, F. A.
Oley, J. C.
Pachelbel, J.
Palme, R. (2)
Papperitz, B. R.
Pepping, E. (4)
Pfeiffer, C. D.
Piutti, K.
Raasted, N. O. (2)
Reda, S.
Reichel, B.
Reinbrecht, F.
Richter, E. H. L.
Riemenschneider, G.
Rinck, J. C. H. (5)
Rudnick, W.
Ruedinger, G.
Rumpf, W.
Saffe, F.
Schneidt, H. M.
Schroeder, H.
Schumacher, M. H. (2)
Schwarz-Schilling, R. (2)
Schwencke, J. F. (2)
Smyth, E. M.
Spiering, G.
Strebel, A.
Thomas, G. A. (2)
Toepfer, J. G. (2)
Vierling, J. G.
Weber, H.
Weismann, W.
Wettstein, H. (2)
Willan, H.
Wolfrum, K.
Zehrfeld, O.

Variants:
Aa hjertens ve

    Gangfloet, S.   Nielsen, L.
    Moseng, S.

Ach, hjaertans ve

    Salonen, S.

Am Kreuz erblasst

    Wedemann, W.

Drag Jesu, mig dog efter dig

    Raasted, N. O. (2)   *Thuner, O. E.

So ruhest du, O meine Ruh

    Gulbins, M.

O unbefleckt empfangnes Herz
(Catholic)

    Boslet, L.

O unbesiegter starker Held, St. Michael
             Gottesheld
See: Unueberwindlich starker Held, St. Michael

O unbezwinglich starker Held, St. Michael
See: Unueberwindlich starker Held, St. Michael

O Ursprung des Lebens (Selle)

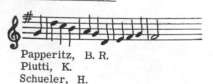

             Z 6940
    Hasse, K.   Papperitz, B. R.
    Koetzschke, H.   Piutti, K.
    Palme, R.   Schueler, H.

O Vader, dat uw

    Mazyk, R. van

O Vater, allmaechtiger Gott
See: Kyrie Magnae Deus

O Welt, ich muss dich lassen
See: Innsbruck

O Welt, sieh hier dein Leben
(Friese)
                 Z 2278

    Haase, K.
    *Hulse, C. Van   Pepping, E.

O Welt, sieh hier dein Leben
See: Innsbruck

O wer alles haet verloren (Freylinghausen)
                 Z 1290

    Fink, C.   Rinck, J. C. H.
Variants:
Her ei ties (German)

    Gangfloet, S.   Pasquet, J.
    Nielsen, L.

Kjemp alvorlig, nu Guds naade

    Rasmussen, A.

O der alles haet verloren

    Haase, K.

Zion's Stille soll sich breiten

    Drischner, M.

O wie selig seid ihr doch, ihr
   Frommen (Crueger)
                 Z 1583

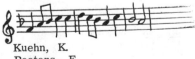

    *Baldamus, F.
    Brahms, J.   Palme, R.
    *Brieger, O.   Pepping, E.
    Claussnitzer, P.   Piutti, K.
    *Faehrmann, H.   *Reda, S.
    *Finzenhagen, L. H. O.   Reger, M.
    Hennig, W.   *Rinck, J. C. H.
    *Hoeller, K.   *Schmidt, F.
    Kickstat, P. (2)   *Sering, F. W.
    Looks, R.   Weinreich, W.
    Morén, J. T.   Wieruszowski, L.

O wie selig seid ihr doch, ihr
Frommen (Stoetzel)
                 Z 1586

    Bouman, P.   Kuehn, K.
    *Grote, H.   Peeters, F.
    Haase, K.   Willan, H.

O wie selig seid ihr doch, ihr
Frommen (Vopelius)
                          Z 1581
     *Albrechtsberger, J. G.

O wir armen Suender
   See: Ach wir armen Suender

O wundergrosser Siegesheld
                          Z 8361
     Pepping, E.
Variant:
Ach wundergrosser Siegesheld

     Pfannschmidt, H.

O wundergrosser Siegesheld
   See: Wie schoen leuchtet

Oberlin (Demuth)

     Jewell, K. W.

Oblation
   See: Lobet den Herren, alle (Crueger)

Ohne Rast und unverweilt
   See: Vienna (Knecht)

Oi Jeesus, autaja (Finnish)

     Parviainen, J.

Oi pyhae Herran (Finnish)

     Kuusisto, T.

Old 25th (Geneva)

     Harwood, B.
     Wood, C.

Old 38th
   See: Psalm 38 (Geneva)

Old 77th
   See: Old 120th (Estes)

Old 81st
   See: Old 120th (Estes)

<u>Old 100th</u> (Geneva)

Z 368

Ashford, E. L.
Best, W. T.
Bristol, L. H.
Buck, D.
Coleman, R. H. P. (2)
Copley, R. E.
Crane, R.
Dressler, J.
Farrar, E. B.
Finney, C. H.
Flesher, G.
Forchhammer, T.
Gardner, J. L.
Gehrm, L. J. , Jr.
Grace, H.

Groom, L. H.
Haase, K.
Hamburger, P.
Heffer, F.
Hegedus, A.
Hulse, C. Van
Joubert, J.
Kousemaker, A.
Leidzen, E.
Loud, J. H.
Markull, F. W.
McKay, G. F.
Nordman, C.
Paine, J. K.
Palmer, C. C.

Parry, C. H. H.
Peeters, F.
Post, P.
Purcell, H.
Reuter, F.
Rohlig, H.
Rowley, A.
Thompson, V. D. (2)
Titcomb, E. H.
Truette, E. E.
Videroe, F.
Wesley, S. S.
Willan, H.
Young, G.

Variants:

<u>Brunn alles Heils</u>

Driessler, J.

<u>Doxology</u>
<u>Dreifaltigkeit, urewig Licht</u>

Jenny, A.

<u>Gjoer doeren hoej, gjoer porten vid</u>

Andersen, E.
Frandsen, H. B.
Frellsen, E.
Gangfloet, S.
Jeppesen, K.
Laub, T.
Moeller, S. O.
Nielsen, L.

Nielsen, O. S.
Nielsen, T. H.
Raasted, N. O.
Rosenkilde-Larsen, E.
Vaerge, A.
Woeldike, M. A.
Wuertz, J.

<u>Herr Gott, dich loben alle wir</u>

Bornefeld, H.
Bossler, K.
*Brede, A.
Drischner, M. (2)
Faehrmann, H.
Fiebig, K.
*Franke, F. W.
*Grote, H.
Hennig, W.
Huth, A.
*Kauffmann, G. F. (2)
Kickstat, P.
*Kittel, J. C.

Krebbs, J. L.
Kuehn, K.
Merkel, G. (2)
Micheelsen, H. F.
Oley, J. C. (2)
Pachelbel, J.
Piutti, K.
Rinck, J. C. H. (2)
Scheidt, S. (2)
Stolze, H. W.
Umbreit, K. G.
Vierling, J. G.
Voullaire, W.

Walcha, H.   Wolfrum, K. (2)
Walther, J. G.   Wurm, A.
Wedemann, W.   Zehrfeld, O.

Kommt Menschenkinder, ruehmt und preisst

Doles, J. F.   Schaab, R.

O Gottes Geist

Koch, J. H. E.

Psalm 134 (Bourgeois)

Rippen, P.   Wilgenburg, D. van
Wieruszowski, L. (2)   Zwart, J.

Song 196 (Dutch)

Wilgenburg, D. van

Old 104th (Ravenscroft)

Christopher, C. S.
Coleman, R. H. P.   Rowley, A.
Palmer, C. C.   Willan, H.
Parry, C. H. H.   Wood, C.

Old 107th (Geneva)

Z 5261

Groves, R.

Old 112th
See: Vater unser

Old 113th
See: O Mensch, bewein dein Suende gross (Strassburg)

Old 116th
See: Windsor (Damon's)

Old 120th (Estes)

also in 3
4

Curry, R. D.   Hulse, C. Van
Haase, K.   Willan, H.
Variants:
Old 77th

Wood, C.

Old 120th (Estes) (cont.)

Old 81st

    Best, W. T.

Old 122nd (Bourgeois)   Z 8234

    Goemanne, N.
Variant:
Psalm 3

    Gagnebin, H.

Old 124th (Geneva)

Blackburn, J.	Harris, W. H.	Peeters, F.
Curry, R. D.	Matthews, H. A.	Warner, R. L.
Haase, K.	Mead, E. G.	Willan, H.

Variants:
Psalm 124 (Geneva)

    Clokey, J. W.   Wood, C.

Toulon

    Duncan, W. E.   Moser, R.

Old 130th (French)   Z 5352

    Peeters, F.
Variants:
Aus diesen tiefen Grunde (Geneva)

    Enckhausen, H. F.

Befall i Herrens haender

    Berg, G.

Du fort de ma détresse
Jeg raaber fast, O Herre

    Laub, T.   Thuner, O. E.
    Raasted, N. O.

Psalm 130 (Geneva)

Groothengel, J. G.	Rippen, P.
Kool, B., Jr.	Schaaf, H. van der
Kousemaker, A.	Speuy, H. J.
Reuland, -	Wilgenburg, D. van

<u>Uverdig er jeg Herre</u> (Strassburg)

 Karlsen, R.

<u>Zu dir von Herzens Grunde</u>

<u>Old 132nd</u>
 See: <u>St. Flavian</u> (Day's)

<u>Old 134th</u> (Estes)

 Variant:
<u>St. Michael</u>

Bender, J.	Peeters, F.
Dicks, E. A.	Rohlig, H.
Haase, K.	Scott, J. S.
Johns, D.	West, J. E.
Peek, R. M.	

<u>Old 136th Psalm</u>

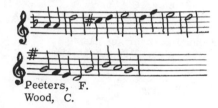

 Wood, C.

<u>Old 137th</u> (Day's)

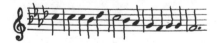

 Haase, K.   Peeters, F.
 Mead, E. G. Wood, C.

<u>Old Dutch Lullaby</u>

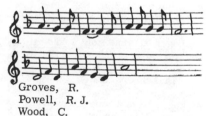

 Dickinson, C.

<u>Old Martyrs</u> (Scotch)

 Best, W. T. Groves, R.
 Dyson, G.   Powell, R. J.
 Grace, H.   Wood, C.

<u>Old Netherlands Song</u>

 Bijster, J.
Variants:
<u>Komt, wilt u spoeden</u>
<u>Lasst uns nun gehen zur</u>
<u>Look Down To Us, St. Joseph</u> (Flemish)

 Nieland, J.

<u>Oldown</u> (Harwood)

 Harwood, B.
 Thatcher, H. R.

Oliphant (Baillot)

    Ashford, E. L.

Olive's Brow (Bradbury)

    Ashford, E. L.

Olivet (Mason)

Arbatsky, Y.	Lindsay, W.
Ashford, E. L.	Lorenz, E. J.
Beck, A.	Matthews, J. S.
Bingham, S.	Mueller, C. F.
Colvin, H.	Peery, R. R.
Diggle, R.	Peeters, F.
Elmore, R. H.	Reuter, F.
Haase, K.	Speed, R. M.
Hokanson, M.	Stults, R. M.
Hulse, C. Van	Thompson, V. D. (2)
Larson, E. R.	

Olmutz (Gregorian-Mason)
    See also: Magnificat-Mode 7
            also in 3
                 2

    Whiting, G. E.

Om himmerigs rige
    See: Min sjael og aand (Tomissoen's)

Om nogen til ondt mig lokke vil
(Haereid)

    Drischner, M.   Karlsen, R.

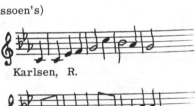

Om nogen til ondt mig lokke vil
(Norsk-Ehrenborg)

    Nielsen, L.

Omni Die Dic Mariae (Corner)

    Peeters, F.

Omni Die Dic Mariae (Trier)

    Kreckel, P. G.
    McGrath, J. J. (2)
    Variant:
Daily, Daily, Sing to Mary

    Kreckel, P. G.

On Christmas Night (English)

    Elmore, R. H.
    Milford, R. H. (2)
Variant:
Sussex Carol

    Miles, G. T.   *Saxton, S. E.

On entend partout (French Noël)

    Borucchia, N.

On freudt verzer ich manchen
   Tag

    Hofhaymer, P.

On ne craint plus dans l'univers
   (French)

    Franck, C.

On This Day, O Beautiful
   Mother (Lambillotte)

    Schehl, J. A.

Once More, My Soul, the Rising
   Day (U.S. Southern)

    Read, G.

Op al den ting som Gud har gjort
   (Freiburg-Schoerrings)

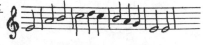

    Bergh, L.   Sandvold, A.
    Karlsen, R.   *Thuner, O. E.
Variant:
Jeg ved et evigt himmerig (German Folk Tune)

    Christensen, B.   Moeller, S. O.
    Frellsen, E.   Noerholm, I.
    Jensen, S.   Raasted, N. O.
    Jeppesen, K.   Woeldike, M. A.
    Laub, T.

Op al den ting (Sletten)
   all

    Nielsen, L.

Op al den ting (Steenberg)

    Karlsen, R.

Op alle folk paa denne jord
              Z 4583
    Raasted, N. O.
    Rosenkilde-Larsen, E.   Videroe, F.
    Thuner, O. E.   Woeldike, M. A.
    Variant:
    Freut Euch des Herren (Schuetz)

Op alle som paa jorden bor (Crueger)
    See: Nun danket all und

Op alle som paa jorden bor (Herman)
    See: Lobt Gott, ihr Christen (Herman)

Op bergen en in dalen (de Pauw)

    Bonset, J.
    Schuurman, A. C.   Vries, H. de
    Variant:
    Song 143 (Dutch)

Op dog, Zion, ser du ej (Hartmann)

    Hamburger, P.   Moeller, S. O.
    Klaebel, F.   Nielsen, J. M.
    Lindorff-Larsen, E.   *Thuner, O. E. (2)

Op dog, Zion, ser du ej
    See: Nun komm der Heiden Heiland

Op gledes alle, gledes nu (Haeffner)

    Nielsen, L.

Op gledes alle, gledes nu (Steenberg)

    Karlsen, R.

Op, I kristne, ruster eder
(Steenberg)

    Nielsen, L.

Op, I kristne, ruster eder (Neander)
    See: Meine Hoffnung stehet feste (Neander)

Op, I kristne, ruster eder
    See: Unser Herrscher (Neander)

Op, min sjael, thi sol er oppe
    See: O Durchbrecher (Halle)

Op Sion, at oplukke   Tune not found

        Wuertz, J.

Op, thi dagen nu frembryder
    (Gade)

        *Hamburger, P.

Op, thi dagen nu frembryder
    (Laub)

        *Wuertz, J.

Op, ti dagen nu frembryder
    (Lindeman)

        Karlsen, R.

Open My Eyes (Scott)

        Thompson, V. D.

Opstanden er den Herre Krist
    See: Surrexit Christus Hodie

Optatus

        Bratt, C. G.

Or dites-nous, Marie
    See: Chartres

Ora Pro Nobis

        Boslet, L.

Orbis Factor
    See: Kyrie Orbis Factor

Ordet om Guds naad
    See: Autuuden ja armon sana

Ordets Herre, du, dom givit
    See: Gott des Himmels

Oremus
See: Morgenglanz der Ewigkeit

Oriel (Ett)

    Titcomb, E. H.   Weston, H. W.

Orientis Partibus (Corbeil)
                also in 4
                     4

    Beck, A.   Plettner, A.
    Goode, J. C.   Reuter, F.
    Haase, K.   Rogers, L.
    Hulse, C. Van   Tatam, J. A.
    Markworth, H. J.
Variants:
Concordi Laetitia

    De Klerk, A.   Weegenhuise, J.
    Hegedus, A.

Redhead 45th

Ortonville (Hastings)

    Proctor, R. E.
    Smith, H. M.   Thompson, V. D.

Ostergaard (Danish)

    Greener, J. H.

Our Lady Trondhjem
See: Paaskemorgen, slukker sorgen (Lindeman)

Our Redeemer (Schreiner)

    Schreiner, A.

Over Kedron
See: Jesus dine dype vunder (Lindeman)

Overmaade fuldt av naade (Norsk
    Folk)

    Baden, C.
    Gangfloet, S.   Nielsen, L.
    Moseng, S.   Sandvold, A.

Overmaade fuldt av naade (Freylinghausen)
See: O Durchbrecher (Halle)

Overstrand (Walker)

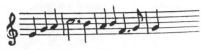

    Walker, E.

Paa dig jeg hoppas, Herre kaer
  See: In dich hab' ich gehoffet (Nuernberg)

Paa Gud alene (Zinck)

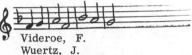

    Cassler, G. W.   Rosenkilde-Larsen, E.
    Godske-Nielsen, H.   Sandvold, A.
    Hamburger, P. (2)   Vaerge, A.
    Nielsen, L.

Paa Jerusalem (Rung)

    Frandsen, H. B.   Videroe, F.
    Hamburger, P.   Wuertz, J.

Paaske vi holde (Laub)

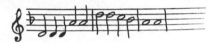

    Nielsen, O. S.
    Thuner, O. E.

Paaskemorgen, slukker sorgen
  (Lindeman)

    Baden, C.   Nielsen, L.
    Bergh, L.   Thorkildsen, J.
    Hokanson, M.   Thuner, O. E.
  Variants:
  Her vil ties, her vil bies (Lindeman)
  Our Lady Trondhjem

    Cassler, G. W.

Paderborn
  See: Maria zu lieben

Paean (Plainsong)

    Rowley, A.

Paedia (Schulz)

    Cassler, G. W.

Palestrina (Palestrina)

    Andrews, M.   Gaul, H.   Hodson, W.
    Bratt, C. G.   Grieb, H.   Hosmer, E. S.
    DeBrant, C.   Haase, K.   Kinder, R.
    Emery, D. R. Henderson, H. Kreckel, P. G.

Palestrina (Palestrina) (cont.)

Lacey, F.	Morrison, R. S.	Wetherill, E. H.
Lorenz, E. J.	Mueller, C. F.	Wyton, A. (2)
Matthews, H. A.	Thatcher, H. R.	Young, G.
Miles, G. T.	Walton, K.	

Variants:
Conqueror

James, A.

Victory

Cassler, G. W.	Powell, R. J.
Fissinger, E.	Rohlig, H.
Graham, R.	Smith, E. H.
Lang, C. S.	

Palisades (Sowerby)

Sowerby, L.

Pange Lingua

Kodaly, Z.

Pange Lingua Gloriosa (Sarum -
     Mode 3)
                    Z 3682a

*Ahrens, J.	Kleber, L.
Anonymous (2)	Kreckel, P. G. (2)
Arresti, G. C.	Latzelsberger, J.
Arnatt, R. K.	Magin, C.
Bairstow, E. C.	Manz, P.
Boëly, A. P. F.	*McGrath, J. J.
Boslet, L. (2)	*Pearce, C. W.
Bratt, C. G.	*Plant, A. B.
Brown, A. G. Y.	Quingnard, R.
Cavazzoni, G.	Sewell, W.
Coleman, R. H. P.	Sicher, F.
David, J. N.	Skop, V. F.
Diemente, E.	Sowerby, L.
Edmundson, G.	Stark, L.
Erbach, C.	Sychra, J. C.
Fasolo, G. B. (4)	Thomson, V.
Gladstone, F. E.	Vierne, R.
Goller, V. (2)	Williams, D. H.
Groves, R.	Woollen, R.

Variant:
Cibavit Eos

Pange Lingua Gloriosa (Plainsong - Mode 3)

Brandon, G.
Dupré, M. J. J. (2)
*Erb, M. J. (5)

*Guilmant, A.
*Peeters, F.
Titelouze, J. (2)

Panis Angelicus (Lambillotte)

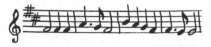

Curry, R. D.
Schehl, J. A.

Papago (American Indian)

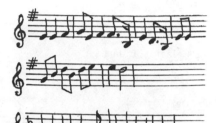

Hulse, C. Van

Parator Nobis

Sister M. G.

Park Street (Venua)

Ashford, E. L.

Parratt (Parratt)

Lynn, G. A.

Pascha Nostra

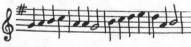

Sister M. T.

Paschal Chorale

Edmundson, G.

Paschal Hymn

Kreckel, P. G.

Pass Me Not (Doane)

Ashford, E. L.
Lorenz, E. J.

Thompson, V. D.

Passion Chorale
See: Herzlich tut mich verlangen

Pater Noster

*Ahrens, J.
Diebold, J.

Pater Noster (Liturgical)
See: Fons Bonitans

Patmos (Havergal)

 Beck, A. (2)   Hulse, C. Van
 Haase, K.   Peeters, F.

Pax (Swedish)

 Variant:
 Ack bliv hos oss

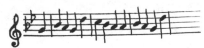

  Aahgren, K. E. Peeters, F.

Pax Celeste (Edinburgh)

 Haase, K.

Pax Dei (Dykes)

 Reuter, F. (2)
 Variant:
 Weiss ich den Weg auch nicht

Pax Tecum (Caldbeck-Vincent)

 Taylor, C. T.

Peace, the Gift of God's Love
(Bilhorn)

 Marshall, P.

Peel Castle (Manx)

 Leitz, D.
 Marshall, C.

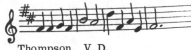

Penitence (Lane)

 Reuter, F.
 Thomas, V. C. Thompson, V. D.

Penitentia (Dearle)

 Walter, S.

Pensum Sacrum (Goerlitz)
See: Herr Jesu Christ, dich zu uns wend (Gotha)

Pentecost (Boyd)

Curry, R. D.
Faulkes, W. Stults, R. M.

Personent Hodie (Piae Cantiones)

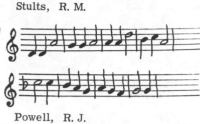

Johnson, D. N.

Petersen (Halle)

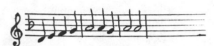

Hayton, R.
Peeters, F. Powell, R. J.

Petra
See: Redhead 76th

Picardy (French)

Bedell, R. L.
Bird, P.   Englert, E.   Owen, H.
Bratt, C. G. (2)   Grieb, H.   Peeters, F.
Burns, W. K.   Healey, D.   Rowley, A.
Casner, M.   Hegedus, A.   Shaw, G. T.
Cassler, G. W.   James, A.   Sowerby, L.
Coleman, R. H. P. (2) Johnson, D. N.   Thiman, E. H.
Cummins, R.   Maekelberghe, A.   Thomson, V.
Diercks, J. H.   Matthews, H. A.   Warner, R. L. (2)
Diggle, R.   Nelson, R. A.   Woodgate, H. L.
Edmundson, G.   Noble, T. T.   Young, G. (2)

Pilgrimage (Herrnhut)
Z 5730
Elmore, R. H.
Variants:
Song 73 (Dutch)

Kremer, G.

Wij knielen voor uw zetel neer

Groothengel, J. G.

Pilgrims (Smart)

Calver, F. L.
Diggle, R. Frost, C. J.

Pilot (Gould)

Ashford, E. L.
Haase, K. Thomas, V. C.
Hustad, D. Thompson, V. D.

Pisgah
 See: <u>Covenanters Tune</u>

<u>Placare Christe</u>

    Dupré, M. J. J.

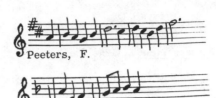

Peeters, F.

<u>Plaistow</u> (Magdalen Hymns)

    Palmer, C. C.
    Roberts, C.

<u>Pleading Saviour</u> (Plymouth)

    Thorkildsen, J.

<u>Pleasant Pastures</u> (Bradbury)

    Thompson, V. D.

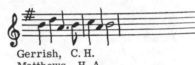

<u>Pleyel</u> (Pleyel)

    Ashford, E. L.   Gerrish, C. H.
    Burnap, U. C.   Matthews, H. A.
    Calkin, J. B.   Thayer, W. E.
    Dickey, M.   Turpin, E. H.

<u>Polish Carol</u>

    Carleton, B.

<u>Polish Christmas Carol</u>

    Reichenbach, H.

Tune not found

<u>Polish Church Song</u>

    Surzyñski, M.

<u>Poplar</u> (Strong)

    Sumsion, C. C.

<u>Posen</u> (Strattner)
           Z 1228
      also in 4
           4
    Baumgartner, H. L.
Variants:
<u>Herr, wir stehen Hand in Hand</u>

    Poppen, H. M.

Himmel, Erde, Luft und Meer

Weber, H.

Potsdam (Bach)

Haase, K.

Praetorius
See: Es ist ein Ros'

Praise (Swedish)

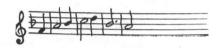

Variant:
Du haver seger vunnit

Salonen, S.

Praise God (American Spiritual)

Schmidt, W. J.

Praise of Christmas
See: Rare Song in Praise of Christmas

Praise to the Holiest (McGrath)

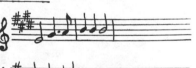

McGrath, J. J.

Prayer for a Clean Heart
(Pennsylvania Dutch)
See: Psalm 86

Prayer Is the Soul's Sincere
Desire (Careless)

Schreiner, A.

Preis, Lob, Ehr, Ruhm, Dank,
Kraft und Mach (Darmstadt)
                    Z 2713
Schueler, H.

Preis, Lob und Dank
See: Psalm 118

Preis und Anbetung bringet ihr
Christen (Rinck)
                    Z 8678
Rinck, J. C. H. (2)

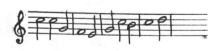

Preiset mit dem Glaubens Mute
See: St. Thomas (Wade)

Pro Omnibus Sanctis (Barnby)

    Variants:
    Sarum

       Calver, F. L.   Stults, R. M.
       Reiff, S. T.

Pro Patria (Armistead)

       Wallbank, N.

Promised Land (U. S. Southern)

       Read, G.

Proprior Deo (Doane)
    See: More Love to Thee (Doane)

Przybieżeli (Polish Carol)

       Labunski, F. R.

Psallite Domino

       Jaeggi, O.

Psalm 1 (Geneva)
              Z 3096
       Dragt, J.
       Gagnebin, H.   Weelden, J. van (2)
    Variants:
    Colur tout à Dieu
    Wer nicht mit den Gottlosen (Marot)

       Rinck, J. C. H.

Psalm 2 (Marot)

       Noordt, A. van
       Schaaf, H. van der   Wolf, C. de
    Variant:
    Wat drift beheerscht

Psalm 3 (Geneva)
    See: Old 122nd (Bourgeois)

Psalm 4 (Bourgeois)
              Z 7823
       Brakman, P. C.
       Wolf, C. de

Psalm 5 (Geneva)

Z 1796

Asma, F.
Gagnebin, H.
Groothengel, J. G.
Variants:
Neem, Heer, mijn bange

Jansen, S. C.
Kee, C.
Speuy, H. J.

Psalm 64

Psalm 6 (Geneva-Marot)

Z 2266

Gagnebin, H. (2)
Groothengel, J. G.
Hekhuis, J.
McKay, G. F.
Noordt, A. van
Variants:
I dag skal allting sjung
I kristne som toer trede

Renooij, B.
Rippen, P.
Tromp, A.
Wilgenburg, D. van
Zwart, J.

Nielsen, L.

Psalm 7 (Bourgeois)

Asma, F.
Variant:
O Heer, mijn God, volzalig Wezen

Noordt, A. van (2)

Psalm 8 (Geneva)

Z 923

Asma, F.
Beek, W. van
Gagnebin, H. (2)
Horst, A. van der
Kerckhoven, A. van den
Kohn, K. G.
Variants:
Der Tag ist hin (Geneva)

Speuy, H. J.
Stulp, G.
Weelden, J. van (2)
Wieruszowski, L. (2)
Zwart, J.

*Claussnitzer, P.
*Franke, F. W.
 Grosheim, G. C.
 Hofmeier, A.
*Merk, G.

Oley, J. C. (2)
Pisk, P. A.
*Piutti, K.
Walcha, H.
Wieruszowski, L.

Det koster mer enn man fra foerst

Karlsen, R

Psalm 8 (Geneva) (cont.)

    Die Sonn' hat sich mit

        Drischner, M.   Kickstat, P.
        Forchhammer, T.   Schaefer, K.
        Hennig, W.   Weber, H.
        Hoeller, K.   Wenzel, E.

    Gott rufet noch

        Gottschick, F.   Reda, S.

    Heer, onze Heer, grootmachtig
    O hoechster Gott

        Rinck, J. C. H.

    Wie herrlich, gibst du, Herr

        Ehinger, H. R.

Psalm 9 (Bourgeois)

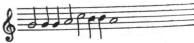

               Z 702

        Speuy, H. J.
    Variants:
    Ik zal met al mijn hart
    Nun lobet Gott im hohen Thron

        Ahrens, J.   Schroeder, H.
        Baumann, M.   *Seckinger, K.
        Romanovsky, E.   Weber, H.

Psalm 12 (Geneva)

               Z 900
        McKay, G. F.
        Speuy, H. J.   Wood, C.
    Variants:
    Behoud, O Heer, wil ons
    Donne Secours

        Bingham, S.

Psalm 15 (Marot)

             Z 1793
        Noordt, A. van
    Variant:
    Wie zal verkeeren

Psalm 16 (Geneva)

             Z 3115

Asma, F.
Gagnebin, H. (2)
Variant:
Bewaar, mij toch

Speuy, H. J.

Psalm 17 (Bourgeois)
Z 5927
Brakman, P. C.
Kee, C.
Variants:
'tBehaag' U, Heer, naar
Psalm 63 (Dutch)

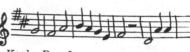

Kool, B., Jr.

Jansen, S. C.

Psalm 19 (Geneva)
Z 8232
Bruin, B.
Gagnebin, H. (2)
Kee, C.
Variants:
Het ruime hemelrond
Song 85 (Dutch)

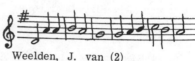

Weelden, J. van (2)
Wilgenburg, D. van

Wilgenburg, D. van

Psalm 21 (Bourgeois)
Z 2506
Blekkenhorst, H.
Variants:
Gak ud, min sjael, betragt med flid

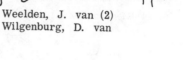

Jansen, S. C.

Vestergaard-Pedersen, C.

Ich hab' mein Sach (Bourgeois)
Song 258 (Dutch)

Psalm 22 (Geneva-Marot)

Asma, F.
Brakman, P. C.
Gagnebin, H.
Kee, C.
Noordt, A. van (2)
Renooij, B.
Variant:
Mijn God, mijn God, waarom verlaut

Schaaf, H. van der
Sumsion, C. C.
Vogel, W.
Weelden, J. van
Wilgenburg, D. van
Zwart, J.

Psalm 23 (Bourgeois)
Z 3199
Berg, J. van den
Dragt, J.
Gagnebin, H. (2)

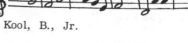

Kousemaker, A.
Oussoren, H. L.
Rippen, P.

Speuy, H. J.
Weelden, J. van (2)

Psalm 23 (Bourgeois) (cont.)

Variants:
De God des heils wil mij
Der Herr ist mein getreuer Hirt (Wittenberg)

*Bornefeld, H.   Reda, S.
Kickstat, P.   Schweppe, J.
Koch, J. H. E.   Weber, H.
Metzger, H. A.   Wenzel, E.
Micheelsen, H. F.   Werner, F.
Pachelbel, J. (2)   Zeggert, G.
Pepping, E.

Gott ist mein Hirt (Bourgeois)

*Eyken, J. A. van   *Menzel, C.

Psalm 24 (Geneva-Marot)
                Z 2665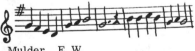

Beek, W. Van   Noordt, A. van
Blankenberg, Q. G. van Rippen, P.
Bruin, B.   Speuy, H. J. (2)
Gagnebin, H. (2)   Vogel, W.
Kee, C.   Weelden, J. van (2)
Mudde, W.   Zwart, J.
Variants:
Al d'aard' en alles
Meine Seele ist still zu Gott

Kaminski, H.   Wieruszowski, L.

Psalm 62 (Bourgeois)

Bijster, J.   Kee, C.
Brakman, P. C.   Vogel, W.

Psalm 95 (Dutch)

Kousemaker, A. (2)   Schaaf, H. van der
Nauta, J.

Psalm 25 (Geneva)
                Z 6678

Bonset, J. (2)   Mulder, E. W.
Brakman, P. G.   Rippen, P.
Bruin, B.   Storm, A.
Gagnebin, H.   Vogel, W.
Hess, C. L.   Weelden, J. van
Kee, C.   Wieruszowski, L.
Kool, B. , Jr.   Zwart, J. (2)

Variants:
'kHef mijn ziel, O God
Ich erhebe mein Gemuete

    Mueller-Zuerich, P.   Reichel, B.

Zu dir ich mein Herz erhebe

    Franke, F. W.   Meissner, H.

Psalm 26 (Bourgeois)
                Z 2185

    Kee, C.
    Vogel, W.
Variant:
O Heer, doe dij Gij recht

Psalm 27 (Geneva)

                Z 6192

    Bijster, J.   Speuy, H. J.
    Gagnebin, H.   Telgen-Vermeulen, H. van
    Mudde, W.   Weelden, J. van (2)
    Schaaf, H. van der Westering, P. C. van
Variants:
Der Herr, mein Licht

    Rinck, J. C. H.

God is mijn Licht
So fuehrst du doch

Psalm 28 (Geneva)

    Brakman, P. C.
Variant:
Ik roep tot U

Gagnebin, H.

Psalm 29 (Bourgeois)

    Rippen, P.
Variant:
Aardsche machten

Psalm 29 (Geneva)

    Gagnebin, H.

Psalm 30 (Geneva)
                Z 2652

    Brakman, P. C.
    Gagnebin, H.

Psalm 30 (Geneva) (cont.)

Variants:
Ik zal met hart
Psalm 139 (Dutch)

Berg, J. van den   Schaaf, H. van der
Mudde, W.   Vogel, W.
Oussoren, H. L.   Wilgenburg, D. van
Rippen, P.

Psalm 31 (Bourgeois)

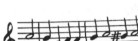

Kee, C.
Schaaf, H. van der

Psalm 32 (Geneva)
                    Z 6225
Berg, J. van den
Gagnebin, H.   Weelden, J. van (2)
Kousemaker, A.   Wilgenburg, D. van
Vogel, W.   Wolf, C. de

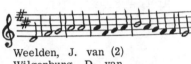

Psalm 33 (Geneva)
                    Z 7990
Gagnebin, H. (2)
Kee, C. (4)   Tromp, A.
Mudde, W.   Weelden, J. van (2)
Rippen, P.   Wieruszowski, L.
Schaaf, H. van der   Wolf, C. de
Schuurman, A. C.   Zwart, J. (3)
Variants:
O Licht geboren aus dem Lichte

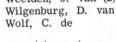

Piutti, K.

Psalm 67 (Dutch)

Psalm 34 (Geneva)
                    Z 5230
Gagnebin, H.
Kee, C.   Vogel, W.
Variant:
Ik loof den Heer

Psalm 36 (Geneva)
See: O Mensch, bewein dein Suende gross

Psalm 37 (Bourgeois)
                    Z 3159

Speuy, H. J.

Psalm 38 (Marot)

Z 3531

Berg, J. van den
Gagnebin, H.
Mudde, W.

Noordt, A. van
Rippen, P.

Variants:
Groot en eeuwig
Grosser Gott, du liebst Erbarmen

Bauer, J.
Metzger, H. A.
Reda, S.

Scholz, H. G.
Weinreich, W.

Hueter, wird die Nacht

Dreier, B.
*Finzenhagen, L. H. O.

*Gerhardt, P.
*Huth, A.

Old 38th

Psalm 40 (Bourgeois)

Speuy, H. J. (2)
Variant:
'kHeb lang den Heer

Psalm 42 (Geneva)
See: Freu dich sehr

Psalm 43 (Bourgeois)

Asma, F.
Berg, J. van den
Blekkenhorst, H.
Dommele, J. van
Kee, C.

Rippen, P.
Tromp, A.
Vogel, W. (2)
Weelden, J. van (3)
Wilgenburg, D. van

Variant:
Geduchte God

Psalm 45 (Bourgeois)

Dragt, J.
Kee, C.
Variant:
Mijn hart, vervuld

Psalm 46 (Bourgeois)

Z 6118

Kee, C.
Rippen, P.

Weelden, J. van (3)

Variant:
God is een toevlucht

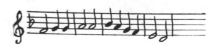

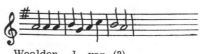

Psalm 47 (Bourgeois)
                          Z 8337

        Asma, F.
        Hess, C. L.
        Jansen, S. C.
        Kee, C.
    Variant:
    Juicht, O volken

Rippen, P.
Wilgenburg, D. van
Zwart, J.

Psalm 48 (Pierre)
                          Z 7988
        Beek, W. van
        Peters, A.
    Variant:
    De Heer is groot

Rippen, P.

Psalm 50 (Bourgeois)
                          Z 3094
        Noordt, A. van
    Variant:
    Der goden God

Psalm 51 (Bourgeois)
                          Z 6151
        Brakman, P. C.
        Rippen, P.
        Schaaf, H. van der
        Speuy, H. J.
    Variant:
    Psalm 69 (Dutch)

        Wilgenburg, D. van

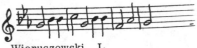

Wieruszowski, L.
Wilgenburg, D. van
Zwart, J.

Psalm 55 (Pierre)

        Wilgenburg, D. van
        Wolf, C. de

Psalm 57 (Pierre)

        Kee, C.

Psalm 61 (Pierre)
                          Z 3532

        Brakman, P. C.
        Buitendijk, B.
    Variant:
    Tu, Herr, mein Geschrei erhoeren

        Rinck, J. C. H.

Kee, C.
Rippen, P.

Psalm 62 (Bourgeois)
  See: Psalm 24 (Geneva)

Psalm 63 (Dutch)
  See: Psalm 17

Psalm 64 (Geneva)
  See: Psalm 5

Psalm 65 (Bourgeois)

Z 5933

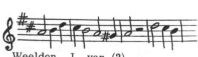

Blekkenhorst, H.
Groothengel, J. G.   Rippen, P.
Kee, C.   Speuy, H. J.
Kousemaker, A.   Weelden, J. van
Mulder, E. W.   Wieruszowski, L. (2)
Variants:
Man betet, Herr, in Zion's stille

  Mueller-Zuerich, P. (2)   Wieruszowski, L.

Psalm 72 (Dutch)

  Bonefaas, J.   Weelden, J. van (2)
  Kool, B., Jr.   Wilgenburg, D. van
  Oussoren, H. L.   Zwart, J.
  Verrips, N.

Psalm 66 (Dutch)
  See: Psalm 118

Psalm 67 (Strassburg)
  See: Es wolle Gott

Psalm 67 (Dutch)
  See: Psalm 33

Psalm 68 (Geneva)
  See: O Mensch, bewein dein Suende gross

Psalm 69 (Dutch)
  See: Psalm 51

Psalm 72 (Dutch)
  See: Psalm 65

Psalm 73 (Bourgeois)

Z 5882

  Rippen, P.   Weelden, J. van (2)
  Stulp, G.   Zwart, J.

Psalm 74 (Geneva)
                        Z 859

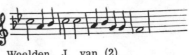

    Fischer, N. Z.   Weelden, J. van (2)
    Rippen, P.   Wilgenburg, D. van
Variants:
Ainsworth 97

    Savage, H. S.

Gott hab' ich lieb, er hoerte

    Franke F. W.

Psalm 116 (deBeze)

    Asma, F.   Schaaf, H. van der
    Beek, W. van   Schuurman, A. C.
    Brakman, P. C.   Speuy, H. J.
    Groothengel, J. G.   Vogel, W. (2)
    Kee, C. (2)   Wilgenburg, D. van
    Noordt, A. van (2)
Song 170 (Dutch)

    Wilgenburg, D. van

Psalm 75 (Geneva)
                        Z 3333

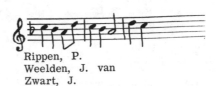

    Beek, W. van
    Bonset, J. (2)   Rippen, P.
    Bruin, B.   Weelden, J. van
    Post, P.   Zwart, J.
Variant:
U alleen U loven

    Mazyk, R. van

Psalm 77 (Dutch)
  See: Psalm 86

Psalm 79 (Geneva)
                        Z 7849

    Beek, W. van
    Brakman, P. C.   Speuy, H. J.
    Rippen, P.   Weelden, J. van (2)

Psalm 80 (Dutch)
  See: Victimi Paschali Laudes (Gregorian)

Psalm 81 (Pierre)
                        Z 3263

    Brakman, P. C.
    Verwoerd, A.

Variant:
Song 71 (Dutch)

Wilgenburg, D. van

Psalm 84 (Geneva)
See: Jervaulx Abbey

Psalm 86 (Geneva)

Z 6863

Barrow, R.
Kee, P.
Kousemaker, A.
Variants:
Geneva 86

Schaaf, H. van der
Weelden, J. van

Goemanne, N.   Larkin, J.

Herr, erhoere meine Klagen

Wieruszowski, L.

Prayer for a Clean Heart (Pennsylvania Dutch)

Johnson, A. H.

Psalm 77 (Dutch)

Cellier, A.   Vogel, W.
Kee, C.   Westering, P. C. van
Post, P.   Wieruszowski, L.
Rippen, P.   Zwart, J.
Tromp, A.

Unveraenderliche Guete

Oley, J. C. (2)

Psalm 87 (Pierre)

Berg, J. van den
Mazyk, R. van   Renooij, B.
                                Rippen, P.

Psalm 89 (Pierre)

Z 3211

Brakman, P. C.	Manueke, D.	Tromp, A.
Bruin, B. (2)	Nauta, J.	Weelden, J. van
Dalm, W.	Reijden, W. van der (2)	Westering, P. C. van
Dragt, J.	Renooij, B.	Westra, E.
Klaassen, J.	Rippen, P. (3)	Wilgenburg, D. van
Kousemaker, A. (2)	Stulp, G.	

Psalm 89 (Pierre) (cont.)

Variants:
Song 132 (Dutch)

    Vogel, W.   Wilgenburg, D. van

Sovereign Grace

Psalm 90 (Bourgeois)
                    Z 3198
    Cellier, A.
    Kousemaker, A.   Kusters, G.

Psalm 91 (Geneva)
                    Z 5694
    Beek, W. van
    Kee, C.   Kousemaker, A.

Psalm 92 (Pierre)

    Klaassen, J.
    Kousemaker, A.   Vogel, W.
    Stam, G.   Wilgenburg, D. van

Psalm 93 (Pierre)
                    Z 819
    Jansen, S. C.
    Post, P.

Psalm 95 (Dutch)
  See: Psalm 24

Psalm 96 (Pierre)

    Klaassen, J.   Vogel, W.

Psalm 97 (Pierre)
                    Z 7191
    Asma, F.
    Bruin, B.   Oussoren, H. L.
    Jansen, S. C.   Wieruszowski, L.
Variant:
Der Herr ein Koenig ist (Goudimal)

    Volckmar, F. W.

Psalm 98 (Dutch)
  See: Psalm 118

Organ - Preludes

Psalm 99 (Pierre)

                    Z 6237

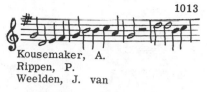

    Bonefaas, J. (2)
    Bruin, B.
    Hoogewoud, H.

    Kousemaker, A.
    Rippen, P.
    Weelden, J. van

Psalm 100 (Geneva)

                    Z 367

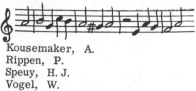

    Asma, F.
    Beek, W. van
    Bijster, J.
    Bonefaas, J.
    Braal, A. de
    Dommele, J. van
    Kee, C.
Variants:
Morgenzang

    Kousemaker, A.
    Rippen, P.
    Speuy, H. J.
    Vogel, W.
    Weelden, J. van
    Zwart, J.

    Zwart, J.

Psalm 131 (Dutch)

    Kee, C.

Song I

    Post, P.

Psalm 101 (Geneva)

                    Z 919

    Post, P.

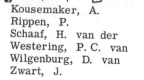

Rippen, P.

Psalm 102 (Pierre)

    Kee, C.

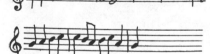

Psalm 103 (Geneva)

                    Z 3187

    Beek, W. van
    Bijster, J.
    Brakman, P. C.
    Dragt, J.
    Gagnebin, H.
    Kee, C.
Variants:
Song 247 (Dutch)

    Kousemaker, A.
    Rippen, P.
    Schaaf, H. van der
    Westering, P. C. van
    Wilgenburg, D. van
    Zwart, J.

    Wilgenburg, D. van

Sus louez Dieu

Psalm 104 (Dutch)
   See: Hanover (Croft)

Psalm 105 (Pierre)
                  Z 2995

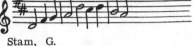

    Beek, W. van
    Bruin, B.
    Hooven, N. van den   Stam, G.
    Jansen, S. C.   Weelden, J. van (2)
    Kee, C.   Wieruszowski, L. (2)
    Rippen, P.   Wilgenburg, D. van
    Variants: Zwart, D. J.
    Aa Herre, lat meg heilt

    Karlsen, R.

I al sin glans

    Woeldike, M. A.   Wuertz, J.

Song 69 (Dutch)

    Wilgenburg, D. van

Psalm 106 (Pierre)

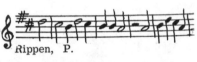

    Kee, C.   Rippen, P.

Psalm 107 (Geneva)

    Barrow, R.
    McKay, G. F.
    Variant:
    Donnez au Seigneur

Psalm 108 (Pierre)

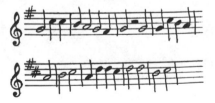

    Groothengel, J. G.

Psalm 113 (Bourgeois)
                  Z 2663
    Tilburg, F. van

Psalm 116 (de Beze)
   See: Psalm 74

Psalm 118 (Geneva)
               Z 6002

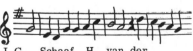

    Barrow, R.   Groothengel, J. G.   Schaaf, H. van der
    Beek, W. Van Huijbers, B.   Speuy, H. J.
    Bonset, J.   McKay, G. F.   Waters, C. F.
    Engels, A.   Nauta, J.   Wilgenburg, D. van (2)

Variants:

Almindelig er Kristi kirke

Rosenkilde-Larsen, E.   Thuner, O. E.

Geneva 118

Schaffer, R. J.

Jauchzt alle Lande, Gott zu Ehren

Brod, K.   Hennig, W.
Eyken, J. A. van   Meissner, H.
Fiebig, K. (2)   Metzger, H. A.
Franke, F. W. (2)   Reda, S.
Grabner, H.   Walcha, H.

Navarre

Haase, K.   Hulse, C. Van

Preis, Lob und Dank

Beyer, M.

Psalm 66 (Dutch)

Asma, F.   Weelden, J. van (3)
Mulder, E. W.   Westering, P. C. van
Rippen, P.   Wilgenburg, D. van (2)
Schaaf, H. van der   Zwart, J.
Schuurman, A. C.

Psalm 98 (Dutch)

Hoogewoud, H.   Wieruszowski, L.
Weelden, J. van   Wilgenburg, D. van

Rendez à Dieu

Clokey, J. W.   Peek, R. M.
Coleman, R. H. P.   Powell, R. J.
Johnson, D. N.   Walter, S.

Singt, singt dem Herren neue Lieder
Jehova
Wieruszowski, L. (2)

Song 181 (Dutch)

Wilgenburg, D. van

Psalm 118 (Geneva) (cont.)

   Song 244 (Dutch)

      Wilgenburg, D. van

   Song 257 (Dutch)

      Wilgenburg, D. van

   Song 268 (Dutch)

      Wilgenburg, D. van

   Song 295 (Dutch)

      Wilgenburg, D. van

Psalm 119 (Geneva)
              Z 3114

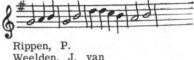

      Kool, B., Jr.
      Noordt, A. van   Rippen, P.
      Post, P.   Weelden, J. van
      Variant:
      O selig sind die in Aufrechtigkeit

      Franke, F. W.

Psalm 121 (Bourgeois)
              Z 2350

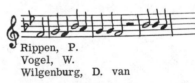

      Asma, F.   Rippen, P.
      Bijster, J.   Vogel, W.
      King, H. C.   Wilgenburg, D. van

Psalm 122 (Geneva)

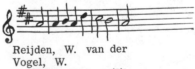

      Beek, W. van
      Brakman, P. C.
      Bruin, B.   Reijden, W. van der
      Jansen, S. C.   Vogel, W.
                    Weelden, J. van (2)

Psalm 123 (Bourgeois)

      Kee, C.
      Kool, B., Jr.   Weelden, J. van (2)

Psalm 124 (Geneva)
   See: Old 124th (Geneva)

Psalm 126 (Bourgeois)
              Z 5864

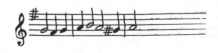

Variant:
Wenn einst der Herr

    Wieruszowski, L. (3)

Psalm 128 (Bourgeois)
              Z 5360
    Bonset, J.

Speuy, H. J.

Psalm 129 (Bourgeois)

    Speuy, H. J.

Psalm 130 (Geneva)
    See: Old 130th (French)

Psalm 131 (Dutch)
    See: Psalm 100

Psalm 133 (Bourgeois)
              Z 3171

    Rippen, P.   Schaaf, H. van der

Psalm 134 (Bourgeois)
    See: Old 100th

Psalm 135 (Pierre)

    Dragt, J.
    Rippen, P.
    Variant:
    Geneva 135

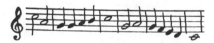

    Bottenberg, W.   Bratt, C. G.

Psalm 136 (Pierre)
              Z 1181
    Rippen, P.
    Wieruszowski, L.
    Variant:
    Holy Name

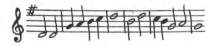

    Peeters, F.

Psalm 137 (Bourgeois)
              Z 3186
    Jansen, S. C.

Psalm 138 (Bourgeois)
    See also: Mit Freuden zart
              Z 8268

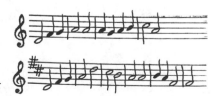

Psalm 138 (Bourgeois) (cont.)

Beek, W. van   Koppenol, J. (2)
Berg, J. van den   Mudde, W.
Bijster, J.   Rippen, P.
Cellier, A.   Tromp, A.
Dommele, J. van   Wieruszowski, L.
Hoogewoud, H.
Variant:
Mein genzes Herz erhebet dich

Wieruszowski, L.

Psalm 139 (Dutch)
  See: Psalm 30

Psalm 140 (Geneva)
  See: Wenn wir in hoechsten Noethen

Psalm 141 (Pierre)
                    Z 749

  Kee, C.
  Mazyk, R. van   Westering, P. C. van

Psalm 143 (Strassburg)
                    Z 1816b

  Hekhuis, J.
  Vogel, W.

Psalm 145 (Pierre)

  Kee, C.
  Rippen, P.   Vogel, W.

Psalm 146 (Pierre)
                    Z 3613

  Bruin, B.
  Dragt, J.   Rippen, P.
  Post, P.   Wilgenburg, D. van

Psalm 146
  See: Herr Jesu Christ, dich zu uns wend

Psalm 150 (Pierre)
                    Z 6370

  Bruin, B.   Rippen, P.
  Johnson, A. H.   Schuurman, A. C.
  Kee, C.   Weelden, J. van (2)
  Mazyk, R. van   Wilgenburg, D. van
  Moolenaar, F.   Zwart, J.

Variant:
Song 26 (Dutch)

    Wilgenburg, D. van

Psalm 202 (Geneva)
  See: Song of Symeon (Geneva)

Psalm Tone - 8th

    Titcomb, E. H.

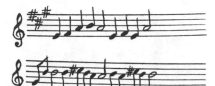

Puer Natus Est Nobis

    Hulse, C. Van (2)
    *Stoegbauer, I.

             Widor, C. M.

Puer Natus Est Nobis
  See: Puer Nobis Nascitur (Praetorius)

Puer Natus in Bethlehem (Old
German)
           Z 192b

Bach, J. S. (2)	Englert, E.
Bedell, R. L.	Marckhl, E.
Bingham, S.	Michl, A.
Bratt, C. G.	Plum, P. J. M.
Buxtehude, D. (4)	Potiron, H.
Doppelbauer, J. F.	Sivert, P.
Dupré, M. J. J.	Walther, J. G.

Variants:
Ein Kind geboren

    Kauffmann, G. F.   Siefert, P.

  Et barn er foedt i Bethleham

    *Videroe, F.

Puer Nobis Nascitur (Praetorius)
  See also: Nun jauchzt dem
  Herren

           Z 1569a

Barlow, W.	Haase, K.	Purvis, R.
Brusey, Dom J. G.	Hulse, C. Van	Rogers, S. E. (2)
Dandrieu, J. F.	Johnson, D. N.	Rohlig, H.
Diemer, E. L.	Lebègue, N.	Shaw, G. T.
Edmundson, G.	Manz, P.	Sweelinck, J. P. (2)
Gaul, H.	Matthews, H. A.	Willan, H.
Guilmant, A.	Powell, R. J.	Wyton, A.

Puer Nobis Nascitur (Praetorius) (cont.)

Variants:
Fra Himlen kom en engel klar

    Frellsen, E.   *Wuertz, J.
    Hamburger, P.

Puer Natus Est Nobis

    Ahrens, J.   *Maleingreau, P. de
    Campbell-Watson, F.   Piechler, A.
    Kreckel, P. G.   Schehl, J. A.
    Lechthaler, J.   *Titcomb, E. H.
    Maekelberghe, A. (2)

Une ist geboren ein Kindelein

    Bull, J.   Taubert, K. H.
    Peeters, F.

Unto Us a Son is Born (Unto Us is Born a Son)

    Gotch, O. H.   Sumsion, H. W.
    Milford, R. H.

Vom Himmel kam der Engel Schaar

    Franke, F. W.

Purer in Heart (Fillmore)

    Greener, J. H.

Quam Dilecta (Jenner)

    Cameron, G.
    Coleman, R. H. P. (3)   Rowley, A.

Quand Dieu naquit
    See: Noël-Quand Dieu naquit

Quare Ergo

    Sister M. G.

Que Dieu se montre
    See: O Mensch bewein dein Suende gross

Que la Grâce de notre Seigneur

    Hess, C. L.

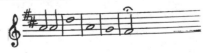

Quebec (Baker)

    Couper, A. B.
    Young, G.
  Variant:
Hesperus

    Baumgartner, H. L.   Peeters, F.
    Curry, R. D.

Quel étonnement (Denizot)

    Boëly, A. P. F.

Quem Pastores
  See: Den die Hirten lobten sehr

Quempas Carol
  See: Den die Hirten lobten sehr

Qu'en cet instant

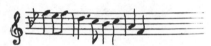

    Noyon, J.

Quies
  See: Elton (Maker)

Quittez, Pasteurs (French)

    Bingham, S.

Quoique soyez petit encore

    Hulse, C. Van

Racine (Diggle)

    Diggle, R.

Radujcie sie bracia mili (Polish
    Carol)

    Labunski, F. R.

Rare Song in Praise of Christ-
    mas (English 1660)

    Best, W. T.
  Variant:
Praise of Christmas

Rathbun (Conkey)

    Bingham, S. (2)
    Cassler, G. W.   Mueller, C. F.
    Haase, K.   Reuter, F.
    Held, W.   Stults, R. M.
    Larson, E. R.   Weiss, C. A.
    Lubrich, F. , Jr.   Young, G.

Ratisbon (Crueger)
   modified from: Z 6801
   Jesu, meine Zuversicht

    Edmundson, G.   Peeters, F.
    Haase, K.   Rohlig, H.
    Hulse, C. Van   Schreiner, A.
    Lang, C. S.
  Variants:
  Eins ist Not, ach Herr (Crueger)

    Baldamus, F.   Piutti, K.
    Bender, J.   Reger, M.
    Bieske, W.   Reuter, F.
    Brieger, O.   Richter, E. H. L.
    Claussnitzer, P. (3)   *Riedel, H.
   *Dienel, O.   Rinck, J. C. H. (2)
   *Engelbrecht, K. F. (2) Rinkens, W.
    Faehrmann, H.   Rudnick, W.
   *Fischer, M. G.   Rumpf, W.
    Fluegel, G.   Schaab, R. (2)
    Franke, F. W. (2)   Schink, H.
   *Geist, P.   Schneider, J.
   *Gruel, E.   Schneider, J. G.
    Haase, R.   Schuetze, W.
   *Hesse, A. F.   Skop, V. F.
    Hoyer, K. (2)   Spar, O.
    Kickstat, P.   Strebel, A.
    Klaus, V.   *Streicher, J. A.
    Kuntze, C.   Wettstein, H. (2)
    Merkel, G.   Wolfrum, P.
    Palme, R.   Zahn, J.
   *Peters, A.

  Ett er noedig, dette ene (Krieger)

   *Gangfloet, S.   Karlsen, R.

  Jeg venter dig, Herre Jesus (Crueger)

    Andersen, E.

Ravenna
  See: Vienna (Knecht)

Ravenshaw
    See: Gottes Sohn ist kommen

Recolitur Memoria (Gregorian)

    Falcinelli, R.

Recordare Virgo

    DeBrant, C.
    Tranzillo, D.

Red Wing Seminary (Dahle)

    Peeters, F.

Redhead 45th
    See: Orientis Partibus (Corbeil)

Redhead 46th

    Archer, J. S.
    Lang, C. S.
    Variant:
    Laus Deo

    Gilbert, N.

Redhead 66th (Metzler)

    Lang, C. S.   Tootell, G.

Redhead 76th

    Edmundson, G.
    Gray, A.   Reuter, F.
    Lang, C. S.   Rowley, A.
    Metzger, H. A.   Schumacher, M. H.
    Variants:
    Ajalon

    Bingham, S.   Powell, N. W.
    Duro, J.

    Gethsemane

    Beck, A.   Lenel, L.
    Haase, K.   Reuter, F.
    Hulse, C. Van

    Petra

    Held, W.   Rogers, S. E.   Taylor, C. T.

Redites-moi l'histoire   Tune not found

    Hess, C. L.

Regent Square (Smart)

    Beck, A.
    Commette, E.   Peeters, F.
    Flesher, G.   Reuter, F.
    Haase, K.   Unkel, R.
    Lang, C. S.   Whitford, H. P.
    Matthews, H. A.   Wilson, R. C.
    Variants:
    Eere zij aan God den Vader

    Mazyk, R. van   Weelden, J. van

    Song 93 (Dutch)

Regina Caeli Jubila (Leisentritt)
  See: Freu dich du Himmelskoenigin

Regina Caeli Laetare (Plainsong-
      Coeli   Mode 6)

    Ahrens, J.
    Bratt, C. G.   Rowell, L.
    Erb, M. J. (4)   *Titcomb, E. H.
    Kreckel, P. G.   Weitz, G.

Regina Mundi

    Sister M. G.

Regina Pacis

    Weitz, G.

Regnator Orbis
  See: O Quanta Qualia

Rejs op, dit hoved, al (Nyegaard)

    *Thuner, O. E.

Rejs op, dit hoved, al (Thomis-
    soen)

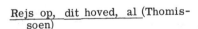

Religion von Gott gegeben
              Z 2909

Variant:
Wie lieblich ist, O Herr, die Staette

Mueller, S.   Steinhaeuser, K.
Ritter, A. G.

Rendez à Dieu
See: Psalm 118 (Geneva)

Requiem Eternam (Kyrial)

Harwood, B.

Requiescat (Dykes)

West, J. E.

Requiescat in Pace   Tune not found

Diebold, J.

Resignation (U. S. Southern)

Wilson, R. C.

Resonet in Laudibus
See: Joseph, lieber Joseph mein

Rest (Bradbury)
See: Asleep in Jesus (Bradbury)

Rest (Maker)
See: Elton

Resurgam

Rowley, A.

Resurgenti Nazarene (Bohemian)

Haase, K.

Resurrection (Slovakian)

Haase, K.

Resurrexi

Sister M. T.

Reuter
See: O Jesu, einig wahres Haupt

Réveillez-vous pastoureaux
(Denizot)

    Boëly, A. P. F.

Rex Gloriae (Smart)

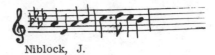

    Haase, K.
    Hulse, C. Van   Niblock, J.

Rhosymedre (Edwards)

    Vaughan-Williams, R.

Richmond (Haweis-Webbe)

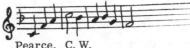

    Coleman, R. H. P.   Pearce, C. W.
    Gray, A. (2)   Rowley, A.
    Groves, R.   Schumacher, M. H.
    Lang, C. S.   Willan, H.
    Variant:
    Chesterfield

    Beck, A.   Peeters, F.
    Haase, K.

Righini (Righini)

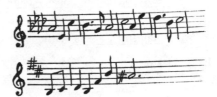

    Zeuner, C.

Rind nu op i Jesu navn (Lully-
Kingo)

    Hamburger, P.
    Jeppesen, K.   Raasted, N. O.
    Moeller, S. O.   Wuertz, J.
    Variant:
    Saligheten er oss naer (Kingo)

    Karlsen, R.

Ringe recht, wenn Gottes Gnade
(Basel)
                Z 1303

    Franke, F. W. (2)   Magnus, E.
    Variant:
    Freuet Euch der schoenen Erde

    Hasse, K.

Ringe recht, wenn Gottes Gnade
(Kuhnau)

Z 1304

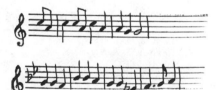

  Bach, J. C.   Markworth, H. J.
  Baldamus, F.   Moser, R.
  *Claussnitzer, P.   Oley, J. C.
  Erbe, K. (2)   Piutti, K.
  Eyken, J. A. van   Rembt, J. E.
  Haase, K.   *Rumpf, W.
  Karg-Elert, S.   Saffe, F. (2)
  Kickstat, P.   Schink, H.
  *Krause, P.   Wettstein, H.
Variants:
Batty

  Cassler, G. W.

Gott will's machen, dass die Sachen

Herrens roest, som aldrig

  *Moeller, S. O.   *Wuertz, J.
  Woeldike, M. A.

Kjemp alvorlig, nu Guds naade

  Karlsen, R.

Rise Up Shepherd

  Saxton, S. E.

Riverton (Bingham)

  Bingham, S.

Rochelle
 See: Seelenbraeutigam (Drese)

Rock of Ages (Hebrew)

  Bingham, S.
  Kohs, E. B.
Variant:
Mooz Tsur

Rocking Carol
 See: Little Jesus, Sweetly Sleep

Rockingham
 See: Rockingham Old

Rockingham Old (Miller)

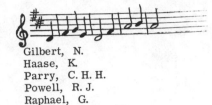

    Archer, V. B.
    Bingham, S.   Gilbert, N.
    Cameron, G.   Haase, K.
    Candlyn, T. F. H.   Parry, C. H. H.
    Coleman, R. H. P. (2) Powell, R. J.
    Conway, M. P.   Raphael, G.
    Dicks, E. A.   Webber, W. S. L.
  Variants:
  Rockingham

    Groves, R.   Noble, T. T. (2)
    Lang, C. S.   Palmer, C. C.
    Mansfield, O. A. (2)   Rowley, A.
    Marchant, A. W.   Silvester, F. C.
    Matthews, H. A.   Thiman, E. H. (2)
    Means, C.   Willan, H.

  Song 48 (Dutch)

    Bijster, J.

Roll, Jordan, Roll (Negro Spiritual)

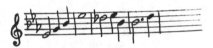

    Archer, J. S.

Rorate Coeli (Rouen - Mode 1)

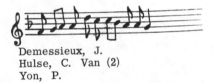

    Benoit, Dom P.
   *Bernard, A.
   *Bratt, C. G.   Demessieux, J.
    Campbell-Watson, F. Hulse, C. Van (2)
                   Yon, P.

Rosa Mystica
  See: Es ist ein Ros'

Rosy Sequence (Sarum)

    Groves, R.

Rouen (Poitiers)

  Variant:
  Iste Confessor (Rouen)

    Egerton, A. H.   Rootham, C. B.
    Harker, C.   Willan, H.

Rouen Church Melody

    Willan, H.

Rouen Melody

  Hurford, P.
  Willan, H.
  Variant:
St. Venantius

  Willan, H.

Rueste dich, Held von Golgotha
  (Gade)

  Variants:
Nun ruest dich, Held

   Raasted, N. O.

 Syng hoejt, min sjael

   Raasted, N. O.

  Udrust dig, helt fra (Gade)

   Amberg, H.   Raasted, N. O.
   Christensen, B.   Thuner, O. E.
   Godske-Nielsen, H. Weinholt-Pedersen, K.
   Houengaard, H.   Woeldike, M. A.
   Messell, E.   Wuertz, J.
   Nielsen, T. H.

Ruhe hier, mein Geist (Darmstadt)
 See: Sieh, hier bin ich (Darmstadt)

Ruhe ist das beste Gut
  (Stoetzel)
       Z 7078

   Buehl, W.   Rumpf, W.
   Rinck, J. C. H. Seyerlen, R.
  Variants:
Himmelan, nur Himmelan (Stoetzel)

   Taeger, A.

 Ruhet wohl, ihr Totenbeine

   Fry, H. S.

Ruhe ist das beste Gut

  Kuehn, K.

Ruhet wohl, ihr Totenbeine
 See: Ruhe ist das beste Gut (Stoetzel)

Russian Hymn (Lwoff)

    Arnold, G. B.   Matthison-Hansen, H.
    Dicks, E. A.   Pye, J. T.
    Freyer, A.   Thayer, W. E.
    Koehler, E.

Rust mijn ziel
    See: Song 179 (Dutch)

Rutherford (Urhan)

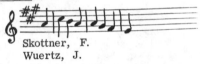

    Mansfield, P. J.
    Reynolds, W. G.

Ruwe stormen mogen woeden   Tune not found

    Moolenaar, F.

Saa tag nu mina haender
    See: So nimm denn meine Haende (Silcher)

Saa vil vi nu sige (Lindeman)

    Alnaes, E.   Skottner, F.
    Nielsen, L.   Wuertz, J.

Sacerdos Et Pontifex   Tune not found

    Weber, C.

Sacramentum Unitatis (Lloyd)

    Sowerby, L.

Sacred Heart of Jesus (Slovak)

    McGrath, J. J.

Sacris Solemnis (Mode 4)

    Dupré, M. J. J.   Langlais, J. F.
    Erb, M. J. (9)   Peeters, F.

Sacris Solemnis (Old English)

    *Tranzillo, D.

Safe in the Arms of Jesus
    (Doane)

    Ashford, E. L.

Safe to the Rock (Sankey)

    Thompson, V. D.
Variant:
O Safe to the Rock

Saffron Walden (Brown)

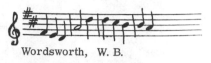

    Coleman, R. H. P.
    Rowley, A.   Wordsworth, W. B.

Sag, was hilft alle Welt
                Z 101
    Walther, J. G.

Sagt an, wer ist doch diese
    mir

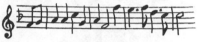

    Brand, T.

St. Agnes (Dykes)

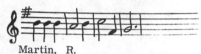

     Ashford, E. L.
     Beck, A.   Martin, R.
     Curry, R. D.   Peeters, F.
     Elmore, R. H.   Shaffer, J. E.
     Haase, K.   Thomas, V. C.
     Hooper, W. L.   Whitford, H. P. (2)
     Hulse, C. Van   Whitney, M. C.
Variant:
St. Agnes (Durham)

St. Agnes (Durham)
   See: St. Agnes (Dykes)

St. Albinus (Gauntlett)

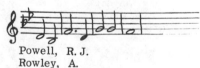

    Dickey, M.   Powell, R. J.
    Groves, R.   Rowley, A.

St. Anatolius (Brown)

    Frost, C. J.
    Haase, K.   Peeters, F.
    Hulse, C. Van   Phillips, C. G.

St. Andrew (Barnby)

    Hulse, C. Van

St. Anne (Croft)

    Archer, J. S.
    Ashford, E. L.
    Bach, J. S.
    Bartlett, H. N.
    Beck, A.
    Best, W. T.
    Buck, D.
    Coke-Jephcott, N.
    Coleman, R. H. P.
    Conway, M. P.
    Copley, R. E. (2)
    Dasher, J. A.
    Diggle, R.
    Edmundson, G.
    Fleischer, H.
    Frost, C. J.
    Gray, A.
    Groves, R.
    Haase, K.
    Harris, C. H. G.
    Harris, C.
    Hulse, C. Van

Krapf, G.
Lang, C. S.
Lowenberg, K.
Matthews, H. A.
Miles, G. T.
Noble, T. T. (2)
Palmer, C. C.
Parry, C. H. H. (2)
Peek, R. M.
Rogers, L.
Rohlig, H.
Silas, E.
Thorne, E. H.
Verrees, L.
Watkinson, J. R.
Wehmeyer, W.
Wesley, S. S.
White, R.
Whitford, H. P.
Willan, H.
Young, G. (4)

Variant:
Song 293 (Dutch)

    Beek, W. van
    Bruin, B.

Wilgenburg, D. van

St. Anselm (Barnby)

    Whitford, H. P. (2)

St. Anthony (Haydn)

    Marier, T. N.

St. Bees (Dykes)

    Lutkin, P. C.
    Matthews, H. A.

St. Bernard (Cologne)

    Archer, J. S.
    Busarow, D.
    Candlyn, T. F. H.
    Goode, J. C.

Haase, K.
Hulse, C. Van
Peeters, F.

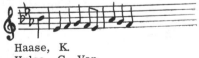

Variant:
Tochter Zion freue dich

    Gulbins, M.

St. Botolph (Smart)

    Hill, L. E.
    Slater, G. A.

St. Bride (Howard)

Beck, A.	Palmer, C. C.
Beck, T.	Peeters, F.
Best, W. T.	Reuter, F.
Farrar, E. B.	Rowley, A.
Haase, K.	Wesley, S. S.
Kitson, C. H.	Willan, H.

St. Catherine (Hemy)

Bingham, S.	Mueller, C. F.
Hulse, C. Van (2)	Rogers, L.
Johnson, D. N.	Schehl, J. A.
Labunski, F. R.	Taylor, C. T.
Lorenz, E. J.	Thompson, V. D.
McKinley, C.	Whitford, H. P.

St. Catherine's Court (Strutt)

    Henschel, G.

St. Cecelia (Hayne)

    Boda, J.
    Conway, M. P.
Variant:
Song 115 (Dutch)

    Kort, J.

St. Christopher (Maker)

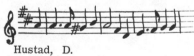

    Colvin, H.
    Curry, R. D.   Hustad, D.
    Elmore, R. H.   Stults, R. M.

St. Clement (Scholefield)

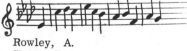

    Bellerby, E. J.
    Cummins, R.
    Mansfield, P. J.   Rowley, A.
    McKinley, C.   Shure, R. D.
Variants: Wallbank, N.
De dag door Uwe gunst

    Bruin, B.   Mazyk, R. van

St. Clement (Scholefield) (cont.)

Song 281 (Dutch)

Kousemaker, A.

St. Colomba (Irish)

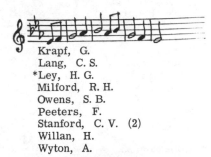

Banks, H.   Krapf, G.
*Cameron, G.   Lang, C. S.
Cassler, G. W.   *Ley, H. G.
Christopher, C. S.   Milford, R. H.
Coleman, R. H. P. (2)   Owens, S. B.
*Groves, R. (2)   Peeters, F.
*Hill, L. E.   Stanford, C. V. (2)
Hinton, J. E. A.   Willan, H.
Kitson, C. H.   Wyton, A.

St. Colomba (Irons)

Lloyd, L. S.
Variant:
Irons

*Grieb, H.

St. Constantine (Monk)

Groves, R.
Reuter, F.   Watkinson, J. R.

St. Crispin (Elvey)

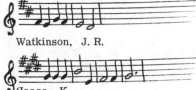

Arbatsky, Y.   Haase, K.
Beck, A.   Hokanson, M.
Bouman, P.   Willan, H.

St. Cross (Dykes)

Beck, A.   Hulse, C. Van
Bingham, S.   Parry, C. H. H.
Goldsworthy, W. A.   Webber, W. S. L.
Haase, K.   Willan, H.

St. Cuthbert (Dykes)

Curry, R. D.
Willan, H.

St. David (Ravenscroft)

    Best, W. T.
    *Sowerbutts, J. A.

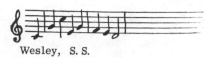
Wesley, S. S.

St. David's Day (Welsh Folk
Tune)

    Vaughan-Williams, R.

St. Denio
    See: Joanna (Welsh)

St. Drostane (Dykes)

        Cassler, G. W. (2)
        Matthews, H. A.

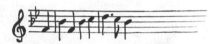

St. Dunstan's (Douglas)

        Boda, J.
        Groom, L.
        Near, G.

Sinzheimer, M.
Sowerby, L.

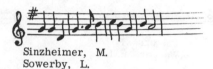

St. Edith (Knecht)

        Reynolds, W. G.
        Thomas, V. C.

Young, G.

St. Elizabeth
    See: Schoenster Herr Jesu (Silesian)

St. Ethelwald (Monk)

        Conway, M. P.
        Farrar, E. B.
    Variant:
    Energy

        Haase, K.

Lang, C. S.
Reuter, F.

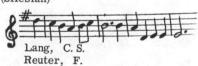

St. Fabian (Barnby)

        Brown, F. R.

St. Flavian (Day's)

        Ashford, E. L.
        Bingham, S. (2)
        Bratt, C. G.
        Candlyn, T. F. H.
        Canning, T.

Farrar, E. B.
Graf, F.
Gray, A.
Haase, K.
Lang, C. S.

St. Flavian (Day's) (cont.)

  Lewis, J. L.   Plettner, A.
  Mead, E. G.   Rogers, S. E.
  Nieland, J.   Smith, R.
  Palmer, C. C.   Taylor, C. T.
  Peeters, F.   Willan, H.
Variant:
Old 132nd

  Harwood, B.   Wood, C.

St. Fulbert (Gauntlett)

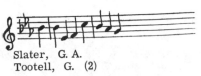

  Guest, D. A.
  Lang, C. S.   Slater, G. A.
  Rowley, A.   Tootell, G. (2)

St. Gabriel (Ouseley)

  Peeters, F.
  Warner, R. L.   Willan, H.

St. George (Gauntlett)

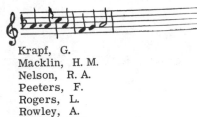

  Coleman, R. H. P.   Lang, C. S.
  Hulse, C. Van   *Mansfield, O. A.
Variant:
St. Olave

  Mansfield, O. A.

St. George (Herman)
 See: Lobt Gott, ihr Christen (Herman)

St. Georges Windsor (Elvey)

  Ashford, E. L.
  Bailey, C. M.   Krapf, G.
  Barlow, W.   Macklin, H. M.
  English, R.   Nelson, R. A.
  Frysinger, J. F.   Peeters, F.
  Gehrke, H.   Rogers, L.
  Griffiths, T. V.   Rowley, A.
  Groves, R.   Saxton, S. E.
  Haase, K.   Woods, F. C.

St. Gertrude (Sullivan)

  Abram, J.
  Achenbach, T.   Diggle, R.
  Ashford, E. L.   Frysinger, J. F.
  Burdett, G. A.   Haase, K.
           Larson, E. R.

Lemare, E. H.
Moolenaar, F.
Pruyn-Hall, E.

West, J. A.
Whiting, G. E.
Young, G.

St. Hilary (Ganther)

Haase, K.

St. Hilda (Barnby)

Ashford, E. L.
Lorenz, E. J.
Rogers, S. E.

Taylor, C. T.
Thompson, V. D.

St. Hugh (English)

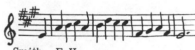

Alderson, A. P.

St. Hugh (Hopkins)

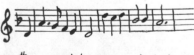

Rowley, A.

St. James (Courteville)

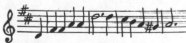

Hulse, C. Van
Krapf, G.
Noble, T. T.
Palmer, C. C.

Smith, E. H.
Stephens, C. E.
Willan, H.

St. John (Dykes)

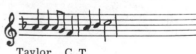

Hulse, C. Van

St. John (Havergal)

Haase, K.

St. Kevin (Sullivan)

Bingham, S.
Hughes, R. J.
Laverty, J. T.
McKay, G. F.
Miles, R. H.

Taylor, C. T.
Thomas, V. C.
Whitford, H. P.
Young, G.

St. Kilda (Broomfield)

Noble, T. T.

St. Leonard (Meiningen)
               Z 3651

   Lynn, G. A.
Variants:
Komm, O komm, du Geist des Lebens (J. C. Bach)

Baldamus, F.	Hulse, C. Van
Beck, A.	*Jenny, A.
*Brieger, O.	Kammeier, H.
Cassler, G. W.	Kickstat, P.
*Claussnitzer, P.	*Kirnberger, J. P.
*Dienel, O.	Klotz, H.
Drischner, M. (2)	*Koch, J. H. E.
*Engelbrecht, K. F. (2)	Krause, P.
Fiebig, K.	Peeters, F.
*Franke, F. W.	Piutti, K.
*Frenzel, H. R.	Raphael, G.
Grabner, H.	Reger, M.
Gulbins, M. (2)	*Rudnick, W.
Haase, K. (2)	Spiering, G.
Hark, F.	Streicher, J. A.
*Hoernig, O.	Wenzel, E.
Hoyer, K.	Wettstein, H.

Liebe, die du mich zum Bilde
Song 107 (Dutch)

   Dragt, J.

Song 205 (Dutch)

   Nauta, J.

St. Louis (Redner)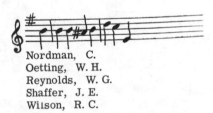

Beck, A.	Nordman, C.
Diggle, R.	Oetting, W. H.
Faulkes, W.	Reynolds, W. G.
Haase, K.	Shaffer, J. E.
Mueller, C. F.	Wilson, R. C.

St. Luke (Clark)

Beck, A.	Markworth, H. J.
Haase, K.	Peeters, F.
Hulse, C. Van	Thorne, E. H.

Variant:
Uffingham

   Palmer, C. C.

St. Magnus (Clark-Playford's)

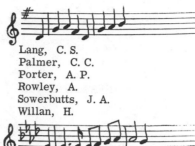

  Barlow, W.
  Conway, M. P.
  Curry, R. D.   Lang, C. S.
  Hasse, K.   Palmer, C. C.
  Hoskins, W. E.   Porter, A. P.
  Hulse, C. Van   Rowley, A.
  Knight, V.   Sowerbutts, J. A.
            Willan, H.

St. Margaret (Peace)

  Colvin, H.
  Diggle, R.   Mueller, C. F.
  Ellingford, H. F.   Stults, R. M.
            Thompson, V. D. (2)

St. Mary (Hackney)   Tune not found

  Stephens, C. E.

St. Mary (Pry's)

  Alderson, A. P.
  Conway, M. P.
  Dicks, E. A.   Matthews, E.
  Dyson, G.   Palmer, C. C. (2)
  Farrar, E. B.   Parry, C. H. H.
  Gray, A. (2)   Pearce, C. W.
  Herbert, P.   Rowley, A.
  Jewell, K. W.   Stanford, C. V. (2)
  Kitson, C. H.   Wesley, S. S.
            Wood, C.

St. Mary Magdalene (Dykes)

  Haase, K.

St. Matthew (Croft)

  Gray, A.
  Palmer, C. C.   Peeters, F.
            Wesley, S. S.

St. Matthias
 See: Song 67 (Gibbons)

St. Michael
 See: Old 134th (Estes)

St. Olave
 See: St. George (Gauntlett)

St. Oswald (Dykes)

  Gray, A.
  Pearce, C. W.

St. Patrick
 See: St. Patrick's Breastplate (Irish)

St. Patrick's Breastplate (Irish)

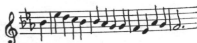

  Clokey, J. W.
  Diggle, R. (2)   Shaw, G. T.
  Fetler, P.   Stanford, C. V.
  Peeters, F.   Wyton, A.
  Variant:
  St. Patrick

  Sowerby, L.

St. Peter (Reinagle)

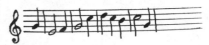

  Archer, J. S.
  Beck, A.   Matthews, H. A.
  Bouman, P.   Noble, T. T. (2)
  Coleman, R. H. P. Peeters, F.
  Conway, M. P.   Powell, R. J.
  Darke, H. E.   Reuter, F.
  Dicks, E. A.   Rowley, A.
  Gray, A.   Stewart, C. H.
  Haase, K.   Thiman, E. H.
  Kitson, C. H.   Tootell, G.
  Lang, C. S.   Willan, H.

St. Petersburg (Bortnianski)

       Z 2964

  Beck, A.
  Dressler, J.   Peeters, F.
  Haase, K.   Shaffer, J. E.
  Markworth, H. J. Wienhorst, R.
  Variants:
  Bortnianski

  Freyer, A.

Ich bete an die Macht der Liebe

  Christiaansz, N. J. Stapf, O.
  Franke, F. W.   Unbehaun, G.
  Rumpf, W.   Wettstein, H.
  Saffe, F.

St. Philip (Monk)

Willan, H.

St. Saviour (Baker)

Haase, K.

St. Stephen (Jones)

Lang, C. S.
Lloyd, L. S.   Peeters, F.
Manz, P.   Willan, H.
Variant:
St. Stephen's Tune

Palmer, E. D.   Wesley, S. S.

St. Stephen's Tune
See: St. Stephen (Jones)

St. Sylvester (Barnby)

Burdett, G. A.

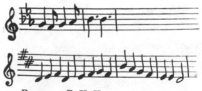

St. Theodulph
See: Valet

St. Theresa (Sullivan)

Abram, J.

St. Thomas (Wade)

Blackburn, J.
Cassler, G. W.   Parry, C. H. H.
Curry, R. D.   *Pearce, C. W.
*Dickey, M.   Taylor, C. T.
Manz, P.   Walton, K.
Variants:
Holywood
Novello
Preiset mit dem Glaubens Mute

Berghorn, A.

Tantum Ergo (Novello)

McGrath, J. J.   Schehl, J. A.
Peeters, F. (3)

St. Thomas (Williams)

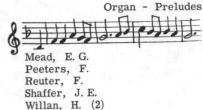

    Baumgartner, H. L.   Mead, E. G.
   *Beck, A.   Peeters, F.
    Burdett, G. A.   Reuter, F.
    Haase, K.   Shaffer, J. E.
    Hulse, C. Van   Willan, H. (2)

St. Venantius
   See: Rouen Melody

St. Vincent (Neukom)

    Sowerby, L.
    Walton, K.

Saligheten er os naer (Lindeman)

    Bergh, L.
    Gangfloet, S.   Karlsen, R.

Saligheten er oss naer (Kingo's)
   See: Rind nu op i Jesu navn (Lully)

Salisbury (Ravenscroft)

    Harwood, B.

Salutio Angelica
   See: Ave Maria (Plainsong)

Salutis Aeterne Dator
   See: Lucis Creator Optime (Sarum-Mode 8)

Salutis Humanae Sator (Mode 4)

    DeKlerk, A.
    Kreckel, P. G.

Salvator (Danish)
   See: Du Herre Krist (Berggreen)

Salvator Natus (Bohemian)

    Haase, K.
    Hulse, C. Van
  Variant:
  Freu dich Erd und Sternenzelt

    Hark, F.

Salve Festa Dies (Calkin)

    Stults, R. M.

Salve Festa Dies (Sarum)

                Z 7149
    Sceats, W. G.

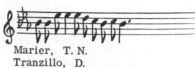

Salve Mater (Plainsong - Mode 5)

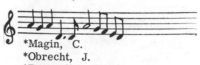

      *Biggs, R. K.
      Kreckel, P. G. (2)   Marier, T. N.
      *Magin, C.   Tranzillo, D.

Salve Regina

      Cornet, P.   *Magin, C.
      Erb, M. J.   *Obrecht, J.
      Heiller, A.   *Ravanello, O.
      *Lopez, M.   Schlick, A.
      Kerckhoven, A. van den *Titcomb, E. H.

Salve Regina

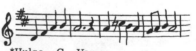

      *Kreckel, P. G.
      Rheinberger, J.
Variant:
Gruss, Himmelskoenigin

Salve Regina (Mode 1)

      *Ahrens, J.
      *Becker, A. C.
      *Campbell-Watson, F.   *Hulse, C. Van
      *Diebold, J.   Kreckel, P. G.
      *Dupré, M. J. J.   Marier, T. N.
      Erb, M. J. (4)   St. Martin, L. de
      Gauss, O.   Stadlmair, H.
      *Hilaire, R. F.   Thomas, V. C.
      Huijbers, B.   *Trexler, G.
                       *Waters, C. F.

Salve Regina Coelitum (Hildesheim) (refrain)

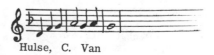

      Kreckel, P. G. (2)
      *Magin, C.   McGrath, J. J.

Salve Sancte Parens

      Boslet, L.
      Erb, M. J. (5)   Hulse, C. Van

Salve Virgo Singularis

    Marier, T. N.

Salvete Flores Martyrum

    Rheinberger, J.

Salzburg (Hintze)

              Z 6778

    Bratt, C. G.   Schultz, R.
    Edmundson, G.   Sinzheimer, M.
    Powell, R. J.   Taylor, C. T.
    Variants:
Alle Menschen muessen sterben - II

    Baldamus, F.   *Koeckert, C.
    Brieger, O.   Kuntze, C.
    Cassler, G. W.   Merk, G. (2)
    Engelbrecht, K. F.   *Middleschulte, W.
    Fluegel, G.   Pachelbel, J. (3)
    Franke, F. W.   Reger, M.
    Gulbins, M. (2)   Reinbrecht, A.
    Haase, K.   Rudnick, W.
    Hoyer, K.   Schink, H.
    Kaeppel, G. C. A.   *Streicher, J. A.
    Karow, K.   Wettstein, H. (2)
    Kickstat, P.

Siegesfuerste, Ehrenkoenig

    Borngaesser, W.   Petzold, J.
    *Gulbins, M. (2)   *Troetschel, H.
    Koch, J. H. E.

Song 238 (Dutch)

    Wilgenburg, D. van

Womit soll ich dich wohl loben

    Schwencke, J. F. (3)

Sancta Mater Istud Agae   Tune not found

    Magin, C.

Sanctorum Meritis (Sarum)

    Breitenbach, C. G. J.
    Pearce, C. W.   Titelouze, J.

Sanctus (Mode 2)

    *Woollen, R.

Sanctus (Mass 4)

    *Lee, J. (2)

Sandell
  See: Tryggare kan ingen vara

Sandon (Purday)

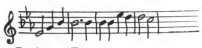

    Smyth, C. F.
    Walter, S.
  Variant:
  Leid, milde ljos

    Nielsen, L.

Sandringham (Barnby)

    Diggle, R.
    Haase, K.   Peeters, F.
    Matthews, H. A.   Stults, R. M.
    Peery, R. R.   Titcomb, E. H.
  Variant:
  O Perfect Love

    Heinrich, A.   Schreiner, A.

Sandys (English)

    Peeters, F.
    Willan, H.
  Variant:
  A Child This Day Is Born

    Warner, R. L.

Sardis (Beethoven)

    Hulse, C. Van

Sarum
  See: Pro Omnibus Sanctis (Barnby)

Savannah
  See: Hoechster Priester (Basel)

Sawley (Walch)

    Hulse, C. Van
    Means, C.

Schaffe in mir, Gott, ein reines
    Herz (Winer)
                Z 8628a

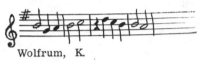

    *Reuter, F.
    Schwencke, J. F.   Walther, J. G.
    *Seeger, K.   Wedemann, W.

Schaffe in mir, Gott, ein reines
    Herz (Witt)
                Z 8628c

    Piutti, K.   Wolfrum, K.

Schatz ueber alle Schaetze
    See: Valet

Schaut, ihr Suender
                Z 8569b

    Werner, J. J.

Scheepke onder Jezus hoede   Tune not found

    Kee, C.

Schlaf suess, mein Kindlein
    (Laub)

    Raasted, N. O.
    Variant:
    Sov soedt barnlille

    Bjerre, J.   *Thuner, O. E.
    Frellsen, E.   Woeldike, M. A.
    Mathiassen, F.

Schmuecke dich, O liebe Seele
    (Crueger)
                Z 6926

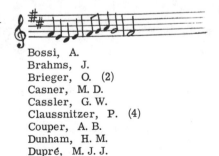

    André, J.   Bossi, A.
    Arbatsky, Y.   Brahms, J.
    Bach, J. S. (2)   Brieger, O. (2)
    Baldamus, F.   Casner, M. D.
    Barlow, W. (2)   Cassler, G. W.
    Barner, A.   Claussnitzer, P. (4)
    Beck, A.   Couper, A. B.
    Beck, T.   Dunham, H. M.
    Bedell, R. L.   Dupré, M. J. J.
    Beyer, M.   Enckhausen, H. F.
    Bibl, R. (2)   Engelbrecht, K. F. (3)

Fischer, M. G. (2)
Fluegel, G.
Forchhammer, T.
Franke, F. W. (2)
Gebhardi, L. E. (2)
Grote, H.
Haase, K.
Haessler, J. W.
Heer, E.
Hennig, W.
Herzog, J. G. (2)
Hessenberg, K.
Hummel, F.
Hurford, P.
Johnson, D. N.
Karg-Elert, S.
Karow, K.
Kickstat, P.
Klaus, V.
Krause, P.
Kuntze, C.
Lang, H. (2)
Lange, S. de
Leupold, A. W.
Lynn, G. A.
Marpurg, F. W.
Merkel, G. (3)
Metzger, H. A.
Mueller, S.
Nicolai, J. G.
Oechsler, E. (2)
Owen, B.
Palme, R. (2)
Papperitz, B. R.
Peeters, F.

Pfaff, H.
Piutti, K. (3)
Poppen, H. M.
Raasted, N. O.
Rebling, G.
Reda, S.
Reger, M.
Reinhardt, A.
Reuter, F.
Riedel, H.
Riemenschneider, G.
Rinck, J. C. H. (2)
Rinkens, W.
Ritter, A. G.
Rudnick, W. (2)
Rumpf, W.
Schaab, R.
Schehl, J. A. (2)
Schmidt, F.
Schoenfeld, H.
Schreiner, A.
Schrenk, J.
Schuetze, W. (2)
Schwencke, J. F. (3)
Straumann, B.
Streicher, J. A.
Telemann, G. P. (6)
Trenkner, W.
Vierling, J. G.
Walther, J. G. (3)
Wedemann, W.
Wettstein, H. (2)
Wolfrum, K.
Zierau, F.

Variants:
Hvo lange skal mit

Aahgren, K. E.

Jesus livets sol og glaede

Christensen, B.
Frandsen, H. B.
Jeppesen, K.
Laub, T. (2)

Laub-Woeldike
Raasted, N. O.
Woeldike, M. A. (2)

Schmueckt das Fest mit Maien
(Folk Tune)

Koch, J. H. E.

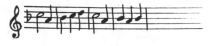

Schmueckt das Fest mit Maien
   (Mendelssohn)

    Franke, F. W.   Wettstein, H.

Schmueckt das Fest mit Maien
   (Witt)
    *Claussnitzer, P.
    Fiebig, K.   Ricek, W.
    Lorenzen, J.   Ziegler, K. M.

Schmueckt das Fest mit Maien
  See: Jesu, meine Freude

Schoenster Emmanuel, Herzog
   der Frommen (Darmstadt)
              Z 4932c
    Coleman, R. H. P.
    Langstroth, I. S.   Schueler, H.
  Variant:
  Liebster Immanuel

    Dupré, M. J. J.   Rembt, J. E.
    Haase, K.   Vierling, J. G.
    Peeters, F. (2)

Schoenster Herr Jesu (Silesian)

              Z 3976
    Ahrens, J.   Johnson, D. N. (2)
    Arbatsky, Y.   Krapf, G.
    Beck, A.   Kreckel, P. G.
    Coleman, R. H. P.   Malling, O.
    Curry, R. D.   Matthews, H. A.
    Curry, W. L.   Matthison-Hansen, G.
    Drischner, M. (2)   McGrath, J. J.
    Edmundson, G.   Merkel, G.
    Elwood, H.   Mueller, C. F.
    Greener, J. H.   Peeters, F.
    Haase, K.   Reuter, F.
    Hoeller, K.   Schehl, J. A.
    Joergensen, G.   Schroeder, H.
  Variants:
  Crusaders Hymn

    Ashford, E. L.   McKay, G. F.
    Biggs, R. K.   Rogers, L.
    Dasher, J. A.   Schmutz, A.
    Hegedus, A.   Young, G. (2)
    Langston, P. T.

Dejlig er jorden

    Birkedal-Barfod, L.   Raasted, N. O.
    Nielsen, J. M. (2)   Wuertz, J.
    Nielsen, L.

Haerlig aer jorden

    Matthison-Hansen, G.   Olson, D.

St. Elizabeth
Song 221 (Dutch)

    Koppenol, J.

Schoenster Herr Jesu (Muenster)
    See: Fairest Lord Jesus (Muenster)

Schoenstes Kindlein
    See: Lovely Infant

Schoepfer
    See: Wir glauben all' an einen Gott, Schoepfer

Schon ist der Tag von Gott bestimmt
    See: Nun freut Euch lieben Christen (Klug)

Schon weicht der Sonne Flammen-
    strahl

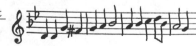

Variant:
Iam Sol Recedit

    Rheinberger, J.

Schumann (Mason & Webb)

    Edmundson, G. (2)
    Haase, K.   Reuter, F.
Variant:
Heath

    Hulse, C. Van   Peeters, F.

Schwing dich auf zu deinem Gott
    (Crueger)
              Z 6309a

    Barner, A. (2)   Luetzel, J. H.
    Buehl, W.   *Oechsler, E.
    Fink, F.   Reichel, B.
    Hark, F.   *Reinhardt, A.
    Kickstat, P.   Rinck, J. C. H. (2)

Schwing dich auf zu deinem Gott (Crueger) (cont.)

    Rudnick, O.   Vierling, J. G.
    Rumpf, W.   Volckmar, W. V.
   *Schweizer, R.   Zipp, F.
Variant:
O du min Immanuel (Crueger)

    Sark, E. T.

Schwing dich auf zu deinem Gott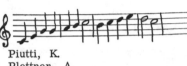
(Ebeling)
                Z 6310
    Claussnitzer, P. (3)   Piutti, K.
   *Grote, H.   Plettner, A.
    Haase, K.   Weber, H.
    Hulse, C. Van   Wolfrum, K.
Variant:
Christe, wahres Seelenlicht

    Gulbins, M. (2)

Schwing dich auf zu deinem Gott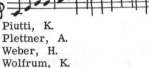
(Franck)
                Z 6352
   *Smyth, E. M.
Variants:
Christus, Christus, Christus ist
Fang dein Werk

    Beck, A.   Haase, K.
    Boeringer, J.   Stellhorn, M. H.

Schwing dich auf zu deinem Gott (Halle)
   See: Christe, wahres Seelenlicht (Halle)

Schwingt heilige Gedanken
   See: Aus meines Herzens Grunde

Se hvor nu Jesus traeder (Kingo - Arrebo)
   See: O Jesu for din pine

Se Jesus aer ett troestrikt namn
   See: Wenn wir in hoechsten Noethen

Se solens skjoenne lys og prakt
(Lindeman)

    Gangfloet, S.   Nielsen, L.
Variant:
Jeg gaar i fare

    Joergensen, G.

Se solens skjoenne lys og prakt
(Norse Folk)

    Baden, C.
    Karlsen, R.   Nielsen, L.

Se, vi gaa upp till Jerusalem
    See: O Jesu, for din pine (Kingo)

Sed Libera Nos

    Erb, M. J. (10)

See How This Tiny Child (Dutch)

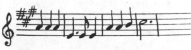

    Shroyens, R.

Seele, dein Heiland

    Schmalz, P.

Seele, geh nach Golgotha
    See: Jesu, meine Zuversicht

Seele, mach dich heilig
    See: Christus der uns selig macht

Seele, was ermuedst du dich
    See: Grosser Gott, wir loben dich

Seele, was ermuedst du dich
    See: Meinen Jesum lass ich nicht (Hammerschmidt)

Seele, was ermuedst du dich (Ulich)
    See: Meinen Jesum lass ich nicht (Ulich)

Seele, was ist schoeneres wohl
    See: Morgenglanz der Ewigkeit

Seelenbraeutigam (Drese)
                   Z 3255

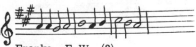

Baldamus, F.	Franke, F. W. (2)
Beck, A.	Haase, K. (2)
Blackburn, J.	Haase, R.
Brieger, O.	Hasse, K.
Claussnitzer, P.	Herzog, J. G.
Edmundson, G.	Hopf, C.
Elmore, R. H.	Hoyer, K.
Engelbrecht, K. F.	Karow, K.
Faisst, I. G. F. von	Kickstat, P.
Fischer, M. G. (3)	Krause, P.
Fluegel, G. (2)	Lang, H.

Seelenbraeutigam (Drese) (cont.)

Leupold, A. W.	Reuter, F.
Lorenz, E. J.	Rinck, J. C. H. (2)
Manz, P.	Rumpf, W.
Mueller, S. W.	Scherzer, O.
Near, G.	Schwencke, J. F. (3)
Oley, J. C.	Streicher, J. A.
Palme, R. (2)	Thomas, O.
Peeters, F.	Vierling, J. G.
Piutti, K. (2)	Weinlig, C. T.
Reger, M.	Wettstein, H. (3)
Reichardt, B.	Young, G.

Variants:
Jesu, geh voran

Beyer, M.	Marx, K.
Borngaesser, W.	Micheelsen, H. F.
David, J. N.	Mueller-Zuerich, P.
Drischner, M.	Raasted, N. O.
Egidi, A.	Reda, S.
Fiebig, K.	Renooij, B.
Hiltscher, W.	Roeder, E. O.
Karg-Elert, S.	Rudnick, W. (2)
Koetzschke, H.	Unbehaun, G.

Rochelle

Clokey, J. W.

Song 222 (Dutch)

Koppenol, J.	Renooij, B.

Vaak, O sjel

Aahgren, K. E.	Drischner, M.

Wer ist wohl wie du
    gut

Fischer, M. G.	Thomas, O.
Rinck, J. C. H.	

Seelenweide, meine Freude
  See: Gott will's machen, dass die Sachen (Freylinghausen)

Sefton (Calkin)

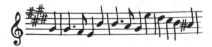

Hulse, C. Van

Segne, Jesu, deine Herde (Breslau)

    Proksch, J.

Sehet, sehet, welche Liebe
   See: O Durchbrecher (Halle)

Seht die Mutter dort voll Schmerzen
   See: Christi Mutter

Seht, er kommt (Handel)
   See: Judas Maccabaeus

Seht nur an

    Neuss, H.

Seht, welch ein Mensch, seh, seh
   See: O Gott du frommer Gott (Hannover)

Seht wie die Sonne schon sinket
(German Folk Tune)

    Schmutz, A.

Sei du mir gegruesset (Luebeck)

    Haase, K.
    Hulse, C. Van

Sei gegruesset

    Kreckel, P. G.

Sei gegruesset, Jesu guetig
(Vopelius)
               Z 8561
    Bach, J. S.

             Dupré, M. J. J.

Sei gegruest, Jesu, du ewiger
Trost
               Z 7157b
    Fischer, M. G.

Sei Lob und Ehr dem (Sohren)
   See: Elbing

Sei Lob und Ehr dem
   See: Es ist das Heil uns (Wittenberg)

Sei Lob und Ehr dem (Crueger)
   See: Wach auf, mein Herz (Lyon)

Sei mir Tausendmal gegruesset
  See: Jesu, deine tiefen Wunden

Sei Mutter der Barmherzigkeit
  See: Mach's mit mir, Gott (Schein)

Seigneur Dieu, ouvre (Denizot)

  Boëly, A. P. F.

Selig sind des Himmels Erben
  See: Wachet auf

Seligstes Wesen (Freylinghuasen)

                Z 6986
  Schwencke, J. F. (2)

Selma (Scotch)

  Orr, R. R. K.

Septem Verba (Schumacher)

  Haase, K.
  Hulse, C. Van

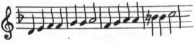

Ser jeg mig i verden om (Skaug)

  Nielsen, L.

Serenity (Wallace)

  Smith, H. M.

Sessions (Emerson)

  Ashford, E. L.

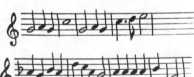

Seymour (von Weber)

  Ashford, E. L.   Stults, R. M.
  Mueller, C. F.   Thomas, V. C.
  Saxton, S. E.   Warner, F. H.

Shall We Gather At the River
  (Lowry)

  Thomson, V.   Young, G.

Shepherd and Virgin Mary
  (Catalonian)
      Castellvi, J. C. Y.

Shepherds of the Mountains

Guilmant, A.

Shirleyn (Harper)

Krapf, G.

Sicilian Mariners

Johnson, D. N.   Schumacher, M. H. (2)
Kessel, G.   Sinzheimer, M.
Kincaid, C.   Thayer, W. E.
Mueller, C. F.   Warner, R. L.
Reuter, F.   Young, G.
Variants:
Ach, wie herrlich

Zwart, J.

O du Froehliche

Gulbins, M.   Rebling, G. (2)
Haase, K.   Seiffert, U.
Heuer, G.   Unbehaun, G.
Janssen, P.   Wenzel, H.
Lampart, K.   Zanger, G.
Landmann, A.

O du Selige

Soederholm, V.

O Sanctissima

Alphenaar, G.   Larkin, J.
Ashford, E. L.   Lux, F.
Bassford, W. K.   Marier, T. N.
Chipp, E. T.   Markworth, H. J.
Curry, R. D.   Meale, J. A.
Diebold, J.   Ore, A.
Frenzel, H. R.   Pfitzner, H.
Hepworth, G.   Rudnick, W.
Hiller, P.   Schehl, J. A.
Hulse, C. Van   Schumacher, M. H.
Kaestel, L.   Springer, M.
Kreckel, P. G.   Stehle, J. G. E.
Kruijs, M. H. Van'T. Truman, E.

Siegesfuerste, Ehrenkoenig
  See: Alle Menschen muessen sterben (Mueller)

Siegesfuerste, Ehrenkoenig
   See: Salzburg (Hintze)

Sieh, hier bin ich Ehrenkoenig
(Darmstadt)
           Z 7324

    Claussnitzer, P. (4)
    Haase, K.   Peeters, F.
    Inderau, H.   Piutti, K.
    Palme, R.   *Rinck, J. C. H.
Variants:
Her vil ties, her vil bies (Darmstadt)
Jeg er rede til aa bede (Darmstadt)

    Nielsen, L.

Ruhe hier, mein Geist

    Koch, J. H. E.

Sieh, hier bin ich Ehrenkoenig
(Koenig)
           Z 7329

    *Baldamus, F.   *Krebs, J. L.
    Drischner, M. (2)   Oechsler, E.
    Faisst, I. G. F. von   Reichardt, T.
    *Fluegel, G.   Rumpf, W.

Siehe, das ist Gottes Lamm   Tune not found

    Fluegel, G.

Sig maanen langsomt haever
   See: Der Mond ist aufgegangen (Schulz)

Silent Night
   See: Stille Nacht

Siloam (Hemy)

    Bitgood, R.

Siloam (Woodbury)

    Reynolds, W. G.

Silver Street (Smith)

    Dickey, M.
    Peeters, F.

Sin vogn goer han (Rung)

    Lindorff-Larsen, E.

Sine Nomine (Vaughan-Williams)

    Crawford, T. J.   Peek, R. M.
    Gehrke, H.   Peeters, F. (2)
    Haase, K.   Sinzheimer, M.
    Howells, H. N.   Sowerby, L.
    Mead, E. G.   Wehmeyer, W.
Variant:
Voor alle heil'gen

    Mazyk, R. van (2)

Singen wir aus Herzens Grund (Horn)
   See: Da Christus geboren war (Bohemian)

Singet dem Herrn ein neues Lied
(Schuetz)
              Z 540
    Bailey, P.

Singet frisch und
   See: Joseph, lieber Joseph mein

Singet, preiset Gott mit Freuden

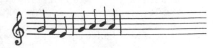

    Schilling, H. L.

Singt dem Koenig Freudenpsalmen
   See: O du Liebe meiner Liebe (Basel)

Singt, singt dem Herren

    Studer, H.

Singt, singt dem Herren neue Lieder
           Jehova
   See: Psalm 118 (Geneva)

Singt und klingt (Praetorius)
           Z 8583
    Goller, F.

Sions vekter hever roesten
         vaegter
   See: Wachet auf

Sitt oega Jesus oeppnat har
   See: Christus Resurrexit

Sjaa, aakrane dei gulnar alt
  (Reimann)
            Z 3119
     Nielsen, L.
     Variant:
     Nun geht mein Leib dem

Sjaa han gjeng inn (Sletten)

     Gangfloet, S.
     Nielsen, L.

Sjaa han gjeng inn til (Vulpius)
   See: Lobet den Herren, ihr Heiden all

Skoen Jomfru hun gang er i rosenlund   Tune not found

     Rung-Keller, P. S.

Skriv dig, Jesus, paa mit hjerte
   See: Freu dich sehr

Skulle jeg dog vaere bange
   See: Froehlich soll mein Herze (Crueger)

Skynd dig frem (Freylinghausen)
   See: Fahre fort (Schmidt)

Slane (Irish)

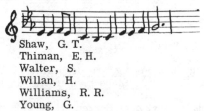

     Arnatt, R.   Shaw, G. T.
     Bohnhorst, F. R.   Thiman, E. H.
     Gehring, P.   Walter, S.
     Hokanson, M.   Willan, H.
     Leitz, D.   Williams, R. R.
     Shaffer, J. E.   Young, G.

Sleep Holy Babe (Schloeder)

     Kreckel, P. G.

Sleep Holy Child (Dutch)

     Peery, R. R.

Sleep of the Child Jesus
   See: Gevaert

Sleep Well, Child of Heaven
   See: Noël Alsacien

Sleepers Wake
   See: Wachet auf

Slukt er dagens lyse flammer
(Norse Folk)

Baden, C.

Snow Lay on the Ground

Powell, R. J.

So fliehen uns're Tage hin
       Z 229
Rinck, J. C. H.

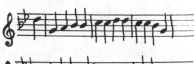

So fuehrst du doch recht selig
(Stoetzel)
      Z 6200
Piutti, K.

So fuehrst du doch recht selig
See: Psalm 27

So gehst du nun, mein Jesu, hin
(Darmstadt)
      Z 7631

 Beck, A.
 Haase, K.
 Hulse, C. Van   Rinck, J. C. H.
Variant: Vierling, J. G.
Du bar ditt kors, O Jesu mild

 Lindroth, H.   Olson, D.

So nimm, denn, meine Haende
(Silcher)
      Z 5234

 Beck, A.
 Haase, K.
 Hoyer, K.   Schilling, A.
 Markworth, H. J.   Stapf, O.
 Reinbrecht, A. (3)   Unbehaun, G.
 Saffe, F.   Wettstein, H. (2)
Variant: Wienhorst, R.
Saa tag nu mina haender

 Melin, H.

So tak daa mine hender (Silcher)

 Karlsen, R.

Song 232 (Dutch)

 Hoogewoud, H. Nauta, J. (2)   Stulp, G.

So ruhest du, O meine Ruh'
    See: O Traurigkeit

So tak daa mine hender (Silcher)
    See: So nimm, denn, meine Haende

Soede Jesu, vi er her
    See: Liebster Jesu (Ahle)

Soendag morgen fra de doede
    See: Herr, ich habe missgehandelt (Crueger)

Soerg, O kjaere Fader, du
    (Lindeman)
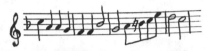

    Baden, C.
    Bergh, L.   Hokanson, M.
    Borg, O.   Nielsen, L.

Soerg, O kjaere Fader, du (K.
    Lindeman)

    Nielsen, L.

Soerger du endnu, min sjael
    See: Jesu, meine Zuversicht

Softly and Tenderly (Thompson)

    Colvin, H.
    Hustad, D.   Thompson, V. D.
    Larson, E. R.   Wilson, R. C.

Sois touché de mes larmes   Tune not found

    Hess, C. L.

Sol Praeceps

    Groves, R.

Soldau (Wittenberg)
                        Z 2029
    Rimmer, F.
    Variants:
    Nu bede vi den Helligaand

    Christensen, B.
    Frandsen, H. B.
    Frellsen, E.   Laub, T.   Rosenkilde-Larsen, E.
    Gangfloet, S.   Moeller, S. O.   Woeldike, M. A. (2)
    Joergensen, G.   Noergaard, P.   Wuertz, J.
    Karlsen, R.   Raasted, N. O. (2)

Nun bitten wir (Walther)

Ahrens, J.
Artmueller, K.
Bausznern, W. von
Beck, A.
Bender, J.
Boehm, G. (2)
Brunner, A.
Buxtehude, D. (4)
Driessler, J.
Enckhausen, H. F.
Fiebig, K.
Fischer, M. G.
Fluegel, G. (2)
Forchhammer, T.
Franke, F. W. (2)
Gerlach, G.
Haase, K.
Hamburger, P.
Hanebeck, H. R.
Hark, F.
Hennig, W.
Hoyer, K. (2)
Humpert, H.
Jenny, A.
Karow, K.
Kickstat, P.
Kittel, J. C.
Kutzer, E.

Lenel, L.
Magnus, E. (2)
Meibohm, D. (2)
Mendelssohn, A.
Micheelsen, H. F. (2)
Mueller, G.
Mueller-Zuerich, P. (2)
Oertzen, R. von
Oley, J. C.
Pepping, E.
Reda, S.
Rinck, J. C. H.
Romanovsky, E.
Schaab, R.
Scheidemann, H. (2)
Scheidt, S.
Schroeder, H.
Schwencke, J. F. (2)
Soenke, H.
Spiering, G.
Steinhaeuser, K. (2)
Stolze, H. W. (2)
Vierling, J. G.
Walcha, H.
Walther, J. G. (3)
Wettstein, H.
Weyrauch, J.

Solemnis Haec Festivitas (Angers)

Harker, C.

Soli Deo Gloria   Tune not found

Lubrich, F. , Sr.

Solid Rock (Bradbury)

Laney, H.

Sollt es gleich bisweilen (Fritsch)
                Z 3512
                Z 1338
     Ritter, A. G.
Variant:
Allenthalben, wo ich gehe (Fritsch)

Gulbins, M.

<u>Sollt es gleich bisweilen</u> (Fritsch) (cont.)

    Gott du bist von Ewigkeit

<u>Sollt es gleich bisweilen</u> (Stoerl)
               Z 1352

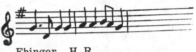

    Claussnitzer, P. (2)   Grosse-Weischede, A. (2)
    Fink, C.   Reichardt, T.

<u>Sollt es gleich bisweilen</u>
   See: <u>Stuttgart</u> (Dretzel)

<u>Sollt es gleich bisweilen</u>
   See: <u>Stuttgart</u> (Gotha)

<u>Sollt ich meinem Gott nicht</u>
   <u>singen</u> (Bertsch)
               Z 7919

    Burkhardt, C.   Ehinger, H. R.

<u>Sollt ich meinem Gott nicht</u>
   <u>singen</u> (Schop)
               Z 7886b
       also in 4
              4

Baldamus, F.	Marx, K.
Barlow, W.	Markull, F. W. (2)
*Bausznern, W. von	Micheelsen, H. F.
Bender, J.	Michel, A.
Brieger, O. (2)	Mojsisovics, R. von
*Claussnitzer, P.	Mueller, S. W.
Doles, J. F. (2)	Oertzen, R. von
Eckardt, A.	Palme, R. (2)
Enckhausen, H. F.	Pepping, E.
Eyken, J. A. van (3)	Piutti, K. (2)
Fiebig, K.	Raphael, G.
Fischer, M. G.	Reger, M.
Fluegel, G. (2)	Reinbrecht, A. (2)
Franke, F. W. (2)	Rembt, J. E.
Frenzel, H. R.	Ricek, W.
Gebhardi, L. E.	Rinck, J. C. H. (3)
*Gulbins, M.	Schaab, R.
Haase, K.	Schilling, A.
Hark, F. (2)	Sechter, S.
*Herrmann, W.	Seiffert, U.
*Hesse, A. F.	Trenkner, W.
Karg-Elert, S. (2)	Troetschel, H.
Karow, K. (2)	Vierling, J. G.
*Kerst, S.	Wedemann, W.
Kuehmstedt, F. (2)	Wettstein, H.
Kuntze, C.	Wickenhausser, R.
Lange, R.	Zipp, F. (2)

Variants:
<u>Geest des Heeren, kom van boven</u>

Reijden, W. van der   Schuurman, A. C.

<u>Halleluia, Lofgezongen</u>

Hoogewoud, H.

<u>Lasset uns den Herren preisen</u>

Hofmeier, A.   Schwencke, J. F. (2)
Kickstat, P. (2)   Theile, A. G.
Kleemeyer, H.   Wettstein, H.
Oley, J. C.   Wolfrum, P. (2)
Rumpf, W.

<u>Lasset uns mit Jesu ziehen</u>

*Claussnitzer, P.   Kammeier, H.
Fiebig, K.   Reda, S.
Hasse, K.

<u>Song 76</u> (Dutch)

Nauta, J.   Wilgenburg, D. van

<u>Song 166</u> (Dutch)

Nauta, J.   Wilgenburg, D. van

<u>Song 173</u> (Dutch)

Asma, F.   Zwart, J.
Hoogewoud, H.

<u>Sollt ich meinem Gott nicht singen</u> (Bolze)
   See: <u>Lasset uns mit Jesu ziehen</u> (Bolze)

<u>Sollt mich die Liebe des Irdschen</u>
   (Koenig)
                    Z 6991

Variant:
<u>Jesu, din soede forening</u> (Koenig)

*Frandsen, H. B.   Joergensen, G.
Frellsen, E.   Karlsen, R.
*Hamburger, P.   Woeldike, M. A.
Jeppesen, K.

<u>Som daggens paerlor glimma</u>
   See: <u>Nyland</u>

Som den gylne sol frembryter (Lindeman)
    See: Nu er frelsens dag

Som den gylne sol frembryter (Schop)
    See: Werde munter

Som dogg paa slegne (Olssoen)

        Karlsen, R.

Som dugg paa slagne (Rung)

        Holstebroe, H. J.   Rung-Keller, P. S.
        Jeppesen, K.   Vestergaard-Pedersen, C.

Som et stille offerlam (Laub)

        Moeller, S. O.
        Raasted, N. O.   Thuner, O. E.

Som foraarssolen (Hartmann)

        Joergensen, G.
        Wuertz, J.

Som toerstige hjoert monne
    (Lindeman)

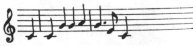

        Gangfloet, S.   Nielsen, L.

Somerset Carol (English)

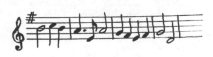

    Variant:
    Come All You Worthy Gentlemen

        Milford, R. H.

Something For Jesus (Lowry)

        Thompson, V. D.
    Variant:
    Something For Thee

        Rand, J.

Something For Thee
    See: Something For Jesus

Sometimes I Feel Like a
    Motherless Child (Spiritual)

        Hancock, E. W.   Thomas, V. C.

Somnar jag in med blicken faest (Nuernberg)
   See: Da Christus geboren war (Bohemian)

Song 1 (Gibbons)
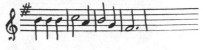

     Peeters, F.   Whitehead, A. E.
     Thiman, E. H.   Willan, H.

Song 1 (Dutch)
   See: Valet

Song 2 (Dutch)
   See: Es kommt ein Schiff

Song 3 (Dutch)
   See: Macht hoch die Tuer (Freylinghausen)

Song 4 (Dutch)
   See: Aus meines Herzens Grunde

Song 5 (Gibbons)

     Christopher, C. S.
     Dyson, G.

Song 7 (Dutch-Franck)
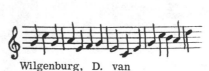

     Kousemaker, A.
     Stulp, G.   Wilgenburg, D. van
   Variant:
   Christmas Carol (Dutch)

     Post, P.

Song 8 (Dutch)
   See: Ach bleib mit deiner (Vulpius)

Song 9 (Old Dutch)
   See: Erhalt uns, Herr

Song 10 (Dutch - Bastiaans)

     Kousemaker, A.
     Stulp, G.   Wilgenburg, D. van
   Variant:
   Daar is uits werelde duistre wolken

     Post, P.   Zwart, J.

Song 11 (Dutch)
   See: Vom Himmel hoch

Song 13 (Gibbons)

    Bullock, E.   Sowerbutts, J. A.
    Cameron, G.   Thiman, E. H.
    Coleman, R. H. P.   Vaughan-Williams, R.
    Groves, R.   Whitlock, P.
    Palmer, C. C.   Willan, H.
Variants:
Canterbury

    Floyd, A. E.   Pullein, J.
    Harwood, B.

Light Divine

    Haase, K.   Noehren, R.
    Hulse, C. Van

Song 14 (Dutch)
    See: Nun sei uns willkommen

Song 15 (Dutch)
    See: Komt verwondert

Song 16 (Dutch)
    See: O Bethleham, hoe blinkt

Song 17 (Dutch)
    See: Es ist ein Ros'

Song 18 (Dutch)
    See: Adeste Fideles

Song 20 (Dutch)

    Beek, W. van
    Dalm, W.

Song 22 (Gibbons)

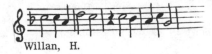

    Dyson, G.
    Stanford, C. V. (2)   Willan, H.

Song 22 (Dutch)
    See: Den die Hirten lobten sehr

Song 24 (Gibbons)

    Coleman, R. H. P.
    Dyson, G.   Thiman, E. H.
    Stanford, C. V. (2)   Willan, H.

Song 26 (Dutch)
    See: Psalm 150 (Pierre)

Song 28 (Dutch)
    See: Kom Christenschaar (Praetorius)

Song 29 (Dutch)
    See: Elbing

Song 30 (Dutch)
    See: Wachet auf

Song 32 (Dutch)
    See: Herzlich tut mich verlangen

Song 33 (Dutch - Gregor)

    Kousemaker, A.

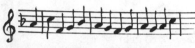

Song 34 (Gibbons)

    Dyson, G.   Hurford, P.
    Gray, A.   Stanford, C. V.
    Variants:
    Angel's Hymn

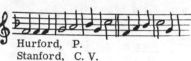

    Palmer, E. D.   Wesley, S. S.

    Angel's Song

    Stanford, C. V.   Willan, H.
    Steele, D. I.

Song 34 (Dutch)
    See: Herzliebster Jesu

Song 35 (Dutch-Bastiaans)

    Schipper, D.

Song 37 (Dutch)
    See: Agnus Dei (Liturgy)

Song 38 (Dutch)
    See: O Lamm Gottes, unschuldig (Decius)

Song 39 (Dutch)
    See: Innsbruck

Song 41 (Dutch)
    See: Kom Christenschaar

Song 42 (Dutch)
    See: Herzliebster Jesu

Song 43 (Dutch)
    See: Herzlich tut mich verlangen

Song 45 (Dutch)
    See: Meine Liebe haengt am Kreuz (Witt)

Song 46 (Dutch)

    Kousemaker, A.

Song 46 (Gibbons)

    Sowerby, L.

Song 47 (Dutch)
    See: Alles ist an Gottes

Song 48 (Dutch)
    See: Rockingham Old

Song 49 (Dutch)
    See: Alle Menschen muessen sterben (Wessnitzer)

Song 50 (Dutch)
    See: Freu dich sehr

Song 51 (Dutch)
    See: O du Liebe, meiner Liebe (Basel)

Song 52 (Dutch)
    See: Die Tugend wird durch's (Halle)

Song 53 (Dutch)
    See: Herr und Aeltster

Song 56 (Dutch)
    See: Allein Gott in der Hoeh'

Song 58 (Dutch)

    Bute, C. J.   Post, P.
    Dragt, J.   Wilgenburg, D. van

Song 61 (Dutch)
    See: Lyra Davidica

Song 62 (Dutch)
    See: Jesu, meine Zuversicht (Crueger)

Song 65 (Dutch)

 Wilgenburg, D. van
Variants:
Song 74 (Dutch)

 Wilgenburg, D. van

Song 207 (Dutch)

 Wilgenburg, D. van

Song 67 (Gibbons)

 Conway, M. P.
 Palmer, C. C.   Peeters, F.
 Pasteur, M.   Willan, H.
Variant:
St. Matthias

 Phillips, C. G.

Song 69 (Dutch-Pierre)
 See: Psalm 105

Song 71 (Dutch)
 See: Psalm 81 (Pierre)

Song 73 (Dutch)
 See: Pilgrimage

Song 74 (Dutch)
 See: Song 65 (Dutch)

Song 76 (Dutch)
 See: Sollt ich meinem Gott (Schop)

Song 78 (Dutch)
 See: Veni Creator Spiritus (Sarum-Mode 8)

Song 80 (Dutch)
 See: O Jesulein suess

Song 82 (Dutch)

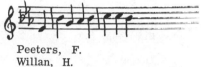

 Wilgenburg, D. van

Song 85 (Dutch)
 See: Psalm 19

Song 89 (Dutch)

    Hasselaar, R.

Song 91 (Dutch)
  See: Allein Gott in der Hoeh'

Song 93 (Dutch)
  See: Regent Square (Smart)

Song 94 (Dutch)
  See: Herr und Aeltster

Song 96 (Dutch)
  See: Ein' feste Burg

Song 98 (Dutch)
  See: Wachet auf

Song 102 (Dutch)
  See: Die Tugend wird durch's (Halle)

Song 103 (Dutch)
  See: Behoed uw kerk

Song 104 (Dutch)
  See: Alle Menschen muessen sterben (Mueller)

Song 105 (Dutch)
  See: O dass ich tausend Zungen (Koenig)

Song 107 (Dutch-Bach)
  See: St. Leonard

Song 112 (Dutch)
  See: Aurelia

Song 113 (Dutch)
  See: Jesu, meine Freude (Crueger)

Song 115 (Dutch)
  See: St. Cecelia (Hayne)

Song 116 (Dutch)
  See: Love Divine (Stainer)

Song 118a (Dutch - Roentgen)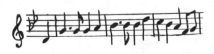

    Nauta, J. (2)

Song 121 (Dutch)
  See: Ellacombe

Song 127 (Dutch)
  See: Jerusalem, du (Franck)

Song 128 (Dutch)
  See: Morgenglanz

Song 132 (Dutch)
  See: Psalm 89 (Pierre)

Song 135 (Dutch)
  See: Nun danket alle Gott

Song 136 (Dutch)
  See: Lobe den Herren, den

Song 138 (Dutch)
  See: Elbing

Song 143 (Dutch)
  See: Op bergen en in dalen

Song 144 (Dutch)
  See: Die Tugend wird durch's (Halle)

Song 146 (Dutch)

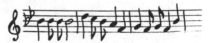

  Bijster, J.
  Wilgenburg, D. van
Variant:
Komt nu met zang (French)

  Bijster, J.

Song 147 (Dutch)
  See: Benedic Anima Mea (Goss)

Song 148 (Dutch-Bastiaans)

Variant:
Van U zyn alle dingen

  Kee, C.

Song 149 (Dutch)
  See: Grosser Gott, wir loben dich

Song 150 (Dutch)
  See: Alle Menschen muessen sterben (Mueller)

Song 151 (Dutch)
  See: Die Tugend wird durch's (Halle)

Song 152 (Dutch)
  See: Lobe den Herren, den

Song 153 (Dutch - Huet)
                  Z 2061
     Post, P.
     Wilgenburg, D. van
Variants:
God enkel licht

     Voogd, T. de   Zwart, J.

  Song 193 (Dutch)

     Wilgenburg, D. van

Song 154 (Dutch)

     Antonisse, A. , Jr.   Dommele, J. van
     Bijster, J.   Stulp, G.

Song 155 (Dutch)

     Dragt, J.
     Post, P.

Song 156 (Dutch - 1609)

     Beek, W. van

Song 162 (Dutch)
  See: Ach bleib mit deiner (Vulpius)

Song 163 (Dutch - Engels)

     Kool, B. , Jr.
     Vogel, W.   Zwart, J.

Song 165 (Dutch - Bastiaans)

     Nauta, J.
     Nieland, H.   Wilgenburg, D. van

Song 166 (Dutch)
  See: Sollt ich meinem Gott (Schop)

Song 168 (Dutch)
  See: Jesu, meine Zuversicht (Crueger)

Song 169 (Dutch)
  See: Love Divine (Stainer)

Song 170 (Dutch)
   See: Psalm 74 (Geneva)

Song 171 (Dutch)

    Kousemaker, A.
    Wilgenburg, D. van

Song 172a (Dutch - Engels)

    Wilgenburg, D. van

Song 173 (Dutch)
   See: Sollt ich meinem Gott (Schop)

Song 174 (Dutch)
   See: Madrid

Song 175 (Dutch)
   See: Freu dich sehr

Song 178 (Dutch)
   See: Alle Menschen muessen sterben (Mueller)

Song 179 (Dutch - Herrnhutter)

    Wilgenburg, D. van
    Variant:
    Rust mijn ziel

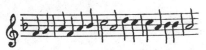

    Groothengel, J. G.

Song 181 (Dutch)
   See: Psalm 118

Song 182 (Dutch - Schuurman)

    Berg, J. J. van den
    Variant:
    D'Almachtig is mijn herder

    Mazyk, R. van (2)   Post, P.

Song 184 (Dutch - Bastiaans)

    Asma, F.
    Beintema, R.   Nieland, H.

Song 186 (Dutch)
   See: Was Gott tut (Gastorius)

Song 189 (Dutch)
   See: Jesu, meine Zuversicht (Crueger)

Song 191 (Dutch)
    See: Alles ist an Gottes

Song 192 (Dutch)
    See: Was mein Gott will

Song 193 (Dutch)
    See: Song 153 (Dutch)

Song 194 (Dutch)
    See: Wer nur den lieben Gott (Neumark)

Song 196 (Dutch)
    See: Old 100th

Song 201 (Dutch)
    See: Allein Gott in der Hoehe

Song 202 (Dutch)
    See: Hanover

Song 205 (Dutch - Bach)
    See: St. Leonard

Song 206 (Dutch)
    See: Alle Menschen muessen sterben (Mueller)

Song 207 (Dutch)
    See: Song 65 (Dutch)

Song 214 (Dutch)
    See: Ach bleib mit deiner (Vulpius)

Song 215 (Dutch - Bastiaans)

      Wilgenburg, D. van

Song 216 (Dutch)
    See: Wachet auf

Song 217 (Dutch)

      Bijster, J.
      Kool, B., Jr.
    Variant:
    Komt, laat ons voortgaan (Bastiaans)

      Mazyk, R. van

Song 218 (Dutch)
    See: Ich will dich lieben (Koenig)

Song 221 (Dutch)
  See: Schoenster Herr Jesu

Song 222 (Dutch)
  See: Seelenbraeutigam (Drese)

Song 223 (Dutch)
  See: Wenn ich ihn nur habe (Breidenstein)

Song 224 (Dutch)
  See: Die Tugend wird durch's (Halle)

Song 225 (Dutch)
  See: Greenland (Haydn)

Song 227 (Dutch)
  See: Die Kirche ist ein altes Haus (Lindeman)

Song 228 (Dutch)
  See: Vienna (Knecht)

Song 229 (Dutch)
  See: Wer nur den lieben Gott (Neumark)

Song 230 (Dutch)
  See: Lux Benigna (Dykes)

Song 232 (Dutch)
  See: So nimm, denn, meine Haende (Silcher)

Song 234 (Dutch)
  See: Jesu, meine Zuversicht (Crueger)

Song 238 (Dutch)
  See: Salzburg

Song 239 (Dutch)
  See: Wer nur den lieben Gott (Neumark)

Song 241 (Dutch)
  See: Innsbruck

Song 243 (Dutch)
  See: Alle Menschen muessen sterben (Mueller)

Song 244 (Dutch)
  See: Psalm 118

Song 247 (Dutch)
  See: Psalm 103

Song 248 (Dutch)
  See: Gott ist mein Lied (Bach)

Song 251 (Dutch)
    See: Wie schoen leuchtet

Song 251: Prelude by Groothengel is on Song 296

Song 252 (Dutch)
    See: Jesu, meine Zuversicht (Crueger)

Song 254 (Dutch)
    See: Kom Christenschaar

Song 257 (Dutch)
    See: Psalm 118

Song 258 (Dutch)
    See: Psalm 21 (Bourgeois)

Song 265 (Dutch)
    See: Wunderbarer Koenig (Neander)

Song 268 (Dutch)
    See: Psalm 118

Song 279 (Dutch)
    See: Erhalt uns, Herr (Klug)

Song 280 (Dutch)
    See: Die Tugend wird durch's (Halle)

Song 281 (Dutch)
    See: St. Clement (Scholefield)

Song 282 (Dutch)
    See: Eventide (Monk)

Song 283 (Dutch)
    See: Angelus (Joseph)

Song 284 (Dutch)

    Wilgenburg, D. van

Song 288 (Dutch)
    See: Winchester New (Halle)

Song 292 (Dutch)
    See: O du Liebe meiner Liebe (Ebeling)

Song 293 (Dutch)
    See: St. Anne (Croft)

Song 295 (Dutch)
    See: Psalm 118

Song 296 (Dutch)
   See: Mache dich, mein Geist (Dresden)

Song 297 (Dutch)
   See: Herr und Aeltster

Song 298 (Dutch - Bastiaans)

   Kusters, G.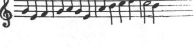

Song 300 A (Dutch)
   See: Beecher (Zundel)

Song 301 (Dutch)
   See: Wilhelmus

Song 303 (Dutch)
   See: Valerius

Song 304 (Dutch)
   See: Gelukkig is het Land

Song A (Dutch)
   See: Wenn wir in hoechsten Noethen

Song B (Dutch)
   See: Lofzang van Maria

Song C (Dutch)
   See: An Wasserfluessen Babylon

Song D (Dutch)
   See: Song of Symeon

Song E (Dutch)
   See: Vater unser

Song I (Dutch)
   See: Psalm 100

Song L (Dutch)
   See: Avondzang

Song of Symeon (Geneva)
                              Z 2126
      Wood, C.
      Variants:
   Lofzang van Simeon

      Zwart, J.

Song of Symeon (Geneva) (cont.)

   Nunc Dimittis (Geneva)

      Haase, K.

   Psalm 202 (Geneva)
   Song D (Dutch)

      Berg, J. J. van den

Sonne der Gerechtigkeit (Bohemian)

      Artmueller, K.   Hennig, W.
      Bender, J.   Hessenberg, K.
      Brod, K.   Pepping, E.
      Hark, F.   Wieruszowski, L.

Sonne und Blume

      Kreckel, P. G.

Sorgen og gleden (Lindeman)

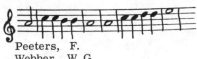

      Alnaes, E.   Gangfloet, S.
      Drischner, M.   Nielsen, L.

Sorrig og glaede (Laub)

      Thuner, O. E.
      Wuertz, J.

Southwell (Damon's)

      Best, W. T.   Peeters, F.
      Canning, T.   Webber, W. G.
      Haase, K.   Wetherill, E.
      Miles, G. T.   Willan, H.
      Palmer, C. C.   Wood, C.

Sov soedt, barnlille (Laub)
   See: Schlaf suess, mein Kindlein

Sovereign Grace
   See: Psalm 89 (Dutch)

Spanish Hymn
   See: Madrid

Spires
   See: Erhalt uns, Herr

Spohr

    Haase, K.
    Peeters, F.

Staa fast, min sjael, staa fast
   See: Nu rinder solen op (Zinck)

Stabat Mater Dolorosa (Mainz)
                Z 40(?)

    DeBrant, C. (2)
    Demessieux, J.   Lemaigre, E.
    Douglas, W.   Marty, A.
    *Dupré, M. J. J.   Mathias, F. X.
    Edmundson, G.   Ravanello, O.
    *Kreckel, P. G.   Schehl, J. A.
    Variant:
    Mater Dolorosa

    Weitz, G.

Stabat Mater Dolorosa (Mechlin -
   Mode 1)

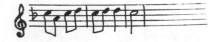

    Dupré, M. J. J.   Ranse, M. de
    Le Bègue, N. A.   *Waters, C. F.

Stans Jesu

    Sister M. G.

Star Spangled Banner (Smith)

    Buck, D.
    Diggle, R.   Paine, J. K.
    Lang, S. de   Peeters, F.

Star Upon the Ocean
   See: Muenster

Stat op, i gry, min Gud   Tune not found

    Thuner, O. E.

Stat op, min sjael
   See: Steh auf, mein Seel (Laub)

Steal Away (Spiritual)

    Lorenz, E. J.
    Thomas, V. C.

Stebbins (Stebbins)

    Lorenz, E. J.

Steh auf in deiner Macht
  See: O Mensch bewein

Steh auf, mein Seel (Laub)

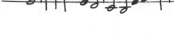

    Raasted, N. O.
Variant:
Stat op, min sjael

    Frandsen, H. B.   Moeller, S. O. (2)
    Jensen, S.   Woeldike, M. A.

Steht auf, ihr lieben Kinderlein
  See: O Heilige Dreifaltigkeit (Hermann)

Steiner
  See: Gott will's machen (Steiner)

Stella Maris
  See: Ave Maris Stella (Mode 1)

Stephanos (Baker)

    Beck, A.
    Haase, K.   Lenel, L.

Still leuchtete der Sterne Pracht

    Lampart, K.

Still, still, weil's Kindlein
  schlafen will

    Spranger, J.

Stille er min sjael (Schop)
  See: Hilf, Herr Jesu, lass gelingen (Schop)

Stille Nacht (Gruber)

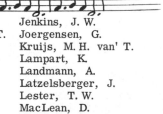

    Beck, A.   Dunn, M. A.   Jenkins, J. W.
    Becker, L. E.   Forchhammer, T. Joergensen, G.
    Birn, M.   Goller, V.   Kruijs, M. H. van' T.
    Bratt, C. G.   Gulbins, M.   Lampart, K.
    Buck, D.   Haase, K.   Landmann, A.
    Carnevali, V.   Haase, R.   Latzelsberger, J.
    Cronham, C. R. Held, W.   Lester, T. W.
    Curry, R. D.   Heuer, G.   MacLean, D.
    DeBrant, C.   Hulse, C. Van   Matthews, H. A.

Mauro-Cottone, M.   Ritter, A. G.   Thomas, O.
McGrath, J. J.   Rogers, S. E.   Thomas, V. C.
Merk, G.   Rohlfing, R. T.   Thompson, V. D.
Midkiff, H. T.   Rudnick, W. (2)   Vail, G. M.
Nielsen, L.   Rumpf, W.   Vibbard, H.
Nordman, C.   Schehl, J. A.   Weelden, J. van
Ore, A.   Schmutz, A.   Weiss, C. A.
Pfretzschner, C. R.   Schulz, H.   Wettstein, H.
Piechler, A.   Schumacher, M. H.   Whitford, H. P.
Purvis, R.   Seely, J. C.   Young, G. (3)
Reger, M.   Stam, G.   Zwart, J. (2)
Reuter, F. (2)   Stiller, K.
Variants:
Glade jul, hellige jul
            dejlige
Nielsen, L.   Wuertz, J.

Holy Night

    Burdett, G. A.

Silent Night

    Ashford, E. L.   Hugle, P. G.
    Barber, S.   Kessel, G.
    Black, C.   Kohlmann, C.
    Dickey, M.   Kreckel, P. G. (2)
    Diggle, R.   Nieland, J.
    Dobritzsch, R.   Rean, G.
    Goller, V.   Stults, R. M. (2)
    Groom, L. H.   Thatcher, H. R.
    Harker, F. F.   Walton, K.

Stille, stille, Jesus lider (Ols-
    soen)

    Gangfloet, S.   Skottner, F.

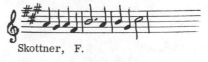

Stockholm (Swedish)

    Peeters, F.
Variant:
Der mange skal komme

    Bergh, L.   Nielsen, L.
    Borg, O.   Peeters, F.
    Haase, K.

Stockport (Wainwright)

    Diggle, R.

Stockport (Wainwright) (cont.)

Variant:
Yorkshire

    Allen, G. P.   Metzger, H. A.
    Haase, K.   Palmer, C. C.
    Hassard, T.   Peeters, F.
    Mead, E. G.

Stockton (Stockton)

    Coleman, R. H. P.

Store Profet med den himmelske
   laere (Mueller)

    Bergh, L.   Nielsen, L.
    Gangfloet, S.   Sandvold, A.

Stort tranen uyt (1584)

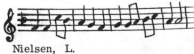

    Bijster, J.

Stracathro (Hutcheson)

    Cameron, G.
    English, R.   Rayburn, R. B.
    Noble, T. T.   Ridout, G.

Straf mich nicht
  See: Mache dich, mein Geist

Strassburg
  See: Aus tiefer Not (Strassburg)

Strength and Stay (Dykes)

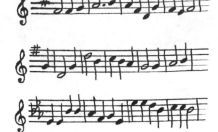

    Conway, M. P.
    Matthews, E.

Stroudwater (Andernach)

    Wilson, J.

Stuttgart (Dretzel)
                Z 1357a
  Variant:
  Sollt es gleich bisweilen

    Karg-Elert, S.   Piutti, K.
    Kickstat, P.   *Schaab, R.
    *Krause, P.

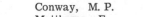

Stuttgart (Gotha)

Z 1353

Bender, J.
Bristol, L. H.
Douglas, W.
Gill, M.
Groves, R.
Haase, K.
Lang, C. S.
Variant:
Sollt es gleich bisweilen

Laverty, J. T.
Matthews, H. A.
Nelson, R. A.
Peeters, F.
Porter, A. P.
Trevor, C. H.

*Rinkens, W.
Schaab, R.

*Vierling, J. G.

Sub Tuum Praesidium (Lambillotte)

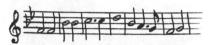

Claussmann, A.

Such wer da will (Stobaeus)

Z 8092

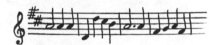

Barlow, W.
Haase, K.
Hasse, K.
Hennig, W.
Hessenberg, K. (2)
Kickstat, P.
Variant:
Wie's Gott bestellt

Micheelsen, H. F.
Oertzen, R. von
Proeger, J.
Walcha, H.
Zipp, F.

Hasse, K.

Such wer da will

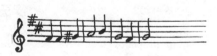

Middle section of Z8092
(above)
Magnus, E.

Such wer da will
See: Lobet den Herrn, ihr Heiden all

Suesser Vater, Herre Gott

Isaac, H.

Suo, Jeesus, paras opettaja
(Finnish)

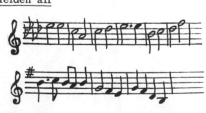

Kuusisto, T.

Suomi (Finnish)

    Peeters, F.
    Raphael, G.

Supplication (Monk)

    Cassler, G. W.

Sur cet autel, ô doux mystère
    (French Noël)

    Erb, M. J.

Surrexit Christus Hodie
              Z 287
              Z 1747a
  Variants:
  Erstanden ist der Heil'ge Christ

    Bach, J. S.   Mueller, G.
    Bender, J.   Pepping, E.
    Dupré, M. J. J.   Walther, J. G. (3)
    Meyer, R.

  Opstanden er den Herre Krist

    Hamburger, P.   Noergaard, P.
    Nielsen, T. H.   Thuner, O. E.

Surrexit Christus Hodie

    Dunn, J. P.

Surrey (Carey)

    Best, W. T.
    Christopher, C. S.   Harwood, B.
    Groves, R.   Palmer, C. C.
    Haase, K.   Rowley, A.
  Variant:
  Carey's

    Wood, C. (2)

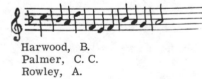

Sursum Corda (Gregorian)

    *Candlyn, T. F. H.

Sursum Corda (Lomas)

    *Hailing, R. G.

Sus bergers en campagne (Denizot)

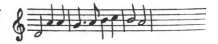

  Boëly, A. P. F.

Sus louez Dieu
 See: Psalm 103 (Geneva)

Sussex Carol
 See: On Christmas Night

Swabia (Spiess)

  Haase, K.
  Peeters, F.

Swedish Litany

  Variant:
  Ack, vad aer dock livet haer

   Salonen, S.

Swedish Melody
 See: Tryggare kan ingen vara

Sweet Bye and Bye (Webster)

  Ashford, E. L.
  Variant:
  In the Sweet Bye and Bye

   Loud, A. E.

Sweet Hour of Prayer (Bradbury)

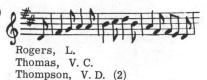

  Ashford, E. L.   Rogers, L.
  Hulse, C. Van   Thomas, V. C.
  Hustad, D.   Thompson, V. D. (2)
  Loud, A. E.

Sweet Name (Sweney)

  Kreckel, P. G.

Sweet Rivers of Redeeming Love
 (Columbian Harmony)

  Groom, L. H.

Swing Low, Sweet Chariot (Negro Spiritual)

      Archer, J. S.   Hancock, E. W.

Synden goer mennesket blind og lam

    *Moeller, S. O.
    *Videroe, F.

Syndernes forladelse (Feuss - Joergensen)

    Woeldike, M. A.

Syng hoejt, min sjael (Gade)
  See: Rueste dich, Held von Golgotha

Synge vi, av hjertens grund
  See: Da Christus geboren (Bohemian)

Taas kukkasilla (Finnish)

    Kuusisto, T.

Taenk naar engang

    Lindberg, O. F.

Taenk naar engang (Baden)

    Nielsen, L.

Taenk naar engang (Berggreen)

    Jeppesen, K.
    Klaebel, F.   Nielsen, L.

Taenk naar engang (Folk Tune)

    Karlsen, R.

Tag des Zorns
  See: Dies Irae (Plainsong)

Tag det sorte kors fra graven (Rung)

    Wuertz, J.

Take the Name of Jesus (Doane)

Thompson, V. D.

Take Time to be Holy (Stebbins)

Thompson, V. D.

Tallis 1st

  Darke, H. E.
  Roberts, C.

Tallis 2nd

  Bratt, C. G.
  Clark, F. S.   Roberts, C.

Tallis 3rd

  Harwood, B.

Tallis Canon

  Best, W. T.
  Conway, M. P.
  Copley, R. E.   Nobel, T. T. (2)
  Edmundson, G. (2)   Peeters, F.
  Gehring, P.   Phillips, C. G.
  Haase, K.   Purvis, R.
  Kitson, C. H.   Rohlig, H.
  Lang, C. S.   Stanford, C. V. (2)
  Manz, P.   Taylor, C. T.
  Meale, J. A.   Thiman, E. H.
  Variant: Young, G.
  Evening Hymn

Tallis Ordinal

  Conway, M. P.
  Larkin, J.   Porter, A. P.
  Palmer, C. C.   Rohlig, H.
  Peek, R. M.   Waters, C. F.
  Peeters, F.   Willan, H.

Talsmand, som paa jorderige
 (Laub)

  Laub, T.

Talsmand, som paa jorderige
(Lindeman)

  *Wuertz, J.

Talsmann, som paa jorderike
(Winter - Hjelm)

  Karlsen, R.

Tantum Ergo (Novello)
 See: St. Thomas (Wade)

Tantum Ergo Sacramentum (German)

  Huijbers, B.
  *Latzelsberger, J.   Ruedinger, G.

Tantum Ergo Sacramentum
(Mozarabic Mode 5)

  Peeters, F.

Tantum Ergo Sacramentum (Phrygian - Mode 3)
 See also: Pange Lingua
    (Sarum - Mode 3)

  Bedell, R. L.   Sychra, J. C.
  Erb, M. J.

Tauet Himmel

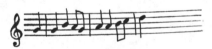

  Miggl, E.
  *Sechter, S. (2)

Tauet Himmel

  Lampart, K.
  Schulz, H.

Te Deum (Vienna)
 See: Grosser Gott, wir loben dich

Te Deum Laudamus (Tone 3)

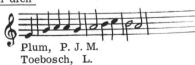

  Fasolo, G. B.   Plum, P. J. M.
  Maessen, A.   Toebosch, L.
  Nieland, J.   Tournemire, C.

Te Deum Laudamus (Tone 8)

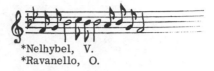

    *Ahrens, J.
    *Dupré, M. J. J.   *Nelhybel, V.
    *Langlais, J. F.   *Ravanello, O.

Te Deum Laudamus (Babst)
  See: Herr Gott, dich loben wir

Te Joseph, Celebrent (Mode 1)

    Peeters, F.

Te Lucis Ante Terminum (Sarum-
    Tone 8)

    Bas, G.   *Gerlach, G.
    *Flay, A. L.   Willan, H.

Te Lucis Ante Terminum (Mode 2)
  See: O Gloriosa Virginum (Mode 2)

Te murheelliset (Finnish)

    Parviainen, J.

Te Splendor Et

    Dupré, M. J. J.

Tempus Adest Floridum

    Christensen, B.
    Nordman, C.   Rohlig, H.
Variant:
Good King Wenceslas

    Andrews, B.   Hulse, C. Van
    Bingham, S.   Kelly, F. S.
    Blair, H.   Plant, A. B.
    Campbell, E. M.   Read, G.
    Cronham, C. R.   Thiman, E. H. (2)
    DeBrant, C.   Thomas, V. C.
    Diggle, R.   Webber, W. S. L.
    Faulkes, W.   West, J. E. (2)
    Gotch, O. H.

Tenbury (Ouseley)

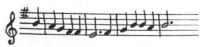

    Haase, K.
    Hulse, C. Van
                Reuter, F.

Ter Sanctus (Rostock)

    Lundquist, M. N.
    Peeters, F.

Terra Beata
  See: Terra Patris (Sheppard)

Terra Patris (Sheppard)

    Yang, J.
    Variant:
    Terra Beata

    Thompson, V. D.

Terribilis Est Locus Iste

    Stoegbauer, I.

Terry
  See: Full of Glory

Teshiniens (Polish)

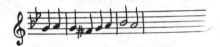

    Hasse, K.
    Peeters, F.

Thatcher (Handel)

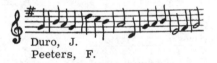

    Buck, D.   Duro, J.
    Cassler, G. W.   Peeters, F.

There's Not a Friend Like the
    Lowly Jesus (Hugg)

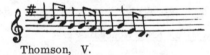

    Thompson, V. D.   Thomson, V.

This Endris Night (English)

    Emery, W. J.
    Jaques, R.   Phillips, C. G.
    Oldroyd, G.   Willan, H.

Thornbury (Harwood)

    Thiman, E. H.

Thou Man of Griefs, Remember
    Us (Dare)

    Read, G.

Though Deepening Trials (Careless)

    Schreiner, A.

Though the Morn (U. S. Southern)

    Read, G.

Three Kings of Orient (Hopkins)

    Cronham, C. R.
Variant:
We Three Kings

Held, W.	Thomas, V. C.
Holden, D. J.	Wyton, A.
Lorenz, E. J.	Young, G.
Nordman, C.	

Thy Life Was Given (MacFarren)

    Hulse, C. Van

Tichfield (Richardson)

    Cassler, G. W.

Tidings (Walch)

    Cook, R. F.
    Olsen, A. L.

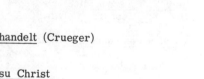

Tiefe, stille, stark und milde
  See: Herr, ich habe missgehandelt (Crueger)

Til dig alene (Wittenberg)
  See: Allein zu dir, Herr Jesu Christ

Til dig jeg raaber, Herre Krist
  See: Ich ruf' zu dir

Til himlene raekker din (Hartmann)

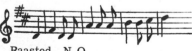

Moeller, S. O.	Raasted, N. O.
Nielsen, T. H.	Videroe, F.
Pedersen, J. V.	Wuertz, J.

Til himmels for den aerens drot
   (Crailsheim)   Z 187b

    Laub, T.
    Moeller, S. O.   Woeldike, M. A.
Variant:
Christus ist heut zum Himmel g'fahr'n

Till haerlichetens
   See: Mach's mit mir, Gott (Schein)

To Jesus' Heart All Burning (German)

    Schehl, J. A.

To Jesus Holy (Holland 1609)

    Huijbers, B.

To Thee We Give Ourselves
   (Hebrew)

    Kohs, E. B.
Variant:
Kee hinay kachomer

Tochter Zion, freue dich

    Wenzel, H.

Tochter Zion, freue dich
   See: St. Bernard (Cologne)

Toer end nogen ihukomme (Laub)

    *Thuner, O. E.

Toer end nogen ihukomme (Lindeman)

Ton-y-Botel (Williams)

    Groves, R.
    Lorenz, E. J.   Purvis, R.
    Maekelberghe, A.   Rogers, S. E.
    Noble, T. T.   Whitford, H. P. (2)
    Parrish, C.   Willan, H.
Variant:
Ebenezer

Tonus Peregrinus

     Titcomb, E. H.

Toplady (Hastings)

      Ashford, E. L.
      Beck, A.
      Bingham, S.
      Burdett, G. A.
      Colvin, H.
      Frazee, G. F.
      Haase, K.
      Hulse, C. Van

      Larson, E. R.
      Lorenz, E. J.
      Mueller, C. F.
      Reuter, F.
      Thomas, V. C.
      Thompson, V. D.
      Wilson, R. C.

Tota Pulchra Es   Tune not found

     Magin, C.

Toulon
  See: Old 124th (Geneva)

Touro-louro-louro

     Hulse, C. Van

Treder op til Herrens bord
  See: Mache dich, mein Geist, bereit

Treuer Gott, ich muss dir klagen
  See: Freu dich sehr

Treuer Heiland, wir sind hier
  (Swiss Hymnal)

     Wieruszowski, L.

Treuer Heiland, wir sind hier
  See: Dix

Treuer Wachter Israel
  See: Da Christus geboren war (Bohemian)

Tribulation (American)

     Schmidt, W. J.

Trinity Office Hymn
  See: Nocte Surgens

Trisagion (Smart)

    Peeters, F.

Triumph, Triumph, es kommt
          Z 2636b

    Piutti, K.

Triumphiere Gottes Stadt
  See: Gott sei Dank durch alle Welt (Halle)

Trods laengselens smerte (Matthi-
    son-Hansen)

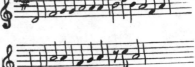

    *Frandsen, H. B.

Trods laengselens smerte (Ring)

Troestet, troestet, spricht der
    Herr (Micheelsen)

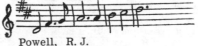

    Micheelsen, H. F. (3)
    Pfeiffer, C. D.

True Hearted (Stebbins)

    Lorenz, E. J.
    Rasley, J. W.

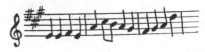

Truro (Burney)

    Bingham, S.   Powell, R. J.
    Cassler, G. W.   Sinzheimer, M.
    Krapf, G.   Weiss, E.

Trust (Mendelssohn)

  Variant:
  Herre, samla nu oss alla

    Salonen, S.

Tryggare kan ingen vara
    (Swedish)

    Bitgood, R.   Hokanson, M.
    Elmore, R. H.   Schmutz, A.

Variants:
Ingen er saa tryg i fare

    Laumann, J.

Sandell

    Nelson, R. A.   Wood, D.
    Peeters, F.

Swedish Melody

    Hustad, D.

Tu auf, tu auf, O Suenderherz

    Doppelbauer, J. F.
    Schroeder, H.   Weber, H.

Tu, Herr, mein Geschrei erhoeren
  See: Psalm 61

Tunbridge (Clark)

    Willan, H.

Tut auf, die schoene Pforte
  See: Gott des Himmels

Tut mir auf die schoene Pforte
  See: Unser Herrscher, unser Koenig (Neander)

Tvang til tro er daarers tale
(Steenberg)

    Karlsen, R.

Twrgwyn (Welsh)

    Morgan, T. J.

Tysk (German)
           Z 7858
      also in 3
           4
    Bencriscutto, F.
Variant:
Wunderbarer Koenig

    Hiltscher, W.
    Hoyer, K.   Kickstat, P.   Ramin, G. (2)
    Karg-Elert, S. Krause, P.   Rinck, J. C. H. (2)
    Karow, K. (2) Piutti, K.   Schwencke, J. F. (2)

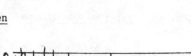

U alleen U loven
   See: <u>Psalm 75</u>

<u>U kan ik niet missen</u>   Tune not found

     Kee, C.

<u>Ubi Caritas Et Amor</u> (Plainsong - Mode 6)

     Benoit, Dom P.
     *Demessieux, J.   *Magin, C.

<u>Udrust dig, Helt fra Golgotha</u> (Gade)
   See: <u>Rueste dich, Held von Golgotha</u>

<u>Uffingham</u> (Clark)
   See: <u>St. Luke</u>

<u>Uforsagt, vaer paa vakt</u> (Losne-dahl)

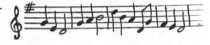

     Nielsen, L.

<u>Uforsagt, vaer paa vakt</u> (Steen-berg)

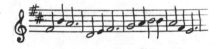

     Nielsen, L.

<u>Un flambeau</u>
   See: <u>Bring a Torch</u>

<u>Unde Et Memores</u> (Monk)

     Edmundson, G.   Hobbs, A.
     Englert, E.   Walter, S.

<u>Underfulle konge</u> (Steenberg)

     Nielsen, L.

<u>Undique Gloria</u> (Elvey)

     Peeters, F.

<u>Une vierge pucelle</u>
   jeune
   See: <u>Von Gott will ich nicht</u> (Erfurt)

<u>Unermesslich, ewig ist Gott</u>

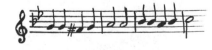

     Toepfer, J. G.
     Wedemann, W.

University (Collignon)

    Grace, H.
    Gray, A.   Sowerbutts, J. A.

University College (Gauntlett)

    Fetler, P.   Matthews, H. A.
    Johnson, D. N.   Pearce, C. W.
    Lang, C. S.   Peeters, F.

Uns Herr Jesu Christ in der
  Nacht

    Rinck, J. C. H.

Uns ist ein Kindlein
  See: Ach, bleib bei uns (Calvisius)

Uns ist ein Kindlein
  See: Ach, bleib mit deiner (Vulpius)

Uns ist geboren ein Kindelein
  See: Puer Nobis Nascitur (Praetorius)

Unser Herrscher, unser Koenig
  (Neander)

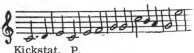

             Z 3735

    Brieger, O.   Kickstat, P.
    Claussnitzer, P.   Mueller, S. W.
    Forchhammer, T. Rinck, J. C. H. (3)
    Franke, F. W.   Schink, H.
    Haas, J.   Schueler, H.
    Hofmeier, A.   Wettstein, H.
    Hoyer, K.   Wolfrum, K. (2)
Variants:
Hilf, Herr Jesu, lass gelingen

    Meyer, R.

Neander

    Beck, A.   Hiltscher, W.
    Candlyn, T. F. H. Hulse, C. Van
    Diggle, R.   Manz, P.
    Fleischer, H.   Peeters, F.
    Haase, K.

Op, i kristne, ruster eder

    *Jensen, S.   *Thuner, O. E.

Unser Herrscher, unser Koenig (Neander) (cont.)

Tut mir auf die schoene Pforte

Bender, J.   Micheelsen, H. F.
Drischner, M.   Oechsler, E.
Hempel, H.   Thate, A.
Hennig, W.   Unbehaun, G.
Hiltscher, W.   Walcha, H.
Huebner, E.   Weber, H.
Metzger, H. A.

Unser Vater, lass uns deine
   Gnade (Raasted)

      Raasted, N. O.
Variant:
Fader milde

Unser Zukunft, Gott, du bist
   See: Aus tiefer Not (Strassburg)

Unter Lilien jener Freuden

      Piutti, K.

Unter Lilien jener Freuden
   (Voigtlaender)
                      Z 3561

      *Claussnitzer, P.

Unto Us a Son Is Born (Unto Us Is Born a Son)
   See: Puer Nobis Nascitur (Praetorius)

Unueberwindlich, starker Held,
   Sankt Michael

      Berghorn, A.
      David, J. N.
                                   Romanovsky, E.
      Roeseling, K.   Weyrauch, J.
Variants:
O unbesiegter starker Held, Sankt Michael
                Gottesheld
      Kraft, K.   Pach, W.
      Miggl, E.

   O unbezwinglich, starker Held, Sankt Michael

Unumschraenkte Liebe (Meyer)
                      Z 7866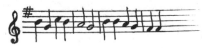

      Enckhausen, H. F.

Unveraenderliche Guete
    See: Psalm 86 (Geneva)

Upp, min tunga (Swedish)

    Aahgren, K. E.

Urbs Beata Jerusalem (Sarum -
    Mode 2)

    Brown, A. G. Y.
    Cassler, G. W.   *Pearce, C. W.
    *Dirksen, R. W.   Peeters, F.
    Faulkes, W.   Phillips, C. G.
    Groves, R.   Titelouze, J.
    James, P.   Willan, H.

Uren, dagen, maanden

    Zwart, J.

Uren, dagen, maanden (Basel)
    See: O du Liebe meiner Liebe (Ebeling)

Ut Queant Laxis (Mode 1)

    Bingham, S.
    Fino, G.   Peeters, F.

Ut Queant Laxis (Rouen Melody)

    *Dupré, M. J. J.
    Fasolo, G. B.   Titelouze, J. (2)

Uverdig er jeg Herre (Strassburg)
    See: Old 130th

Uxbridge (Mason)

    Bingham, S.
    Haase, K.

Vaagn
    See also: Vaakn

Vaak, O sjel
    See: Seelenbraeutigam (Drese)

Vaakn op, du som sover (Linde-
    man)

    Bergh, L.
    Karlsen, R.

Vaakn op, og slaa paa dine strenge
  See: Winchester New (Crasselius)

Vaar Frelsar, yver jordi (Lindeman)

    Nielsen, L.

Vaar Gud han er saa fast en borg
  See: Ein' feste Burg

Vaar Gud han held vaar framtid
  loeynd (Klein)
              Z 1675

    Karlsen, R.
    Variant:
    O Gott, wie soll ich danken dir

Vaar Gud, han signe Norges land
  (Steenberg)

    Nielsen, L.

Vaenligt oever jorden glaenser
  (Wallin)

 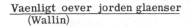

    Cassler, G. W.

Vaer troestig, mitt hjerte (Folk
  Tune)

    Nielsen, L.

Vaer troestig, mitt hjerte
  (Lindeman)

    Karlsen, R.

Vaer velkommen, Herrens aar
  (Berggreen)

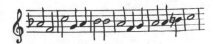

    Christensen, B.
    Frellsen, E.
    Godske-Nielsen, H.
    Jeppesen, K.
    Joergensen, G.
    Laub, T.

    Laub-Woeldike
    Nielsen, J. M. (2)
    Nielsen, T. H.
    Raasted, N. O.
    Wuertz, J.

Vaj nu, korsets flag, paa voven
    dannebrog   (Laub)

    Jensen, S.
    Moeller, S. O.

    Nielsen, O. S.
    Videroe, F.

Vakna upp, sjaa soli lyser (Mon-
sen)

Nielsen, L.

Valerius

Variants:
O Heer die daar

Zwart, J.

Song 303 (Dutch)

Valet will ich dir geben (Teschner)   Z 5404

Bach, J. S. (2)	Kunze, K.
Bachem, H.	Lang, H. (3)
Baldamus, F.	Leupold, A. W. (2)
Beck, A.	Looks, R.
Bender, J. (2)	Lorenz, J. F.
Birn, M. (2)	McCollin, F.
Brieger, O.	Merkel, G.
Brosig, M. (2)	Micheelsen, H. F. (2)
Brown, A. G. Y.	Nieland, J.
Claussnitzer, P. (3)	Oley, J. C.
Diercks, J. H.	Palme, R.
Dressler, J.	Peeters, F.
Drischner, M. (2)	Pfatteicher, C. F.
Dupré, M. J. J.	Piutti, K.
Eckardt, A.	Post, P.
Enckhausen, H. F.	Raasted, N. O.
Engelbrecht, K. F. (2)	Reda, S. (2)
Fischer, M. G. (2)	Reger, M. (2)
Franke, F. W. (3)	Reinbrecht, A. (2)
Grosheim, G. C.	Reinhardt, A.
Grote, H.	Reuter, F. (2)
Guilmant, A.	Ricek, W.
Haase, K.	Rinck, J. C. H. (4)
Hark, F.	Ritter, A. G. (2)
Hasse, K. (3)	Rudnick, W.
Hennig, W.	Rumpf, W.
Herzog, J. G.	Sassmannshausen, W.
Hesse, A. F.	Schrenk, J.
Karow, K.	Schwencke, J. F. (3)
Kauffmann, G. F. (4)	Stiller, K. (2)
Kickstat, P.	Stolze, H. W.
Klaus, V.	Strebel, A.
Koch, M.	Umbreit, K. G.
Koeckert, C.	Vierling, J. G.
Koetzschke, H.	Volckmar, F. W.
Kuehn, K.	Wagner, E. (2)

Valet will ich dir geben (cont.)

    Wendt, E. A.   Wettstein, H. (4)
    Werner, J. G.   Weyrauch, J.
Variants:
Du hast, O Herr, dein Leben

    Kauffmann, G. F.

Hvorledes skal jeg moede

    Jeppesen, K.   Thuner, O. E.
   *Laub, T.   *Videroe, F.
    Raasted, N. O. (2)   Wuertz, J.
    Rosenkilde-Larsen, E.

Lass mich dein sein und bleiben

    Gerhardt, C.   Stiller, K.
    Poppen, H. M.   Wagner, A.

St. Theodulph

    Bender, J.   Lorenz, E. J.
    Bratt, C. G. (2)   McKinley, C.
    Broadhead, G. H.   Peery, R. R.
    Cassler, G. W.   Rohlig, H.
    Diggle, R.   Walcha, H.
    Elmore, R. H.   Westrup, J. A.
    Green, R.   Willan, H.
    Hokanson, M.   Wyton, A.
    Jackson, B.

Schatz ueber alle Schaetze

    Doles, J. F.   Schaab, R. (2)
    Kuntze, C.

Song 1 (Dutch)

    Antonisse, A. , Jr.   Stulp, G.
    Braal, A. de   Wilgenburg, D. van
    Kousemaker, A.

Wie soll ich dich empfangen

    Fluegel, G.   Mueller-Zuerich, P.
    Krause, P.   Rinck, J. C. H. (2)
    Merk, G.   Schwartz, G. von

Van U zyn alle dingen
  See: Song 148

Vanaeret vor drot kom i sin grav
  (Laub)

      Videroe, F.

Var haelsad skoena morgonstund
  See: Wie schoen leuchtet

Var i ikke Galilaeer   Tune not found

      Lindorff-Larsen, E.

Var man maa nu
  See: Nun freut Euch, lieben Christen (Nuernberg)

Varina (Root)

      Richolson, G. H.
  Variant:
  Land of Pure Delight

Vater, krone du mir Segen
  See: Freu dich sehr

Vater, Sohn, Heiliger Geist   Tune not found

      Rohwer, J.

Vater unser im Himmelreich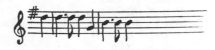
  (Leipzig)
                        Z 2561

      Bach, J. C.   Hellenberg, K.
      Bach, J. S. (7)   Hesse, A. F.
      Baldamus, F.   Heussenstamm, G.
      Bausznern, W. von   Huber, K.
      Beck, A.   Johns, D.
      Boehm, G. (3)   Kaminski, H.
      Brieger, O.   Kammeier, H.
      Busch, A. G. W.   Karges, W.
      Buxtehude, D. (8)   Kauffmann, G. F.
      David, J. N. (2)   Kickstat, P. (2)
      Doppelbauer, J. F.   Kluge, M.
      Dragt, J.   Krause, P.
      Dupré, M. J. J.   Krieger, J. (4)
      Edmundson, G. (2)   Kuhne, F.
      Enckhausen, H. F.   Leupold, A. W.
      Grabner, H.   Manz, P.
      Grote, H.   Mendelssohn-Bartholdy, F.
      Haase, K.   Micheelsen, H. F.
      Hasse, K.   Middleschulte, W.
      Hassler, H. L.   Moore, M.
      Heiller, A.   Mueller-Zuerich, P. (2)

Vater unser im Himmelreich (Leipzig) (cont.)

Pach, W.   Schwencke, J. F. (2)
Pachelbel, J. (5)   Snow, F. W.
Papperitz, B. R.   Speuy, H. J.
Pasquet, J.   Steigleder, J. U. (2)
Peeters, F. (2)   Stolze, H. W.
Pisk, P. A.   Sweelinck, J. P.
Piutti, K. (2)   Telemann, G. P. (4)
Post, P.   Vierling, J. G.
Praetorius, M.   Walcha, H.
Reger, M.   Wedemann, W.
Rheinberger, J.   Weinmann, J.
Richter, E. F.   Wettstein, H.
Rinck, J. C. H.   Wiemer, W.
Ritter, A. G.   Wieruszowski, L.
Rumpf, W.   Wolfrum, K.
Schaab, R.   Zachau, F. W. (2)
Scheidt, S. (5)   Zipp, F.
Schneider, J. (3)   Zwart, J.
Schreiner, A.

Variants:
Herr Jesu Christ, wahr Mensch und Gott

Hennig, W.   *Toepfer, J. G.

Nimm von uns, Herr, du treuer Gott

Kittel, J. C.   Zipp, F.

O du vaar Herre, Jesu Krist

Berg, G.

O Fader vaar i himmerik

Borg, O.

O hjertekaere Jesus Krist

Laub, T.   Videroe, F.
Thybo, L. (2)

Old 112th

White, L.

Song E (Dutch)

Wilgenburg, D. van

Vor Fader udi himmerig

    Raasted, N. O.

Vekter, skal da moerkets rike
(Huus-Hansen)

    Nielsen, L.

Vel moedt, i kristne fromme
(German)
                 Z 5356

    Thuner, O. E.
Variant:
Wohlauf, ihr Christen frommen

Velkommen igen, Guds (Berggreen)

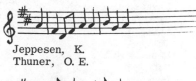

    *Frandsen, H. B.   Jeppesen, K.
    Jensen, S.   Thuner, O. E.

Venez bergers (French Noël)

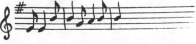

    Borucchia, N.

Venez Divin Messie (French
Noël)

    Alain, A.
    Benoit, Dom P.   Erb, M. J.
    Borucchia, N.   Plum, P. J. M.

Venez Pasteurs (French Noël)

    Piché, P. B.

Veni Creator

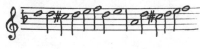

    *Boslet, L.

Veni Creator Spiritus (Lambillotte)

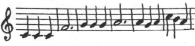

    Bratt, C. G.
Variant:
Come Holy Ghost (Lambillotte)

    McGrath, J. J.

Veni Creator Spiritus (Sarum -
Mode 8)
                         Z 295

Adams, T.
Ahrens, J. (2)   Kreckel, P. G. (2)
Andriessen, H.   Latzelsberger, J.
Archer, J. S.   *Litaize, G.
Bartmuss, R.   Manz, P.
Beltjens, G.   Milford, R. H.
Bermudo, J.   Nelson, R. A.
Bourdon, E.   Nieland, J.
Brandon, G.   Peeters, F. (3)
Breydert, F. M.   Pepping, E.
Cabezon, A. de   Phillips, C. G.
Capocci, F.   Plum, P. J. M.
Cavazzoni, G.   Rodriguez, M.
Clokey, J. W.   Roeseling, K.
Cook, J.   Romanovsky, E.
David, J. N.   Ruijgrok, J. J.
*Demessieux, J.   Scheidt, S. (2)
Dragt, J.   Schilling, H. L.
Dunstable, J.   Schindler, W.
Dupré, M. J. J.   Schroeder, H.
Duruflé, M.   Skop, V. F.
Edmundson, G.   Sowerby, L.
Fasolo, G. B.   Strohofer, J.
Gardner, J. L.   Thiman, E. H.
Gindele, C.   Titcomb, E. H.
Groves, R.   Titelouze, J. (2)
Hulse, C. Van (3)   *Vadon, J.
*Jacob, Dom C.   Woollen, R.
Jacob, G.   Wyton, A.
Kauder, H.   Zachau, F. W.

Variants:
Kom Hellig Aand med skapermakt

    Karlsen, R.   *Thorkildsen, J.

Komm, Gott, Schoepfer, Heil'ger Geist (Klug)

    Bach, J. S. (2)   Pranschke, J.
    Bornefeld, H. (2)   Rinck, J. C. H.
    Brosig, M. (2)   Schwencke, J. F. (2)
    Driessler, J.   Titelouze, J.
    Dupré, M. J. J.   Toepfer, J. G.
    Knab, A.   Vierling, J. G.
    Metzler, F. (3)   Walcha, H.
    Pachelbel, J. (2)   Walther, J. G.
    Peeters, F.   Weber, H.
    Pepping, E.   Zachau, F. W. (2)

Kom Heil'ger Geist

Schroeder, H.   Walton, K.
*Sechter, S.

Komm, O Gott, Schoepfer

Stolze, H. W.

Komm Schoepfer, Geist

Ahrens, J.   *Romanovsky, E.
*Doebler, K.

Song 78 (Dutch)

Kremer, G.   Wilgenburg, D. van

Veni Domine

Chihara, P.
Yon, P.

Veni Emmanuel (Plainsong)

Andriessen, H.   Lutkin, P. C.
Arnold, C.   MacNutt, W.
Bairstow, E. C.   Matthews, H. A.
Barlow, W. (2)   Milford, R. H.
Betteridge, L.   Moser, R.
Bratt, C. G. (2)   Peeters, F.
Burdett, G. A.   Phillips, C. G. (2)
Candlyn, T. F. H.   Phillips, J. G.
Cassler, G. W.   Purvis, R.
Clokey, J. W.   Reichel, B.
Curry, R. D.   Rogers, S. E.
Dressler, J.   Rohlig, H.
Edmundson, G.   Rowley, A.
Egerton, A. H.   Saxton, S. E.
Elmore, R. H.   Schafer, G.
Englert, E.   Sowerby, L.
Floyd, H. A.   Statham, H.
Fromm, H.   Stone, D. M.
Groves, R.   Thomas, V. C.
Halsey, E.   Walton, K.
Harris, C. H. G.   Wehmeyer, W.
Held, W.   Westering, P. C. Van
Hughes, R. J. (2)   Whitford, H. P.
Hulse, C. Van   Williams, D. H.
Krapf, G.   Wyton, A. (2)
Lorenz, E. J.   Yon, P. A.

Veni, O Sapientia (Plainsong)

   Variants:
O komm, O komm, Emanuel

    Doebler, K.

   Veni, Veni, Emmanuel

    Kreckel, P. G.　　　　　　　Schehl, J. A.

Veni Redemptor I

    Preston, T.
    Tallis, T.

Veni Redemptor II

    *Redford, J.
    Tallis, T.

Veni Redemptor Gentium
  See: Nun komm der Heiden Heiland

Veni Sancte Spiritus (Dublin -
   Mode 1)
               Z 34

    Hulse, C. Van
    Kreckel, P. G.　　　　　　　Tachezi, H.
    Latzelsberger, J.　　　　　Titcomb, E. H.
    Moser, R.　　　　　　　　　Tranzillo, D.
    Plum, P. J. M.　　　　　　　Trexler, G.
    Stoegbauer, I.　　　　　　　Vranken, J.
   Variant:
Kom, Gud, Helligaand, kom brat

    Andersen, E.　　　　　　　　*Wuertz, J.

Veni Sancte Spiritus (Webbe)

    Groves, R.
    *Lang, C. S.　　　　　　　　Palmer, C. C.
    Oldroyd, G.　　　　　　　　Rowley, A.

Veni, Veni, Emmanuel
  See: Veni, O Sapientia (Plainsong)

Venite Adoremus (Traditional)

    Gehrenbeck, D.

Venner, sagde Guds engel blidt
  (Laub)

    Jensen, S.
    Thuner, O. E.   Wuertz, J.

Verbum Supernum (Plainsong -
  Mode 8)

    Guilmant, A.   Peeters, F.
    Langlais, J. F.   Togni, V.
  Variant:
  O Nata Lux De Lumine (Mode 8)

    Peeters, F.

Verbum Supernum Prodiens
  (Mechlin - Mode 8)

    *Dupré, M. J. J.   Oldroyd, G.
    Erb, M. J. (10)   Peeters, F.

Verbum Supernum Prodiens
  (Sarum- Mode 2)

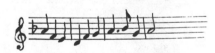

    *Coleman, R. H. P.
    *Redford, J.   Rogers, S. E.

Verden i det onde senkers
  (Flitner)

    Nielsen, L.

Verden, O verden (Holter)

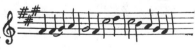

    Karlsen, R.

Verden, O verden, hvi frister
  (Laub)

    *Thuner, O. E.

Vergangen ist der lichte Tag
  (Danish)
         also in 2 and in major
             4
   Leifs, J. T.
  Variants:
  Den lyse dag forgangen er (Kingo)

    Karlsen, R.   Raasted, N. O.
    Laub, T.   Rung-Keller, P. S.
    Noerholm, I.   Woeldike, M. A. (2)

Vergangen ist der lichte Tag (Danish) (cont.)

   Der helle Tag vergangen ist

      Raasted, N. O.

Verlass mich nicht

      Karg-Elert, S. (2)

Verleih uns Frieden gnaediglich
   (Nuernberg)
   Based on Veni Redemptor
               Z 1945a

*Ahrens, J.	Metzger, H. A.
*Bausznern, W. von	Micheelsen, H. F.
Bender, J.	Piutti, K.
David, J. N.	Poppen, H. M.
Drischner, M. (2)	Poser, H.
Fiebig, K.	Rinck, J. C. H.
Karow, K.	Schlick, A. (3)
Koch, J. H. E.	Thieme, K.
Krause, P.	Vierling, J. G.

Verzage nicht, du Haeuflein
   klein (Altenburg)
              Z 2516

      Franke, F. W.
      Hessenberg, K.   Traegner, R.

Verzage nicht, du Haeuflein klein (Leipzig)
   See: Kommt her zu mir, spricht Gottes Sohn (Leipzig)

Vesper Hymn (Bortnianski)

Ashford, E. L.	Morrison, R. S.
Conway, M. P.	Truette, E. E.
Matthews, H. A.	Whiting, G. E.
Melville, C. E.	Whitney, S. B.

Vetter
   See: Das walt Gott, Vater

Vexilla Regis (German)

      DeBrant, C.

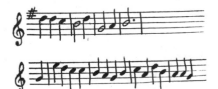

Vexilla Regis (Hampton)

      Barlow, W. (2)
      Haase, K.   *Whiting, G. E.

Vexilla Regis Prodeunt (Sarum -
Mode 1)
                Z 315

    Ahrens, J.   Edmundson, G.
    *Amelsvoort, J. van   Evans, P. A.
    Bairstow, E. C.   *Fleury, A.
    Bas, G.   Held, W.
    Brandon, G.   Hulse, C. Van
    Bratt, C. G.   Lenel, L.
    Bull, J.   Peeters, F.
    Bedell, R. L.   Pepping, E.
    *Campbell, S. S.   Piedelievre, P.
    *Cashmore, D. J.   Purvis, R.
    *Delestre, C. R.   Titcomb, E. H.
    *Demessieux, J.   Willan, H.
    Dupré, M. J. J.
  Variant:
  O Crux, Ave, Spes Unica

    Ahrens, J.   Erb, M. J.

Vi baerer til dig vaar (P. Lindeman)

    Nielsen, L.

Vi kommer, Herre Jesus Krist
  See: Wenn mein Stuendlein

Vi tacke dig, O Jesu god

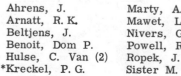

    Bengtsson, C.
    *Berg, G.

Vi takka dig, O Jesu god
  See: Wir danken dir, Herr Jesu Christ (Wittenberg)

Vi tro, vi alle tro
  See: Wir glauben all an einen Gott, Schoepfer (Wittenberg)

Vi tror og troester (Walther)
  See: Wir glauben all an einen Gott, Schoepfer (Wittenberg)

Victimae Paschali Laudes
Victimi   (Gregorian)(Mode 1)
        Z 8759

    Ahrens, J.   Marty, A.   Thomas, V. C.
    Arnatt, R. K.   Mawet, L.   Tombelle, F. de la
    Beltjens, J.   Nivers, G. G.   Tournemire, C.
    Benoit, Dom P.   Powell, R. J.   Trexler, G.
    Hulse, C. Van (2) Ropek, J.
    *Kreckel, P. G.   Sister M. T.

Victimae Paschali Laudes (Gregorian-Mode 1) (cont.)

    Variant:
    Psalm 80 (Dutch-Pierre)

Victimae Paschali Laudes
Victimi (Traditional Catholic)

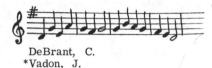

    Bratt, C. G.   DeBrant, C.
    David, T. C.   *Vadon, J.
    Variant:
    Christ the Lord Is Risen Today

    Faessler, G.   Nieland, J.

Victory
    See: Palestrina

Vidi Aquam (Kyrial)

    Bibl, A.
    Erb, M. J. (5)

Vidunderligst af alt paa jord

    Raasted, N. O.

Vienna (Knecht)
               Z 1238

    Haase, K.   Peeters, F. (3)
    Harwood, B.   Thiman, E. H.
    Variants:
    Ohne Rast und unverweilt

    Schmid, K.

    Ravenna

    Canning, T.

    Song 228 (Dutch)

    Bijster, J.   Hekhuis, J.

Vigil (Swedish)

    Hokanson, M.
    Variant:
    Hvo tranes lampa

Vigiles Et Sancti
    See: Lasst uns erfreuen (Cologne)

Ville de Havre (Bliss)

    Colvin, H.
Variant:
It Is Well With My Soul

    Rogers, L.

Vincent (Palmer)

    Thompson, V. D.

Virgin Most Pure (English)

Best, W. T.	Plant, A. B.
Blair, H.	Thiman, E. H.
Faulkes, W.	Thomas, V. C.

Virgin Unspotted (American)

    Drakeford, R.
    Hastings, E. H.

Virgo Dei Genitrix

    Dupré, M. J. J.

Viri Galilaei

    Gindele, C.
    Jaeggi, O.

Vita Sanctorum Decus Angelorum
                Z 5005

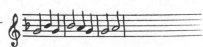

    Scheidt, S.

Voici la première (Denizot)

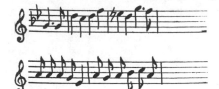

    Boëly, A. P. F.

Voici le Noël (French Noël)

    Barlow, W.

Voix séculaire   Tune not found

    Hess, C. L.

Vol van pracht   Tune not found

    Zwart, J.

Voller Wunder (Ebeling)
              Z 3371

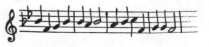

Haase, K.
Hulse, C. Van   Unkel, R.

Vom Himmel hoch da komm ich
    her (Luther)   Z 346

Abel, O.	Grabert, M.
Ahrens, J.	Grote, H.
Andrews, M.	Gulbins, M. (3)
Bach, J. B.	Haase, K.
Bach, J. S. (6)	Haase, R. (2)
Baldamus, F.	Hamburger, P.
Barner, A.	Helmbold, C. A.
Beck, A.	Hering, K. E.
Beckmann, G. (2)	Herrmann, K. H.
Bender, J.	Herzog, J. G.
Blumenthal, P.	Hesse, A. F.
Boehm, G. (2)	Hoyer, K. (2)
Borg, O.	Huth, A.
Bornefeld, H.	Janssen, P.
Briegel, W. C.	Karg-Elert, S. (2)
Brieger, O. (2)	Kickstat, P.
Brosig, M. (3)	Kirnberger, J. P.
Buttstedt, J. H. (2)	Koetzschke, H.
Cebrian, A.	Kousemaker, A.
Claussnitzer, P. (7)	Krause, P.
Conze, J. (2)	Krieger, J.
Crane, R.	Kuehn, K.
David, J. N. (2)	Kuntze, C.
David, T. C.	Kunze, K.
Driessler, J.	Landmann, A.
Drischner, M.	Langstroth, I. S. (2)
Dupré, M. J. J.	Lechthaler, J.
Dyckerhoff, W. (2)	Leupold, A. W.
Ebhardt, G. F.	Looks, R.
Edmundson, G. (2)	Lubrich, F. , Jr.
Enckhausen, H. F.	Magnus, E.
Engelbrecht, K. F.	Marckhl, E.
Eyken, J. A. van (3)	Markull, F. W.
Faehrmann, H.	Marpurg, F. W.
Faisst, I. G. F. von (2)	Markworth, H. J.
Fischer, A.	Matthison-Hansen, F.
Fleck, M.	Merk, G.
Fluegel, E. P. (2)	Merkel, G. (5)
Fluegel, G. (3)	Micheelsen, H. F. (2)
Franke, F. W.	Mojsisovics, R. von
Gall, H.	Moser, R.
Geist, P.	Mudde, W.
Genzmer, H.	Mueller, G.
Goetze, H.	Mueller, S.

Mueller, W. A.
Near, G.
Olsson, O. E.
Pachelbel, J. (5)
Palme, R.
Papperitz, B. R.
Peeters, F.
Pepping, E. (2)
Peters, A.
Pfaff, H.
Piechler, A.
Piutti, K. (4)
Post, P.
Powell, R. J.
Purvis, R.
Reda, S.
Reger, M. (4)
Reijden, W. van der
Reinbrecht, A.
Reuter, F. (4)
Riedel, H.
Riemenschneider, G.
Rinck, J. C. H. (8)
Ritter, A. G.
Romanovsky, E.
Rudnick, W. (3)
Rumpf, W.
Schaab, R. (2)
Scheidt, S.
Schilling, A.
Schilling, H. L.
Schmid, J.
Schneider, J. J.
Schoenfeld, H.
Schoenherr, C.

Schulz, H.
Schumacher, M. H.
Schurig, V.
Schwarz-Schilling, R.
Schwencke, J. F. (2)
Seiffert, U. (3)
Soenke, H.
Stiller, K. (3)
Stolze, H. W. (2)
Thieme, K.
Thomas, G. A. (2)
Thomas, O. (2)
Toepfer, J. G. (2)
Trautner, F. W.
Vierling, J. G.
Vogel, P. (2)
Volckmar, F. W. (2)
Wagner, E.
Walcha, H.
Walther, J. G. (2)
Weber, H.
Wedemann, W.
Wehmeyer, W.
Weiss, C. A.
Wendt, E. A.
Wettstein, H. (3)
Winter-Hjelm, O.
Wolfrum, K.
Wyton, A.
Young, G.
Zachau, F. W. (7)
Zehrfeld, O. (2)
Zwart, J.

Variants:
Ach mein herzliebes Jesulein
Dies ist der Tag den Gott gemacht
Es kam ein Engel

Doebler, K. (2)
Goetze, H.

Romanovsky, E.

Fra himlen hoejt kom budskab her

Alnaes, E.
Frellsen, E.
Hamburger, P. (2)
Henschkel, J.
Hoegenhaven, K. J.
Jensen, S.

Jeppesen, K.
Laub, T.
Nielsen, T. H.
Raasted, N. O. (2)
Videroe, F.
Woeldike, M. A.

Vom Himmel hoch da komm ich her (cont.)

  Gute Maer

    Ritter, A. G.   Rudnick, W.

  Song 11 (Dutch)

    Berg, J. J. van den

  Wir singen dir, Emmanuel

    *Gulbins, M.

Vom Himmel hoch ihr Englein kommt
  See: Vom Himmel kam der Engel Schaar (Susanni)

Vom Himmel kam der Engel
  Schaar (Piae Cantiones)

    Bach, J. S.
    Buttstedt, J. H.   Dupré, M. J. J.

Vom Himmel kam der Engel
  Schaar (Erfurt)
             Z 297b
    Pasquet, J.

Vom Himmel kam der Engel
  Schaar (Klug)
             Z 344a
    Schwarz-Schilling, R.
    *Soenke, H.

Vom Himmel kam der Engel
  Schaar (Susanni)

    Bingham, S.
    *Schwencke, J. F. (2)
  Variants:
  A Little Child There Is Y-Born
  Vom Himmel hoch ihr Englein kommt

    Lampart, K.   Weinreich, W.

Vom Himmel kam der Engel Schaar
  See: Puer Nobis Nascitur (Praetorius)

Von Gott will ich nicht lassen
  (Crueger)
          Z 5266b

Brieger, O.
Franke, F. W.
Goodhart, A. M.
Variant:
Kommt Kinder, lasst uns gehen (Crueger)

Kickstat, P.
Rudnick, W.
Wettstein, H.

Wieruszowski, L.

Von Gott will ich nicht lassen
(Erfurt)

Z 5264

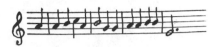

Abel, O.
Bach, J. C.
Bach, J. M.
Bach, J. S.
*Baldamus, F.
Barlow, W.
Beck, C.
*Breuker, C.
Buxtehude, D. (4)
*Claussnitzer, P.
*Dienel, O.
Dupré, M. J. J.
Enckhausen, H. F.
*Fischer, M. G.
Haase, K.
*Hanebeck, H. R.
Hark, F.
*Hesse, A. F. (2)
*Hessenberg, K.
Karow, K.
Kickstat, P.
Krause, P.
Krebs, J. L. (2)

Manicke, D.
Marpurg, F. W.
Meissner, H.
Merkel, G.
Micheelsen, H. F.
Nagel, W.
Peeters, F.
Pepping, E. (2)
Peters, A.
Pfaff, H.
Piutti, K.
Raasted, N. O.
Reger, M.
Reiter, J.
Schink, H.
Schwencke, J. F. (2)
*Steinhaeuser, K. (2)
*Stiller, K.
Stolze, H. W.
Vierling, J. G.
Walther, J. G. (3)
Weber, H.
Zipp, F.

Variants:
Guds godhed vil vi prise

Debois, C. H.
Godske-Nielsen, H. (3)

Raasted, N. O. (2)
Woeldike, M. A.

Helft mir Gott's Guete preisen

*Hoeller, K.
Kuntze, C.

*Palme, R.
*Spiering, G.

I doeden Jesus blundet

Laub, T.

Von Gott will ich nicht lassen (Erfurt) (cont.)

Mit Ernst, O Menschenkinder

Abel, O.   Magnus, E.
Bach, J. C.   Micheelsen, H. F.
Bender, J.   Reda, S.
Bornefeld, H.   Schneider, M. G.
Herrmann, K. H.   Schwartz, G. von
Karg-Elert, S.   Walcha, H.
Luedders, P.

O Gud, som tiden vender

Steenberg, P.

Une vierge pucelle
   jeune

Daquin, L. C.   Lebègue, N. A. (3)

Von Liebe kommt gross Leiden

Peeters, F.

Voor alle heil'gen
See: Sine Nomine

Vor (Fuer) deinen Thron
See: Wenn wir in hoechsten Noethen

Vor Fader udi himmerig
See: Vater unser

Vor Gud er idel
See: Mit haab og troest (Thomissoen)

Vor Gud han er saa fast en borg
See: Ein' feste Burg

Vor Herre han er en konge stor
   (Hartmann)

      *Godske-Nielsen, H.

Vor Herre Jesu mindefest
See: Lasst uns zum Kreuze (Danish)

Vor Herre, til dig maa jeg ty
   (Laub)

      Woeldike, M. A.

Vor Jesus kan ej noget herberg
  finde (Laub)

      Thuner, O. E.
      Videroe, F.

Vor tro er den forvisning paa
  (Laub)

      Thuner, O. E.

Vous qui désirez sans fin (French
  Noël)

      Boëly, A. P. F.   Corrette, M.

Vox Clara Ecce Intonat (Landshuter)

      Schehl, J. A.

Vox Dilecti (Dykes)

      Beck, A.
      Calver, F. L.   Lynn, G. A.
      Haase, K.   Reuter, F.

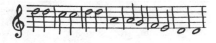

Vreden din avvend (Crueger)
  See: Herzliebster Jesu

Vreuchten
  See: Awake Thou Wintry Earth

Všichni věrni (Czech Advent
  Hymn)

      Michálek, F.

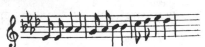

Vulpius
  See: Gelobt sei Gott in hoechsten Thron

W zlobié leży (Polish Carol)

      Labunski, F. R.

Waarheen Pelgrims   Tune not found

      Asma, F.

Wach auf, du Geist (Halle)
  See: Winchester New (Crasselius)

Wach auf, mein Herz, die Nacht
ist hin (Lyon)

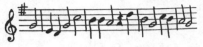

Variants:
Nun freut Euch hier und ueberall

    Ehinger, H. R.

Sei Lob und Ehr dem (Crueger)

Becker, A.	*Otto, H.
Bender, J.	*Piutti, K.
*Doles, J. F.	Proeger, J.
*Egidi, A.	*Rinck, J. C. H.
*Gartz, F.	*Schaab, R. (2)
Genzmer, H.	*Stiller, K.
*Gruel, E.	*Toepfer, J. G.
*Herzog, J. G.	*Vierling, J. G.
*Hesse, A. F.	Walcha, H.
*Hoepner, C. G.	Wenzel, E.
*Kickstat, P.	*Wettstein, H.
*Oley, J. C.	*Wurm, A.

Wach auf, mein Herz, und singe
(Crueger)
              Z 171

*Bach, A. W.	*Schurig, V.
Bender, J.	*Seiffert, U.

Wach auf, mein Herz, und singe (Selnecker)
See: Nun lasst uns Gott dem Herrn Dank sagen

Wach auf, meins Herzens Schoene
(Nuernberg)
           Z 4327b
    Magnus, E.

                    Weber, H.

Wach auf, wach auf, du Deutsches
Land (Walther)
           Z 8761

David, J. N. (2)	
Driessler, J.	Hoyer, K.
Drischner, M.	Jobst, M.
Fiebig, K.	Weber, H.
Franke, F. W.	Wettstein, H.
Hark, F.	Zipp, F. (2)

Wach auf, wach auf, du sich're
Welt (Freylinghausen)
           Z 5918
    Hasse, K.

Wach auf, wach auf, 's ist hohe Zeit
  See: <u>Der Tag brich an</u> (Vulpius)

<u>Wachet auf, ihr faulen Christen</u>
  (Darmstadt)
                        Z 4986
    Fischer, M. G.

<u>Wachet auf, ruft uns die Stimme</u>
  (Nicholai)
                        Z 8405

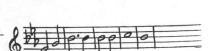

Ahrens, J.	Hennig, W.
Albrecht, G.	Herzog, J. G. (2)
André, J.	Hesse, A. F.
Bach, J. S.	Hoernig, O.
Baldamus, F. (2)	Jackson, F. A.
Bausznern, W. von	Karg-Elert, S. (2)
Beck, A.	Karow, K.
Bender, J.	Kee, P.
Boehner, J. L.	Kickstat, P.
Bratt, C. G.	Kimstedt, C.
Breydert, F. M.	Koehler-Wumbach, W.
Brieger, O.	Koetzschke, H.
Claussnitzer, P. (4)	Krause, P.
David, J. N.	Krebs, J. L.
Dienel, O.	Kuehmstedt, C. (3)
Distler, H.	Kuntze, C.
Driessler, J.	Lang, H.
Drischner, M.	Leopold, A. W. (2)
Dupré, M. J. J.	Luetzel, J. H.
Eckardt, A.	Manz, P.
Enckhausen, H. F.	Markull, F. W. (2)
Engelbrecht, K. F. (3)	Markworth, H. J.
Ertel, J. P.	Merkel, G. (3)
Eyken, J. A. van	Micheelsen, H. F.
Faehrmann, H.	Moisisovics, R. von
Faisst, I. G. F. von	Mueller, S.
Fischer, C. A.	Mueller, S. W.
Fleck, M.	Mueller-Zuerich, P.
Fluegel, G.	Nagel, W.
Forwald, R. M.	Nelson, R. A.
Franke, F. W. (3)	Oertzen, R. von
Frenzel, R.	Palme, R. (2)
Genzmer, H.	Peeters, F.
Glaus, A.	Peters, A.
Grote, H.	Piutti, K. (3)
Gulbins, M.	Raphael, G. (2)
Haase, K.	Reda, S.
Haase, R.	Reger, M. (3)
Hanebeck, H. R.	Reinbrecht, A.
Hark, F. (2)	Reuter, F.
Hasse, K.	Riedel, H.

Wachet auf, ruft uns die Stimme (Nicholai) (cont.)

Rinck, J. C. H. (4)   Stolze, H. W. (2)
Rinkens, W.   Straumann, B.
Roeder, E. O.   Sulyok, I.
Rogers, S. E.   Sumsion, C. C.
Rudnick, W.   Thomas, G. A.
Rumpf, W.   Thomas, O. (2)
Rundnagel, C.   Videroe, F.
Saffe, F.   Vierling, J. G.
Schaab, R. (2)   Walther, J. G. (5)
Schaper, G.   Weber, H.
Scheidt, S.   Wedemann, W.
Schink, H.   Weigl, B.
Schmid, J.   Wenzel, E.
Schreiner, A.   Wettstein, H. (3)
Schwencke, J. F. (4)   Wieruszowski, L.
Sechter, S.   Wolfrum, P.
Seyerlen, R.   Wyton, A.
Siebenbrodt, R.

Variants:
Einer ist's an dem wir hangen

Hasse, K.

Halleluya, jauchzt ihr Choere

Wenzel, H.

Selig sind des Himmels Erben

Krause, P.

Sions vaegter hever roester
     vekter
Forwald, R. M.   Moseng, S.
Gangfloet, S. (2)   Nielsen, T. H.
Laub, T.   Thuner, O. E.
Moeller, S. O.   Videroe, F.

Sleepers Wake

Frank, R.   Martin, M. I'a.

Song 30 (Dutch)

Wilgenburg, D. van

Song 98 (Dutch)

Wilgenburg, D. van

Song 216 (Dutch)

Christiaansz, N. J.

Waer Gott nicht mit uns dieser
  Zeit (Walther)
                    Z 4434

    Bach, J. C.
    Borris, S.   Reda, S.
    Buxtehude, D.   Vierling, J. G.
    Hanff, J. N.   Walther, J. G.
    Metzger, H. A.   Wenzel, E.

Waer Gott nicht mit uns dieser
  Zeit (Slovak)
                    Z 4435

    Franke, F. W.   Haase, K.
Variant:
O Come and Mourn

Wahrer Gott, wir glauben dir

    Ahrens, J.
    Doebler, K.

Wainwright (Wainwright)

    Peeters, F.

Walder (Walder)

    Haase, K.

Walle Stets, O Christ

    Claussnitzer, P. (2)
    Wagner, E. (2)
Variant:
Wir sind dein, Herr

    *Koetzschke, H.

Walle stets, O Christ

    Piutti, K.

Wallog (Davies)

    Parrish, C.

Walsall (Purcell)

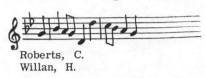

 Milvain, H.
 Noble, T. T.   Roberts, C.
 Peeters, F.   Willan, H.

Waltham (Calkin)

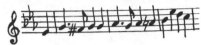

 Stults, R. M.

Waltham (Albert)
 See: Gott des Himmels

Walther

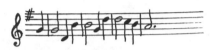

 Haase, K.
 Variant:
 Erstanden! Erstanden!

Walton
 See: Germany

Wandle leuchtender und schoener

 Kunz, E.

Wann einer schon ein Haus aufbaut
 See: Andernach (French Psalm)

Wann endlich, eh' es Zion meint
 (Gregor)
     Z 2679

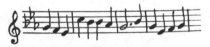

 Hasse, K.

Wann Gott einst uns're Bande

 Franke, F. W.
 Meissner, H.   Witteborg, A.

Wann sich die Sonn' erhebet

 Wieruszowski, L.

Wareham (Knapp)

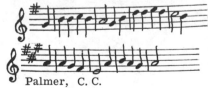

 Best, W. T.   Palmer, C. C.
 Coleman, R. H. P.   Sinzheimer, M.
 Haase, K.   Smith, H. M.
 Hunt, W.   Thiman, E. H.
 Lang, C. S.   Wetherill, E.
 Mead, E. G.   Willan, H.
 Milford, R. H.   Wright, M. S.
 Murrill, H. H. J.

Waring (Barnby)

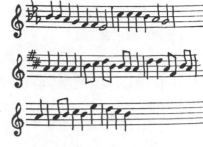

    Hulse, C. Van

Warrenton

    Pfautsch, L.

Warum betruebst du dich, mein
   Herz (Eler's)
                Z 1689a
    Bach, J. C. (2)
    *Karow, K.   Schaab, R.
    Krebs, J. L.   Scheidt, S. (5)
    Oley, J. C.   *Vierling, J. G.
    Pachelbel, J. (5)   Walther, J. G. (2)
    Piutti, K.   Zachau, F. W.

Warum sind der Thraenen
   See: Arbeid, ti natten (Schulz)

Warum sollt ich mich denn graemen
   See: Ebeling

Warum willst du doch

    Oley, J. C.

Warum willst du draussen stehen
   See: Freu dich sehr

Warwick Haven (Walker)

    Walker, E.

Was frag' ich nach der Welt
   (Fritsch-Darmstadt)
               Z 5206b

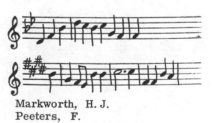

    Beck, A.   Markworth, H. J.
    Brieger, O.   Peeters, F.
    Grote, H.   Schwencke, J. F. (2)
    Haase, K.   Streicher, J. A.
    Herzog, J. G.   Vierling, J. G. (2)
    Hillert, R.
   Variants:
   Ach Gott, verlass mich nicht (Darmstadt)

    Krause, P.

Darmstadt

    Faxon, N. P.

Was frag' ich nach der Welt (Fritsch-Darmstadt) (cont.)

Ich halte treulich still

    Haase, K.

O Gott, du frommer Gott (Darmstadt)

Brieger, O.	Piutti, K.
Franke, F. W.	Reger, M.
Karg-Elert, S.	Richter, E. F.
Kickstat, P.	Schaab, R. (2)
Krebs, J. L. (2)	Stolze, H. W.
Kuehn, K.	Streicher, J. A.
Kuntze, C.	Vierling, J. G.
Merkel, G. (2)	

Was frag' ich viel nach Geld und Gut (Weimar)
Z 2370

    Stolze, H. W.

Was fuercht'st du, Feind Herodes, sehr (Franck)
Z 530

    *Litzau, J. B.
Variants:
Nun freut Euch, Gottes Kinder all

    Hasse, K.

Willkommen sei die froehlich Zeit

Was Gott tut, das ist wohlgetan (Gastorius)
Z 5629

Abel, O.	Franke, F. W. (2)
André, J.	Goetze, H.
Baldamus, F.	Gronau, D. M.
Barner, A. (2)	Guilmant, A. (2)
Beck, A.	Haas, J.
Beck, T.	Haase, R.
Bender, J.	Hasse, K.
Bonitz, E.	Hesse, A. F.
Brieger, O. (2)	Janssen, J.
Chaix, C.	Karg-Elert, S. (2)
Claussnitzer, P. (2)	Kellner, J. P. (2)
Doebler, K.	Kickstat, P.
Doles, J. F.	Klaus, V. (2)
Eckardt, A.	Krause, P.
Enckhausen, H. F.	Krebs, J. L.
Fischer, M. G.	Kreckel, P. G.
Fluegel, G.	Kuntze, C.

Lcupold, A. W.

Loewe, J. K. G.

Lorenz, C. A.

Manz, P.

Markull, F. W.

Marpurg, F. W. (2)

Mazyk, R. van

Meister, J. G.

Merkel, G. (2)

Micheelsen, H. F.

Mudde, W.

Mueller, S.

Mueller, S. W.

Neumann, F.

Nicolai, J. G.

Niepel, P.

Oley, J. C.

Pachelbel, J. (5)

Papperitz, B. R.

Peeters, F.

Piutti, K.

Raphael, G.

Rebling, G.

Reda, S.

Reger, M. (3)

Reichardt, B.

Reinbrecht, A.

Rembt, J. E.

Reuter, F.

Ricek, W.

Riemenschneider, G.

Rinck, J. C. H. (3)

Ritter, A. G. (3)

Roeder, E. O.

Rudnick, W. (2)

Rumpf, W.

Sattler, H.

Schaab, R. (2)

Schaper, G.

Schilling, A.

Schneider, J. G.

Schoenfeld, H.

Schrenk, J.

Schueler, H.

Schuetze, W.

Schwencke, J. F. (3)

Sering, F. W.

Stade, F. W.

Stolze, H. W. (3)

Streicher, J. A. (2)

Thomas, G. A.

Toepfer, J. G. (2)

Umbreit, K. G.

Vierling, J. G.

Volckmar, F. W.

Waldstein, W.

Walther, J. G. (6)

Wedemann, W.

Weeber, J. C.

Wettstein, H. (5)

Wolfrum, K. (2)

Zehrfeld, O. (2)

Zoellner, K. H.

Variant:

Song 186 (Dutch)

Bruin, B.

Storm, A.

Wilgenburg, D. van (2)

Was kann uns kommen an
See: Nun freut Euch, lieben Christen (Klug)

Was mein Gott will, das g'scheh
allzeit (French)
Z 7568

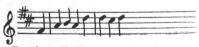

Bach, W. F.

Baldamus, F.

Bausznern, W. von

Borngaesser, W.

Busch, A. G. W.

Claussnitzer, P.

Dallmann, W.

Droebs, J. A.

Fischer, M. G.

Franke, F. W.

Grabner, H.

Haase, K.

Hark, F.

Herrmann, W.

Herzog, J. G.

Kickstat, P.

Kindermann, J. E.

Krause, P.

Krebs, J. L.
Kuntze, C.
Marpurg, F. W.
Meister, J. G.
Merkel, G.
Mendelssohn-Bartholdy, F.
Oley, J. C.
Pachelbel, J. (3)
Palme, R.
Papperitz, B. R.
Piutti, K.
Raphael, G.
Reger, M.
Rinck, J. C. H.
Rinkens, W.
Rudnick, W.

Rumpf, W.
Schaab, R. (2)
Schmidt, F.
Schwarz-Schilling, R.
Schwencke, J. F. (3)
Stade, F. W. (2)
Steinhaeuser, K.
Stolze, H. W.
Telemann, G. P. (2)
Toepfer, J. G.
Vierling, J. G.
Walther, J. G.
Wedemann, W. (2)
Wettstein, H.
Zachau, F. W. (2)

Variants:
Ich hab' in Gottes Herz und Sinn

Doles, J. F.

Song 192 (Dutch)

Nauta, J.   *Zwart, J.

Wer Gott vertraut hat wohl gebaut

Stoeber, H.

Wassail

Hulse, C. Van

Wat drift beheerscht
See: Psalm 2

Watchman (Mason)

Bingham, S.
Mader, C.   Noble, T. T.

Water Meadow (Walker)

Walker, E.

Wayfaring Stranger (U. S. Folk
Tune from Irish)

Whitney, M. C.

We Three Kings
See: Three Kings of Orient

Webb (Webb)

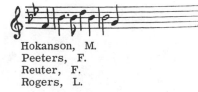

Arbatsky, Y.
Beck, A.
Clark, L. S.
Frazee, G. F.
Haase, K.

Hokanson, M.
Peeters, F.
Reuter, F.
Rogers, L.

Weg mit allem, was da scheinet
(Bernburg)
            Z 3733
    Oley, J. C.

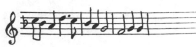

Weicht, ihr Berge
    See: Jesus, Jesus, nichts als Jesus

Weil ich Jesu Schaeflein bin
(Brueder)
            Z 3417
    *Beck, A.   Haase, K.

Weimar (K. P. E. Bach)

    Haase, K.

Weimar (Vulpius)
    See: Jesu, Leiden, Pein und Tod

Weiss ich den Weg auch nicht
    See: Pax Dei (Dykes)

Welche neuer Lieder dringen

    Sister M. F.

Welcome, Son of Mary
    See: Nun sei uns willkommen

Welt ade, ich bin dein muede
(Darmstadt)
            Z 6533
    Franke, F. W.

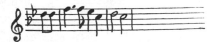

Welt ade, ich bin dein muede
(Rosenmueller)
            Z 6531

    *Brieger, O.   Egidi, A.

Welwyn (Scott-Gatty)

    Beebe, E. J.
    Gore, R. T.

Wem in Leidenstagen
  See: Bemerton

Wend ab deinen Zorn, lieber
  Gott, in Gnaden
                    Z 967
    Schwencke, J. F. (2)   Walther, J. G.

Wenn dich Unglueck tut greifen an
  (Vulpius)
                    Z 499
    Armsdorff, A.   Walther, J. G.

Wenn einst der Herr
  See: Psalm 126

Wenn ich einmal soll scheiden
  See: Herzlich tut mich verlangen

Wenn ich ihn nur habe (Breiden-
  stein)
                    Z 3283
    Claussnitzer, P.   Rudnick, W.
    Erbe, K. (2)   Saffe, F.
    Fluegel, E. P.   Seyerlen, R. (2)
    Krause, P.   Stapf, O.
    Piutti, K.   Streicher, J. A.
    Reuter, F.   Wettstein, H. (2)
  Variants:
  Als ik Hem maar kenne

    Hoogewoud, H.

  Song 223 (Dutch)

    Hoogewoud, H.

Wenn ich in Angst und Not
  (Loewenstern)
                    Z 4233
    Hasse, K.

Wenn ich in Todesnoeten bin
                    Z 4491

    Franke, F. W.

Wenn ich, O Schoepfer
  See: Es spricht der Unweisen Mund (Walther)

Wenn mein Stuendlein vorhanden
  ist (Wolff)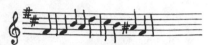
                Z 4482

Bach, J. C.	*Piutti, K.
Bach, J. M. (2)	*Riedel, H.
Claussnitzer, P.	Rinck, J. C. H.
David, J. N. (2)	Rinkens, W.
Haase, H. H.	Schaeffer, A.
Haase, K.	Schink, H.
Kempff, W.	Schwencke, J. F. (3)
Krebs, J. L. (2)	Vierling, J. G.
Kropfreiter, A. F.	Wieruszowski, L.
Pachelbel, J.	Zachau, F. W. (2)

Variant:
Vi kommer, Herre Jesus Krist

Wenn meine Seel' den Tag
  bedenket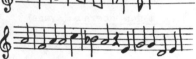

    Enckhausen, H. F.

Wenn meine Suend' mich kraenken

    Oley, J. C.

Wenn meine Suend' mich kraenken
  (Praetorius)
                Z 4337
    Haase, K.

Wenn meine Suend' mich kraenken (Leipzig)
  See: Hilf Gott, dass mir's gelinge (Dresden)

Wenn wir in hoechsten Noethen
  sein (Bourgeois)
             Z 394
             Z 750

Anonymous	Haase, K.
Bach, J. C. (2)	Hark, F.
Bach, J. M. (2)	Helm, J.
Bach, J. S.	Herzog, J. G.
Barlow, W.	Hulse, C. Van
Bausznern, W. von	Jacobi, M.
Bender, J.	Krause, P.
Brown, A. G. Y.	Kuehn, K.
Clausing, F.	Magnus, E.
Claussnitzer, P. (2)	Merkel, G. (2)
Doles, J. F.	Micheelsen, H. F.
Draht, T.	Pachelbel, J. (2)
Driessler, J.	Peeters, F.
Fiebig, K.	Piutti, K. (2)
Fischer, M. G. (4)	Reda, S.
Franke, F. W. (2)	Reichard, G. H.

Wenn wir in hoechsten Noethen sein (Bourgeois) (cont.)

Reinbrecht, A. (3)   Toepfer, J. G.
Richter, C.   Umbreit, K. G.
Rinck, J. C. H. (2)   Vierling, J. G.
Rumpf, W.   Walcha, H.
Schaab, R. (2)   Walther, J. G.
Scheidt, S.   Wedemann, W.
Schwencke, J. F. (2)   Wenzel, E.
Sittard, A. (3)   Wolfrum, K.
Stecher, H.
Variants:
Errett' mich, O mein lieber Herr

Kickstat, P.   Pfaff, H.

Jesus, Thy Name Hath Power To Bless

Olsson, O. E.

Les Commandemens

McKay, G. F.

Naar i den stoerste (Lyons)

Borg, O.   Frandsen, H. B.

Naar vi i stoerste (Lyons)

Gangfloet, S.   Nielsen, L.

O dass doch bald

Hennig, W.   Weber, H.

O Jesu Krist, dig till oss

Aahgren, K. E.

Psalm 140 (Geneva-Dutch)

Kee, C.   Sweelinck, J. P. (2)

Se Jesus aer ett troestrikt namn

Melin, H.

Song A (Dutch)

Zwart, J.

Vor deinen Thron

    Bach, J. S.   Schaab, R.
    Dupré, M. J. J.

Wenn zur Vollfuerung deiner
  Pflicht (Kuhnau)
             Z 5897b
    Helmbold, C. A.

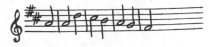

Wer Gott vertraut (Calvisius)
          Z 8207
    Oley, J. C.
    Umbreit, K. G.   Walther, J. G.
    *Vierling, J. G.   Zachau, F. W.

Wer Gott vertraut hat wohl gebaut
  See: Was mein Gott will, das g'scheh allzeit

Wer ist der Herr, der so (Rembt)

          Z 865
    Umbreit, K. G.   Walther, J. G.

Wer ist wohl wie du
      gut
  See: Seelenbraeutigam (Drese)

Wer kann der Treu vergessen
  (Ebeling)

    Drischner, M. (2)
    Werner, F.

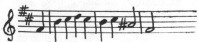

Wer nicht mit den Gottlosen geht zu Rath (Marot)
  See: Psalm 1

Wer nur den lieben Gott laesst
  walten (Neumark)
          Z 2778
    Bach, J. S. (5)   Cassler, G. W.
    Baldamus, F.   Chemin-Petit, H.
    Bausznern, W. von Claussnitzer, P. (8)
    Beck, A.   Copley, R. E.
    Bender, J.   Curry, W. L.
    *Besemann, I. C.   David, J. N.
    *Boehm, C.   *Davis, W. R.
    Boehm, G.   Dienel, O.
    *Boehner, J. L.   Doebler, K.
    Blok, R.   *Doles, J. F.
    Brieger, O.   Drischner, M.
    Brosig, M.   Dupré, M. J. J.
    Burkhard, W.   Eckardt, A.

Wer nur den lieben Gott laesst walten (Neumark) (cont.)

Edmundson, G.	Mueller-Zuerich, P.
Enckhausen, H. F.	Neumann, F.
Eyken, J. A. van (3)	Nicolai, J. G.
*Fischer, A.	Niepel, P.
Fleck, M.	Palme, R.
Fluegel, E. P.	*Papperitz, B. R.
Forchhammer, T. (2)	Peeters, F.
Franke, F. W. (3)	Pepping, E. (2)
*Grabert, M.	Piutti, K.
Gradehand, F.	Raasted, N. O.
*Grote, H.	Reger, M. (3)
Haase, K.	Reichardt, C.
Hasse, K.	Rembt, J. E.
Heilmann, H.	Reuter, F. (2)
Herzog, J. G. (3)	*Richter, E. F.
*Hesse, A. F.	Rinck, J. C. H. (4)
Hoepner, C. G. (3)	*Ritter, A. G.
*Hoernig, O.	*Roeder, E. O.
Homilius, G. A. (2)	Rudnick, W. (2)
Hulse, C. Van (2)	*Rudolph, C. F.
Huth, A.	Rumpf, W. (2)
Kaeppel, G. C. A.	Sachs, J. G.
Karg-Elert, S.	Saffe, F.
Kaun, H.	Schaab, R.
Kehrer, A.	*Scherzer, O.
*Kellner, J. C.	*Schoenfeld, H.
Kickstat, P. (2)	*Schoenfelder, E.
*Kirnberger, J. P.	Schrenk, J.
Kittel, J. C. (2)	Schuetze, W. (2)
*Klauer, F. G.	Schumann, G.
Klaus, V.	Seckinger, K.
Knuth, F.	Seyerlen, R.
*Koeckert, C.	Stade, F. W. (4)
Koehler, E.	Stecher, H.
Koehler-Wumbach, W.	Stiller, K.
Krause, P. (2)	Strebel, A.
Krebs, J. L. (2)	Streicher, J. A.
*Kuehmstedt, F. (2)	Thomas, G. A. (2)
Kuntze, C.	*Toepfer, J. G.
Kunze, K.	Trautner, H.
Landahl, C. W.	Trenkner, W.
Landmann, A.	Umbreit, K. G. (2)
Leupold, A. W. (2)	Vetter, H. R.
*Ludwig, C. A.	Vierling, J. G. (2)
Markull, F. W.	*Visser, Y. G.
Marpurg, F. W. (2)	*Volckmar, F. W.
Merk, G.	Walcha, H.
Merkel, G. (2)	Walther, J. G. (2)
Mojsisovics, R. von	Wedemann, W. (3)
Mueller, S.	Wettstein, H. (6)
Mueller-Hartung, C.	Wiemer, W.

*Wolfrum, K.   Zoellner, K. H.

Variants:
Bremen

   Rohlig, H.

Dein Jesus rufet

   Rudnick, W.

Du gehest in den Garten beten

   Wenzel, H.

Hvo ene later Herren

   Drischner, M.   Nielsen, L.
   Gangfloet, S.   Sandvold, A.

Hvo ikkun lader Herren

   Christensen, B.   Lindeman, L. M.
   Holstebroe, H. J.   Moeller, S. O. (2)
   Jensen, S.   Rosenkilde-Larsen, E.
   Jeppesen, K.   Thomsen, P. (2)
   Laub, T.   Woeldike, M. A.

Min sjael och sinne

   Lindberg, O. F.

Mir ist Erbarmung widerfahren

   Chemin-Petit, H.   *Rumpf, W.

Neumark

   Diemer, E. L.

Song 194 (Dutch)

   Bruin, B.   Wilgenburg, D. van

Song 229 (Dutch)

   Asma, F.   Nauta, J.

Song 239 (Dutch)

   Wilgenburg, D. van

Wer nur den lieben Gott (Neumark) (cont.)

Wer weiss wie nahe mir mein Ende

    Schwencke, J. F. (3)   Telemann, G. P. (2)

Wer nur den lieben Gott laesst
  walten
             Z 2795

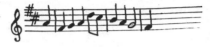

    Enckhausen, H. F.
    *Hess, C.

Wer nur den lieben Gott laesst walten (Hamburg)
  See: Winchester New (Crasselius)

Wer nur den lieben Gott laesst walten (2nd Tune)
  See: Geht hin, ihr glaeubigen Gedanken

Wer Ohren hat zu hoeren
  See: My Gospel (Pennsylvania Dutch)

Wer weiss wie nahe mir mein
  Ende (Hamburg)

    Fink, C.   Lang, H.

Wer weiss wie nahe mir mein
  Ende (Moeck)

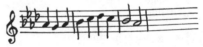

    Brieger, O.
    Haase, K.   Hulse, C. Van
    Hiss, F.   Zahn, J.

Wer weiss wie nahe mir mein
  Ende (Rudolfstadt)
           Z 2839b

    *Bach, K. P. E.   *Matthison-Hansen, G.
    Baldamus, F.   Micheelsen, H. F.
    *Breuker, C.   Pepping, E.
    *Brosig, M.   Pfaff, H.
    Claussnitzer, P. (6)   Piutti, K.
    *Fricke, R.   Reger, M. (2)
    Grabner, H.   *Riemenschneider, G.
    *Herrmann, W.   *Rinck, J. C. H. (3)
    *Herzog, J. G.   Roeder, E. O.
    Karg-Elert, S.   Rudnick, W.
    Kickstat, P.   Schmidt, F.
    Krause, P.   Streicher, J. A.
    Kuehmstedt, F.   Walcha, H.
    Kuehn, K.   Wettstein, H.

Variant:
Du bester aller Menschenkinder

    Klaus, V.

Wer weiss wie nahe mir mein Ende (Neumark)
See: Wer nur den lieben Gott (Neumark)

Werde Licht, du Stadt der Heiden
(Koenig)
                Z 3776

    Kickstat, P.   Piutti, K.

Werde Licht, du Stadt der Heiden (Schop)
See: Hilf, Herr Jesu (Schop)

Werde Licht, du Volk der Heiden
(Kocher)
              Z 3680

    Luedders, P.

Werde munter, mein Gemuete
(Schop)
             Z 6551

         also in $\frac{3}{4}$

Bach, J. S.	Mattheson, J.
Baldamus, F.	Merkel, G. (2)
Brieger, O.	Oley, J. C. (2)
Claussnitzer, P.	Pachelbel, J. (2)
Drischner, M. (2)	Palme, R.
Enckhausen, H. F.	Papperitz, B. R. (3)
Fiebig, K.	Piutti, K. (2)
Fink, C.	Reger, M.
Fischer, M. G.	Reichardt, B.
Franke, F. W. (2)	Reinbrecht, A.
Grabner, H.	Rembt, J. E.
Grote, H.	Reuter, F.
Grundmann, O. A. (2)	Rinck, J. C. H.
Haase, K.	Schaper, G.
Heinrich, J. G.	Schwencke, J. F. (3)
Karg-Elert, S.	Stolze, H. W. (2)
Kickstat, P.	Streicher, J. A. (2)
Koehler-Wumbach, W.	Vierling, J. G.
Krause, P.	Walther, J. G. (2)
Kunz, E.	Weber, H.
Kunze, K.	Wedemann, W.
Leupold, A. W.	Whitlock, P.
Magnus, E.	Wurm, A.
Marpurg, F. W.	

Variants:
Jesu, meiner Seelen Wonne
    Hokanson, M.

Werde munter, mein Gemuete (Schop) (cont.)

Nu velan, vaer frisk til mode

Frellsen, E.   Raasted, N. O. (2)
Hamburger, P.   Wuertz, J.
Moeller, S. O.

O du allersuesste Freude

Koch, J. H. E.

Som den gylne sol frembryter (Schop)

Gangfloet, S.   Sandvold, A.

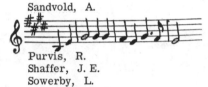

Were You There (Spiritual)

Felton, W. M.   Purvis, R.
Gaul, H.   Shaffer, J. E.
Hancock, E. W.   Sowerby, L.
McClain, C. S.   Young, G.

Wesley (Mason)

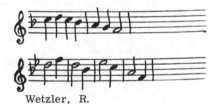

Bingham, S.
Mason, D. G.

Westminster (Cooke)

Wordsworth, W. B.

Westminster Abbey (Purcell)

Harker, C.
Steel, C.   Wetzler, R.

Westminster Carol
See: Les Anges dans nos

Westminster New (Nares)

Wesley, S. S.

Weymouth (Ferris)

Snow, F. W.

What a Friend (Converse)

Mazyk, R. van
Thompson, V. D. (2)   Young, G.

Variants:
Converse

    Biggs, R. K.   Reuter, F.
    Felton, W. M.

Friend

    Beck, A.   Haase, K.

What Is This Lovely Fragrance
  See: Fragrance

When Jesus Wept (Billings)

    Vaughan, C.

When Morning Gilds the Skies

    McGrath, J. J.
  Variant:
  O Esca Viatorum (Haydn)

Whence Comes This Goodly Fragrance
  See: Fragrance

Where Charity and Love (Benoit)

    Englert, E.

While By Our Flocks (German)

    Hastings, E. H.
  Variants:
  Als ich bei meinen Schafen wacht

    Roeseling, K.

  Echo Carol

    Lorenz, E. J.

White Rock (Welsh)

    Vaughan-Williams, R.

Whiter Than Snow (Fischer)

    Thompson, V. D.

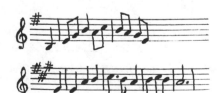

Whither the Burden (Pennsylvania
    Dutch)

    Johnson, A. H.

Whittier
    See: Elton (Maker)

Wie der Hirsch
    See: Freu dich sehr

Wie feierlich erhebt die Stille
    (Bourgeois)

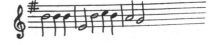

    Franke, F. W.

Wie Gott mich fuehrt
    See: Es ist das Heil uns kommen her

Wie gross ist des Allmaecht'gen
                    Z 6020

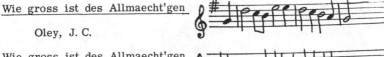

    Rumpf, W.

Wie gross ist des Allmaecht'gen

    Oley, J. C.

Wie gross ist des Allmaecht'gen

    Wedemann, W.

Wie gross ist des Allmaecht'gen
    (Bach)

    Roth, F.
    Schwencke, J. F.

Wie gross ist des Allmaecht'gen
    (Hiller)
                    Z 6028

    Schaab, R. (2)

Wie gross ist des Allmaecht'gen (Halle)
    See: Die Tugend wird durch's (Halle)

Wie gross ist des Allmaecht'gen (Knecht)
    See: Die Tugend wird durch's (Knecht)

Wie heilig ist die Staette hier
    See: Aus tiefer Not (Strassburg)

Wie herrlich gibst du, Herr
   See: Psalm 8

Wie herrlich ist's ein Schaeflein
   Gottes werden (Grimm)
                        Z 3143a
      *Fricke, R.

Wie herrlich ist's ein Schaeflein Gottes werden
   See: Mein Freund zerschmilzt

Wie in den Wiesengrunde

      Leifs, J. T.

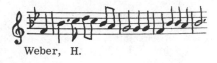

Wie lieblich ist das Haus
   See: Jervaulx Abbey

Wie lieblich ist der Maien
   (Steuerlein)

      Hennig, W.   Weber, H.

Wie lieblich ist, O Herr, die Staette
   See: Religion von Gott gegeben

Wie lieblich schoen, Herr Zabaoth
   See: Jervaulx Abbey

Wie nach einer Wasserquelle
   See: Freu dich sehr

Wie schoen ist unsers Koenigs
   Braut
                        Z 2632
      Hasse, K.

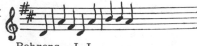

Wie schoen ist's doch
   See: Wie schoen leuchtet

Wie schoen leucht uns der Morgenstern (Nicolai)
   See: Wie schoen leuchtet

Wie schoen leuchtet der Morgenstern (Nicolai)
                        Z 8359

      Aahgren, K. E.   Behrens, J. J.
      Ahrens, J.   Bender, J. (2)
      Armsdorff, A.   Bornefeld, H.
      Bach, J. C.   Brieger, O. (2)
      Bach, J. S. (2)   Busch, A. G. W.
      Baldamus, F.   Buttstedt, J. H.
      Barlow, W. (2)   Buxtehude, D. (6)

Wie schoen leuchtet der Morgenstern (Nicolai) (cont.)

Cassler, G. W.

Claussnitzer, P. (2)

Copley, R. E.

David, J. N. (2)

Dienel, O.

Distler, H. (2)

Doppelbauer, J. F.

Drischner, M. (2)

Drwenski, W.

Dupré, M. J. J.

Edmundson, G.

Enckhausen, H. F.

Faehrmann, H.

Faisst, I. G. F. von

Fiebig, K.

Fink, C. (2)

Fischer, M. G. (2)

Fluegel, G. (2)

Forchhammer, T. (3)

Franke, F. W. (3)

Fricke, R.

Gaebler, E. F.

Gerhardt, P.

Gindele, C.

Haase, K.

Hark, F.

Hasse, K.

Heinrich, J. G.

Herrmann, K. H.

Herzog, J. G.

Huth, A.

Kaminski, H.

Karg-Elert, S. (2)

Kauffmann, G. F. (2)

Kempff, W.

Kickstat, P.

Kienzl, W.

Kimstedt, C.

Kirnberger, J. P.

Kittel, J. C.

Knab, A.

Koehler-Wumbach, W.

Koetsier, J.

Koetzschke, H.

Krapf, G.

Krause, P.

Kuehn, K. (2)

Kummer, E.

Kuntze, C.

Landmann, A.

Lang, H.

Lenel, L.

Leupold, A. W. (2)

Lorenz, J. F.

Luetzel, J. H.

Lux, F.

Magnus, E.

Manz, P.

Markull, F. W.

Markworth, H. J.

Merkel, G. (3)

Meyer, R.

Micheelsen, H. F. (2)

Michel, A.

Michl, A. (2)

Miles, G. T.

Mojsisovics, R. von

Mueller, S.

Mueller, S. W.

Mueller, W. A.

Mueller-Zuerich, P. (3)

Oertzen, R. von

Oley, J. C.

Olsson, O. E.

Pach, W.

Pachelbel, J. (4)

Palme, R. (3)

Peeters, F.

Pepping, E.

Peters, A.

Petzold, J.

Piutti, K.

Poppen, H. M.

Praetorius, M.

Raasted, N. O. (2)

Raphael, G.

Reda, S.

Reger, M. (4)

Reichardt, A.

Reichel, B.

Reimann, H.

Reinbrecht, A. (2)

Reinhardt, A.

Reuter, F. (2)

Ricek, W.

Richter, E. F.

Riedel, H.

Rinck, J. C. H. (4)

Rinkens, W.

Ritter, A. G.

Rohlig, H.

Rudnick, W. (2)

Rumpf, W.
Samuel, P.
Schaab, R.
Schaper, G.
Scheidt, S. (3)
Schmid, J.
Schneider, J. J.
Schuetze, W.
Schumann, G.
Schwencke, J. F. (3)
Seiffert, U.
Seyerlen, R.
Sittard, A.
Stade, F. W. (2)
Stein, K. (2)
Stiller, K.
Straumann, B.
Streicher, J. A.

Telemann, G. P. (2)
Thomas, G. A. (2)
Thomas, O.
Tod, E. A.
Trenkner, W.
Tuerke, O. (2)
Unbehaun, G.
Vierling, J. G.
Voigtmann, R. J.
Volckmar, F. W. (3)
Walcha, H.
Wedemann, W.
Wettstein, H. (6)
Weyrauch, J.
Wieruszowski, L.
Wolfrum, K.
Zachau, F. W.
Zwart, J.

Variants:
Af hoejheden oprunden er

Hamburger, P.
Laub, T.
Moeller, S. O.

Noerholm, I.
Raasted, N. O. (2)
Wuertz, J.

Av hoeyheten opprunnen er

Drischner, M.
Gangfloet, S.

Moseng, S.
Thorkildsen, J.

Dich seh' ich wieder, Morgenlicht

Schaab, R.

Frankfort

Schreiner, A.

Ich und mein Haus

Gottschick, F.

Morgenstern
O Heil'ger Geist, kehr bei uns ein

Breitenbach, C. G. J.
Doles, J. F.
Egidi, A.
Gulbins, M.
*Janssen, P.

Ritter, A. G.
Rudnick, W.
Wenzel, H.
Werner, F.

Wie schoen leuchtet der Morgenstern (Nicolai) (cont.)

O Jesu, Jesu, Gottes Sohn

   Hasse, K.

O wundergrosser Siegesheld

   Gruel, E.

Song 251 (Dutch)

   Dragt, J.   Mulder, E. W.
   Mudde, W.   Wilgenburg, D. van

Var haelsad skoena morgonstund

   Kullnes, A.

Wie schoen ist's doch

   Abel, O.

Wie schoen leucht uns
   (Listed under Wie schoen leuchtet)

Wo ist ein solcher Gott wie du

   Hasse, K.

Wie selig ist die kleine Schaar
   See: Hvor salig er den lille flok

Wie sie so sanft ruh'n
                      Z 4105

   Franke, F. W.   Schiffner, R.
   Reuter, F.   Wettstein, H.

Wie soll ich dich empfangen
   (Crueger)
                      Z 5438

   Bornefeld, H.   Hulse, C. Van
   Bredack, W.   Jucker, B.
   *Driessler, J.   Kammeier, H.
   Drischner, M. (2)   Kickstat, P.
   *Egidi, A.   Luedders, P.
   Fiebig, K.   Magnus, E.
   Fra.:e, F. W. (3)   Micheelsen, H. F.
   *Gulbins, M.   Oley, J. C.
   Haase, K.   *Pepping, E. (3)
   Hark, F.   Reda, S.
   Hennig, W.   Ricek, W.

Wie soll ich dich empfangen
  See: Herzlich tut mich verlangen

Wie soll ich dich empfangen
  See: Valet

Wie soll ich doch die Guete dein
  See: Mach's mit mir Gott

Wie sollt ich dich, mein Gott,
  nicht lieben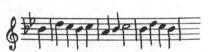

        Sachs, J. G.

Wie wohl ist mir, O Freund der
  Seelen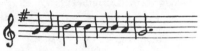

        Wedemann, W.

Wie wohl ist mir, O Freund der
  Seelen (Freylinghausen)
                Z 7792

Wie wohl ist mir, O Freund der
  Seelen (Hiller)
                Z 7795

Wie zal verkeeren
  See: Psalm 15

Wie's Gott bestellt
  See: Such wer da will (Stobaeus)

Wigan (Wesley)

   Cassler, G. W.

Wigtown (Scotch)

   Peeters, F.

Wij knielen voor uw zetel neer
  See: Pilgrimage (Herrnhut)

Wilhelmus (Valerius)

   Zwart, J.
Variant:
Song 301 (Dutch)

Will There Be Any Stars In My
  Crown (U. S. Southern)

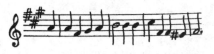

   Thompson, V. D.
   Thomson, V.

Willkommen, heil'ge Stunde   Tune not found

   Brosig, M.

Willkommen, Held im Streite
  (Lang)

   Buehl, W.

Willkommen, Held im Streite (Vulpius)
  See: Ach, bleib mit deiner Gnade

Willkommen sei die froehlich Zeit
  See: Was fuercht'st du, Feind Herodes (Franck)

Wiltshire (Smart)

   Coleman, R. H. P.
   Frost, C. J.

Winchester New (Crasselius)
              Z 278b

   Barlow, W.
   Bratt, C. G.   Smith, E. H.
   Haase, K.   Thiman, E. H.
   Lang, C. S. (2)   Tootell, G.
   Mead, E. G.   Webber, W. S. L.
   Rowley, A.   West, J. E.

Variants:
Crasselius

    Metzger, H. A.

Dig skall min sjaal

    Lindberg, O. F.   Thyrestam, G.

Dir, Dir, Jehova (Halle) (Wach auf, du Geist)

Abel, O.	Reger, M.
Claussnitzer, P. (4)	Reichardt, A.
Fluegel, G. (2)	Reichardt, B.
Haase, K.	Reinbrecht, A.
Karg-Elert, S. (2)	Reuter, F. (2)
Karl, W. F.	*Richter, E. F.
Karow, K. (2)	Rinck, J. C. H. (3)
Kaun, H.	*Rudnick, W.
Kempff, W.	Schilling, A.
Kimstedt, C.	Schink, H.
*Kittel, J. C.	Seiffert, U. (2)
Klaus, V.	*Stiller, K.
Kuntze, C.	Stolze, H. W.
Merkel, G. (2)	Streicher, J. A.
Micheelsen, H. F.	*Wenzel, H.
Ramin, G. (2)	Wettstein, H. (3)
Raphael, G.	*Zehrfeld, O.
Reda, S.	

Dir, Dir, Jehova (Hamburg)

*Baake, F.	Kaeppel, G. C. A.
Baldamus, F.	*Kegel, K. C.
Boehner, J. L.	Klaus, V. (2)
*Brandt, A.	Krause, E.
Bredack, W.	Krause, P.
Brieger, O.	*Kuehmstedt, F.
*Brosig, M.	Leupold, A. W.
*Cebrian, A.	Luetzel, J. H.
*Davin, K. H. G. (2)	Merkel, G.
Drischner, M.	Mueller-Zuerich, P.
Ebhardt, G. F.	Oley, J. C.
Faehrmann, H. (2)	Piutti, K.
Fischer, M. G. (3)	Reinhardt, A.
*Fleck, M.	*Ritter, A. G.
Franke, F. W.	Rumpf, W. (2)
*Gebhardi, L. E.	Schaab, R. (2)
*Gerhardt, P.	Toepfer, J. G.
*Grote, H.	Vierling, J. G.
Grundmann, O. A.	Wedemann, W.
Heinrich, J. G. (2)	*Wendt, E. A.
Hoyer, K.	Wenzel, E. (2)

Winchester New (Crasselius) (cont.)

Dir Gott, dir will ich (Crasselius)

   Michel, A.

Song 288 (Dutch) (Halle)

   Nauta, J.

Vaakn op, og slaa paa dine strenge (Crasselius)

   Baden, C.   Laub, T.
   Frellsen, E.   Sandvold, A.
   Karlsen, R.

Wach auf, du Geist (Halle)

   Bender, J.   Ehinger, H. R.
   Egidi, A.

Wer nur den lieben Gott laesst walten (Crasselius)

   Enckhausen, H. F.   Mueller, S.
   Franke, F. W.   Schaab, R. (2)
   Gerke, A.   Schwencke, J. F. (4)
   Huth, A.   Tuerke, O.
   Kickstat, P.   Vierling, J. G.
   Krause, P.   Wedemann, W.

Winchester Old (Tye)

   Beck, A.   Mansfield, O. A.
   Bichsel, M. A.   Markworth, H. J.
   Coleman, R. H. P.   Palmer, C. C.
   Farrar, E. B.   Peeters, F.
   Groves, R.   Reuter, F.
   Haase, K.   Rowley, A.
   Hopkirk, J.   Walter, S.
   Howard, J. T.   Whitehead, A. E.
   Langstroth, I. S.   Wood, C.

Windham (Read)

   Haase, K.
Variant:
Jesus Crucifixus (Read)

   Edmundson, G.

Windsor (Damon's)

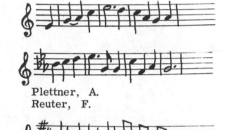

    Best, W. T.
    Cameron, G.   Hulse, C. Van
    Coleman, R. H. P.   Macfarren, G. A.
    Cowell, C. P.   Pearce, C. W.
    Emery, W. J.   Smith, R.
    Goodman, J.   Wesley, S. S.
    Groves, R.   Westrup, J. A.
    Haase, K.   Willan, H. (2)
    Variant:
    Old 116th

Windy Peak (Walker)

    Walker, E.

Winterton (Barnby)

    Beck, A.   Plettner, A.
    Haase, K.   Reuter, F.

Wir beten an die Macht

    Gauss, J.

Wir Christenleut hab'n jetzo Freud' (Fritsch)
   See: Ecce Agnus (Dresden)

Wir Christenleut hab'n jetzo Freud' (Crueger)
   See: O Jesu Christ, dein Krippelein

Wir danken dir, Gott, fuer und
  fuer

    Bergt, B. F.
    Troppmann, J. A.

Wir danken dir, Herr Jesu Christ,
  dass du fuer uns (Wittenberg)

           Z 366

    Bornefeld, H.
    Driessler, J.   Hulse, C. Van
    Grabner, H.   Micheelsen, H. F.
    Haase, K.   Pepping, E.
    Hennig, W.   Walcha, H.
    Variants:
    Das Wort geht von dem Vater aus

    Birck, W.

Wir danken dir, Herr Jesu Christ, dass du
  fuer uns (Wittenberg) (cont.)

  Vi takka dig, O Jesu god

        Aahgren, K. E.   Olson, D.

Wir danken dir, Herr Jesu Christ
  See: Breslau

Wir danken dir, Herr Jesu Christ
  See: Herr Jesu Christ, wahr Mensch und Gott (Eccard)

Wir danken dir, Herr Jesu Christ, dass du von Tod (Fischer)
  See: Erschienen ist der herrlich Tag

Wir danken Gott fuer seine Gab'n
  (Herman)
                Z 382
        Weiss, E.

Wir glauben all' an einen Gott,
  Schoepfer (Langenoels)
                Z 7972

        Brieger, O.
        Haase, K.   Piutti, K.
        Merk, G.   Reuter, F. (2)

Wir glauben all' an einen Gott,
  Schoepfer (Wittenberg)
                Z 7971
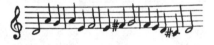

        *Ashford, E. L.   Micheelsen, H. F.
         Bach, J. C. (2)   Pachelbel, J.
         Bach, J. S. (3)   *Papperitz, B. R. (2)
        *Besemann, I. C.   *Peters, A.
         Bornefeld, H.   Pfeiffer, C. D.
         Copley, R. E.   Piutti, K.
         Driessler, J.   Praetorius, M. (2)
        *Droebs, J. A.   *Reichardt, B.
         Dupré, M. J. J.   Rinck, J. C. H. (3)
        *Fluegel, G.   *Schaab, R.
         Franke, F. W.   Scheidt, S. (5)
         Grabner, H.   Schwencke, J. F. (2)
         Grote, H. (2)   *Sorge, G. A.
         Haase, K.   Sweelinck, J. P.
         Kaeppel, G. C. A. (2)   Tuerke, O. (2)
        *Kaminski, H.   Vierling, J. G.
        *Karow, K.   Walther, J. G.
         Kauffmann, G. F.   Wenzel, E.
         Krebs, J. L. (3)   *Wolff, C. M.
         Mettenleiter, B.   Zachau, F. W. (2)
         Metzger, H. A.   Zier, E.

Variants:
Das Credo

   Zipp, F.

Schoepfer
Vi tro, vi alle tro

   Andersen, E.   Laub, T.

Vi tror og troester (Walther)

   Borg, O.

Wir glauben all' an einen Gott,
  Vater, Sohn (Darmstadt)
             Z 4000

   Bach, J. S.   Peeters, F.
   Dupré, M. J. J.   Piutti, K.
   Franke, F. W.   Plettner, A.
   Grote, H.   Rembt, J. E.
   Haase, K.   Rinck, J. C. H.
   Herrmann, K. H.   Tuerke, O. (4)
   Kaeppel, G. C. A.   Umbreit, K. G.
   Kickstat, P.   Vierling, J. G.
   Krebs, J. L.   Walther, J. G.
  *Papperitz, B. R.   Wedemann, W.

Wir glauben Gott im hoechsten
  Thron (Lahusen)

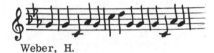

   Bieske, W.   Weber, H.
Variant:
Ein neues Glaubenslied

   Abel, O.

Wir Menschen sind zu dem, O Gott
  See: Es ist das Heil uns kommen her

Wir pfluegen und wir streuen
  (Schulz)

   Groves, R.   Peeters, F.
   Langstroth, I. S.   West, J. E.

Wir sind dein, Herr
  See: Walle stets, O Christ

Wir singen dir, Emmanuel
  See: Vom Himmel hoch

Wir stolzen Menschenkinder

Variant:
Herr, schaue auf uns nieder

Hasse, K.

Wir treten zum beten
See: Netherlands (Valerius)

Wir werfen uns darnieder

Assmayr, I.

Wir wollen alle froehlich sein
(Spangenberg)
                    Z 25b

Borngaesser, W.
Driessler, J.   Micheelsen, H. F.
Franke, F. W.   Pepping, E.
Heilmann, H.   Soenke, H.
Kickstat, P.   Vogel, G.

Wir wollen singen ein Lobgesang
(Gesius)
                    Z 385a

Bornefeld, H.   Pepping, E.
Kammeier, H.   Weber, H.
Variant:
Gott Vater, Herr, wir danken dir

Senftleben, G.

Wird das nicht Freude sein
                    Z 4287
       Claussnitzer, P.

Wither's Rocking Hymn (Vaughan-
Williams)

Pearson, W. D.

Wo findet die Seele die Heimat
(Folk Tune)

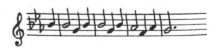

Ashford, E. L.
Forchhammer, T.   Rahn, E.

Wo Gott der Herr nicht bei uns
   haelt (Wittenberg)
                    Z 4441

Bach, J. C.

Barbe, H.

Dueben, A.

Enckhausen, H. F.

Franke, F. W.

Krebs, J. T.

Metzger, H. A.

Oley, J. C.

Pachelbel, J. (3)

Pepping, E.

Proeger, J.

Reda, S.

Schwencke, J. F. (3)

Sweelinck, J. P. (2)

Vierling, J. G.

Walter, J.

Zachau, F. W. (2)

Zipp, F.

Variant:

Ach lieben Christen, seid getrost

Wo Gott zum Haus nicht gibt sein Gunst (Klug)
Z 305

Bach, J. C.

Bauer, J.

Beck, A.

Claussnitzer, P. (4)

Distler, H.

Fischer, M. G.

Grote, H.

Haase, K.

Jenne, N.

Metzger, H. A.

Michel, A.

Othmayr, K.

Pachelbel, J. (3)

Peeters, F. (2)

Piutti, K. (2)

Plettner, A.

Reda, S.

Rinck, J. C. H.

Toepfer, J. G.

Umbreit, K. G.

Vierling, J. G.

Walther, J. G. (2)

Zehrfeld, O.

Zier, E.

Zipp, F.

Variants:

Auf, jauchzet dem Herrn

Stolze, G. C.

Ich komme vor dein Angesicht

Straumann, B.

Mein Gott, ich danke herzlich dir

Doles, J. F.   Schaab, R.

Gall, H.

Nun wolle Gott, dass unser Sang

Meyer, R.

Wo ist das Kind, das uns gebor'n

Ruedinger, G.

Wo ist ein solcher Gott wie du

See: Wie schoen leuchtet

Wo soll ich fliehen hin (Nuern-
    berg)
                Z 2177

      Haase, K.
      Walther, J. G.

Wo soll ich fliehen hin (Regnart)
    See: Auf meinen lieben Gott (Regnart)

Wo willst du hin
    See: Ach blein bei uns (Calvisius)

Wohl dem, der Gott verehret
             Z 5427(?)

      Franke, F. W.

Wohl dem Menschen der nicht
    wandelt (Ebeling)
             Z 6602

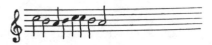

      Doles, J. F.

Wohl denen, die da wandeln
    (Schuetz)
             Z 4341

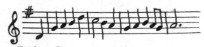

      Hennig, W.   Reda, S.
      Koch, J. H. E.   Schneider, M. G.
      Metzger, H. A.   Weber, H.

Wohlauf, die ihr hungrig seid
    (Bohemian)
             Z 1613

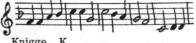

      Drischner, M. (2)
      Hennig, W.   Knigge, K.
      Hessenberg, K.   Metzger, H. A.
                           Wagner, A.

Wohlauf, ihr Christen frommen
    See: Vel moedt, i kristne

Wohlauf, tut nicht versagen
    (Helder)
             Z 5428

      Shaw, G. T.

Wohlauf, wohlauf, du edles Blut

      Ruedinger, G.

Wohlauf, wohlauf, zum letzten Gang
    See: Ich hab' mein Sach (Stuttgart)

Wollt ihr wissen, was mein Preis
  (Cammin)

          Z 1863

     *Brieger, O.

Wollt ihr wissen, was mein Preis
  (Reimann)

          Z 1861

    Kuehn, K.
    Piutti, K.   Roeder, E. O.

Womit soll ich dich wohl loben
  (Silcher)

          Z 6836

    Breuninger, K. K.   Buehl, W.

Womit soll ich dich wohl loben
  See: Salzburg

Wonderful Words Of Life (Bliss)

    Thompson, V. D.

Wondrous Love (American)

    Barber, S.
    Bohnhorst, F. R.   Schmidt, W. J.
    Johnson, D. N.   Young, G.

Woodbird
  See: Es flog ein kleins Waldvoegelein
       Taeublein weisse

Woodworth (Bradbury)

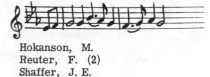

    Ashford, E. L.
    Beck, A.   Hokanson, M.
    Bingham, S.   Reuter, F. (2)
    Colvin, H.   Shaffer, J. E.
    Goode, J. C.   Thompson, V. D.
    Haase, K.   Wetzler, R.
  Variant:
  Just As I Am (Bradbury)

    Langston, P. T.

Worcester (Tomkins)

    Atkins, I. A.

Worcester (Whinfield)

    Haase, K.
    Sassmannshausen, W.

Worgan
   See: <u>Lyra Davidica</u>

Work For the Night Is Coming
(Mason)

    Ashford, E. L.
    Bingham, S.
Variant:
Work Song

    Goode, J. C.

Work Song
   See: <u>Work For the Night Is Coming</u>

Worship (Moravian)

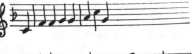

    Elmore, R. H.

Wort aus Gottes Mund (Witt)
             Z 8052
    Ehinger, H. R.
    Vogel, P.
Variant:
Jesu, meine Liebe

    Fink, C.   Reichardt, T.
    Fink, F.   Rumpf, W.

Wsród nocnej ciszy (Polish Carol)

    Labunski, F. R.

Wuertemburg
   See: <u>Mache dich, mein Geist, bereit</u>

Wunderanfang, herrlich Ende
   See: <u>Alles ist an Gottes Segen</u>

Wunderbarer Gnadenthron
   See: <u>Da Christus geboren war</u> (Bohemian)

Wunderbarer Koenig, Herrscher
  von uns allen (Neander)
           Z 7854

Baldamus, F.   Metzger, H. A.
Barner, A.   *Muehling, A.
Bender, J.   Oechsler, E. (2)
Claussnitzer, P.   Oertzen, R. von
Drischner, M. (2)   Oley, J. C.
Fiebig, K.   Palme, R.
Fischer, M. G.   Pfaff, H.
Fluegel, G.   *Rabich, E.
*Forchhammer, T. (3)   Reda, S.
Franke, F. W.   Reger, M.
Frenzel, H. R.   Rinck, J. C. H.
Genzmer, H.   Rudnick, W.
Haase, K.   Rumpf, W.
Hasse, K. (2)   Schaeffer, A.
Hennig, W.   Schauss-Flake, M.
*Herzog, J. G.   Schmid, K.
Huth, A.   *Schneider, F. C.
Karg-Elert, S. (2)   *Streicher, J. A.
Kickstat, P.   Wagner, A.
*Koeckert, C.   Weber, H.
Leupold, A. W.   Wettstein, H. (2)
*Lorenz, C. A.
Variants:
Arnsberg

Beck, A.   Fromm, H.
Bitgood, R.   Peeters, F.

Gott ist gegenwaertig

Ehinger, H. R.   Kee, P.
Hanebeck, H. R.   Metzger, H. A.
Herzog, J. G.   Wieruszowski, L.

Song 265 (Dutch)

Kee, P.   Nauta, J.
Kousemaker, A.   Wilgenburg, D. van

Wunderbarer Koenig
See: Tysk

Wunderschoen, praechtige

Schroeder, H.

Wunderschoen, praechtige
(Corner)

Kreckel, P. G. (2)

Wunderschoen, praechtige
(Folk Tune)

 Ahrens, J.
 *Schmalz, P.

Y Delyn Aur (Welsh)

 Jenkins, C.
 Stocks, H. C. L.
Variant:
Golden Harp

Yattendon 46 (Wooldridge)

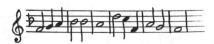

 Peeters, F.

Ye Watchers and Ye Holy Ones
 See: **Lasst uns erfreuen** (Cologne)

Yigdal
 See: **Leoni**

Yoe synkkae on jo haelvennyt
(Finnish)

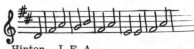

 Kuusisto, T.

York (Scotch)

 Bingham, S.   Hinton, J. E. A.
 Dunham, H. M.   Sowerbutts, J. A.
 Dyson, G.   Wood, C.
 Emery, W. J.

Yorkshire
 See: **Stockport** (Wainwright)

Zephyr (Bradbury)

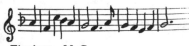

 Miles, R. H.

Zeuch an die Macht
 See: **Lobet den Herrn, ihr Heiden all** (Vulpius)

Zeuch ein zu deinen Toren
 (Crueger)
       Z 5294

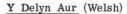

 Bornefeld, H.   Fischer, M. G.
 Brieger, O. (2)   Franke, F. W. (2)
 Buehl, W.   *Hennig, W.
 *Driessler, J.   Herrmann, K. H.
 Faisst, I. G. F. von *Hulse, C. Van

Huth, A.   Pepping, E.
Karow, K.   Rembt, J. E.
Kickstat, P.   Rumpf, W.
Koch, J. H. E.   Studer, H.
Lang, H.   Wagner, F.
Marx, K.   Werner, F.
*Oechsler, E.   Wieruszowski, L.
Variant:
Kommt her, ihr seid geladen

Hennig, W.

Zeuch ein zu deinen Toren

Kunze, K.

Zeuch ein zu deinen Toren

Bender, J.

Zeuch ein zu deinen Toren
See: Helft mir Gott's Guete preisen (Magdeburg)

Zeuch meinen Geist, triff meine
Sinnen (Koenig)
Z 788
Claussnitzer, P.
Piutti, K.   Rinck, J. C. H.

Zeuch mich, zeuch mich
See: Liebe die du mich zum Bilde (Darmstadt)

Zeuch uns nach dir
See: Ach Gott und Herr (Schein)

Zhvězdy vyšlo slunce (Czech)

Michálek, F.

Zion (Hastings)

Colvin, H.

Zion (Moreley)

Haase, K.
*Reuter, F.

Zion klagt mit Angst und
Schmerzen (Crueger)
Z 6550

Zion klagt mit Angst und Schmerzen (Crueger) (cont.)

Claussnitzer, P.	Rinck, J. C. H.
Enckhausen, H. F.	Rudnick, O.
Franke, F. W.	Steinhaeuser, K.
Gulbins, M.	Stolze, H. W.
Haase, K.	Vierling, J. G.
Karow, K. (2)	Voullaire, W.
Piutti, K.	Wolfrum, K.
Reinbrecht, F.	

Zion's Stille soll sich breiten
    See: O wer alles haet verloren

Zu Bethlehem geboren

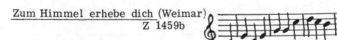

Ahrens, J.	Kutzer, E.
Berghorn, A.	Miggl, E.
Bonvin, L.	Monar, A. J.
Doebler, K.	Sister M. F.
Doppelbauer, J. F.	Sorge, E. R.
Koch, K.	Walcha, H.

Zu dir ich mein Herz erhebe
    See: Psalm 25

Zu dir ist meine Seele stille

    Franke, F. W.

Zu dir von Herzens Grunde
    See: Old 130th (French)

Zum Himmel erhebe dich (Weimar)
                Z 1459b

    Unbehaun, G.

Zween der Junger
    See: Alle Menschen muessen sterben (Mueller)

Music Publishers Mentioned in the Index
(Many now non-existent)

Abingdon Press - Nashville, Tenn.
J. Aible - Leipzig, Germany
Allegro - Straubedruck - Berlin, Germany
Alsbach & Co. - Amsterdam, Netherlands
American Composers Alliance - New York, N. Y.
American Music Edition - New York, N. Y.
AMSCO Publishing Co. - New York, N. Y.
J. André - Offenbach, Germany
Appun - Bunzlau, Poland
Arnold - Dresden, Germany
Ars Nova - Goes, Netherlands
Ars Viva - Mainz, Germany
Artia - Prague, Czechoslovakia
Asch & Co. - London, England
Aschehoug & Co. - Oslo, Norway
Ascherberg, Hopwood & Crew - London, England
E. Ashdown - London, England
Associated Music Publishers - New York, N. Y.
Atelier Elektra - Copenhagen, Denmark
Augener - London, England
Augsburg Press - Minneapolis, Minn.
Avant Music Press - Los Angeles, California

B. M. I. - Toronto, Canada
Bachem - Koeln, Germany
Baedeker - Essen, Germany
Baerenreiter Verlag - Kassel, Germany
Bahn - Heinrichshofen, Germany
M. Bahn - Berlin, Germany
Annie Bank - Amsterdam, Netherlands
G. Basse - Regensburg, Germany
Bayley & Ferguson - London, England
Beal & Co. - London, England
Bech - Munich, Germany
Beck - Rothenburg, Germany
A. Beck - River Forest, Illinois
Beckerschen Buchhandlung - Gotha, Germany
Beco Musikverlag - Hamburg, Germany
Belgo-Canadian - Montreal, Canada
Belwin Music Co. - New York, N. Y.
A. J. Benjamin - Hamburg, Germany
W. Bergmans - Tilbury, Ontario, Canada

Berra - Prague, Czechoslovakia
C. Bertelsmann - Guetersloh, Germany
H. Beyer & Soehne - Langensalza, Germany
Birchard - Evanston, Ill.
Birnbach - Berlin, Germany
L. J. Biton - France
A. Boehm & Soehne - Augsburg, Germany
J. A. Boehme - Hamburg, Germany
Boesens Musikforlag - Copenhagen, Denmark
F. Bongiovanni - Bologna, Italy
Boosey & Hawkes - London, England and New York, N. Y.
S. Bornemann - Paris, France
Bernard Bosse - Regensburg, Germany
Boston Music Co. - Boston, Mass.
Bosworth & Co. - Koeln, Germany
Bote & Bock - Berlin, Germany
Brauer - Dresden, Germany
Brattfisch - Nuernberg, Germany
B & H - Breitkopf & Haertel - Wiesbaden, Germany
Broadcast Music Co. - New York, N. Y.
Broadman Press - Nashville, Tenn.
M. Brockhaus - Loerrach, Germany
Brodt Music Co. - Charlotte, N. C.
Broekmans & van Poppel - Amsterdam, Netherlands
Broude Bros. - New York, N. Y.
Brueggemann - Halberstadt, Germany

Carisch & Jaenichen - Milan, Italy
Chantry Music Press - Fremont, Ohio
Chappell & Co. - London, England
J. W. Chester - London, England
Christophorus Verlag - Freiburg, Germany
Cieplik - Beuthen, Poland
Clementi - London, England
Comptoir - Langensalza, Germany
Concordia Publishing House - St. Louis, Mo.
A. Coppenrath - Regensburg, Germany
Cos Cobb Press - New York, N. Y.
Costallat & Co. - Paris, France
J. B. Cramer - London, England
A. Cranz - Wiesbaden, Germany
F. S. Crofts - New York, N. Y.
Cron Luzern - Lucerne, Switzerland
Cumberland Press -
Curwen & Son - London, England

Ed. Dania - Copenhagen, Denmark
F. Decourcelle - Nice, France
Deichert - Leipzig, Germany
Demets - Paris, France
Diabelli - Wien, Austria

J. Diener - Mainz, Germany
O. Ditson - Boston, Mass.
L. Doblinger - Wien, Austria
E. Donajowski - London, England
Donemus Foundation - Amsterdam, Netherlands
A. Durand - Paris, France

Edition Musicus (Bedell) - Brooklyn, N. Y.
Ed. Musicus de la Schola Cantorum - Paris, France
Elkin-Vogel - Philadelphia, Pa.
Elkin & Co. - London, England
Engstroem & Soedring - Copenhagen, Denmark
Evangelisches Verlagsanstalt - Stuttgart, Germany

A. Fassio - Lachute, Quebec, Canada
Feuchtinger & Gleichauf - Regensburg, Germany
Fine Arts Corp. - New York, N. Y.
C. Fischer - New York, N. Y.
J. Fischer - Glen Rock, N. J.
H. T. FitzSimons - Chicago, Ill.
H. Flammer - New York, N. Y.
C. G. Foerster - Berlin, Germany
Foetisch - Lausanne, Switzerland
R. O. Forberg - Bad Godesberg, Germany
Frazer - Helsinki, Finland
Freeman - Brighton, England
R. Friese - Leipzig, Germany
Adolf Fuerstner - Berlin, Germany

F. W. Gadow & Son - Hildburghaussen, Germany
Galaxy Music Press - New York, N. Y.
H. Gall - Wien, Austria
Galleon Press - New York, N. Y.
Galliard, Ltd. - London, England
J. M. Gallup - Hartford, Conn.
Gamble Hinged Music Co. - New York, N. Y.
Gebetner & Wolf - Austria
Gebhardi - Brieg, Poland
Carl Gehrmans Musikforlag - Stockholm, Sweden
C. Geissler - Heinrichshofen, Germany
Gensel - Grimma, Leipzig, Germany
H. Gerig - Geneva, Switzerland & Koeln, Germany
C. Glasser - Schleusingen, Germany
Gleichauf - Regensburg, Germany
F. Gloeggl - Wien, Austria
Fr. W. Goedsche - Meissen, Germany
Goerlich - Breslau, Germany
O. H. Gotch - Worthing, England
H. W. Gray - New York, N. Y.
Gregorian Institute - Toledo, Ohio
Gressler - Langensalza, Germany

Gries & Schornagel - Hannover, Germany
G. A. Grieshammer - Leipzig, Germany
H. Grote - St. Louis, Mo.
Guttenberg - Berlin, Germany
A. J. Guttmann - Wien, Austria

K. Haase - Lincoln, Nebraska
J. Hainauer - Breslau, Germany
Ed. J. Hamelle - Paris, France
Wilhelm Hansen - Copenhagen, Denmark
Hargail Music Press - New York, N. Y.
Harmonia - Hilversum, Netherlands
Harth - Leipzig, Germany
Harvard University Press - Cambridge, Mass.
R. Hasslwanter - Koeln, Germany
Job de Heer - Rotterdam, Netherlands
Heidelmann - Bonn, Germany
Heinrichshofen - Wilhelmshaven, Germany
Helbig - Altenberg, Germany
Helwing - Hannover, Germany
Henn - Geneva, Switzerland
Herder - Freiburg, Germany
H. Herelle - Paris, France
Max Hesse - Berlin, Germany
Heugel & Co. - Paris, France
Heuser - Neuwied/Rhein, Germany
Heuwekemeijer - Amsterdam, Netherlands
Hinrichsen Edition - London, England
Hochstein - Heidelberg, Germany
Hoereth - Beiruth, Lebanon
L. Hoffarth - Dresden, Germany
Hofmeister - Hofheim, Germany
F. Hofmeister - Leipzig, Germany
L. Holle - Wolfenbuettel, Germany
Hope Publishing Co. - Chicago, Ill.
Hudby & Umeni   )
Hudebni Matice Umelecke Besedy) - Prague, Czechoslovakia
Huellenhagen & Griehl - Hamburg, Germany
Hug & Co. - Zuerich, Switzerland

Janin Frères - Lyons, France
J. Jehle - Ebingen, Germany
Junfermann - Paderborn, Germany
Otto Junne - Munich, Germany & Leipzig, Germany

Kaabers Musikforlag - Aarhus, Denmark
C. F. Kahnt - Lindau/Bodensee, Germany
Kaiser - Munich, Germany
Kallmeyer - Wolfenbuettel, Germany
Edwin F. Kalmus - New York, N. Y.

Kell's Buchhandlung - Plauen, Germany
J. S. Kerr - Glasgow, Scotland
G. Kessel - St. Paul, Minn.
Kesselring - Hildburghausen, Germany
Kistner & Siegel - Leipzig, Germany
Kittaase (See Concordia)
Kjos Music Co. - Detroit, Mich.
C. A. Klemm - Berlin, Germany
C. Klemm - Berlin, Germany
Klinkhard - Leipzig, Germany
Klinkicht - Meissen, Germany
C. Klinner - Bremen, Germany
Koeppel - Germany
Koerner - Erfurt, Germany
G. W. Koerner - Leipzig, Germany
C. Kothe - Leobschuetz, Germany
Kranz - Germany
C. F. Kranz - Baltimore, Md.
H. Kreisler - Hamburg, Germany
L. Krenn - Wien, Austria
Krumpholz & Co. - Bern, Switzerland
Kuehn - Weimar, Germany
Kummer - Leipzig, Germany

Langensalza - Germany
Langlais - Paris, France
Laudy & Co. - London, England
A. Leduc - Paris, France
Leeds Music Corp. - New York, N. Y.
Ed. LeGrand Orgue - Brooklyn, N. Y.
H. Lemoine - Paris, France
A. Lengnick - London, England
Leonard, Gould & Boltler - London, England
R. Lerotte & Cie - Paris, France
F. LeRoux - Nantes, France
F. E. C. Leuckart - Munich, Germany
Lichtenauer - Rotterdam, Netherlands
Litaize - Paris, France
Litolff - Frankfurt, Germany
Liturgical Music Press - New York, N. Y.
Loebel - Leipzig, Germany
O. Lohses - Copenhagen, Denmark
Lorenz Music Publishers - Dayton, Ohio
H. Lyche - Oslo, Norway

Machar & Noel - Paris, France
E. B. Marks - New York, N. Y.
McL. & R. - McLaughlin & Reilly - Boston, Mass.
Mercury Music Corp. - New York, N. Y.
Merrymount Music - New York, N. Y.
Merseburger Verlag - Berlin, Germany

Meserchen Kunsthandlung - Germany
J. B. Metzler - Stuttgart, Germany
Mills Music Co. - New York, N. Y.
Moeseler - Wolfenbuettel, Germany
Morelia - Mexico City, Mexico
E. H. Morris - New York, N. Y.
H. Mosman's - Hertogenbosch, Germany
G. Mueller - Rudolfstadt, Germany
Willy Mueller Edition - Heidelberg, Germany
L. Muraille - Liege, Belgium
Music Manuscript Service - Canton, Ohio
Music Press - New York, N. Y.
Music Publishers Assoc. - London, England
Ed. Musicus (Bedell) - Brooklyn, N. Y.
Musikalische Fundgrube - Schoenebeck, Germany
Musikk-Huset A/S - Oslo, Norway
Ed. Musique Sacrée - Paris, France

Nagel's Musikarchive - Kassel, Germany
O. Nahmacher - Berlin, Germany
Nederlandsche Orgelmuziek - Zaandam, Netherlands
New England Conservatory - Boston, Mass.
Pierre Noel - Paris, France
Norberg Musikforlag - Vaesteraas, Sweden
Nordiska Musikfoerlaget - Stockholm, Sweden
Norsk Musikforlag - Oslo, Norway
Novello & Co. - London, England

Oertel - Hannover and Munich, Germany
Oesterreichische Bundesverlag - Wien, Austria
Oppenheimer - Hameln, Germany
Organistengilde zu Eckernfoerde - Eckernfoerde, Germany
Oxford University Press - London, England and New York, N. Y.

Pabst - Delitzsch, Germany
Paezschen - Leipzig, Germany
Pallma - Beaumont, California
Paterson's - London, England
W. Paxton - London, England
Peer International - Montreal, Canada
Peer Musikverlag - Munich, Germany
C. F. Peters - Frankfurt/Main, Germany and New York, N. Y.
Phillippo - Paris, France
Plainsong and Medieval Society - London, England
F. R. Portius - Stuttgart, Germany
Theodore Presser Co. - Philadelphia, Pa.
Pro Musica - Leipzig, Germany
Keith Prouse Music Publisher - London, England
F. Pustet - Regensburg, Germany

Albert Rathke - Magdeburg, Germany
R. Reibenstein - Germany
Reimer - Berlin, Germany
Reinecke Bros. - Leipzig, Germany
Reinhardt - Elberfeld, Germany
Reussner - Germany
F. Reuter - New Ulm, Minn.
Richards & Co. - London, England
G. Ricordi - Milan, Italy
Riegel - Potsdam, Germany
Ries & Erler - Berlin, Germany
Rieter-Biedermann - Leipzig, Germany
DeRing - Antwerp, Belgium
Winthrop Rogers - London, England
Frank K. Root Co. - Chicago, Ill.
Roothaan - Utrecht, Netherlands
G. F. Rosche - Chicago, Ill.
Rothe - Leipzig, Germany
R. D. Row - Boston, Mass.
Rózsavoelgyi - Budapest, Hungary
C. Rozsnyai - Budapest, Hungary
Rubach - Magdeburg, Germany
Rudolfstadt - Germany
Rob Ruehle - Berlin, Germany
Ruh & Walser - Adliswil/Zuerich, Switzerland
C. Ruhle - Leipzig, Germany
Ruhle & Wendling - Wiesbaden, Germany
Rushworth & Dreaper - London, England

Sacred Music Press - Dayton, Ohio
Saechsische Buchhandlung - Meissen, Germany
St. Cecelia - London, England
St. Gregory Guild - Philadelphia, Pa.
St. Mary's Press - New York, N. Y.
Sandersleben - Germany
Sassmannshausen - Chicago, Ill.
M. Schauenburg - Lahr/Bayern, Germany
E. C. Schirmer - Boston, Mass.
G. Schirmer - New York, N. Y.
Schlesinger - Berlin, Germany
Schlimpert & Pueschel - Meissen, Germany
W. Schmid - Nuernberg, Germany
Schmidl - Trieste, Italy
A. P. Schmidt - Boston, Mass.
Schmitt, Hall & McCreary - Chicago, Ill.
Schola Cantorum (Litaize) - Paris, France
Schola Paroissiale - Paris, France
Schott & Co. - London, England
Schott Frères - Brussels, Belgium
B. Schott & Soehne - Mainz, Germany
Ed. Schuberth - New York, N. Y.
J. Schuberth - Wiesbaden, Germany

Schuelter - Altona, Germany
Schulbuchhandlung des Thuringien Lehrer Vereins - Langensalza,
  Germany
C. L. Schultheiss - Tuebingen, Germany
Schultze - Berlin, Germany
L. Schwann - Duesseldorf, Germany
Schweers & Haake - Bremen, Germany
J. G. Seeling - Dresden, Germany
J. Seiling - Regensburg, Germany
Senart - Paris, France
Seyffardt - Amsterdam, Netherlands
Shattinger - St. Louis, Mo.
Shawnee Press - Delaware Water Gap, Pa.
C. F. W. Siegel - Munich, Germany
Sikorsky - Hamburg, Germany
Carl Simon - Berlin, Germany
N. Simrock - Hamburg, Germany
Sirius Verlag - Berlin, Germany
Skandinavisk or Borups Musikforlag - Copenhagen, Denmark
Ethel Smith Music Corp. - New York, N. Y.
Societé Anonyme - Nantes, France
C. Sorgenicht - Hagen, W. Germany
Spinal - Wien, Austria
Sprague-Coleman - New York, N. Y.
Stainer & Bell - London, England
Steingraeber - Offenbach, Germany
A. Stender - Regensburg, Germany
W. Stumpf - Bachem, W. Germany
R. Sulzer - Berlin, Germany
Summy - Chicago, Ill.

Tarto Music Co. - Somerville, N. J.
Tascher'schen - Kaiserlautern/Bavaria, Germany
Tetzner - Langensalza, Germany
Thelen - Berlin, Germany
G. V. Thompson, Ltd. - Toronto, Canada
Tischner & Jagenberg - Koeln, Germany
P. J. Tonger - Rodenkirchen, Germany
Transatlantique - Paris, France
Transcontinental Music Corp. - New York, N. Y.
Trautwein - Berlin, Germany

Ugrino - Hamburg, Germany
United Music Publishers - London, England
Universal Verlag - Wien, Austria
Fr. A. Urbánek & Son - Prague, Czechoslovakia

Van den Hoeck & Ruprecht - Goettingen, Germany
G. H. Van Eck - den Haag, Netherlands
J. R. Van Rossum - Utrecht, Netherlands

Verein der Organistengilde Kiel - Kiel, Germany
T. L. Verne - Langensalza/Saxony, Germany
C. F. Vieweg - Berlin, Germany
Viking Musikforlag - Copenhagen, Denmark
Vincent Music Co. - London, England
W. C. de Vletter - Rotterdam, Netherlands
Voigt - Weimar, Germany
Volksverein - Gladbach, Germany
Volkwein Bros. - Pittsburgh, Pa.

J. A. H. Wagenaar - Utrecht, Netherlands
J. G. Walde - Loebau, Germany
Waldheim-Eberle - Wien, Austria
Waterloo Music Co. - Waterloo, Ontario, Canada
Wattenbach - Gotha, Germany
Waysenhaus - Kassel, Germany
Weekes & Co. - London, England
J. Weinberger - Wien, Austria
Weinhold - Breslau, Germany
Weiss-Feil - Chicago, Ill.
Westerlund - Helsinfors, Finland
Western International Music - Los Angeles, Calif.
Wesphalen - Flensburg, Denmark
Whistling - Leipzig, Germany
White-Smith - Boston, Mass.
J. C. Willemsen - Amersfoort, Netherlands
J. Williams - London, England
H. H. Willis - Chicago, Ill.
R. Winkler - Leipzig, Germany
M. Witmark & Sons - New York, N. Y.
B. F. Wood - Boston, Mass.
Darwin Wood - Fruitvale, California
WLSM (World Library of Sacred Music) - Cincinnati, Ohio

Year Book Press - London, England

Zaandam (Nederlandshe Orgelmuziek) - Koog/Zaan, Netherlands
Zanibon - Padova, Italy
Zimmerman - Frankfurt, Germany
Zoller - Ebingen, Germany
C. A. Zumsteeg - Hamburg, Germany
J. Zwart - Koog/Zaan, Netherlands

N. B.   I have included the locations of publishers no longer in
existence as a clue to where to look in archives and libraries
to locate compositions.